Making Sense of
Modula-2

Making Sense *of*
Modula-2

Eric W. Tatham and
Irene Glendinning

School of Mathematical and Information Sciences
Coventry University
UK

INTERNATIONAL THOMSON COMPUTER PRESS
I(T)P An International Thomson Publishing Company

London • Bonn • Boston • Johannesburg • Madrid • Melbourne • Mexico City • New York • Paris • Singapore
Tokyo • Toronto • Albany, NY • Belmont, CA • Cincinnati, OH • Detroit, MI

Making Sense of Modula-2

Copyright © 1994 Eric Tatham and Irene Glendinning

I⊤P   A division of International Thomson Publishing Inc.
      The ITP logo is a trademark under licence

British Library Cataloguing-in-Publication Data
A catalogue record for this book is available from the British Library

First published by Chapman and Hall 1994
Reprinted by International Thomson Publishing 1995
Printed in England by Clays Ltd, St Ives plc

ISBN 1-85032-278-3

International Thomson Computer Press   International Thomson Computer Press
Berkshire House   20 Park Plaza
High Holborn   14th Floor
London WClV 7AA   Boston MA 02116
UK   USA

`http://www.thomson.com/itcp.html`

Imprints of International Thomson Publishing

To our families

Contents

viii   *Contents*

The prologue

In the past, our own first year BSc Computer Science students have been introduced to programming using the Pascal language. That is, until it became increasingly apparent that this was not providing the most appropriate foundation for the software engineering concepts taught in the subsequent years of their courses. A review of possible alternatives concluded that Modula-2 would provide a more suitable first programming language, and could be coupled with a complementary, parallel study of a functional language and formal methods. More recently, with the introduction of a modular degree scheme, here at Coventry, we found that increasing numbers of students from other disciplines are being required or are electing to include an element of computer software development as a part of their studies. Our module, which was originally intended for main-stream computer scientists, has rapidly expanded its enrolment to include students with diverse educational background and experience. We found many such students uncomfortable with the technical style of existing programming texts and further disadvantaged by the often heavy reliance on mathematically based programming examples. This prompted us to produce this text to satisfy the needs of this diverse student population.

Although we have organized the book's contents to facilitate use as a reference, we have sought primarily to produce an easy-to-follow programming design course, rather than a definitive guide to the intricacies of Modula-2 syntax. We believe that a first programming course should provide a solid foundation of good practice and transferable skills. To some extent the language chosen is less important than the software engineering principles covered and the transfer of skill to another procedural language should present few problems.

The book's emphasis is on design and planning to create well structured, maintainable, understandable software. To this end, two different design methodologies have been used. We start by exploring functional decomposition before introducing object-oriented design via a comparative case study.

Learning to program has some similarity with learning to play a musical instrument. Programming, like music, demands a blend of technical precision and creativity that requires both knowledge and skill, and for some this comes more easily than for others.
The results can be highly rewarding and satisfying, but there's an account to be settled in that the process can, unfortunately, be fraught with regular frustration and seemingly insurmountable hurdles to understanding. If you let these get the better of you, all you will end up with is the frustration.
We hope that our book will help you over the hurdles by supporting your lecture course and/or your own personal study. However, the fact remains that there is no substitute for practice. As with any skill, the way to learn to do it is by doing it and to persevere, being inspired rather than discouraged when others about you seem to be more expert. If an accomplishment is hard-won the personal satisfaction is all the greater and well worth the effort.

If you were learning to play a musical instrument, a good tutorial book would probably have you playing real tunes as soon as possible rather than requiring that you start by wading through a lot of musical theory. Similarly, in this book, we'll start you programming in Chapter 1 and deal with the theory largely in the context of practical examples.

Inevitably, some topics are more difficult to understand than others. If you find a particular section difficult, read through it a few times, try the example programs, the self test questions and the associated exercises. Don't be afraid to explore and to experiment.

If you do find moments when you're at screaming point then our advice is:

SCREAM!

go for a coffee, go for a walk, go to bed and sleep on it - things often seem better in the morning (although admittedly not always). Solutions to seemingly intractable problems often come when you take a rest from thinking about them.

Above all, we want the experience of learning to design programs to be fun as well as rewarding.

The source text of the software is available free of charge through HENSA (The Higher Education National Software Archive) using `ftp`. The host is `micros.hensa.ac.uk`, the login is `hensa`, the password is `hensa` and the file you require is `micros/ibmpc/dos/a/a001/tatham` (all in lower case). The source text is in ASCII.

The apologue

Again on a musical note; a friend of our's occasionally plays the piano. He plays entirely by ear and punctuates his renditions with several discordant notes. Unfortunately, he cannot read music at all, having learned to play in a pub in the East-end of London. If he wanted to practise and play to concert standard you might think he at least has a head start but, by his own admission, he would find it harder now than if he could start entirely from scratch. He would have too many bad habits to 'unlearn' first.

The moral of this?
If you are completely new to programming be reassured, it may well be an advantage. If, on the other hand, you already have many programs to your name, fine, but be prepared for new ideas and new ways of doing things.

Acknowledgements

We thank our friends and colleagues at Coventry University for their constructive comments before and during compilation of this book. We also thank the many students who have grappled with and helped us to refine much of the material.

We are particularly grateful to John Turner of Staffordshire University for reviewing the book, and to John Tatham who donated his time and copy writing skills in providing detailed comments on the proofs.

Our thanks also go to Dave Hatter of Chapman & Hall for instigating the writing and for his unflagging enthusiasm and encouragement.

Finally, we thank our spouses, Lynda and Guy, without whose support this book would never have been written.

1   Getting started

1.1   Programming languages

The earliest computers had their instructions permanently wired in, which meant that they were able to perform only one task. It was a great leap forward when computers were designed with plugs and plug-boards to change the connections of the wires. This enabled computers to be re-programmed to perform many different tasks, but required considerable expertise and patience in devising the tasks for the computer to solve in a way that could be 'programmed' into a set of 'machine code' instructions, and then in translating the program into a set of wiring diagrams.

1.1.1   Machine code

Machine code is a digital computer's own language with each instruction represented as a sequence of binary (two state) digits, which are usually represented using the symbols 0 and 1. Each different type of computer processor has its own machine code instruction set which it 'understands' and when a computer's processor is presented with its particular instruction code it will respond in a pre-defined and predictable way. Machine code is described as low level with each machine code instruction performing a single, simple computer task such as LOAD, STORE or ADD.

A machine code program to add two numbers might look like this:

```
0010 0000 0000 0110
0001 0000 0000 0111
0011 0000 0000 1000
```

1.1.2   Assembly language

Dealing with the long binary digit sequences of machine code may be acceptable to a computer, but even programmers who work with low level code prefer to use a symbolic language, which can be written down, typed into a computer, remembered and understood by colleagues. This more usable alternative to machine code is known as assembly language. There is an assembly language for each type of computer processor with instructions that correspond one-to-one with the machine code instruction set.

An assembly language program to add two numbers might look like this:

```
LDA 006
ADD 007
STA 008
```

1.1.3   High level languages

Each high level programming language, such as BASIC, C, COBOL, Pascal and Modula-2, has its own instruction set.
This has two significant advantages.

1. High level languages are not peculiar to specific computer processors so, in theory at least, when you write your program it doesn't matter which make of computer it is to be used on. In other words, high level languages have a greater machine independence.

2. High level languages make programming easier as each high level instruction translates into several machine code instructions.
    For example, high level languages allow you to evaluate a complex arithmetical expression like (b * c / (e - f)) using a single program statement. It would take many machine code instructions to achieve the same result.

The high level language, Modula-2, was developed by Niklaus Wirth from his earlier language, Pascal. He designed Modula-2 to address the shortcomings of Pascal. As its name implies, the newer language is highly modular; it also allows individual parts of a program to conceal information from other sections and so stop them interfering with parts that don't concern them.
It incorporates a number of features, absent or loosely defined in Pascal and, thus, further enforces 'good programming' practice.

1.1.4   A layered view

Our aim, when designing a program, is to get a computer to do something useful for us or for others. A high level language is a convenient tool for creating the machine code for the applications we require. Just as our computer hardware may require many machine code instructions in order to carry out one of our high level language instructions, it may take many high level instructions to provide the basic facilities in our application program.

So, in fact, there are a number of different levels at which we could interact with a computer: the application level, the high level language level, the assembler/machine code level, or the actual hardware level. These levels can be represented diagrammatically as concentric circles, much like the skins around an onion.

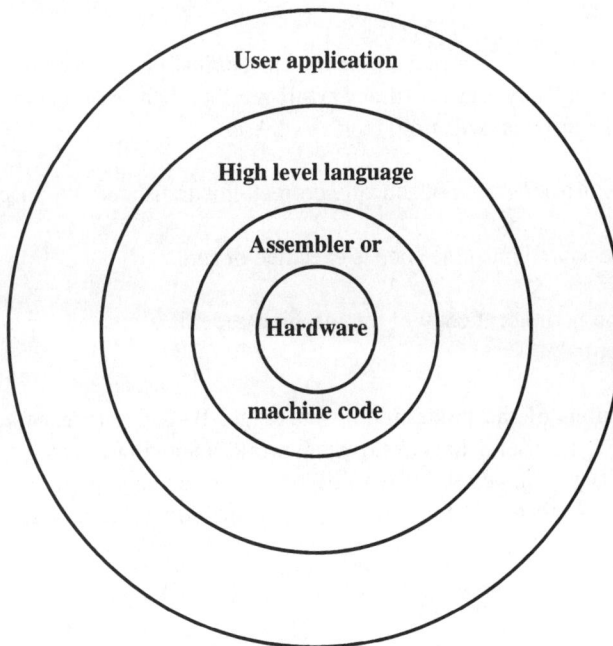

User application

High level language

Assembler or

Hardware

machine code

As we move outward from the hardware core, adding software 'skins', the computer should become easier to use, as successive sets of available instructions are designed to correspond more closely to the end user's basic task requirements and the user is progressively more insulated from having to be concerned about specific hardware details.

1.2   Interpreters, compilers and linkers

Fortunately you do not need to translate your assembler or high level code into machine code because special computer programs are available to do this for you. Assembly language programs are translated via an assembler and high level programs are translated using either an interpreter or a compiler.

1.2.1   Interpreters

An interpreter is itself a program which works its way through the program instructions converting them to machine code equivalents, which are not stored but are carried out straightaway. This allows a computer program to be run directly from the programming code.

To do its job of carrying out each instruction in turn the interpreter performs three functions:

1. a syntax check is carried out on the current instruction to determine whether it is 'grammatically' correct (if any errors are found an error message will be displayed and the program will stop) then

2. if the instruction is syntactically correct, it is translated into machine code, and then

3. the generated machine code is executed or run.

There is no permanent copy of the machine code; it is created for a single instruction and then discarded.

Most versions of the programming language, BASIC, are executed via an interpreter. Interpreters are useful for development work, achieving a very rapid response to minor modifications. However, for reasons such as efficiency at run-time and security of the code, most high level language programs, including Modula-2, are translated using a compiler.

1.2.2   Compilers

As with an interpreter, a compiler is itself a program which turns the programmer's high level source program into the corresponding machine code. However, unlike an interpreter, a compiler generates complete machine code without immediately executing any of it.

A compiler performs the first two functions of the interpreter, syntax checking and code translation, in two distinct phases, using the whole source program. The second phase, the code translation, can only begin if the whole program is free from errors in the syntax of the language. If any errors are detected they are reported back to the programmer for correction and the compiler stops.

When a program is free of syntax errors the code generation phase begins. A compiler produces an object program, which is the machine code version of the source program. Some compilers may produce an executable program directly; that is a program which can be executed by just typing in its name. In other cases it is necessary to initiate a separate linking stage after compiling the program.

1.2.3   Linkers

When a program is composed of several distinct modules or sub-program parts it is necessary to provide a list of the different components which need to be included. The linker is a program whose job is to combine separately compiled object programs to form a single executable program.

All compiled programs have to go through this phase, but sometimes the compiler will take care of it automatically and the programmer is not required to initiate the linking process explicitly.

1.3   Writing your own program

1.3.1   Six steps to your first program

There are six basic steps involved in creating your own Modula-2 program:

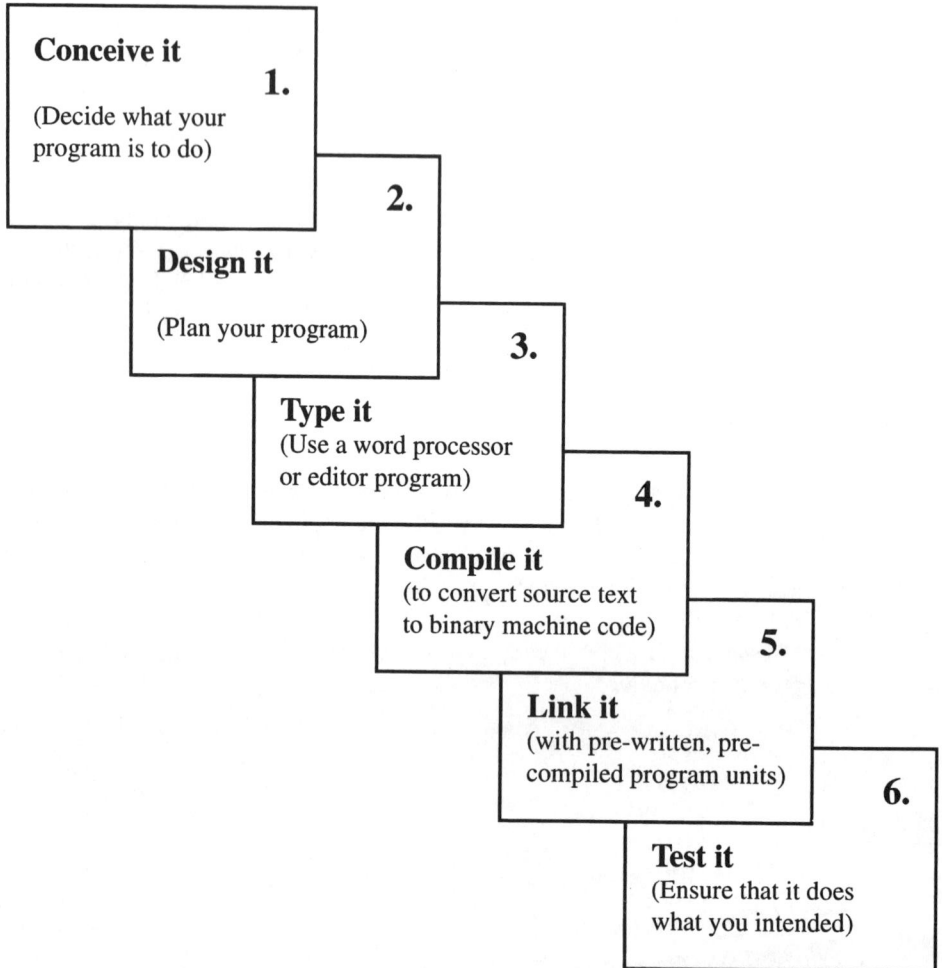

Conceive it   **1.**

(Decide what your
program is to do)

2.

Design it

(Plan your program)

3.

Type it
(Use a word processor
or editor program)

4.

Compile it
(to convert source text
to binary machine code)

5.

Link it
(with pre-written, pre-
compiled program units)

6.

Test it
(Ensure that it does
what you intended)

Trying to learn a programming language without writing any programs of your own would be like trying to learn to swim without getting wet. Rather than throw you in at the deep end (the strategy of my old PE teacher) we'll provide you with some sample programs to begin with and some ideas for small programs which you can write yourself.

When you are creating your own programs make sure that you follow all six stages. It may be tempting to miss out **Conceive it** and **Design it** for the early programs at least, but remember that all program writing must be approached systematically or you are much more likely to end up in a tangle.

1.3.2   Watching your Ps and Qs!

Computer programming languages, like spoken languages, have grammatical rules. However, as computer programs need to be translated precisely and unambiguously into the equivalent machine code instructions, you will find that a computer is much less tolerant than a human when the rules of its 'grammar' are broken.

While you are learning we will try to introduce the available instructions gradually. You need to be clear about the grammatical rules (or syntax) of each instruction to avoid making **syntactic errors** that will prevent your program working at all.

It is also important that you understand exactly what each instruction does and how it works, otherwise you may make some false assumptions, resulting in **semantic errors**, or 'bugs' which may not completely stop your program, but may make it behave in a way that you didn't intend.

If this will be your first experience of programming languages your task will not be complicated by any pre-conditioning or bad habits. If you have seen or perhaps written programs in some other language, such as BASIC or Pascal, you will find some instructions familiar, but beware, there are some significant differences.

1.3.3   Case study: *A limerick to try your Patience*

With the first example we'll explain the basic structure of Modula-2 programs and will show you how to write to the standard output device, which is probably a computer screen.

The program simply displays a five line, amusing rhyme called a limerick.
Here are the steps:

Step 1.   Conceive it:
The program is to display a limerick.

Step 2.   Design it:
For each line of the limerick:
    output a line, then start a new line.

Step 3.   Type it:

Here's the program code for the program module Patience.

```
MODULE Patience;
(*
**Purpose: Program to display the lines of a limerick
**Uses module: InOut
*)
FROM InOut IMPORT WriteString, WriteLn;

BEGIN
    WriteString("A student from South Woodham Ferrers");
    WriteLn;
    WriteString("Usually cool in the face of all terrors");
    WriteLn;
    WriteString("Put his boot through the screen");
    WriteLn;
    WriteString("And said something obscene");
    WriteLn;
    WriteString("When his program showed 96 errors");
    WriteLn
END Patience.
```

If your Modula-2 compiler is supplied with a built-in word processor or text editor then use this to type in the program, otherwise you can use any standard text editor, such as **vi** or **emacs**, or any available word processing package. Once you have typed your program you will need to save it, giving it a file name ending in .mod. In this case, we suggest, Patience.mod. This is called the source program.

If you are familiar with programming in BASIC the first thing you may notice is that with Modula-2 the format is much more flexible and would even allow a program to be written entirely on one line. However, this would not help its legibility, so for the sake of those who will have to read your program later (yourself included) it is wise to follow a standard pattern of format.

For the time being at least, we suggest that you follow the style of our sample programs using indentation exactly as we have done. Most TAB, RETURN and SPACE characters are ignored by the compiler so they should not affect the working of your program.

Step 4.   Compile it:

If you have an integrated program development environment this stage is simply a matter of selecting the appropriate menu choice and the option to compile.

If you have a command driven compiler then you need to study the command syntax, and the available options, from the manual that came with your compiler, or seek the help of your tutor.

It is worth finding out if your compiler provides any short-cut methods to save you from entering long command lines and to reduce the risk of typing errors. There is no point in making life more difficult than necessary.

What if it doesn't compile?

Unless you are a very accurate typist your program won't compile first time and you will be presented with a list of syntax errors, so we could perhaps introduce another step here:

Debug it

Dealing with errors

When learning to program, a very frustrating aspect is dealing with error messages, removing syntax errors and getting your program to compile.

The first thing to come to terms with is that, in general, compilers can seem totally stupid. They are not able to apply common sense like us; they simply follow a set of rigid logical rules. If any such rule is violated, then an error will be detected and the most appropriate error message will be output to help you to track down the mistake. Sometimes the error messages are helpful, but some can be incredibly cryptic.

The error message may occur at the location of the error or, when it is detected, somewhere later in the program. This is because some errors, such as a missing statement separator symbol ';', are not detected until the compiler attempts, unsuccessfully, to translate the two instructions as though they are one. For this reason compilers often produce inappropriate error messages, which are not as helpful as they might be.

A trivial typing mistake can cause a plethora of error messages. In fact, when first programming in Modula-2, students sometimes become very competitive to see who can generate the most errors from a program as short as `Patience`.

Often the best approach to solving errors is to correct the obvious ones and then try compiling again. However, there are occasions when you get error messages that were not reported on the first compilation. This might mean that the compiler found so many mistakes the first time, it stopped looking. Alternatively you could be introducing new errors!

Most importantly, keep cool and don't give up! As you continue to correct errors and re-compile, the number of syntax errors should steadily reduce and eventually you will have an executable program to test.

One way that you can get to know your compiler better is to keep a log of different error messages and their cause. This means that you might spend quite a lot of time recording errors at first, but save a great deal of time later when you come to debug much larger programs.

Step 5.   Link it:
The Patience program makes use of some pre-written facilities, supplied with your compiler, to output lines of text on the screen. This code must be linked with your program code. For small programs like this many Modula-2 systems will compile and then link automatically, while others require that you initiate the compile and link operations separately. The manual for your compiler, or your tutor, will be able to tell you what is required for your system.

Step 6.   Test it:
Before you can shout "Eureka, my program works!" you must satisfy yourself that the program behaves according to the rules that were set in the design. You must test your Patience! This simply means you consider whether the output from the program, in this case the limerick, is correct. If there are mistakes, perhaps in the format or the spelling, then it is necessary to correct the source program once again and re-compile and link it. Errors detected at the testing stage are usually **semantic errors**, as opposed to **syntax errors**. They affect the working or logic of the program rather than its compilation. Here's the output from our limerick program:

```
A student from South Woodham Ferrers
Usually cool in the face of all terrors
Put his boot through the screen
And said something obscene
When his program showed 96 errors
```

Most of the programs we will test will have some interaction with 'the user', that is the person who is running the program. Different input values may require different actions by the program, resulting in different output values. We will consider how to test more complex programs as we meet them.

1.3.4 Working with windows

When a program is run on some computer systems, particularly those with a window environment, the output window may flash on the screen and then disappear before you have had a chance to read it. If you find this happens on your system you should find that your InOut library module contains a procedure to hold the display until a key or mouse button is pressed. The procedure will probably be called HoldScreen and a call to it needs to be included at the end of your programs. You must also include its name in the IMPORT list near the beginning of your programs.

```
MODULE Patience;
...
FROM InOut IMPORT WriteString, WriteLn, HoldScreen;

BEGIN
    .....
    .....
    WriteLn;
    HoldScreen
END Patience.
```

Self test 1.1

If things go wrong with your program the fault may be due to syntax errors or semantic errors. Referring to the six steps for creating a Modula-2 program,
a)   which step would you be unable to pass if your program contains:
    (i)   a syntax error?
    (ii)   a semantic error?
and
b)   which step would you need to go back to if:
    (i)   a syntax error has occurred?
    (ii)   a semantic error has occurred?

1.4   Program features

1.4.1   Naming your program

Each program module is given a unique name, e.g. `Patience`, usually assigned by the program designer. This name is used both inside the program, featuring on the first line, and outside the program, to identify the program files.

There will be three different program files after successful compilation. These files are distinguished by using a suffix or extension (such as .mod) to the file name.

For example,

The source program	`Patience.mod`
The object program	`Patience.obj`
The executable program	`Patience`

Note that the naming conventions do vary between compilers, particularly the extension used to identify the object code. Also, your system may limit the number of characters that can be used in a file name, in which case you may have to abbreviate the names of some of the example programs in this book.

1.4.2   Identifiers

The program name is just one example of an identifier. From Chapter 2 onwards we will need to define other names, for example, to identify parts of a program module and to refer to places in the computer's memory. To avoid ambiguity and confusion, both for the programmer and the compiler, a single set of rules is provided in Modula-2 specifying what constitutes a valid identifier. The syntax chart below is a graphical and concise way of specifying a legal identifier:

Identifier:

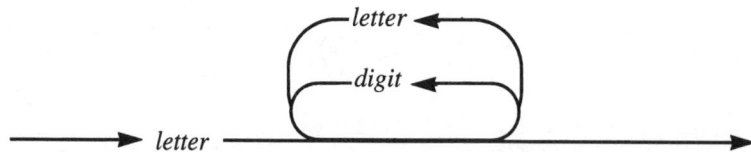

A **syntax chart** is a useful way of showing program constructs. For example, to show the syntax for a legal identifier start at the left-hand side of the chart and follow the arrows to the right. Each path through the chart yields a syntactically valid identifier.

When the chart contains a loop the portion in the loop can be repeated, therefore, an identifier must start with a letter, followed by any number of letters and digits. In practice there will be a limit to the number of characters allowed depending on your computer/compiler combination.

Thus,

```
a    Names   num1        p8Sensor
```

are valid identifiers but

```
2BorNot2B      %$@$   num_1
```

are not, although some compilers will accept the last, treating the underscore character as a valid letter.

1.4.3 Reserved words

A further restriction on identifiers is that an identifier cannot be the same as any of the 40 special Modula-2 words recognized by the compiler. These are known as **reserved words** and they are:

```
AND            ELSIF            LOOP           REPEAT
ARRAY          END              MOD            RETURN
BEGIN          EXIT             MODULE         SET
BY             EXPORT           NOT            THEN
CASE           FOR              OF             TO
CONST          FROM             OR             TYPE
DEFINITION     IF               POINTER        UNTIL
DIV            IMPLEMENTATION   PROCEDURE      VAR
DO             IMPORT           QUALIFIED      WHILE
ELSE           IN               RECORD         WITH
```

1.4.4 Case sensitivity

Note that the reserved words must all be typed using capital letters. Modula-2 is case sensitive, which means that End, end and END are considered to be three different words. Of the three only END is a reserved word.

1.4.5 Procedures

Most programs are likely to be more complex than Patience and, as you may imagine, correspondingly more difficult to design, test and maintain. Unfortunately, there is a limited amount of complexity the human brain can cope with at any one time, and large monolithic programs are like 'king-size' chocolate bars - not easy to digest in one go without making yourself ill.

Procedures are program blocks that allow you to divide your programs into manageable chunks of code - the programmer's equivalent of 'fun-size' bars. Procedures can be pre-written or you can write your own. You have already met the pre-written variety in Patience where we made use of WriteString and WriteLn which are 'calls' to the computer instructing it to run these particular library procedures. By the end of Chapter 3 you'll be writing your own.

1.4.6   **Importing**

The program `Patience` makes use of some procedures which have been written and tested by someone else. These are to be found in a library module called `InOut`, which is a fairly standard feature included with Modula-2 compilers. We'll explore the concepts of procedures and libraries more fully a little later.

The instruction:

```
FROM InOut IMPORT WriteString, WriteLn;
```

directs the compiler to make available to the program (i.e. to import) the two named PROCEDURES, `WriteString` and `WriteLn`, from the library module `InOut`. The code for these procedures will be combined with your program during the linking stage. If this `IMPORT` line is omitted the program will not be able to recognize the identifiers `WriteString` and `WriteLn`, and the linking step will fail.

As an experiment try deleting the import line from `Patience`, then re-compiling and linking, and you'll see what we mean.

It is possible that a program may need to import two procedures that have the same identifying name, for example we could have import instructions of the form:

```
FROM LibModA IMPORT Xproc;
FROM LibModB IMPORT Xproc;
```

If you then called `Xproc` from within the program, the compiler would not be able to determine whether you were referring to `LibModA`'s `Xproc` or `LibModB`'s.

To overcome this potential problem Modula-2 allows you to import facilities with an alternative instruction format.

Instead of;

```
FROM LibModA IMPORT Xproc;
FROM LibModB IMPORT Xproc;
```

you may import using instructions of the form:

```
IMPORT LibModA;
IMPORT LibModB;
```

or simply;

```
IMPORT LibModA, LibModB;
```

and then when you use anything provided by the imported library modules you must qualify the identifying name by prefixing it with the library module identifier so that, using our example, the respective calls become:

    LibModA.Xproc and LibModB.Xproc

You may find that you prefer to always use this method.

1.4.7 Parameters (or arguments)

Consider one of the lines of the Patience program containing a reference to the procedure WriteString:

    WriteString("And said something obscene");

The phrase contained in the brackets is called a parameter or an argument; the terms really amount to the same thing. The procedure WriteString needs just one parameter which must contain printable characters. In Patience, the parameter of WriteString is, in each case, a line of the limerick enclosed in quotation marks (double quotes). Each line of the limerick is in the form of a literal character string. WriteString outputs the value of the parameter to the standard output device, usually a computer screen.
Note that the procedure WriteLn does not require any parameters. It simply outputs an end of line character to the standard output device, causing the next output to appear on the line below.

1.4.8 Literals

The arguments used in Patience are all character string literals. Such literals are simply printable characters enclosed in either single or double quotes. The opening quotes tell the compiler that it should not attempt to translate any of the following characters as Modula-2 instructions. The closing quotes determine the end of the literal.
Modula-2 allows literals to be enclosed in either single or double quotes in order that literals may actually contain quotation marks. Single quotes enclosed in double quotes are treated as literal characters and, similarly, double quotes can be included in a literal by enclosing it in single quotes, so:

    WriteString(' "I love you," she said. ');

will output:

            "I love you," she said.
and

    WriteString(" Sarah's shoes. ");

will output:

            Sarah's shoes.

It is not possible for a single literal string to contain both single and double quotes.

1.4.9   Comments

Comments can be included within your Modula-2 source code by delimiting the comment with the symbols (* and *). The compiler will ignore all characters between these symbols.

For example, we used a comment as a header to give information about Patience.

```
MODULE Patience;
(*
**Purpose: Program to display the lines of a limerick
**Uses module: InOut
*)
FROM InOut IMPORT WriteString, WriteLn;

BEGIN
    .....
    .....
END Patience.
```

The ** at the beginning of each new line within our comment is not essential, but we have included these asterisks simply to make the lines stand out as part of the comment.

Although, in this example, it happens to be spread over several lines, single line comments can be used and comments can be included in lines containing program code.

The compiler treats comments as spaces and, therefore, they cannot be used in places where spaces would not be acceptable, such as in the middle of an identifier or literal.

Comments can be nested inside one another, which at first may sound a strange thing to want to do. However it can be useful when debugging (i.e. removing errors from programs) as whole sections of code can be commented out by enclosing in (* and *) even if the sections already contain comments.

1.4.10   Statements

The body of a program or procedure is the part between the reserved words BEGIN and END.

Within it are a sequence of statements each separated from the next by a semi-colon ';'.

(The last statement in a block of statements is followed by the word END and does not need a semi-colon; thus the last WriteLn in the Patience program has no semi-colon. It would not be syntactically wrong to put a separator here and would have no effect on the working of the program; it would simply cause the compiler to include an extra empty statement at this point in the executable machine code.)

There are only eleven sorts of statement in Modula-2 and they are:

- procedure call,
- assignment,
- RETURN,
- IF,
- FOR,
- WHILE,
- REPEAT,
- LOOP,
- EXIT,
- CASE,
- WITH.

Every statement used in Patience is a procedure call. We will be looking at the other possible statements in the chapters that follow.

Self test 1.2

Which of the following are legal identifiers?

a) sausage
b) IMPORT
c) import
d) num3
e) 34numbers
f) sausage&mash

Self test 1.3

Decide what is wrong with the following literal character string and put it right.

```
'Mine's a large brandy'
```

1.4.11   Dissecting Patience

The `Patience` program contains several features which will be used in all the programs you will write so let's slice it up for a closer look.

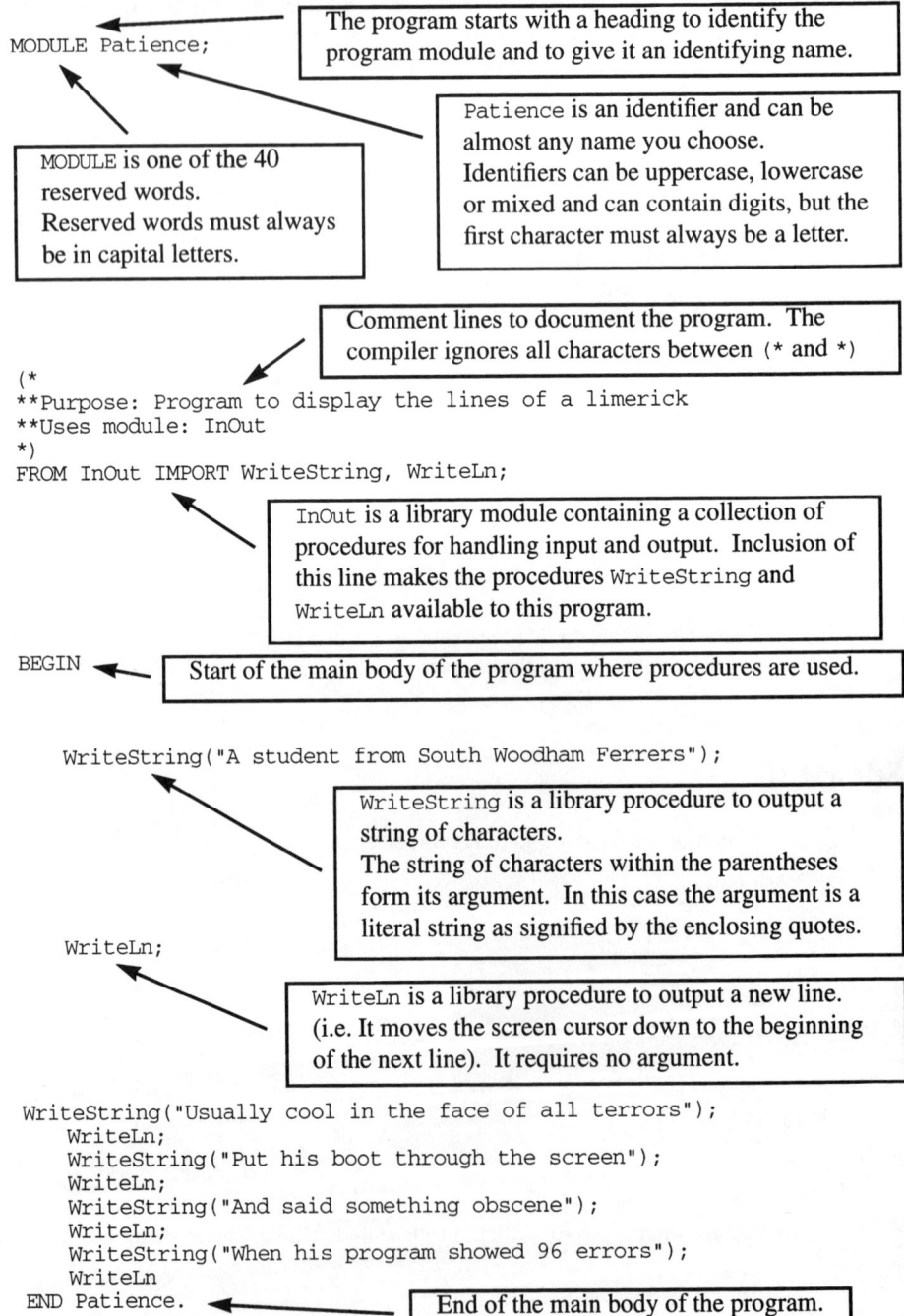

`MODULE Patience;`

> The program starts with a heading to identify the program module and to give it an identifying name.

> `MODULE` is one of the 40 reserved words.
> Reserved words must always be in capital letters.

> `Patience` is an identifier and can be almost any name you choose.
> Identifiers can be uppercase, lowercase or mixed and can contain digits, but the first character must always be a letter.

> Comment lines to document the program. The compiler ignores all characters between (* and *)

```
(*
**Purpose: Program to display the lines of a limerick
**Uses module: InOut
*)
FROM InOut IMPORT WriteString, WriteLn;
```

> `InOut` is a library module containing a collection of procedures for handling input and output. Inclusion of this line makes the procedures `WriteString` and `WriteLn` available to this program.

`BEGIN`

> Start of the main body of the program where procedures are used.

`    WriteString("A student from South Woodham Ferrers");`

> `WriteString` is a library procedure to output a string of characters.
> The string of characters within the parentheses form its argument. In this case the argument is a literal string as signified by the enclosing quotes.

`    WriteLn;`

> `WriteLn` is a library procedure to output a new line. (i.e. It moves the screen cursor down to the beginning of the next line). It requires no argument.

```
    WriteString("Usually cool in the face of all terrors");
    WriteLn;
    WriteString("Put his boot through the screen");
    WriteLn;
    WriteString("And said something obscene");
    WriteLn;
    WriteString("When his program showed 96 errors");
    WriteLn
END Patience.
```

> End of the main body of the program.

Exercise 1.1

Here is a program which contains six deliberate syntax errors.

```
MODULE Tabulate;
(*
**This program contains six syntax errors
*)
From InOut IMPORT WriteString; WriteLn;

BEGIN
     WriteString('                 ');
     WriteString('Column 1  ');
     WriteString('Column 2  ');
     WriteLn;
     Writestring("Row 1");
     WriteLn
     WriteString("Row 2);
     WriteLn
END.
```

a) Try to find all the errors before typing in the program by comparing it to Patience.
b) See if you can work out exactly what the program is supposed to do.
c) Compile the program with the errors in and make a note of the error messages produced by your compiler for each error,
d) Correct the errors, re-compile and run the program.
e) Compare your expectations with the actual result.

Exercise 1.2

Using Patience and Tabulate to guide you, write a program which will output your name and address, as it would appear on an envelope.

Exercise 1.3

Write a program which outputs a poem or limerick of your choice.

2   Dealing with data

The most sensible starting point for writing any piece of computer software is to determine what the user is going to want to do with it. For example, a software engineer may be thinking of writing a word processor application, a drawing package, or even software to control an automatic washing machine.

In the case of a word processor the user would expect to be able to accomplish tasks such as entering words, deleting, copying, moving blocks of text, or changing type style to bold or italic.

The user of a drawing package would probably expect to be able at least to draw lines and other simple shapes, and perhaps to fill areas.

A washing machine control program would probably allow the user to carry out tasks such as to wash cotton, woollen, or synthetic garments, as well as to rinse and spin. To accomplish these tasks the program must be able to control tasks such as switching the main motor, the heater and pumps on and off, and sampling water volume and temperature.

Notice that in all of these cases there are operations (e.g. delete, copy, draw, fill, sample) to be made available and there are objects (things) on which the operations will act.

An operation should represent a task that a user may wish to carry out and is usually specifically related to a particular object so it does not usually make sense to mix them.

For example, it doesn't really make sense to try to delete a pump or to switch on a word even though inside a digital computer all objects, whether words, pumps or pictures, and all operations, such as delete, draw or sample, are ultimately represented as electrical ons and offs. Most operations only make sense when applied to the appropriate objects.

Some types of object and their associated operations are so fundamental and universally useful that they are included as basic building blocks in Modula-2. For example, numbers and alphabetic characters are likely to be required by almost any program. Similarly, arithmetic operations such as add, subtract, multiply and divide, are likely to be in regular demand. Even with these, the principle that most operations only make sense when applied to the appropriate objects still applies. Using the add operation on objects that are numbers may be appropriate, but it is not sensible in 'real-world' terms to try adding 'd' to 'z' without some reinterpretation of the operation 'add'.

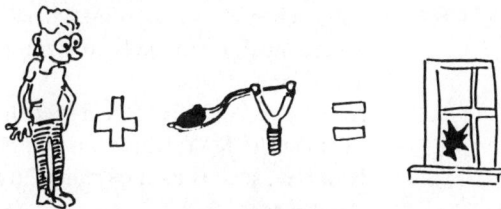

Thinking back to the layered view of a computer system introduced in Section 1.1.4, the user application level deals with the objects and operations associated with the user's tasks. At the high level language level these objects are represented by data of appropriate type and structure, while all are represented ultimately at the hardware level as electrical ons and offs.

2.1 Data types

2.1.1 Simple data types

We'll start by looking at the simplest data (object) types provided by Modula-2. These types each cover a range of related values.

Data type	Range of allowed values
INTEGER	An INTEGER value can in theory be any whole number, positive or negative. In practice the upper and lower limits depend on your computer/compiler combination. e.g. -34, -1, 0, 3, 2345
CARDINAL	A CARDINAL value is similar to INTEGER in that it can be any whole number but, unlike INTEGER, CARDINAL values are always positive. The lower limit is 0 and the upper limit depends on your computer/compiler combination. e.g. 0, 7, 456
REAL	A REAL value is a decimal number. It is not restricted to being a whole number as it includes a fractional part. REAL numbers can be, and often are, represented using scientific notation, e.g. 2.45E-04 (which represents 2.45×10^{-4}, or 0.000245) or they can be represented in the more familiar floating point format, e.g. -0.034, 0.0, 234.4563
BOOLEAN	The BOOLEAN type incorporates just two values: TRUE and FALSE
CHAR	A CHAR value can be any single character contained in the ASCII character set, e.g. A,B,g,*,@, etc. (See Appendix A for a full list of the ASCII character set.)
ARRAY OF CHAR	Single characters may sometimes be useful, but in our programs we are much more likely to want to use whole strings of characters in the form of words. An ARRAY OF CHAR is a special case of a more general type called an ARRAY, which we will be looking at in Chapter 7. However, such is its importance, it is worth knowing something about it now. Items of data type ARRAY [0..Length] OF CHAR can be any string of characters (Length+1) long. (The allowable length is (Length+1) because the range is [0..Length]; the first character is the 0th.) You can substitute for Length any cardinal number you wish.

2.1.2 Ordinal types

Data types such as CARDINAL, INTEGER, CHAR and BOOLEAN are called ordinal types. They all have a clearly defined set of values that could be written out in sequential order.

This is not true of the data type REAL, which is not an ordinal type. For example, between the CARDINAL values 2 and 6 there are clearly three other values, whereas the number of values actually available between REAL 2.0 and 6.0 would be difficult to determine and dependent upon the computer system being used.

2.1.3 Strong typing

Modula-2 is a strongly typed language, which means that the compiler can determine whether operations that are performed on objects are consistent with the object's type. At first you may find this somewhat annoying as the compiler acts in an extremely pedantic way, but it does help to enforce better programming style and can prevent mistakes that would cause hard-to-find programming bugs.

2.2 Operators

Having looked briefly at some of the data types provided by Modula-2, here are some of the built-in operators that can be applied to CARDINAL, INTEGER and REAL numbers:

Operator	Operation and, in brackets, the allowed operand types (i.e. the types the operation can be applied to)
+	Add (CARDINAL, INTEGER and REAL)
−	Subtract (CARDINAL, INTEGER and REAL)
*	Multiply (CARDINAL, INTEGER and REAL)
/	Decimal division (REAL only)
DIV	Integer division (CARDINAL and INTEGER)
MOD	Remainder from integer division (CARDINAL and INTEGER)

2.3   Expressions

Any of the above operators can be used with operands of the appropriate type to form expressions, for example:

```
2.5 * 3.0
```

is an expression which evaluates directly to 7.5 and in which two data values of type REAL are to be combined using the * operator.

To distinguish them from CARDINAL or INTEGER values, REAL numbers in a Modula-2 program must contain a decimal point with at least one digit before the point. So,

```
0.3        0.342      24.      15.8       9.0        0.21E07
```

are all valid REAL values, but

```
5          .23        .79E07
```

are NOT.

We cannot mix the operand types within an expression, so we cannot multiply 2.5 by 3 when 2.5 is a REAL and 3 is a CARDINAL or an INTEGER. Generally, we cannot even use a CARDINAL and an INTEGER in the same expression.
Modula-2 insists that the operands in an expression are compatible with one another. We'll look at this issue in a little more depth later.

Self test 2.1

Which of the following are illegal expressions:

a)   0.3 + 2.8
b)   24.0 * 2
c)   23 MOD 8
d)   4.8 DIV 2.0

2.3.1   Order of precedence

If several operators are included in a single expression Modula-2 evaluates the expression in a strict order of operator precedence. Arithmetic expressions have two levels of precedence:
   * / DIV MOD have the highest precedence so are evaluated before
   + and – which have the lowest precedence.

Operators with the same precedence in an expression are evaluated from left to right.

2.3.2   Using parentheses () to change the order of precedence

To change the order of precedence or to make the order of evaluation of an expression less ambiguous than it might otherwise appear, parentheses can be included. Just as in mathematics, the expressions inside parentheses are evaluated first. Although operator precedence means parentheses are not always necessary in complex expressions, it is a good idea to include them if they make your intention clearer.

For example, without parentheses the expression:

```
6.2 - 3.2 * 2.0
```

evaluates to -0.2 due to precedence of * over - , whereas

```
(6.2 - 3.2) * 2.0
```

evaluates to 6.0

The first expression can be written less ambiguously as

```
6.2 - (3.2 * 2.0)
```

2.4   Variables

To allow programs the flexibility of handling a variety of data values in a particular situation, data values can be represented by variables which have identifying names. These names must follow the rules for identifiers described in Section 1.4.2.

A variable identifier can be thought of as a label for an area of storage in the computer's memory big enough to hold a value of a particular data type. Before a variable can be used its data type must be declared. So, for example, for a variable of type INTEGER we might choose an identifying name, num. We must declare num as being of type INTEGER so the computer can set aside a portion of free memory large enough to hold an INTEGER value. We don't need to know exactly which bit of memory is used; we simply refer to it with our identifier, num, and the computer should know where to find it. The actual value stored in num can be changed during the execution of the program.

When space is first set aside for our num variable the initial value is undefined. The portion of memory the computer selected as free could already contain any old rubbish value so we must be careful not to use the stored value until we are sure it contains something sensible.

The value of a variable is undefined until you store something in it.

Dealing with data

We can use variables in expressions in a similar way to using unknowns in algebraic expressions.

For example, if we had declared two variables, degC and degF, both of type REAL to represent temperature values in degrees Celsius and degrees Fahrenheit respectively, the expression to convert Celsius to Fahrenheit would be:

```
(degC * 9.0 / 5.0) + 32.0
```

and to convert Fahrenheit to Celsius:

```
(degF - 32.0) * 5.0 / 9.0
```

2.4.1   Assignment

Assignment statements are used to change the state of a variable, i.e. to change the contents of its associated memory space. Either actual values or values resulting from the evaluation of an expression can be assigned to a variable using an assignment statement. For example:

```
degC := 23.2;
```

assigns the value 23.2 to the variable degC.

The assignment statement:

```
degF := (degC * 9.0 / 5.0) + 32.0;
```

assigns the result of evaluating the right hand side expression to the variable degF.

Syntax chart for assignment

Assignment:

———▶ *variable identifier* ———▶ := ———▶ *expression* ———▶

Notice that even though assignment expressions may look similar to normal algebraic equations they are not the same.

The symbol := does not mean 'equals'; it means something nearer to 'is now to contain.'

The expression:

```
degF = degF + 23.0;
```

is algebraically impossible; `degF` represents an unknown value and there is no value of `degF` that can possibly satisfy it, but

```
degF := degF + 23.0;
```

is perfectly acceptable because `degF` identifies an area of computer memory.
`degF + 23.0` adds 23.0 to whatever `degF` currently contains and the statement directs that `degF` 'is now to contain' the result of the addition replacing the value originally stored in `degF`.

2.4.2   Declaring variables

To set aside memory for our variables we need to declare their types. The variable declarations follow the reserved word VAR.
Using `degF` and `degC` as examples, here's how to do it:

```
MODULE Convert;
(*
**Purpose: To convert temperatures between the
**Celsius and Fahrenheit scales
*)
FROM ..... IMPORT ........
VAR
     degF, degC : REAL;
BEGIN
(*Main program code to convert between temperature scales
**using the variables degF and degC which have both been
**declared as being of type REAL*)
END Convert.
```

(This is not a complete program but shows the position of the variable declarations.)

`degF` and `degC` are both of type REAL so they are declared together in the same type declaration, however, the effect is exactly the same as if we had declared them separately, thus:

```
VAR
     degF : REAL;
     degC : REAL;
```

If we require more variables of different types we can declare these in a similar way:

```
VAR
     degF, degC : REAL;
     num : INTEGER;
     success : BOOLEAN;
```

Self test 2.2

Assuming the following variable declarations have been made:

```
VAR
    balance, sum : INTEGER;
    total : REAL;
```

which of the following are syntactically correct assignment statements?

(a) `total := .78;`
(b) `sum := 0.21E06;`
(c) `balance := sum;`
(d) `total := total + 78.0;`
(e) `total := balance + sum;`
(f) `sum := balance MOD 2;`
(g) `total := sum DIV 2.0;`
(h) `sum := balance * balance;`
(i) `balance := sum / balance;`
(j) `sum := (sum - 5);`

Self test 2.3

Write a single statement which could replace the two statements below.

```
class := 12 - 3 * class;
class := class DIV 3 + 15;
```

2.5   Library modules

2.5.1   Input and output

Besides the operators described above, other operations we are likely to wish to apply to data include output to a standard output device, usually the display screen, and input from a standard input device, usually the keyboard. Unfortunately, the I/O (input/output) parts of computer programs are often highly specific to the computer system being used; screens are different and input devices vary, so no one set of I/O facilities is going to meet all possible needs. Therefore, unlike its predecessor Pascal, Modula-2 has no input or output commands built into the language. As its name suggests, it takes a modular approach and allows hardware specific program modules to be written independently from the main program parts. So you could write a program that takes its input from a keyboard and possibly convert it to mouse input simply by changing the appropriate module.

Although Modula-2 compilers normally come complete with I/O library modules containing fairly standard procedures based on Niklaus Wirth's recommendations, the fact remains that these library modules sometimes differ. We will try to stick to using facilities you are almost certain to find with your compiler, but be warned that you might find some slight differences.

All Modula-2 compilers that we know of have a library module called InOut, which provides some of the basic I/O facilities.

Here's a list of some procedures you should find available in InOut, including WriteString and WriteLn, which you have already met as they were imported by Chapter 1's Patience program:

FOR INPUT:

Purpose	Procedure with its arguments
To read in a character of type CHAR	Read(ch) (*Where ch is any variable of type CHAR*)
To read in a string or array of CHARs	ReadString(str) (*Where str is any variable of type ARRAY OF CHAR *)
To read in an INTEGER value	ReadInt(num) (*Where num is any variable of type INTEGER*)
To read in a CARDINAL value	ReadCard(num) (*Where num is any variable of type CARDINAL*)

AND FOR OUTPUT:

Purpose	Procedure with its arguments
To write out a character of type CHAR	`Write(ch)` (*Where ch is any value, constant or variable of type CHAR*)
To write out a string or array of CHARs	`WriteString(str)` (*Where str is any value, constant or variable of type ARRAY OF CHAR*)
To terminate the current line and move on to the next	`WriteLn` (*No arguments*)
To write out an INTEGER value	`WriteInt(num,width)` (*Where num is any value, constant or variable of type INTEGER to be output and width is any value, constant or variable of type CARDINAL to describe the minimum output field width*)
To write out a CARDINAL value	`WriteCard(num,width)` (*Where num is any value, constant or variable of type CARDINAL to be output and width is any value, constant or variable of type CARDINAL to describe the minimum output field width*)

You may notice that amongst these input and output procedures there are none to handle type REAL.

It is possible that your InOut module includes facilities for REALs but you are more likely to find them in another library module called RealInOut. This module, perhaps with one or two other things, should include the following procedures:

Purpose	Procedure with its arguments
To read in a real number	`ReadReal(num)` (*Where num is any variable of type REAL*)
To write out a real number	`WriteReal(num,width)` (*Where num is any value, constant or variable of type REAL to be output and width is any value, constant or variable of type CARDINAL to describe the number of characters to use for that output*)

For example:

```
WriteReal(23.76,12)
```

would produce output something like this:

```
2.376E+01
```

with leading blanks to fill out the 12 character space specified.

2.5.2   Dealing with fixed point format

Unfortunately, Wirth's description of RealInOut does not include a procedure for outputing real numbers in fixed point format, e.g. 23.76, which makes life a little more difficult. Lack of such a procedure is such a glaring omission that most compilers do provide one.

Here's a fairly typical example:

```
WriteFixPt(num,width,places)
```
(*Where num is any value, constant or variable of type REAL to be output; width is any value, constant or variable of type CARDINAL to specify the number of characters to be used for output and places specifies the number of digits to be shown after the decimal point*)

So,
```
WriteFixPt(23.76,6,1);
```

would output

```
23.8
```

which has one digit after the decimal point and two leading blanks to make up the required width.

However, such procedures are not all quite the same.

Self test 2.4

Write a series of statements that use the procedures from the InOut library module to read a CARDINAL value from the keyboard into variable, card, then write it to the screen in a minimum field width of 10 characters.

2.6   Case study: *Beans, beans, good for the heart...*

The following series of short programs are all designed to do the same simple calculation but each differs slightly from the others in order to illustrate some further features of Modula-2.

When I cook there is one thing on the menu: baked beans; consequently when I replenish my supplies I have one kind of item in my supermarket trolley: tins of beans!
At the checkout the assistant (trying politely to keep a healthy distance from a customer with such a dietary habit) enters the price for one tin, then the number of tins in my trolley.
A short program can be written to allow this to be done and to total up my bill.
To avoid the problem of outputing REAL numbers, our first version of this program will work only with whole numbers of pence rather than £s and pence. Our values are, therefore, all going to be whole numbers and should never need to be negative so CARDINAL is a suitable type for both the quantities and the prices.

```
MODULE Beans1;
(*
**Purpose: To calculate my Bean bill
**Uses module: InOut
*)

FROM InOut IMPORT WriteString,ReadCard,WriteLn,WriteCard;

VAR
    beanPrice,noOfTins : CARDINAL;
BEGIN
    WriteString("Enter price of a tin of beans in pence:");
    ReadCard(beanPrice);

    WriteLn;
    WriteString("Enter the number of tins: ");
    ReadCard(noOfTins);
    WriteLn;



    WriteCard((beanPrice * noOfTins),1);
    WriteString(" pence");
    WriteLn

    END Beans1.
```

Imports four library procedures from `InOut`.

Declares two variables of type CARDINAL for use by the program.

Program pauses until a CARDINAL value is typed in and the RETURN key is pressed. The value is placed in part of the computer's memory known as `beanPrice` by this program.

The result is calculated by multiplying the value held in `beanPrice` by the value held in `noOfTins`, and then output directly.

Although the width is specified as 1, this does not truncate numbers with more than one digit. It simply ensures there are no leading spaces however small the number.

This second version of the Beans program uses an extra variable, bill, in which the result of the calculation is placed using an assignment statement. This makes the argument to WriteCard clearer and can also be useful if the result is to be used later in the program.

```
MODULE Beans2;
(*
**Purpose: To calculate my Bean bill using assignment
**Uses module: InOut
*)
FROM InOut IMPORT WriteString, ReadCard, WriteLn, WriteCard;
VAR
     beanPrice,noOfTins,bill : CARDINAL;
BEGIN
     WriteString("Enter price of a tin of beans in pence: ");
     ReadCard(beanPrice);
     WriteLn;
     WriteString("Enter the number of tins: ");
     ReadCard(noOfTins);
     WriteLn;
     bill := (beanPrice * noOfTins);
     WriteCard(bill,1);
     WriteString(" pence");
     WriteLn
END Beans2.
```

2.6.1   Constants

A variable is so named because it is allowed to change its value during the execution of a program. There are many problems which involve fixed or constant values. One way to specify these is to use literal values within the program itself. For example, to calculate the circumference of a circle from the radius the formula required is;

```
(2 x π x radius)
```

and can be expressed as:

```
circumference := 2.0 * 3.14159 * radius;
```

Alternatively, important constants such as π can be defined at the start of the program and given a suitable identifier.

The reserved word CONST must be used before constant declarations. For example:

```
MODULE ....
FROM ....
CONST
    PI = 3.14159;
VAR
    circumference, radius:REAL;
BEGIN
    ....
    circumference:=2.0*PI*radius;
    ....
END ....
```

A value, such as the 2.0 in the above example, is usually kept as a literal, unless it has special significance in a particular formula which needs to be made clear.

The type of a constant is determined by its value. Given the constant declarations:

```
CONST
    PI = 3.14159;
    CREDIT = 23;
    DEBIT = -57;
```

PI is of type REAL, CREDIT is of type CARDINAL and DEBIT is of type INTEGER.

Using constants can help to clarify parts of a program. Constants can also help with maintenance. If, for example, we decided to increase the accuracy of the value of π, then no matter how many times π is used in the program it is only necessary to alter one line, the constant declaration. Had we not used a constant we would have to find and change every occurrence of the literal value.

Constant syntax chart

Constant:

$\longrightarrow$ *constant identifier* $\longrightarrow$ = $\longrightarrow$ *constant expression* $\longrightarrow$

A constant may be used in place of any literal value of the same data type.

In the following example, the Beans program has been simplified slightly by making the assumption that the price of a tin of beans will be a constant value of 28 pence:

```
MODULE Beans3;
(*
**Purpose: To calculate my Bean bill using a constant
**Uses module: InOut
*)
FROM InOut IMPORT WriteString, ReadCard, WriteLn, WriteCard;
CONST
    PRICE = 28;
VAR
    noOfTins,bill : CARDINAL;
BEGIN
    WriteString("Enter the number of tins of beans: ");
    ReadCard(noOfTins);
    WriteLn;
    bill := (PRICE * noOfTins);
    WriteCard(bill,1);
    WriteString(" pence");
    WriteLn
END Beans3.
```

2.6.2   Non-printable characters

Most modern computers use an internal character set based on ASCII (American Standard Code for Information Interchange). So far all the characters we have used as values of type CHAR have been printable, keyboard characters. However, some ASCII characters have no simple printable symbol to represent them. To be used as input data some non-printable characters can be typed by pressing the Ctrl (Control) key at the same time as pressing an alphabetic character; others can be entered using a standard keyboard key such as Esc (Escape). If you need to include such characters inside your program you cannot use the keyboard to enter the value when typing in your source code, since source code must consist of printable characters.

Modula-2 provides an alternative way of expressing individual characters, by using the octal (base 8) representation of the character's ordinal number followed by a letter C. (The octal number system uses only the figures 0 to 7, so decimal 8 becomes octal 10.)

ASCII characters are in the range 0C to 177C. For example the ordinal number 27 has an octal equivalent 33, so 33C and represents the Escape character and is treated as being of type CHAR. The ASCII character 7C represents Bell, so the statement:

```
Write(7C);
```

will cause your terminal to beep.

It can be useful to set up character constants to use within a program, for example:

```
CONST
     NULL = 0C;
     ESC = 33C;
     BELL = 7C;
```

Such constants can be used in expressions wherever a CHAR type is valid. You may find that your system provides a library module which makes these constants available for import by your programs.

The table in Appendix A lists the ASCII character set together with decimal and octal values.

2.6.3   Subranges

If it is known in advance that only a limited range of values is to be used it is possible to define a variable with a subrange of a data type. This subrange is specified in square brackets. The type must be ordinal and is implied by the values used, for example the statement:

```
VAR
     num:[0..24];
```

means that the variable num may contain any CARDINAL value between 0 and 24 inclusive. CARDINAL rather than INTEGER type is assumed because the lower limit is not negative.

In a similar way, the statement:

```
VAR
     letter: ['a'..'j'];
```

means that letter may contain any CHAR value between 'a' and 'j' inclusive.

Subranges may be used in place of data types in type declarations.

2.6.4   Compatibility

Modula-2 is a strongly typed language and, as such, does not generally let you mix variables of different type in the same expression. Therefore, you cannot directly add a REAL value to a CARDINAL, or assign an INTEGER to a CHAR variable without the compiler complaining. However, the rules concerning this are not as clear-cut as you might suppose. There are, in fact, four levels relating to compatibility and data types may be:

- THE SAME
  which means they are identical and can always be used together.
  As you will see shortly, this degree of compatibility is required in respect of some procedure parameters.

- COMPATIBLE
  which means they are not necessarily identical, but can usually be used together in an expression without problems.
  For example, CARDINALs and CARDINAL subranges are not the SAME, but they are COMPATIBLE and can be used together in expressions.

- ASSIGNMENT COMPATIBLE
  which means they are not necessarily identical (i.e. the SAME) or COMPATIBLE, but can be used as the variable and the expression in an assignment statement.
  For example, INTEGERs and CARDINALs are not COMPATIBLE, so cannot normally be used together in the same expression. However, the value of an INTEGER variable can be assigned to a CARDINAL variable provided that the INTEGER value is within the range of CARDINAL values. e.g. not negative.

- NOT COMPATIBLE
  in which case they cannot normally be used together in any of the above ways.

The full implications of these levels will, we hope, become more apparent to you as we look at further language features.

As a reference guide, and to help you determine the level of compatibility between two data types, we have included a flow chart in Appendix B.

In the following example it is assumed that beans are being rationed and that the number of tins of beans sold to a customer can never exceed 24 and will never be less than 0.

Thus a subrange [0..24] is used.

```
MODULE Beans4;
(*
**Purpose: To calculate my Bean bill using subrange
**Uses module: InOut
*)
FROM InOut IMPORT WriteString, ReadCard, WriteLn, WriteCard;
CONST
    PRICE = 28;
VAR
    noOfTins : [0..24];
    bill : CARDINAL;
BEGIN
    WriteString("Enter the number of tins of beans: ");
    ReadCard(noOfTins);
    WriteLn;
    bill := (PRICE * noOfTins);
    WriteCard(bill,1);
    WriteString(" pence");
    WriteLn
END Beans4.
```

Unfortunately, the statement;

```
ReadCard(noOfTins);
```

is now illegal. Because ReadCard returns a value via its parameter, it permits only parameters that are the SAME as CARDINAL type. A subrange of CARDINAL cannot be used. (You may find that some compilers do not detect this error.)

A CARDINAL subrange could, on the other hand, be used with WriteCard, as this does not return a value via its parameter. (See Section 3.1.2 where this is explained in more detail.)

The expression;

```
(PRICE * noOfTins)
```

is legal, because the constant PRICE is of CARDINAL type and noOfTins is a CARDINAL subrange. These types are not the SAME but they are COMPATIBLE and can be used together in an expression.

Take a look at Beans5:

```
MODULE Beans5;
(*
**Purpose: To calculate my Bean bill using subrange
**Uses module: InOut
*)
FROM InOut IMPORT WriteString, ReadCard, WriteLn, WriteCard;
CONST
    PRICE = 28;
VAR
    noOfTins : [0..24];
    quantity, bill : CARDINAL;
BEGIN
    WriteString("Enter the number of tins of beans: ");
    ReadCard(quantity);
    noOfTins := quantity;
    WriteLn;
    bill := (PRICE * noOfTins);
    WriteCard(bill,1);
    WriteString(" pence");
    WriteLn
END Beans5.
```

This time the program will work.

The assignment of the CARDINAL, quantity, to CARDINAL subrange, noOfTins, is legal as they are ASSIGNMENT COMPATIBLE. However, we have a potential problem. If quantity contains a value outside the specified range, [0..24], it will be 'bad news' for our program. It will crash!

We could use a constant to set the upper range limit in Beans4 and thus increase ease of maintenance:

```
CONST
    LIMIT = 24;
VAR
    noOfTins : [0..LIMIT];
```

To put it to its full advantage, any reference to the upper limit of the subrange in the program should make use of LIMIT rather than the literal value 24.

The use of a subrange might seem to have caused more trouble than it was worth. However, in practice, we should make the program more robust by providing checks to ensure that the input value is within the range limits. The use of subrange does ensure that nothing can happen within the program to take the value of noOfTins outside the allowed range.

2.6.5   Declaring your own data types

In addition to the standard data types provided by Modula-2, such as CHAR and
CARDINAL, it is possible to declare your own data types with appropriate identifiers.
The simplest form of user declared data type is a subrange type declaration, as used in the
program below. The reserved word TYPE must be used before type declarations.

```
MODULE Beans6;
(*
**Purpose: To calculate my Bean bill using Ration type
**Uses module: InOut
*)
FROM InOut IMPORT WriteString, ReadCard, WriteLn, WriteCard;
CONST
    PRICE = 28;
TYPE
    Ration = [0..24];
VAR
    noOfTins: Ration;
    quantity, bill : CARDINAL;
BEGIN
    WriteString("Enter the number of tins of beans: ");
    ReadCard(quantity);
    noOfTins := quantity;
    WriteLn;
    bill := (PRICE * noOfTins);
    WriteCard(bill,1);
    WriteString(" pence");
    WriteLn
END Beans6.
```

Once again, we could use a constant to increase maintainability:

```
CONST
    LIMIT = 24;
TYPE
    Ration=[0..LIMIT];
VAR
    noOfTins:Ration;
```

Once a data type has been declared, its identifier can be used inside the program in place
of the equivalent type declaration. This can have many advantages, especially when
writing large programs.

Exercise 2.1

To find out more about your own compiler, experiment with Beans5 and Beans6, using out of range values.

Exercise 2.2

Write a program to allow input of a temperature in degrees Celsius and to calculate and output the equivalent temperature in degrees Fahrenheit.

Exercise 2.3

Write a program which reads in a REAL number representing the radius of a circle, calculates the area (π * r * r) and outputs the result.

To do this you will need to locate and import the procedures supplied with your compiler for reading and writing REALs.

Make sure that you use a constant declaration for π.

3 Structuring programs

3.1 Using procedures

A good strategy for solving large problems is to 'divide and conquer' by breaking up a complex problem into smaller, more manageable pieces. The question is: how best do we divide a program design problem?

One way is to divide the program into simpler, subprogram parts, with each part functionally separate from the others. That is, with each part having its own specific job to do. Procedures provide a mechanism for doing this and, as well as using procedures provided in pre-written library modules, we can write our own.

Each procedure that we write should be viewed as a functionally separate subprogram with its own local constant and variable declarations.

Looking at the Beans2 example from Chapter 2, we'll redesign it from scratch; this time using procedures.

Here it is again for reference:

```
MODULE Beans2;
(*
**Purpose: To calculate my Bean bill using assignment
**Uses module: InOut
*)
FROM InOut IMPORT WriteString, ReadCard, WriteLn, WriteCard;
VAR
    beanPrice,noOfTins,bill : CARDINAL;
BEGIN
    WriteString("Enter price of a tin of beans in pence: ");
    ReadCard(beanPrice);
    WriteLn;
    WriteString("Enter the number of tins: ");
    ReadCard(noOfTins);
    WriteLn;
    bill := (beanPrice * noOfTins);
    WriteCard(bill,1);
    WriteString(" pence");
    WriteLn
END Beans2.
```

When applying the divide and conquer principle to the Beans program, the first step is to recognize that its overall job consists of three functionally separate parts:

```
BEGIN
    GetBeanData
    CalculateBill
    DisplayBill
END
```

This is fairly typical of small programs in that we have an input, a calculation and an output part, i.e.

```
    GetInput
    Process
    DisplayOutput
```

Each procedure communicates with other program parts via the data passed through its parameters so an important part of its design is the decision about what data needs to be passed in and out. So next we need to think about the data that each procedure requires to communicate to the others.

If we regard GetBeanData, CalculateBill and DisplayBill as procedure calls, what will the parameters be?

Well, GetBeanData needs to obtain the price and quantity of tins from the keyboard and make these available to CalculateBill, which needs this data in order to calculate the total bill, which it, in turn, must pass on to DisplayBill, which needs the final bill amount in order to display it on the screen.

Therefore, we need to pass beanPrice, noOfTins and bill between the procedures as follows:

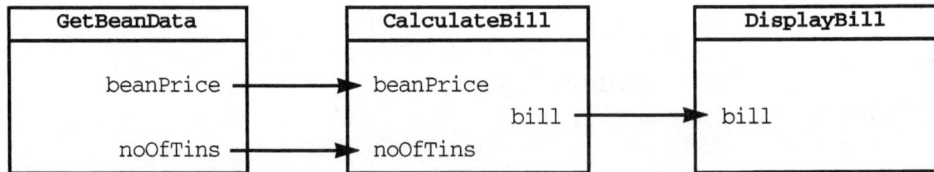

GetBeanData	CalculateBill	DisplayBill
beanPrice →	beanPrice	
	bill →	bill
noOfTins →	noOfTins	

3.1.1   Actual parameters and formal parameters

Parameters are used to pass data into and out of procedures. The parameters in a procedure call statement are called actual parameters. That is, they are the actual parameters with which we will call the subprogram. Each one corresponds to a formal parameter (or parameter template) declared in the corresponding procedure heading. The correspondence is by position rather than by name, so the first actual parameter maps to the first formal parameter, the second actual parameter to the second formal parameter, and so on, even if the parameter names differ.

Actual parameters

```
GetBeanData(beanPrice, noOfTins);
(*Call*)
```

Formal parameters

```
PROCEDURE GetBeanData(VAR beanPrice, noOfTins : CARDINAL);
(*Procedure heading*)
```

3.1.2   Variable parameters and value parameters

In the above example, the parameters are to be used for passing values OUT OF the procedure so they can be used by the main program. These parameters must be variables so that they can be assigned values within the procedure.
The reserved word VAR is used in front of these formal parameter declarations to indicate that they are indeed variable parameters.
Variable parameters are used to pass data OUT OF or INTO AND OUT OF subprograms. The corresponding calling arguments MUST be variables (actual values cannot be used).
Consider InOut's input procedures such as Read and ReadString.
These must always be called using variable parameters through which to pass input data back to your program.

A call to the GetBeanData procedure in the form:

```
GetBeanData(beanPrice, noOfTins);
```

is acceptable because all the arguments are variables, but the call:

```
GetBeanData(28,16);
```

is not acceptable because the parameters are values and as such cannot be assigned new values from within the procedure.

In the case of:

```
PROCEDURE DisplayBill(bill : CARDINAL);
```

the parameter `bill` is for passing a value INTO the procedure. Notice that the reserved word VAR is not used. This is called a value parameter and the calling parameter can be a variable or it can be an actual value.

So, the procedure call:

```
DisplayBill(bill);
```

is legal and so is the call:

```
DisplayBill(56);
```

A procedure declaration can contain both variable and value parameters.
e.g.
```
PROCEDURE CalculateBill( beanPrice,noOfTins : CARDINAL;
                              VAR bill : CARDINAL);
```

Here, `beanPrice` and `noOfTins` are value parameters for values into the procedure and `bill` is a variable parameter.

The rules are that:

- the number of actual parameters must match the number of formal parameters,

- the order of the actual parameters must be the same as the order of the formal parameters because the parameters are matched by position, not by name,

- in the case of value parameters, the type of each actual parameter must be ASSIGNMENT COMPATIBLE with the type of the corresponding formal parameter and

- in the case of variable parameters, each actual parameter must be of the SAME type as the corresponding formal parameter.

(See Section 2.6.4 and Appendix B for more information on compatibility.)

Here is `Beans2` rewritten as `Beans7`; this time using procedures:

```
MODULE Beans7;
(*
**Purpose: To calculate my Bean bill using procedures
**Uses module: InOut
*)
FROM InOut IMPORT WriteString, ReadCard, WriteLn, WriteCard;

VAR
    beanPrice,noOfTins,bill : CARDINAL;

PROCEDURE GetBeanData(VAR beanPrice, noOfTins : CARDINAL);
BEGIN
    WriteString("Enter price of a tin of beans in pence: ");
    ReadCard(beanPrice);
    WriteLn;
    WriteString("Enter the number of tins: ");
    ReadCard(noOfTins);
    WriteLn
END GetBeanData;

PROCEDURE CalculateBill( beanPrice, noOfTins : CARDINAL;
                         VAR bill : CARDINAL);
BEGIN
    bill := (beanPrice * noOfTins)
END CalculateBill;

PROCEDURE DisplayBill(bill : CARDINAL);
BEGIN
    WriteCard(bill,1);
    WriteString(" pence");
    WriteLn
END DisplayBill;

BEGIN (*Main Beans7 program*)
    GetBeanData(beanPrice, noOfTins);
    CalculateBill(beanPrice, noOfTins, bill);
    DisplayBill(bill)
END Beans7.
```

Although in `Beans7` we have chosen to use the same identifiers for actual and formal parameters, this is not necessary.

For example, consider the `InOut` procedure `ReadCard`. `Beans7` makes use of `ReadCard` twice: once with the identifier `price` and the second time with identifier `tins`. It will work with any identifier as the actual parameter name as long as there is only one actual parameter and its type is CARDINAL.

3.1.3   Block structure

Here's yet another helping of beans: Beans8. Everything is pretty much the same as Beans7 except that this time each procedure uses its own unique identifiers.

```
MODULE Beans8;
(*
**Purpose: To calculate my Bean bill and to show that
**actual and formal parameter names can differ
**Uses module: InOut
*)
FROM InOut IMPORT WriteString, ReadCard, WriteLn, WriteCard;
(*************************************************************)


VAR
    beanPrice,noOfTins,bill : CARDINAL;

PROCEDURE GetBeanData(VAR price, tins : CARDINAL);
BEGIN
    WriteString("Enter price of a tin of beans in pence: ");
    ReadCard(price);
    WriteLn;
    WriteString("Enter the number of tins: ");
    ReadCard(tins);
    WriteLn
END GetBeanData;

PROCEDURE CalculateBill(unitPrice, quantity : CARDINAL;
                                    VAR total : CARDINAL);
BEGIN
    total := (unitPrice * quantity)
END CalculateBill;

PROCEDURE DisplayBill(cost: CARDINAL);
BEGIN
    WriteCard(cost,1);
    WriteString(" pence");
    WriteLn
END DisplayBill;
(*************************************************************)

BEGIN (*Main Beans8 program*)
    GetBeanData(beanPrice, noOfTins);
    CalculateBill(beanPrice, noOfTins, bill);
    DisplayBill(bill)
END Beans8.
```

The procedure `CalculateBill` could be used for calculating the total price of commodities other than beans. This fact is much more apparent once its parameters do not specifically refer to beans.

Modula-2 programs actually consist of three distinct regions which we have separated, in `Beans8`, using comment lines.
The first part of the program contains the module heading and import list and the second consists of all the necessary declarations. In this case we have had to declare three global variables and three procedures to be used by the main program. In this declaration region we could also have declared any constants or types to be used by the program. The last region of the program code is the main program body which, in this case, consists of just three procedure calls. When the program is run it is the sequence of instructions in the main program body that are executed and the program only executes the procedures if and when they are called from the main program.

The program is a module and is said to constitute a block, which is a sequence of optional declarations followed by a sequence of executable program statements between BEGIN and END.
Modula-2 allows this block structure to be nested within itself rather like the hollow Russian dolls which each open to reveal another. In this way procedure declarations each form their own block consisting of optional, local declarations and a sequence of executable statements. As you will see, the declarations within a procedure can include constants, types, variables and more procedures, which in turn can contain their own constants, types, variables and more procedures, which in turn can contain their own constants, types, variables and more procedures, which in turn ....

We'll take a closer look at this in Chapter 4.

Self test 3.1

Assuming the variable declarations:

```
VAR
    price, noOfTins, total : CARDINAL;
    amount : REAL;
    quantity, cost : INTEGER;
```

and the procedure:

```
PROCEDURE CalculateBill(unitPrice, quantity : CARDINAL;
                            VAR total : CARDINAL);
```

which of the following are legal calls to `CalculateBill`:

```
a)  CalculateBill(price, noOfTins, total);
b)  CalculateBill(23, 4, total);
c)  CalculateBill(price, noOfTins, 46);
d)  CalculateBill(price, amount, total);
e)  CalculateBill(price, quantity, total);
f)  CalculateBill(price, quantity, cost);
```

Self test 3.2

In the procedure heading:

```
PROCEDURE CalcTAX(price, rate : REAL; VAR tax : REAL);
```

which of the following correctly describes `tax`:

a) it is a formal variable parameter,
b) it is an actual variable parameter,
c) it is a formal value parameter or
d) it is an actual value parameter.

Self test 3.3

Which one of the following best describes an ACTUAL PARAMETER?

a) It is one of the identifiers included in brackets in a PROCEDURE heading.
b) It is a value which is passed back from a procedure.
c) It is a variable or value in brackets in a procedure call.
d) It is a value which is input to a procedure but not output.

3.1.4   Parameter passing

When a procedure has a formal parameter that is a value parameter (i.e. not preceded by a VAR) it acts in a similar way to a variable which is local to (i.e. declared within) the procedure's block, in that a new area of memory is allocated for it each time the procedure is called. The difference between a value parameter and a local variable is that a value parameter has an initial value: that of the corresponding actual parameter with which the procedure is called.

When a procedure has a formal parameter that is a variable parameter, then no new space is allocated for it. Instead, the actual parameter itself is used by the procedure. This variable is known to the procedure by the formal parameter identifying name, which acts like a synonym during the procedure call. Thus, any changes to the variable parameter within the procedure are also changes to the actual parameter.

As value parameters are used for passing values into procedures, corresponding actual parameters can be either values, or variables which contain a value.

As variable parameters are used for passing values in and out, or just out of procedures, corresponding actual parameters can only be variables to which the procedure can assign new values.

To illustrate what happens when Beans8 is run, consider the following explanation, then try explaining it to an understanding friend using your own words and diagrams.

Here are the procedures with their parameters; the arrows show how the parameters are passed between the main program and the procedures:

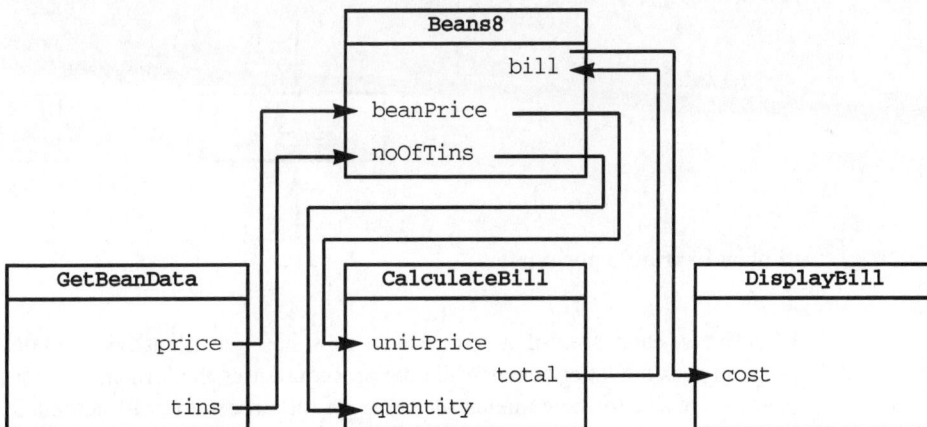

In the diagrams that follow the rectangular boxes represent memory space and matching space letters identify shared portions of memory.

The main program, Beans8, first uses VAR to set aside memory space for three CARDINAL variables, beanPrice, noOfTins and bill.

```
VAR
    beanPrice, noOfTins, bill : CARDINAL;
```

Structuring programs

This effectively sets aside three areas of appropriate sized memory labelled `beanPrice`, `noOfTins` and `bill`.

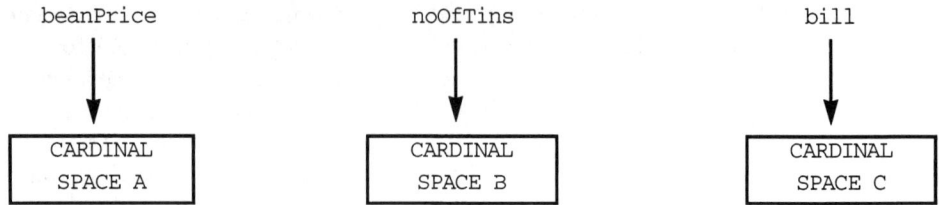

```
      beanPrice                    noOfTins                      bill

          |                           |                           |
          v                           v                           v
   +-------------+             +-------------+             +-------------+
   | CARDINAL    |             | CARDINAL    |             | CARDINAL    |
   | SPACE A     |             | SPACE B     |             | SPACE C     |
   +-------------+             +-------------+             +-------------+
```

The main program calls `GetBeanData` with the actual parameters `beanPrice` and `noOfTins`.

```
GetBeanData(beanPrice, noOfTins);
```

These map onto the corresponding formal parameters `price` and `tins`.

```
PROCEDURE GetBeanData(VAR price, tins : CARDINAL);
```

As these are variable parameters, `price` relates to the portion of memory labelled `beanPrice` and `tins` relates to `noOfTins`.

Actual variable parameters: beanPrice   noOfTins

```
                                 |                           |
                                 v                           v
                          +-------------+             +-------------+
                          | CARDINAL    |             | CARDINAL    |
                          | SPACE A     |             | SPACE B     |
                          +-------------+             +-------------+
                                 ^                           ^
                                 |                           |
```

Formal variable parameters: price   tins

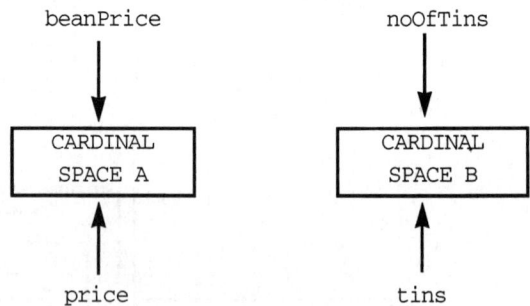

Effectively, each area of memory used now has two identifying names. The main program uses the latter names while the procedure uses the former. So, for example, any alteration made to the contents of `price` in the procedure will automatically apply to `beanPrice` and thus be communicated back to the main program.

These values are then passed via the actual parameters `beanPrice` and `noOfTins` in the main program's call to `CalculateBill`.

```
CalculateBill(beanPrice, noOfTins, bill);
```

Actual value parameters: beanPrice   noOfTins

```
   ┌──────────────┐          ┌──────────────┐
   │   CARDINAL   │          │   CARDINAL   │
   │   SPACE  A   │          │   SPACE  B   │
   └──────────────┘          └──────────────┘
```

These map to the formal value parameters unitPrice and quantity.

```
PROCEDURE CalculateBill( unitPrice, quantity : CARDINAL;
                   VAR total : CARDINAL);
```

As these are value parameters two new portions of memory are set aside labelled
unitPrice and quantity.

Formal value parameters: unitPrice   quantity

```
   ┌──────────────┐          ┌──────────────┐
   │   CARDINAL   │          │   CARDINAL   │
   │   SPACE  D   │          │   SPACE  E   │
   └──────────────┘          └──────────────┘
```

The values of the corresponding actual parameters are copied into these to be used by the
procedure. As unitPrice and quantity contain copies, any changes to these will not be
communicated back via beanPrice and noOfTins.

total is a variable formal parameter which corresponds to the calling actual parameter
bill. As it is a variable parameter no new portion of memory is set aside for total.
total is simply another label for memory allocated for bill. total is the identifier used
within CalculateBill and bill is the identifier used by the main program.

Actual variable parameter: bill

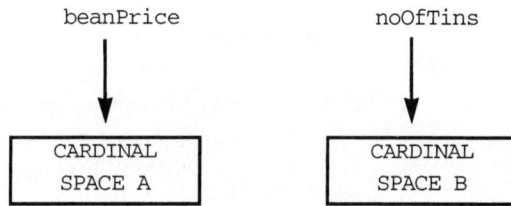

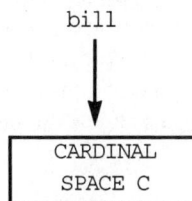

```
           ┌──────────────┐
           │   CARDINAL   │
           │   SPACE  C   │
           └──────────────┘
```

Formal variable parameter: total

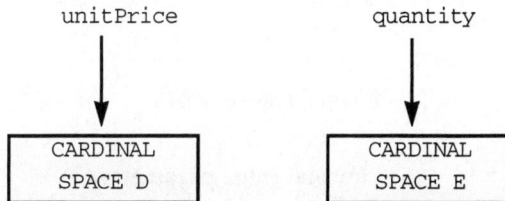

Finally, the actual parameter `bill` is used by the main program to call `DisplayBill`:

```
DisplayBill(bill);
```

which has formal parameter `cost`.

```
PROCEDURE DisplayBill(cost : CARDINAL);
```

This is a value parameter so memory is allocated for it and the value of the corresponding actual parameter `bill` is copied into `cost` for display on the screen.
So,

Actual value parameter: `bill`

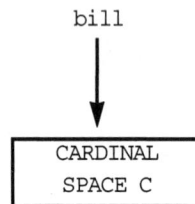

$$\downarrow$$

```
CARDINAL
SPACE C
```

is copied into `cost`.

Formal value parameter: `cost`

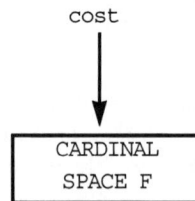

$$\downarrow$$

```
CARDINAL
SPACE F
```

3.1.5   Comparing `Beans2` and `Beans8`

Comparing the programs `Beans2` and `Beans8`, it is much easier to tell what the program `Beans8` is doing. Simply reading the procedure calls in the main program shows clearly what the program does and it actually made the job of writing the program simpler, in that the task was broken down into three smaller ones which could be dealt with separately. Although this program was a simple one the same technique of 'divide and conquer' can help us cope with the design of much larger programs.

When learning a new programming language, experiment. Try modifying the sample programs. If you are not sure if something is going to work, write a small program and try it out.

3.1.6   Standard procedures

Modula-2 has five built-in procedures; DEC, INC, EXCL, INCL and HALT.
Now's a good time to look at the first two of these. We'll deal with the others when we need them.

Standard procedure	Argument type	Purpose
DEC ( )	Any variable of ordinal type, with an optional second parameter; usually INTEGER or CARDINAL	Decrements the value of its first argument.
INC ( )	Any variable of ordinal type, with an optional second parameter; usually INTEGER or CARDINAL	Increments the value of its first argument.

INC(x, i) is equivalent to x := x + i, while

DEC(x, i) is equivalent to x := x - i

With a single argument the size of the increment is (+1), and the size of the decrement is (-1).

3.2   Functions

A function, like a procedure, is another type of subprogram available to Modula-2 programmers. Like a procedure, a function can require one or more arguments and is called by its identifying name.

One of the ways a function differs from a procedure is that it represents a value of a specific type and is used in place of a value or variable inside an expression, most commonly in assignment statements.

There are three basic types of functions:

- standard functions provided as part of the Modula-2 language,

- user-defined function procedures which you can write yourself for use in particular programs,

- pre-defined library functions which may be imported into programs.

3.2.1   Standard functions

An example of a function which you will need to use shortly is FLOAT.

FLOAT is a standard function requiring one argument, which may be CARDINAL or INTEGER. It converts this value to the equivalent REAL value and 'returns' this to be used in the expression. In the example, the parameter intValue is unchanged by the function.

```
RealResult:=FLOAT(intValue) / 4.0;
```

A list of standard functions with a description of their operation begins on the following page.

Standard function	Argument type	Result type	Purpose
ABS( )	INTEGER or REAL	as argument	Returns the absolute (positive) or REAL value of the parameter, disregarding the sign if negative.
CAP( )	CHAR	CHAR	If the parameter is a lower case letter (range 'a' to 'z'), then the function returns the equivalent capital letter, or else the parameter value is returned.
CHR( )	CARDINAL	CHAR	Each CHAR is stored inside a computer using a 7 bit (ASCII) code, which can be represented as a CARDINAL value. CHR returns the character equivalent to the CARDINAL parameter value.
FLOAT( )	INTEGER or CARDINAL	REAL	Returns the REAL number equivalent to the given parameter value.
HIGH( )	open array	INTEGER or CARDINAL	Returns the length (number of components minus 1) of an open array parameter.
MAX( )	typeID	as argument	Returns the maximum value possible for the given data type.
MIN( )	typeID	as argument	Returns the minimum value possible for the given data type.
ODD( )	INTEGER or CARDINAL	BOOLEAN	If the parameter value is an odd number then the result is TRUE, otherwise the result is FALSE.
ORD( )	ordinal type	CARDINAL	Returns the ordinal position of the given value.
SIZE( )	typeID	CARDINAL	(Used in conjunction with pointers), returns the space allocation requirements for a particular data type.
TRUNC( )	REAL	INTEGER	Returns the integer part of the given REAL value, (with no rounding).
VAL( )	typeID and CARDINAL	as argument	Returns the value of the data type in the given ordinal position.

3.2.2   **Case study:** *Decimalize*

In this case study we'll take you through the six stages of program development to produce a program that makes use of some of Modula-2's built-in functions.

Step 1.   (Conceive it)
In 1971 British currency changed from an old system based on 12 pennies to a shilling, and 20 shillings to the pound, to a decimalized currency system with 100 new pence to the pound.
The requirement is to write a program to convert pre-decimalized British money, specified in pounds, shillings and old pence to the nearest new penny.

Step 2.   (Design it)
Apply a divide and conquer strategy.

This problem fits fairly nicely into the simple program pattern we have identified in the `Beans` example,
i.e.
```
GetInput
Process
DisplayOutput
```

Our main program, `ConvertMoney`, could consist of these three procedure calls; but so could a lot of other programs.

We should select procedure identifying names that are descriptive enough to make it obvious what our program does.
A procedure name should clearly identify what the procedure does and each procedure should carry out just ONE well defined job.

So our main program might consist of the following three procedure calls:

Decimalize:
```
BEGIN
    GetOldMoney
    ConvertOldToNew
    DisplayNewMoney
END Decimalize.
```

The next task is to decide what data needs to be passed between these procedures. All communication between them should be via parameters.
After the call to `GetOldMoney` we would expect to have values for `oldPounds`, `shillings` and `oldPence`. These need to be passed on to `ConvertOldToNew` which should use them to calculate and return the equivalent `newPence`. `newPence` should then be passed to `DisplayNewMoney` so it can be displayed on the screen.

So our main program becomes:

Decimalize:
```
BEGIN
    GetOldMoney(oldPounds, shillings, oldPence);
    ConvertOldToNew(oldPounds,shillings,oldPence,newPence);
    DisplayNewMoney(newPence)
END Decimalize.
```

The main program requires four variables, oldPounds, shillings, oldPence and newpence.

We are now in a position to write a skeletal program consisting, as previous programs, of the elements:
* the module identifier,
* any library imports required,
* the main program variable declarations,
* procedure declarations,
* the main program.

```
MODULE Decimalize;

IMPORT IO;  (*Required for keyboard input and screen output*)
VAR
    oldPounds, shillings, oldPence, newPence : CARDINAL;

PROCEDURE GetOldMoney(VAR    oldPounds, shillings,
                             oldPence: CARDINAL);

PROCEDURE ConvertOldToNew(  oldPounds, shillings,
                            oldPence: CARDINAL;
                            VAR newPence: CARDINAL);

PROCEDURE DisplayNewMoney(newPence: CARDINAL);

(*Main program*)
BEGIN
    GetOldMoney(oldPounds, shillings, oldPence);
    ConvertOldToNew(oldPounds,shillings,oldPence,newPence);
    DisplayNewMoney(newPence)
END Decimalize.
```

All that remains is to fill in the detail of each procedure.

GetOldMoney and DisplayNewMoney are very straightforward as they simply handle input and output.

ConvertOldToNew needs to assign the converted money value to newPence, so we will need an assignment statement of the form:

```
newPence := (Convert old pounds) + (Convert shillings)
                                  + (Convert old pence);
```

There are 100 new pence in an old pound.
A shilling is equivalent to 5 new pence (symbol **p**), and as 12 old pence (symbol **d**) make one shilling,
So,
$$12d = 5p$$
therefore
$$1p = 12d \div 5d$$
and
$$1p = 2.4d$$

Thus the expression becomes:

```
newPence :=(oldPounds * 100)    + (shillings * 5)
                                 + (oldPence / 2.4);
```

The calculation is correct, but can you see why this won't work in our Modula-2 program?
The problem is one of type compatibility, or should we say type incompatibility?
oldPence is of CARDINAL type while 2.4 is REAL and / is a REAL operator.
We need to convert temporarily, the value of oldPence to REAL, do our division and then convert the result back to CARDINAL in order for it to be compatible with the rest of the expression.

We can achieve this using two built-in functions, TRUNC and FLOAT.

```
TRUNC(x)
```
returns the 'whole' part of its REAL argument as an INTEGER, so
```
TRUNC(8.6)    returns 8
```

(Note that on some systems, the result returned by built-in functions, such as TRUNC, is CARDINAL rather than INTEGER.)

```
FLOAT(x)
```
returns its INTEGER argument as a REAL value, so
```
FLOAT(8)    returns 8.0
```

The expression becomes:

```
newPence :=(oldPounds * 100) + (shillings * 5) +
                          TRUNC(FLOAT(oldPence) / 2.4);
```

We are not quite home and dry yet.
To illustrate why let's assume the value of oldPence is 9.

FLOAT(9) gives 9.0

FLOAT(9)/2.4 gives 3.75

and TRUNC(FLOAT(9) / 2.4) knocks off the decimals giving 3.

TRUNC does not round to the nearest whole number.
So, for example, 4.2 or 4.9 would be truncated to 4.
We can ensure values are properly rounded by adding 0.5 before truncating.

TRUNC((FLOAT(9) / 2.4) + 0.5) results in 4.

So, the expression becomes:

```
newPence :=(oldPounds * 100) + (shillings * 5) +
                        TRUNC((FLOAT(oldPence) / 2.4) + 0.5);
```

Remember from Chapter 2, CARDINAL and INTEGER types are assignment compatible but **NOT** otherwise compatible, so we can't mix the two within an expression. (See Appendix B.)

TRUNC may in practice return a CARDINAL or an INTEGER value. The other parts of the expression are all CARDINAL, so to make this work properly in either case we'll first assign the TRUNC part to a CARDINAL variable.
So, at last:

```
newPence := TRUNC((FLOAT(oldPence) / 2.4) + 0.5);
newPence := (oldPounds * 100) + (shillings * 5) + newPence;
```

This example is a case in which the strong type checking of Modula-2 is somewhat irritating, but in other circumstances it can prevent more serious hassle.

Here is the complete Decimalize program. Compile, link and run it. See if it works. Remember to experiment. Try some of the intermediate expressions above. See for yourself what happens.

```
MODULE Decimalize;
(*
** Purpose:    Program to convert pre-decimalized money into
**post-decimalized new pence
** Uses module: InOut
*)
FROM InOut IMPORT WriteString,WriteLn, ReadCard, WriteCard, Write ;
(*Required for keyboard input and screen output*)
CONST
    NewPenceInPound = 100;    (*Constant is of type CARDINAL*)
    NewPenceInShilling = 5;(*Constant is of type CARDINAL*)
    OldPenceInNew = 2.4;   (*Constant is of type REAL*)
VAR
    oldPounds, shillings, oldPence, newPence : CARDINAL;

    PROCEDURE   GetOldMoney(VAR oldPounds, shillings,
                                oldPence: CARDINAL);
    (*Get old fsd from user*)
    BEGIN
        WriteString("Please enter value of old pounds  ");
        ReadCard(oldPounds);
        WriteLn;
        WriteString("Please enter value of shillings  ");
        ReadCard(shillings);
        WriteLn;
        WriteString("Please enter value of old pence  ");
        ReadCard(oldPence);
        WriteLn
    END GetOldMoney;

    PROCEDURE ConvertOldToNew(oldPounds,shillings,
                                oldPence: CARDINAL;
                                VAR newPence:CARDINAL);
    (*Convert fsd to new pence*)
    BEGIN
        newPence:=TRUNC((FLOAT(oldPence)/OldPenceInNew)+ 0.5);
        newPence :=(oldPounds * NewPenceInPound) +
                (shillings * NewPenceInShilling ) + newPence
    END ConvertOldToNew;
```

```
      PROCEDURE DisplayNewMoney(newPence: CARDINAL);
      (*Display new pence value on screen*)
      BEGIN
          WriteString("The equivalent value in new pence is  ");
          WriteCard(newPence,1);
          Write("p");
          WriteLn
      END DisplayNewMoney;


  BEGIN  (*Main program*)
      GetOldMoney(oldPounds, shillings, oldPence);
      ConvertOldToNew(oldPounds,shillings,oldPence,newPence);
      DisplayNewMoney(newPence)
  END Decimalize.
```

3.2.3   Converting between types

The Decimalize program illustrates the use of FLOAT and TRUNC to convert between whole numbers (INTEGER and CARDINAL) and REAL numbers. It is also possible to convert ordinal data types, such as CHAR, into CARDINAL numbers using the standard function ORD. This function returns the ordinal number of its actual parameter. The ordinal number of a CHAR value is its ASCII equivalent. Conversion to CARDINAL allows non-numeric data to be used indirectly in arithmetic operations.

To convert back to the original data type from CARDINAL there are two standard functions. CHR can be used to convert from CARDINAL (ASCII) to CHAR, and VAL can be used to convert from CARDINAL to a named ordinal type.

Here's an example program to illustrate type conversion.

```
  MODULE Encryption;
  (*Purpose: A single input character is encrypted using
  **a simple calculation on the ordinal value of the
  **character, then the new character is output
  **Uses module: InOut *)
  FROM InOut IMPORT Read, Write, WriteLn;
  VAR
      inChar, outChar : CHAR;
      valChar : CARDINAL;
  BEGIN
      Read(inChar);
      WriteLn;
      valChar := ORD(inChar);
      outChar := CHR(valChar + 3);
      Write(outChar);
      WriteLn
  END Encryption.
```

A problem could arise with this simple encryption problem. Can you see what it is?

(Hint: Look at the range of ASCII values in Appendix A.)

The standard Modula-2 procedure, INC, can produce the same result as above in a single statement.

```
INC(inChar,3);
```

In this case the result replaces the original input value in inChar.

3.2.4   Function procedures

Besides writing your own procedures, Modula-2 allows you to create your own functions. These may be individual functions within particular programs or may be written in a general purpose format, suitable for inclusion in your own library. A function is a special type of procedure, often called a function procedure.

A normal procedure call is a program statement and a procedure's results should be passed using parameters but, just like the standard functions described above, a function procedure computes a single value and a call to a function procedure may appear in an expression.

A function declaration differs slightly from the declaration of a normal procedure in that:

- the heading must specify the TYPE of the value to be returned and

- the body of the function must include a RETURN statement that, when executed, evaluates to the result to be returned by the function.

Here is the procedure CalculateBill from the Beans8 program rewritten as a function procedure. Compare it with the original.

```
PROCEDURE CalculateBill(unitPrice,quantity:CARDINAL):CARDINAL;
BEGIN
    RETURN (unitPrice * quantity)
END CalculateBill;
```

and here is the calling statement:

```
bill := CalculateBill(unitPrice, quantity);
```

Here's the complete program, Beans9 with CalculateBill written as a function procedure:

```
MODULE Beans9;
(*Purpose: Calculate my Bean bill using a function procedure
**Uses module: InOut*)
FROM InOut IMPORT WriteString, ReadCard, WriteLn, WriteCard;
VAR
    beanPrice,noOfTins,bill : CARDINAL;

PROCEDURE GetBeanData(VAR price, tins : CARDINAL);
BEGIN
    WriteString("Enter price of a tin of beans in pence: ");
    ReadCard(price);
    WriteLn;
    WriteString("Enter the number of tins: ");
    ReadCard(tins);
    WriteLn
END GetBeanData;

PROCEDURE CalculateBill(unitPrice, quantity : CARDINAL): CARDINAL;
BEGIN
    RETURN (unitPrice * quantity)
END CalculateBill;

PROCEDURE DisplayBill(cost: CARDINAL);
BEGIN
    WriteCard(cost,1);
    WriteString(" pence");
    WriteLn
END DisplayBill;

(************************************************************)

BEGIN (*Main Beans9 program*)
    GetBeanData(beanPrice, noOfTins);
    bill := CalculateBill(beanPrice, noOfTins);
    DisplayBill(bill)
END Beans9.
```

Exercise 3.1

Rewrite Decimalize; this time using a function procedure for ConvertOldToNew.

3.2.5 Side effects

A side effect occurs when a variable is altered by another procedure in an unpredictable fashion. This can happen if a variable parameter is used when a value parameter would have been appropriate.

Although not strictly illegal in Modula-2, variable parameters should not be used at all with function procedures. This is because the purpose of a function is to return a single value to the calling statement and a function's parameters are seen as inputs to the computation of that value. Should a function have a variable parameter then a change to the actual parameter value, as a result of a function call, would be considered a side effect.

You should always seek to avoid the possibility of side effects. If a function you are writing needs to return more than one value, then your function is trying to do too much or you should be using a normal procedure.

Self test 3.4

Can you determine which of the formal parameters in module Decimalize are value parameters and which are variable parameters, and why?

Self test 3.5

If the Decimalize program had been written to convert decimalized British money, specified to the nearest penny, to pre-decimal money in pounds, shillings and pence, specified to the nearest pre-decimal penny, why wouldn't a function procedure have been appropriate for implementing ConvertNewToOld?

Self test 3.6

A ConvertNewToOld procedure would need to convert newPounds into oldPounds, shillings and oldPence. Complete the three assignment statements that would need to be contained in ConvertOldToNew.

```
oldPounds :=
shillings :=
oldPence :=
```

(Assume newPounds is entered as a REAL value of the form 24.67 and that oldPounds, shillings and oldPence are all to be of CARDINAL type.)

Self test 3.7

In which one of the following Modula-2 statements is `Calc` a function procedure?

a) `Calc(value1 + value2, value3);`
b) `Calc;`
c) `Calc := total + value;`
d) `Result := 6 + Calc(value1, value2);`

3.2.6   The `MathLib0` library module

Some library functions may be provided with your compiler with particular applications in mind. Other library modules may be created for a particular project, perhaps to support a team of programmers. These functions are made available to your program via the IMPORT command.

The library module `MathLib0` (the last character is a zero) should be provided with all Modula-2 compilers. It contains a selection of common mathematical and trigonometrical functions which are summarized below:

`MathLib0` library functions

Function	Argument	Result type	Purpose
`sqrt(x)`	a REAL value	REAL	Returns square root of x
`ln(x)`	a REAL value	REAL	Returns natural logarithm of x: $\log_e x$
`exp(x)`	a REAL value	REAL	Returns exponential e^x
`sin(x)`	a REAL value	REAL	Returns the sine of x; x must be given in radians.
`cos(x)`	a REAL value	REAL	Returns the cosine of x; x must be given in radians.
`arctan(x)`	a REAL value	REAL	Returns the arctangent of x; x must be given in radians.
`entier(x)`	a REAL value	INTEGER	Returns the greatest integer less than or equal to x.

`MathLib0` does not contain the trigonometric function tangent. The main reason for this is that it is relatively easy to compute the value of tan(x) using the standard functions sin and cos, since;

```
tan(x) = sin(x) / cos(x)
```

If you use this method be careful, as there are some values of x for which tan(x) is infinite; something your computer will have trouble coping with.

Ignoring this problem at this stage, except for a warning in the comment at the beginning, here is a way of calculating tan(x), where x is in degrees.

```
MODULE Tangent;
(* Purpose: Calculates the tangent of an angle in degrees
**but beware, the program does not check for angles which
**produce an infinite result
**Uses modules: InOut, RealInOut, MathLib0
*)
FROM MathLib0 IMPORT sin, cos;
FROM InOut IMPORT WriteLn, WriteString, ReadInt;
FROM RealInOut IMPORT WriteReal;
CONST
    PI=3.14159;
VAR
    radians, tangent:REAL;
    degrees:INTEGER;
BEGIN
    WriteString("Program to calculate tan(x)");
    WriteLn;
    WriteString("Please enter the value of x in degrees: ");
    ReadInt(degrees);
    WriteLn;
    (*Convert degrees to radians*)
    radians:=FLOAT(degrees)*PI/180.0;
    tangent:=sin(radians) / cos(radians);
    WriteString("tan(x)=");
    WriteReal(tangent, 10);
    WriteLn
END Tangent.
```

Exercise 3.2

Rewrite Tangent as a function procedure:

```
PROCEDURE tan (angle : REAL) : REAL;
```

3.2.7   **Case study:** *Using the `MathLib0` library to help Eratosthenes*

During the fourth, third and second centuries B.C. one of the most enlightened places on earth was the city of Alexandria situated near the mouth of the river Nile. It was a place that attracted the foremost scholars of the time including the Greek astronomer Eratosthenes. In about 300 B.C. a school of astronomy was founded at Alexandria and an occupation of great interest was that of trying to quantify the size of the earth. This was a problem that occupied the mind of Eratosthenes who used some clever thinking and some simple trigonometry to come up with a radius for the earth which was very close to today's measured value of 6380 km.

At that time, and in that enlightened place, the earth was believed to be spherical. Eratosthenes started with this assumption and the realization that the sun was so far away that its rays could be considered to be parallel to one another when striking the earth's surface. He reasoned that if he could measure the angle of the suns rays simultaneously at two points sufficiently far apart on the earth's surface, the difference between the angles would give him the angle of arc subtended at the centre of the earth, and from this he could easily estimate the earth's circumference and radius.

His first problem was synchronizing the measurement with no accurate clocks. However, he was aware that places due north or south of one another experienced noon (i.e. the sun at its highest point) at the same time, so he chose Alexandria and Syene (now Aswan) about 801 km. due south (although Eratosthenes's measurement would have been in stadia) as his measurement sites. Another good reason for choosing Syene was the fact that there was a deep well there and it was known that at exactly noon on midsummer day the sun was directly over the well and could be seen reflected in the water at the bottom. All Eratosthenes had to do was measure the angle of the sun's rays at noon on midsummer day in Alexandria. He did this by placing a stick of known height vertically in the ground and measuring the length of the shadow cast at the appropriate moment. The stick and shadow formed a right-angled triangle from which he could determine the angle of the sun's rays. Pretty clever, huh!

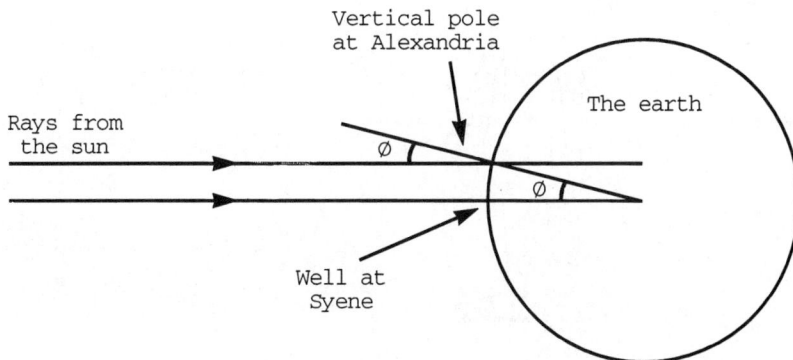

Here are the equations he might have used:
To find the angle of the sun's rays, Ø, given the pole height, h, and shadow length, s

$$\text{Ø} = \arctan(s \, / \, h)$$

To find the earth's circumference c where d is the distance between Syene and Alexandria:
$$c = d * 2 * \pi \, / \, \text{Ø}$$

To find the earth's radius r:
$$r = c/(2*\pi)$$

These can be combined into a single equation to calculate radius:

$$r = d \, / \arctan(s/h)$$

The program, Eratos, uses a function procedure to calculate the final result using this equation.
(If you don't understand the maths involved, don't worry, it's not important as far as your understanding of Modula-2 is concerned, but it does provide an interesting example of the use of the MathLib0 library module.)

If Eratosthenes's pole had had a height of 1000 mm he would have found the shadow to be about 131 mm long.

Had a computer been available at the time, Eratosthenes could have pre-programmed it to compute the earth's radius and circumference quickly as soon as he'd taken the shadow measurement.

Here's the program he might have used.

```
MODULE Eratos;
(*
**Purpose: To calculate the radius of the Earth for
**Eratosthenes
**Uses modules: InOut, RealInOut, MathLib0
*)
FROM InOut IMPORT WriteString, WriteLn;
FROM RealInOut IMPORT ReadReal, WriteReal;
FROM MathLib0 IMPORT arctan;
VAR
    radius, shadow : REAL;

PROCEDURE GetLength(VAR shadow : REAL);
BEGIN
    WriteString("Enter the length of the shadow in mm ");
    ReadReal(shadow);
    WriteLn
END GetLength;

PROCEDURE CalcRadius(shadow : REAL) : REAL;
CONST
    POLE = 1000.0;  (*mm*)
    DISTANCE = 801.0 ;(*km*)
BEGIN
    RETURN  (DISTANCE / arctan(shadow/POLE))
END CalcRadius;

PROCEDURE DisplayRadius(radius : REAL);
BEGIN
    WriteString("The radius of the earth is ");
    WriteReal(radius,10);
    WriteString(" km");
    WriteLn
END DisplayRadius;


BEGIN (* Main program *)
    GetLength(shadow);
    radius := CalcRadius(shadow);
    DisplayRadius(radius)
END Eratos.
```

Self test 3.8

Which one of the following problems can be solved most appropriately using a function procedure rather than a procedure?

a) Exchange the values of two CHAR variables.
b) Find the cube root of a number.
c) Increment an existing variable.
d) Print a value.

Self test 3.9

Explain how a function procedure differs from a normal procedure in Modula-2.

Self test 3.10

The program Eratos contains two constant declarations; POLE and DISTANCE.
Re-examine the program and determine an alternative place to put these declarations. What are the pros and cons of each of the alternatives?

Exercise 3.3

Run the Eratos program using 131.0 (mm) as the input shadow length.

Exercise 3.4

Create a function procedure, Square, which has one REAL parameter x, and returns the REAL value x^2.
Test the function by embedding it in a simple program which takes as input a REAL value, x and outputs x^2.

Exercise 3.5

If the lengths of two sides, **b** and **c**, of a triangle, and the size of the enclosed angle, **A**, are known, then the length of the third side, **a**, can be calculated. Use your function Square from Exercise 3.4 in a program to calculate the length of side **a** using the formula:

$$a := sqrt(b^2 + c^2 - 2bcCosA)$$

You will need to import cos and sqrt from the library module MathLib0.

4   Block structure and scope

In Section 3.1.3 we introduced the concept of block structure. To recap: a program is a module and constitutes a block, which is a sequence of optional declarations followed by a sequence of program statements enclosed between BEGIN and END.
This is described by the syntax chart:

Block structure:

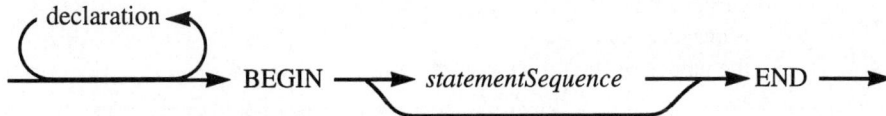

declaration

BEGIN → statementSequence → END →

At the beginning of a block is an optional sequence of declarations which may contain:

>   constants,
>   types,
>   variables and
>   procedures.

(In addition, a block may contain module declarations.)

Procedure declarations also form their own blocks and these may, in turn, contain optional declarations of:

>   constants,
>   types,
>   variables and
>   procedures.

(Note that IMPORT is not classed as a declaration and cannot be used from within a procedure.)

Some programming languages do not allow you to nest procedures inside one another. Although permitted in Modula-2, we suggest that you do not get into the habit of doing this, as it can make your programs difficult to understand.

4.1   Global and local declarations, and scope rules

The identifier used for a declaration in one block could, quite possibly, have the same identifying name as that used in another block, therefore, we need some rules to avoid ambiguity and confusion. These rules are called scope rules and they govern the range of 'visibility' (or scope) of the following declared entities:

constant names,
type names,
variable names,
procedure names and
the names of formal parameters.

The principle of scope is perhaps best illustrated by analogy to fame or power. For example, the fame and power of the President of the United States extends over the whole of the United States and to a large extent over the whole world, while the fame and power of the Vice-Chancellor of a University extends, at least, over the staff and students of the University. At the other end of the scale I am known to just a few select individuals and the scope of my power extends only over my dog; sometimes!

In a Modula-2 program, constants, types, variables, procedures, and even modules, can have limited visibility (or 'fame') as far as other program parts are concerned. The scope of an object refers to the extent of its visibility; i.e. the block (or portion) of the program in which it can be seen and used.

A module forms one type of Modula-2 block. The scope of global declarations to a module is such that globals are visible throughout the program module. This is somewhat akin to the 'global visibility' of the US President.

However, it is possible to 'mask' a global declaration, making it unavailable in part of the program, because a local declaration uses the same identifier. Using our analogy, this is like referring to the President when in the Student's Union, it being assumed you mean the Union President rather than any other. This 'masking' is sometimes referred to as a **'hole in scope'** of the global entity.

A procedure is another kind of Modula-2 block. Local declarations are visible only inside the procedure in which they are declared. A formal parameter is also classed as a variable local to its procedure. A procedure's local declarations are visible to any procedures nested inside it, subject to any masking through use of the same identifier.

Take another look at the Eratos program from Chapter 3, which is reprinted here in skeletal form, with boxes around each of the component blocks:

```
MODULE Eratos;
......
VAR
     radius, shadow : REAL;


     PROCEDURE GetLength(VAR shadow : REAL);
     BEGIN

         ......
     END GetLength;


     PROCEDURE CalcRadius(shadow : REAL) : REAL;
     CONST
         POLE = 1000.0;  (*mm*)
         DISTANCE = 801.0 ;(*km*)
     BEGIN

         ......
     END CalcRadius;


     PROCEDURE DisplayRadius(radius : REAL);
     BEGIN

         ......
     END DisplayRadius;


BEGIN (* Main program *)
     ......
END Eratos.
```

The program has:

a main program module block with two global variables;	radius, shadow
a procedure block, GetLength, with a local formal parameter;	shadow
a procedure block, CalcRadius, with a local formal parameter and two local constants;	shadow POLE, DISTANCE
a procedure block, DisplayRadius, with a local formal parameter;	radius

Entities are visible within the block in which they are declared and within any nested inner blocks, provided the entity name has not been re-declared locally.

The following shows the program blocks and the entities that are visible within each.

```
Eratos
Visible entities:
Global: radius
Global: shadow
Procedure GetLength
Procedure CalcRadius
Procedure DisplayRadius
```

```
GetLength
Visible entities:
Global: radius
Local: shadow
Procedure GetLength
Procedure CalcRadius
Procedure DisplayRadius
```

```
CalcRadius
Visible entities:
Global: radius
Local: shadow
       POLE
       DISTANCE
Procedure GetLength
Procedure CalcRadius
Procedure DisplayRadius
```

```
DisplayRadius
Visible entities:
Global: shadow
Local: radius
Procedure GetLength
Procedure CalcRadius
Procedure DisplayRadius
```

`shadow` is used as a formal parameter of `GetLength` and it is a variable parameter as it is required to return a value to the main program. The global identifier, `shadow`, and `GetLength`'s local identifier, `shadow`, are distinct and separate yet both reference the same area of memory.

Main program's actual calling variable parameter: shadow

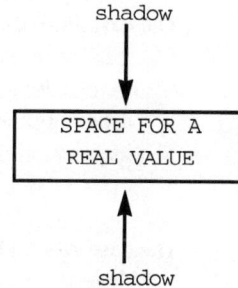

```
SPACE FOR A
REAL VALUE
```

`GetLength`'s formal variable parameter: shadow

Three instances of `shadow` exist, one global and two local, within each of `GetLength` and `CalcRadius`. If statements in either of these procedures refer to `shadow`, it is their respective local variables that are used.
`POLE` and `DISTANCE` are local to, and only visible from within, `CalcRadius`.

The global identifying name, `radius`, has been re-declared locally by `DisplayRadius`, so two separate instances of the name, `radius`, exist. When statements within `DisplayRadius` refer to `radius` it is the local variable that is used, while a reference anywhere else throughout the program refers to the global variable.

There is no nesting of procedures in `Eratos`, so all are visible within the main program block where they are declared, and each procedure is visible from within the others. Thus, for example, `CalcRadius` could include a call to `DisplayRadius` if required or, indeed, could contain a call to itself. (This is the principle of recursion which we'll have more to say about later.)

Block structure and scope

As you have already seen, there is no requirement to use the same names for formal and actual parameters. Indeed, in reusable procedures, such as ReadChar, it would make no sense to use the same name for the actual parameter each time.

There are reasons for and against using the same identifiers.

The case FOR using the same identifiers:
• it helps to make the data flows clear and
• in the case of value parameters, there is no possibility of the procedure code accessing the actual parameter variable directly, since local identifiers make any identical global names inaccessible.

The case AGAINST using the same identifiers:
• there is less likelihood of confusion about whether variables are local or global if different names are used and
• where possible procedures should be designed with reusability in mind, not specific to one program.

On the following page you will find a more complex and general example to illustrate scope when there are nested procedures.

When evaluating the scope of entity, start at the innermost declarations and work outward; i.e. start with the block (procedure or module) in which it is used. If it is not declared in this block, search the declarations of the enclosing block, and so on, until the declaration is found.

```
MODULE ScopeTest;
IMPORT X,Y,Z;
CONST c1,c2...
TYPE t1,t2...
VAR v1,v2,v3...

    PROCEDURE First (v1,v2,v4.....);
    (*Cannot include additional imports*)
    CONST c3..
    TYPE t3..
    VAR v5,v6..

        PROCEDURE Second (v2,v3,v4...);
        (*Cannot include additional imports
        **but could additionally include local type
        **and constant declarations*)
        VAR v6..
        BEGIN (* code for nested procedure Second *)
            (* visible locals: v2,v3,v4,v6
            ** visible from First: c3,t3,v1,v5,Second,Third
            ** visible from ScopeTest: X,Y,Z,c1,c2,t1,t2,
            **                                  First,Fourth
            *)
        END Second;

        PROCEDURE Third (v1..);
        (*Cannot include additional imports
        **but could also include local type declarations*)
        CONST c1..
        VAR v2...
        BEGIN (* code for Nested procedure Third *)
            (* visible locals: c1,v1,v2
            ** visible from First: c3,t3,v2,v4,v5,v6,
            **                                  Second,Third
            ** visible from ScopeTest: X,Y,Z,c2,t1,t2,v3,
            **                                  First,Fourth
            *)
        END Third;

    BEGIN (* code for procedure First *)
        (* visible locals c3,t3,v1,v2,v4,v5,v6,Second,Third
        ** visible from ScopeTest X,Y,Z,c1,c2,t1,t2,v3,
        **                                  First,Fourth
        *)
    END First;

    PROCEDURE Fourth(v1,v2,v3);
    (*Cannot include additional imports but could
    **additionally include local type declarations*)
    TYPE t1
    VAR v4
    BEGIN (* code for procedure Forth *)
        (* visible locals t1,v1,v2,v3,v4
        ** visible from ScopeTest X,Y,Z,c1,c2,t2,
        **                                  First,Fourth*)
    END Fourth;

BEGIN (* main program *)
    (* visible globals X,Y,Z,c1,c2,t1,t2,v1,v2,v3,
    ** plus procedures First and Fourth
    *)
END ScopeTest.
```

Self test 4.1

For each region (or block) in the following skeletal program, indicate which variables and procedures are visible in that region.

```
MODULE Scope;
VAR
    a : REAL;
    d : BOOLEAN;
    e : CHAR;

    PROCEDURE ProcA(a : CARDINAL);
    VAR
        c : CHAR;
        d : INTEGER;
    BEGIN (*ProcA*)
        ....
    END ProcA;

    PROCEDURE ProcB(VAR f : REAL);
    VAR
        a : CHAR;
        b: INTEGER;
        c : CARDINAL;

        PROCEDURE ProcC(g : REAL);
        VAR
            b : CARDINAL;
            d : BOOLEAN;
            f : REAL;
        BEGIN (*ProcC*)
            ....
        END ProcC;

    BEGIN (*ProcB*)
        ....
    END ProcB;

BEGIN (*Scope*)
    ....
END Scope.
```

Self test 4.2

a)   Find the syntax error in the incomplete program below:

```
MODULE SelfTestQuest;
VAR
    value, answer : REAL;

PROCEDURE GetRadius(VAR radius : REAL);
BEGIN
    (******)
END GetRadius;
```

```
PROCEDURE CircleArea(radius, area : REAL);
CONST
    PI = 3.142;
BEGIN
    area:=PI * (radius * radius)
END CircleArea;

PROCEDURE PrintResult(area : REAL);
BEGIN
    (******)
END PrintResult;

BEGIN (*Main Program *)
    GetRadius (value);
    CircleArea (value, answer);
    PrintResult (area)
END SelfTestQuest.
```

b) When the syntax error is corrected and the missing statements are completed, the program compiles but always returns an area of zero. Find the reason for this and describe how you would correct the program.

5   Design

So far we have looked at a few small programs and you may be excused for thinking that all the extra typing just for the sake of clarifying programs that are easy to follow anyway is a lot of additional effort for little real benefit. However, although we may be thinking small now, our aim is to be able to think BIG.

We expect that, so far, the largest slice of your time in writing programs has been spent sitting typing at the keyboard, so you may be surprised to hear that in a commercial environment writing the original program code is a relatively small part of the overall software development process. Analysis, design and testing usually take up a far larger proportion of the time. Even after testing, programs need maintenance to iron out bugs or to add new facilities. This can be more expensive than the original development costs. In the 1970s it led to a serious problem.

5.1   The software crisis

Let us start with an analogy.
Imagine you were planning to write your autobiography. You might collect together some photographs and write the facts you could remember in a note book. Then, perhaps, having put the job aside for a few weeks, you read your work once again, decide to add a few points you've remembered recently, or to move a few paragraphs around as you recall a particular event more clearly. So you draw some arrows and write some notes in the margin of your book to show the changes. After another couple of months the same thing happens. You find your notebook but there is no more space in the margins, so you insert scraps of paper indicating changes. You are beginning to find your own notes hard to decipher so you resolve to rewrite the whole thing when you have time. You never get around to it. After you've become famous and died someone picks up your notes in order to publish your biography. But, sadly for posterity, the photographs are unlabelled and your notebook almost impossible to understand.

Unfortunately, this is not very removed from what has frequently been the situation with software development. Programs have been written then modified and patched until even the original programmer has trouble understanding them. When (s)he leaves the company, what chance has anyone else got? In the 1970s this problem led to what has become known as the Software Crisis, with a growing amount of time being spent on maintaining badly-structured, hard-to-understand, difficult-to-modify programs. The maintenance itself often made the programs even more incomprehensible and increased the risk of introducing unwanted side effects.

Our aim is to develop software that is reliable, usable and maintainable, so it is no use trying to justify a messy, over-complicated program with the claim;

BUT IT WORKS!

In this case, the end certainly does not justify the means.

5.2   Software life cycle

The stages in the life of a piece of software are usually referred to as the Software Life Cycle. To illustrate these stages we'll use an analogical parallel (in italics) which we hope will make things a little easier to relate to and remember.

5.2.1   Requirements analysis

Trying to determine exactly what is needed by the user of our proposed piece of software.

Mr and Mrs Wirth are a young professional couple who want a house that they can call home. They have a friend who is an architect so they ask him to build them an economical house with space for themselves and to accommodate occasional visits from their parents. They are both out at work most of the day, so don't have a lot of time for gardening, but would like a bit of garden in which to sit or to entertain friends in the summer.

5.2.2   Specification

Expressing the users' requirements in a more formal way, to ensure that these are complete and consistent.

Mr and Mrs Wirth's house is to have two bedrooms, a living room, a kitchen and a bathroom. The garden is to be small to medium in size and easy to maintain, with a patio area, lawn and shrubbery.
Plot size: 50 x 80 metres
Bedroom 1: At least 12 sq metres
Bedroom 2: At least 10 sq metres
Living room: At least 16 sq metres
Kitchen: At least 10 sq metres
Bathroom: At least 8 sq metres

The kitchen should have direct access to the outside. There should be easy access to the bathroom from all rooms, but no direct connection between the kitchen and bathroom. The house is to be of brick construction. Building regulations must be followed.

5.2.3   Design

This involves planning the form of a program or set of programs that will meet the users' requirements.

The architect draws up proper plans of the house and garden, with a list of materials required.
He may even have a model made to ensure all is as required. It would be a good idea if he were to talk things over with Mr and Mrs Wirth at this stage.

(Unfortunately, in the case of computer software development, the customer is sometimes left out at this stage of the process.)

5.2.4   Implementation

Coding and constructing the program(s).

The brickies, carpenters, plasterers, plumbers and electricians all do their thing to make Mr and Mrs Wirth's dream a reality.

5.2.5   Testing

Checking to see that each program conforms to the specification and also that it meets the users' requirements.

The finished house is inspected during construction by a building inspector to ensure all regulations are being complied with, and by the architect to ensure his design is being carried out as intended. Mr and Mrs Wirth visit the site now and again to see how things are progressing. A final check and Mr and Mrs Wirth can move into their new home.

5.2.6   Maintenance

Correcting any errors that are discovered or adapting the software to meet new requirements.

A few settling cracks appear in the plaster of Mr and Mrs Wirth's house, so this is put right.
After 9 months in their new home, Mrs Wirth gives birth to triplets so Mr Wirth goes to see his architect friend about building an extension.

Self test 5.1

Which one of the following statements describes the main cause of the so-called Software Crisis of the 1970s?

a) The cost of computer hardware.
b) Increasing proportion of programmer time being spent on testing.
c) Lack of available computer software.
d) Significant amount of programming time being spent on maintenance.

5.2.7   Waterfall model

The sequence of steps in the software life cycle is rarely linear. Design is an iterative process that at any stage may necessitate revision of an earlier step. The model that results has been likened to a series of waterfalls where at any level the water can be pumped back to a previous level.

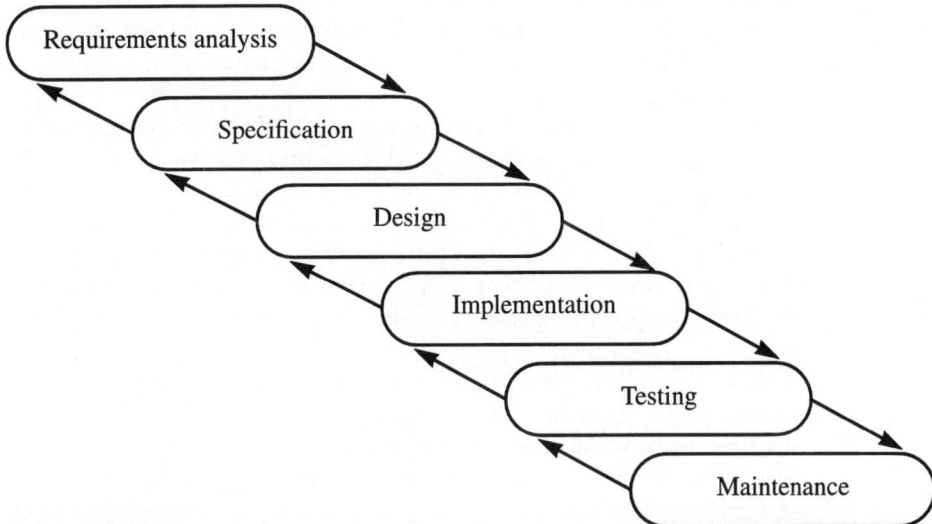

5.2.8   Task analysis

Traditionally, the software life cycle was as we have described but, more recently software developers have become aware of the need to design programs that are easy for humans to use. In the past, software has been discarded, not because it didn't work, but because people did not find it easy enough to use or did not like using it. There is now considerable interest in designing 'user-friendly' or user-centred software but, as yet, no comprehensive or widely accepted methodology for accomplishing this has been developed.

However, it does seem certain that the life cycle should begin with some form of task analysis to determine exactly what tasks are to be carried out by a user. What does the user want to do and how does (s)he want to do them?

User-centred task analysis could, on its own, form the subject of a complete book, so we need to focus our discussion, concentrating particularly on design, implementation, and testing.

5.2.9   Formal specification

Programs can be specified using a formal notation that is verifiable mathematically. Using this as the basis for implementation should result in programs that can be 'proved' correct without the need for extensive testing.

5.3   Functional decomposition using data flow diagrams

The programs encountered so far in this book have been simple enough to demand very little formal design. Indeed, the very act of describing a problem often suggests a sensible way of solving it. With more complex problems there may be a number of alternative approaches to a solution and the structure of the final program will depend on the planning and design technique used.

In this book you will meet two design strategies. The first is based on functional decomposition and the second is an object-oriented design approach, which we'll introduce later.

Functional decomposition is based on a principle known even to ancient military leaders: to divide and conquer. A complex problem is broken down and dealt with in more easily manageable parts. Complex functions are broken down, or decomposed, into a number of simpler ones, until a reasonable level of detail has been achieved and each part is simple enough to be specified in terms of an English-cum-programming language description, called pseudocode. The pseudocode description can then be translated into the desired programming language code.

Data flow diagrams (or DFDs for short) can be used to illustrate the way we plan to decompose our program. They provide a graphic way of describing the functions and the data passing between them. They show the data flow through a system and the processes or transformations performed on the data. From a data flow diagram it is relatively straightforward to create a structure chart showing the subprograms to be used and the interaction between them.

The four elements of a data flow diagram are:

1. Data flows
   represented by

2. Processes
   represented by

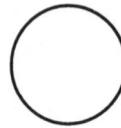

3. Data stores
   represented by

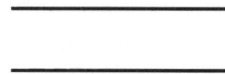

4. Data sources and sinks
   represented by

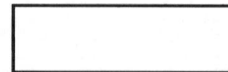

Each line with an arrow represents some data flowing through the system.
Each bubble represents a transformation that converts an input flow into an output flow.
Parallel lines represent data stores or files.
Rectangular boxes represent sources or sinks for data, e.g. keyboard and display screen.

The aim is to create a design with the best possible decomposition by producing subprograms that only communicate with each other via input and output of serial streams of data.

The method is also based partly on the observation that most programs have a similar overall structure. That is, they have some input data, perform some action on it, and then output the result.

Many design methods incorporate data flow diagrams and consequently there are also many different ways of drawing them.

5.3.1   Context diagram (also called the level 0 data flow diagram)

It is usual to start a design with a context diagram which gives an overview of the relationship between the software and the input and output data flows.

The only details which should be included in a context diagram are those which are external to the system. It is usual to omit any data files used by the software from the context diagram as these are shown in one of the more detailed data flow diagrams.

The diagram is usually very simple, consisting of sources (such as a keyboard input device), sinks (such as a screen output device), labelled data flows to document the inputs and outputs, all connected to a single bubble, which represents the main software process.

Here's an example:

A simple spell checking program reads input lines of text, extracts words and checks them against the words held in a dictionary file. If an input word is found in the dictionary it is deemed to be spelled correctly. The program reports on whether each input word is spelled correctly or not.

The context diagram:

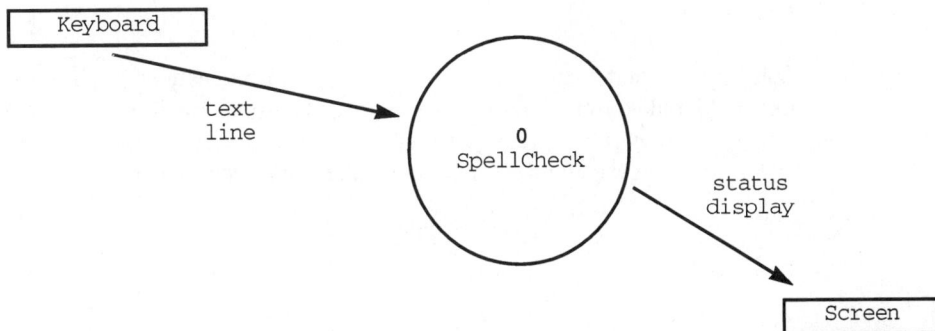

5.3.2   Stepwise refinement of the data flow diagram

The next stage after determining the context diagram is to refine the main bubble into a set of smaller bubbles, so the overall process becomes subdivided into functionally simpler constituents. This is the level 1DFD.

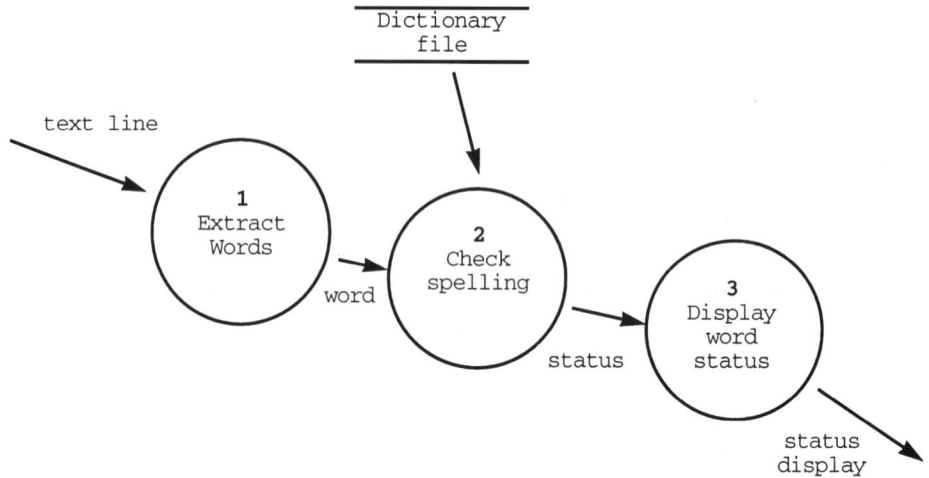

```
                        Dictionary
                           file

    text line

                    1                    2
                 Extract              Check
                  Words      word    spelling              3
                                                        Display
                                                         word
                                            status      status

                                                              status
                                                              display
```

Stepwise refinement continues until the whole system has been decomposed into a set of simple processes each of which performs one basic task and is hopefully straightforward to implement.

If necessary, level 2 DFDs could be constructed to decompose each of the processes in the level 1 DFD. It makes the relationship between levels clear if the process bubbles are numbered. If ExtractWords is process 1, then its level 2 DFD would have processes numbered 1.1, 1.2, etc. (a similar system to the one used for numbering the section headings in this book).

Some programming languages with parallel processing features (such as Ada and to some extent Modula-2) or systems with 'piping' facilities (such as Unix) allow the direct implementation of a data flow diagram. However, for a sequential program it is helpful to transform the data flow diagram into a hierarchical structure chart.

5.3.3   Deriving the structure chart

As its name suggests, a structure chart is used to create a diagrammatic model of the structure of a program. It provides a plan of the parameters passed between procedures and the main program, and whether they need to be value or variable parameters. It also shows from what part of the program different procedures and functions are called. Where there are a number of DFDs at level 2 or higher, the structure chart provides a way of assembling all the components of the design into a single diagram which represents the required program structure.

To derive the structure chart, we must identify three main regions of processing: the input flows, the transform flows and the output flows.

- Input flows handle data that is essentially input even though it may have undergone a number of transformations,
- transform flows are central and can be described as neither input nor output, and
- output flows handle data that is essentially output.

Most programs will consist of a number of input processes, transform processes and output processes. In order to pass data between these regions we need an executive program module. In our spell check example, the division is very easy; ExtractWord is the only input process, CheckSpelling the central transform, and DisplayStatus the only output transform.

We can name our executive program SpellCheck, which when activated will perform the entire task of the system by calling subordinate procedures. The procedures can be grouped as input procedures, central transformation procedures and output procedures, and can be represented in a structure chart as:

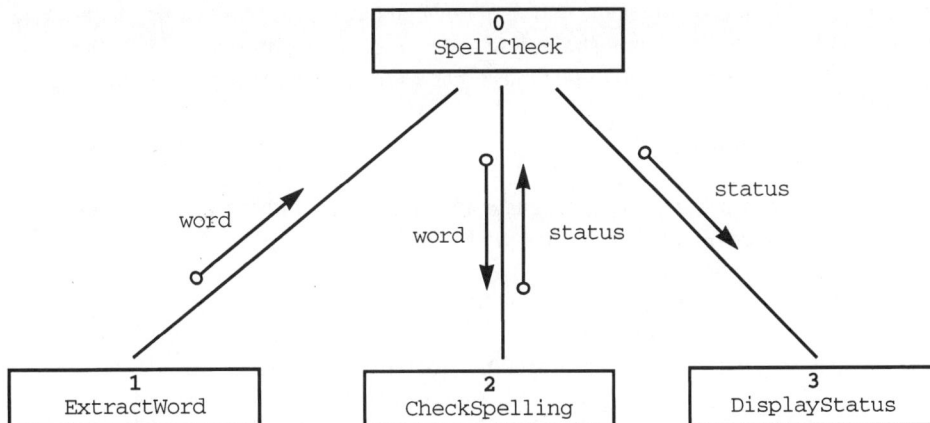

The main program, SpellCheck, calls three procedures, ExtractWord, CheckSpelling, and DisplayStatus.

Along the lines connecting the process boxes are placed directed data flows representing the parameter to be passed between different parts of the program design.

The SpellCheck example is a very simple one to illustrate the technique but, as we are sure you can imagine, data flow diagrams can become very complex indeed and it is not always quite so easy to determine which process is the central one. A trickier example is the subject of Chapter 14.

5.3.4   Pseudocode

The final stage of the design is to express the problem in algorithmic form, usually called pseudocode. Pseudocode is a hybrid between English and programming language. Unlike an actual programming language the precise syntax is not important so it is a useful way of expressing initially how a procedure is to work.

There are many advantages to using pseudocode at this stage rather than coding directly into the chosen programming language.

•   If the design is independent of a particular language, the program could be
     implemented in different ways.

•   The DFDs and structure charts show the processes and data flows, but do not
     describe the internal structure of the program. It is as important to plan the detail as
     to plan the relationship between the building blocks.

•   The design can be hand-checked in an abbreviated format before language
     translation begins. If major design flaws are detected after the program has been
     created then restructuring and debugging of program code will be necessary. This is
     a much more difficult task than restructuring at the pseudocode stage.

Pseudocode syntax

As there is no formal language for pseudocode it is up to the programmer to arrive at a set of descriptions for the design which are:
•   consistent,
•   precise,
•   unambiguous, and
•   independent of any specific programming language.

The level of formality used in pseudocode descriptions varies depending on author. There is a case for making pseudocode formalized to the extent that it is almost a programming language in itself; a precise description, yet implementation language independent. The language independence of pseudocode is especially important if the target language is not decided at the time of the design.

We suggest that, for the time being, you follow the style used in this book. The pseudocode does not need to be expressed at the same level of detail as the program code. If the pseudocode is word-processed for your documentation then you should be able to construct your source code directly from it.

There is a pseudocode block for each 'procedure' identified in the structure chart. For the SpellCheck example the pseudocode may look like this:

0   SpellCheck: (*main routine*)
BEGIN
    ExtractWord   (word)
    CheckSpelling   (word,status)
    DisplayStatus   (status)
END SpellCheck.

1   ExtractWord:
BEGIN
    Display prompt for word
    Read word
    (* may incorporate some checking or validation of input data*)
END ExtractWord;

2   CheckSpelling:
BEGIN
    Open dictionary file for reading
    Search the dictionary file for the word
    IF the word is found THEN
        status is 'found'
    ELSE
        status is 'not found'
    END IF
    Close file
END CheckSpelling;

3   DisplayStatus:
BEGIN
    IF status is 'found' THEN
        display "Word OK"
    ELSE
        display "Word not in dictionary"
    END IF
END DisplayStatus;

The pseudocode has identified what needs to be done. Before the program is written in the chosen programming language the designer needs to investigate different ways to perform the search and identify a match in the dictionary to complete the design. We'll look at this particular program again in the form of an exercise in Chapter 9.

5.3.5   Implementation

The job of actually writing the code for a computer program is easier if we can work from a complete set of pseudocode. If any design flaws are detected during this coding stage then the design should be adjusted as well as the code. At the end of the coding phase the design should reflect the true structure of the program; the program code and design should correspond.

However, don't forget that ultimately the source code is the place a programmer would look to correct a bug, or to make some other modifications. Even if the programmer wrote the code there is no guarantee that (s)he will remember it in detail six months or more later. Along with good design, the format and documentation of the source code are the key to the maintainability of software.

5.3.6   Comment on the use of data flow design

There is a lot of interest in data flow design, in particular because of its suitability for designing programs for parallel systems (i.e. systems in which separate subprograms can be executing at the same time).
The technique seems especially popular for real-time applications, such as process control, but the only essential ingredient for its use is that flows of data can be identified.

5.4   Further design issues

5.4.1   Modularity

If you were a design engineer working on a new vehicle for a car manufacturer, rather than carrying out the detailed design of every component yourself, the job is likely to be divided up into reasonably independent sub-systems which can be worked out in detail by a specialist design team. So you might find yourself working on engine design, the braking system or perhaps the electrical system. Although one person may be over-seeing the whole project, it is possible to split the task into subsystems which are as independent of one another as possible. It makes good sense to follow the same principle when designing computer hardware or software.

Although the computer being used to prepare this book is now several years old, we are fortunate that, in common with most modern hardware, it has a modular design. If we wanted to upgrade its memory, we need only undo a single screw and plug a further memory circuit board into one of the spare sockets provided. Similarly, if something goes wrong, the faulty circuit can, in theory, be identified, unplugged and (if the bank balance will stand it) replaced. Compare this with most early pieces of electronic equipment with spaghetti-like wiring between components. Faults could be very difficult to trace, and when identified required a soldering iron to fix. Modern design is simpler and faults are dealt with more easily because each sub-circuit has a single well defined function and requires a minimal number of connections to other circuits. Despite increased functionality, modern electronic design, implementation, testing and maintenance is manageable because the designers take a modular approach. This means that each sub-system can be designed, created and tested independently of the others, but a common standard used to connect them together. The parts must be functionally independent, so that a change to one will not necessitate a change to any other.

A modular approach can do similar things for software.

The aim is to produce software that is easy to create, test and maintain. To this end we need procedures that can be changed with minimal effect on other procedures. We can achieve this by ensuring that we:

- design each procedure so that it carries out a single, well defined task,
- select, for each procedure, an identifying name that is informative about the nature of the procedure's task, and
- avoid accessing global variables within procedures by ensuring that all data flow between procedures is via the procedures' parameters. Don't be tempted to omit parameters by using global variables instead.

5.4.2   Subprogram size

How do you know when to stop sub-dividing?
How big should a subprogram be?

Opinion as to actual size seems to vary from about 7 lines of code to about 40 lines (or one page of text), depending on the problem being solved.

Some computer scientists argue that the smaller the subprogram, the easier it will be to understand, while others feel that very small subprograms mean that there will need to be more of them and that decreasing complexity in one way only increases it in another.

It is impossible to specify an optimum size precisely but, as a general principle in this case, good things do come in little packages although obviously a compromise is required. A good time to stop sub-dividing is when the subprogram does one specific job and when it is easy to see how to implement it. Also, we should be able to study the detailed logic of one subprogram in isolation from the others and understand what subprograms do in relation to one another without having to worry about how they do it.

5.4.3   Cohesion

Ideally, every statement in a subprogram should contribute towards the performance of a single well-defined task. Subprograms that do this are said to be functionally cohesive.

5.4.4   Coupling

To allow subprograms to be designed, implemented, tested and maintained with minimal effect on other parts of the system, it is important to decompose the software in such a way that there is minimal interaction between the subprograms. The fewer the number of objects that connect the subprograms, the better, so few parameters should be passed between modules in procedure calls. All data in and out of subprograms should be via a well defined interface, i.e. the parameters in the case of procedures. Subprograms that break this rule are like circuits with wires soldered straight onto the micro-chip pins. You can no longer easily unplug and change them.

5.5   Testing

Once your program is free of syntax errors and the compilation and linking is successful then the program needs to be tested. This means that the performance of the program is monitored, under controlled conditions, in a number of different circumstances. It is usually possible to provide the appropriate conditions for most tests by varying the data values input to the program.

In commercially produced software, failure to test properly can be a very expensive mistake. Not only might the customers be inconvenienced by having inoperable software, but the software developer will have to undertake the possibly costly process of tracking down the errors and issuing corrections to all customers, thereby engendering a lack of confidence in future products. When customers pay a great deal of money for software they have a right to expect it to be reliable.

If we consider a piece of commercial software in widespread use, such as a word processor or spreadsheet package, we should assume that every possible eventuality will occur at some time in its life. Ideally the tester of such programs should incorporate all such cases in the testing, but this would be a very difficult, if not impossible task!

Apart from designing programs that can be mathematically verified the best we can do is devise sensible testing strategies to boost our confidence that our software is going to behave itself.

5.5.1   Testing strategies

There are several possible approaches to testing depending on the nature of the software.

Bottom-up testing involves testing each component procedure separately and independently of the others.

Stub testing involves starting with the main program and dummy procedures or stubs, which do nothing. The testing is done in incremental stages, and once a test is satisfactory the next building block is added and tested, until the program is complete.

Black box testing is a way of preparing test data from the viewpoint of the DFD context diagram. The software is considered to be a black box, with the property that a given input will produce a specific output. The test data is designed to assess the ability of the software to match the specification, with no regard for the internal workings.

White box testing, unlike black box testing, is about designing test data which will test the internal workings and structure of the software; the opposite to black box testing. The actual program statements can be used to help to construct test data which will explore possible routes through the code.

A combination of different methods is the usual way to achieve a comprehensive testing strategy. Black and white box testing are used together to ensure that the software is tried and checked both externally and internally. Tested components may be introduced into a stub program, to ascertain whether the assembled program functions as a unit.

A test harness can be constructed instead of just using the keyboard as an input device. This is a specially written program which sets up the test data and conditions for each procedure to be tested. This is one way to relieve the monotony of testing for the programmer and it can be rerun as many times as required.

Testing is generally an unpopular duty, but under no circumstances should it be ignored or done half-heartedly. In a way it is a destructive process because a tester is trying to break the program; to find conditions for which the programmer has not allowed and see how the program stands up to the worst events it can be expected to encounter.

It is not the quantity of test data which is important. There are specific data values for every program which are likely to cause errors. Such values must be identified and tried.

Testing and debugging is an iterative process, which should continue until a satisfactory set of test results is achieved.

5.5.2   Test tables

A good way to demonstrate that you have tested your software correctly and to present the results, is to use a tabular format called a test table. This will have one entry for each test, with the headings as shown in the following possible test table compiled for SpellCheck:

Test values	Reason for test	Expected outcome	Actual outcome	Resolution of result
A	Lower boundary. i.e. First word in dictionary, and one of the shortest	Word found	Word found	Successful
ZYMOTIC	Upper boundary. i.e. Last word in dictionary	Word found	Word found	Successful
happy	Typical word, lower case	Word found	Word found	Successful
HaPPy	Mixed case	Word found	Word found	Successful
AAAA	Invalid word at start of dictionary	Word not found	Word not found	Successful
ZZZ	Invalid word at end of dictionary	Word not found	Word not found	Successful
MNPRQ	Invalid word in middle	Word not found	Word not found	Successful
i	Only valid if a capital	Word not found	Word found	Correction required
12345	Non alphabetics	Word not found	Word not found	Successful

There are many other tests that could be incorporated to test SpellCheck more thoroughly, for example, the longest word in the dictionary, plurals, and the use of apostrophes. Testing provides a means to explore how the program deals with normal, invalid and exceptional data. It often raises questions which have not been considered until this stage of the development, such as how to handle lower case **i** in the SpellCheck program. If errors are discovered the program should be corrected, then subjected to ALL the tests again. This may seem an unnecessary waste of time and effort but a small change to a program can affect other parts of the software, so you cannot be sure it works unless it is retested in full; and even then you can't be absolutely sure.

5.6   Documentation

Most commercial software is developed using teams of design and programming specialists. For ease of communication the team members must work to a common design method and standardized programming technique, so that members may understand each other's work and share common program code.

An important, but often neglected duty for a programmer, is to 'write up' or document software, so that other programmers can understand it, make use of it and maintain it in the future. This is known as technical documentation.
Some software must also be documented in a way that enables a non-technical user to understand it and make use of it. This is called a user guide or a user manual.

At this stage we will look at what needs to be included in the technical documentation.

Here's a guide to what a complete set of technical documentation could contain:

- contents page;
- a brief statement of the problem;
- requirements specification including input/output requirements;
- the design which, using our chosen design method, will consist of:
    - context diagram,
    - levelled set of DFDs,
    - structure chart,
    - pseudocode, and
    - data dictionary;
- commented source code / compilation listing;
- testing strategy;
- test table with results;
- test data and sample runs;
- operating instructions;
- maintenance log.

Documentation is not a 'do once and forget it' process. It should be developed alongside the software and maintained with the software.
Corrections and enhancements to the software should be incorporated in all parts of the documentation, so that at any time the documentation reflects the current state of the operating software.

5.6.1   Data dictionary

A data dictionary contains a list and description of all the entities used by a program.

Each identifier used by the program should be recorded in the data dictionary, together with relevant information on, for example, what it represents, where in the program it can be used or viewed and any restrictions which apply to it.

Data dictionary entries should be included for each module, procedure, constant, data type and variable declared in the software. It provides a means of keeping track of all identifiers used in the program.

A data dictionary may be simply drawn up on paper. However, there are obvious advantages in maintenance and presentation if it can be word processed, put in a spreadsheet or even entered on a database. If specialized drawing tools or CASE (Computer Aided Software Engineering) tools are used to construct the diagrams then it may be possible to arrange for a data dictionary, with some of the required information, to be created automatically.

The information stored in a dictionary entry for a particular identifier depends on what the identifier represents; it could be a module, a procedure, a constant, a type or a variable.

Item	typical data dictionary information
MODULE	module name, brief description, imports, exports, date written, author, date last amended, by whom, scope
PROCEDURE	name, brief description, parameters, pre-conditions, post-conditions, scope
CONST	name, value, scope
TYPE	name, definition, scope
VAR	name, type, value restrictions, scope

5.6.2   Meaningful identifiers

A simple but effective means of aiding the readability of source code is to use identifiers which describe their purpose. An identifier such as `stockLevel` may take slightly longer to code and type in than `sl`, but the first identifier conveys much more to the reader than the second.

5.6.3   Comments

In addition to the comment block at the start of the module, there should be a comment with every procedure to convey any information not obvious from the procedure header. This comment should include a statement about pre-conditions (i.e. the assumed state of parameters on entry to the procedure), and post-conditions (i.e. the state of parameters on exit from the routine).

5.6.4   Pre-conditions and post-conditions

The documentation of a sub-program should contain a statement about the parameter requirements or assumed conditions at the start of the procedure (the pre-conditions), and a statement about the contents and significance of any variable parameters belonging to the procedure (the post-conditions).

The pre-conditions and post-conditions of a section of code provide the basis on which to prove its correctness. Mathematically expressed, they can be used to guide the design specification to achieve a verifiably correct program.

5.6.5   Indentation

Modula-2 is a block-structured language. Indenting blocks of code to emphasize a program's structure enhances its readability.

A maintainable and readable program should incorporate all the above features.

Exercise 5.1

Design a set of test cases for the `Encryption` program listed in Section 3.2.3. Present the results in the form of a test table.

5.7   Case study: *Food energy*

To illustrate the design process we will apply the full DFD technique to producing a program for calculating energy from food intake.

5.7.1   Requirements

The requirement is to write a program to calculate the energy obtained from eating fats and carbohydrates.

5.7.2   Specification

The program is to prompt the user and accept input, via the keyboard, of a value representing the quantity of fats consumed and a value representing the quantity of carbohydrates consumed; both in grammes. The program is then to calculate the energy, in kiloJoules (kJ), provided by each of these. The total energy intake is to be calculated and then converted to Calories. The program is to output, to the screen, the energy obtained from fats, in kJ, the energy obtained from carbohydrates, in kJ, and the total energy, in Calories.
Fats provide energy at the rate of 38 kJ/g, while carbohydrates yield 17 kJ/g.
There are 4.2 kJ in 1 Calorie.
(The daily energy requirement for an adult varies, but is about 2600 Calories.)

5.7.3   Design

First, the context diagram (level 0 DFD).

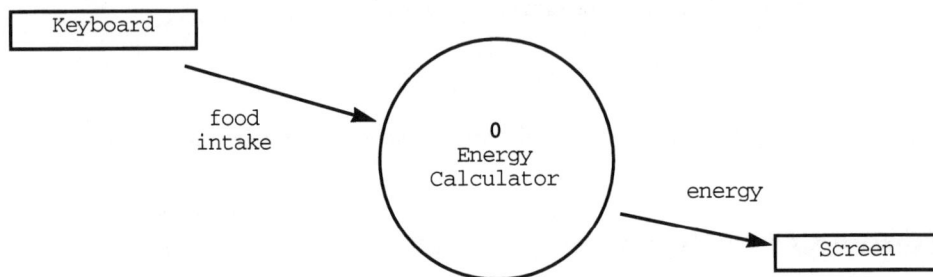

Refining to the level 1 DFD:

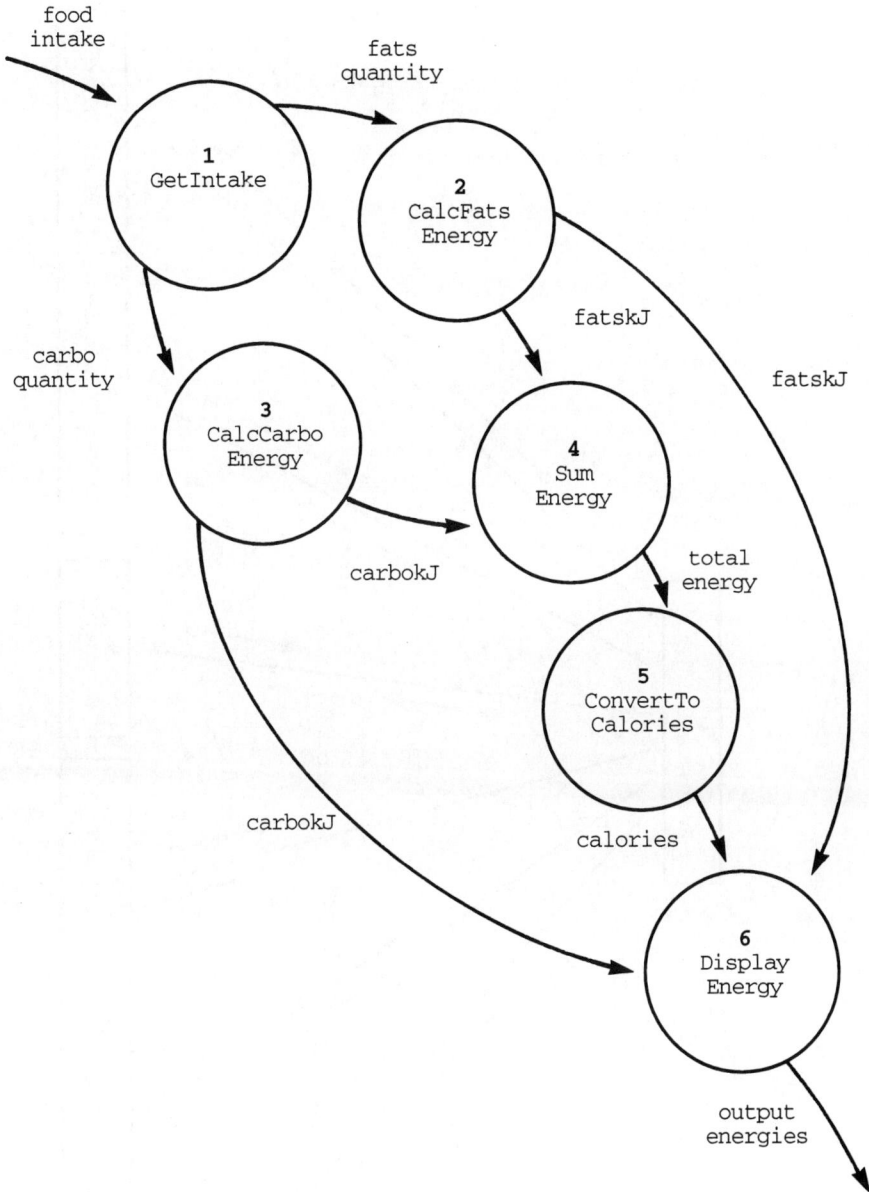

And the structure chart:

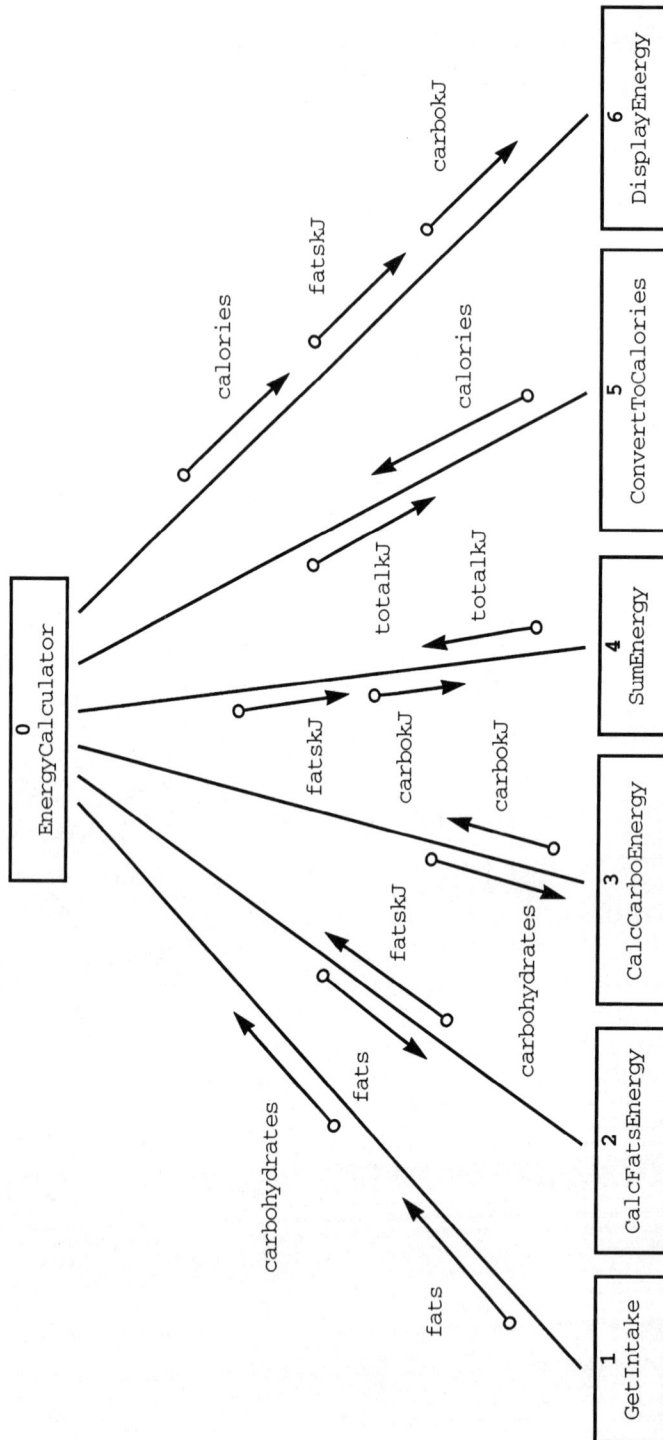

Each box in the structure chart represents a procedure to be implemented.

Remember that each procedure should carry out a single well defined and easily implementable task.

A sensible decision, when to stop the process of refinement, has to be made. We think that it is reasonable to treat GetIntake as a single task but we could, arguably, have refined it further into GetFats and GetCarbohydrates. Do you think, that in this case, it would have enhanced program clarity or ease of implementation? What other subdivisions seem reasonable?

Although, in order to compile, the final code must conform to correct Modula-2 syntax, during the initial design process and before actual coding in Modula-2, remember from the earlier discussion, it is useful to express our program parts in pseudocode.

First the main program,

0   EnergyCalculator:
BEGIN
    GetIntake   (fats, carbohydrates)
    CalcFatsEnergy   (fats, fatskJ)
    CalcCarboEnergy   (carbohydrates, carbokJ)
    SumEnergy   (fatskJ, carbokJ,totalkJ)
    ConvertToCalories   (totalkJ, calories)
    DisplayEnergy   (fatskJ, carbokJ, calories)
END EnergyCalculator.

then each of the procedures,

1   GetIntake:
BEGIN
    Get quantity of fats intake in grammes
    Get quantity of carbohydrates intake in grammes
END GetIntake;

2   CalcFatsEnergy:
BEGIN
    fatskJ := $38kJg^{-1}$ * fats quantity
END CalcFatsEnergy;

3   CalcCarboEnergy:
BEGIN
    carbokJ := $17kJg^{-1}$ * carbohydrates quantity
END CalcCarboEnergy;

4   SumEnergy
BEGIN
    totalkJ := fatskJ + carbokJ
END SumEnergy;

5   ConvertToCalories
```
BEGIN
    calories := totalJ / 4.2kJ
END ConvertToCalories;
```

6   DisplayEnergy
```
BEGIN
    display fatskJ
    display carbokJ
    display calories
END DisplayEnergy;
```

SumEnergy is a very simple calculation and there is nothing to be gained by making it a separate procedure.

CalcFatsEnergy, CalcCarboEnergy and ConvertToCalories are simple calculations also, but each represents a conversion operation that may be useful in other contexts, so we will implement these as separate function procedures.

It is now a relatively straightforward step to convert the pseudocode into actual code for the implementation language we are using.

5.7.4   Implementation

```
MODULE EnergyCalculator;
(*
** Purpose: Program to calculate energy from food intake
** Uses modules: InOut, RealInOut
*)
FROM InOut IMPORT WriteString, WriteLn;
FROM RealInOut IMPORT ReadReal, WriteReal;
 (*Required for keyboard input and screen output*)
VAR
    fats,carbohydrates,fatskJ,carbokJ,totalkJ,calories:REAL;

PROCEDURE GetIntake(VAR fats, carbohydrates: REAL);
(*Gets values for fats and carbohydrates intake from user
**Pre-conditions: None
**Post-conditions: fats contains the quantity of fats intake
**and carbohydrates contains the quantity of carbohydrates
**intake as input from the keyboard*)
BEGIN
    WriteString("Intake of fats in grammes? ");
    ReadReal(fats);
    WriteLn;
    WriteString("Intake of carbohydrates in grammes? ");
    ReadReal(carbohydrates);
    WriteLn
END GetIntake;
```

```
PROCEDURE CalcFatsEnergy(fats:REAL) : REAL;
(*Calculates the energy provided by amount of fats given
**by parameter fats
**Pre-conditions: fats contains a REAL value
**Post-conditions: Returns the energy provided
**assuming 38kJ per gram*)
CONST
    FATSENERGY = 38.0;   (*kJ per gram*)
BEGIN
    RETURN (fats * FATSENERGY)
END CalcFatsEnergy;


PROCEDURE CalcCarboEnergy(carbohydrates:REAL) : REAL;
(*Calculates the energy provided by amount of carbohydrates
**given by parameter carbohydrates
**Pre-conditions: carbohydrates contains a REAL value
**Post-conditions: Returns the energy provided
**assuming 17kJ per gram*)
CONST
    CARBOENERGY = 17.0;   (*kJ per gram*)
BEGIN
    RETURN (carbohydrates * CARBOENERGY)
END CalcCarboEnergy;

PROCEDURE ConvertToCalories(totalkJ:REAL) : REAL;
(*Converts kJ to Calories
**Pre-conditions: fatskJ and carbokJ contain REAL values
**Post-conditions: Returns the sum of fatskJ
**and carbokJ*)
CONST
    kJinCAL = 4.2;   (* 4.2kJ = 1 Calorie *)
BEGIN
    RETURN (totalkJ / kJinCAL)
END ConvertToCalories;


PROCEDURE DisplayEnergy(fatskJ, carbokJ, calories:REAL);
(*Display energy from fats and carbohydrates in kJ
**and total energy in Calories
**Pre-conditions: fatskJ and carbokJ contain REAL values
**representing kJ and calories contains total energy
**in Calories
**Post-conditions: None*)
CONST
    WIDTH = 10;
BEGIN
    WriteString("Energy from fats is ");
    WriteReal(fatskJ,WIDTH);
    WriteString(" kJ");
    WriteLn;

    WriteString("Energy from carbohydrates is ");
    WriteReal(carbokJ,WIDTH);
    WriteString(" kJ");
    WriteLn;

    WriteString("Total energy is ");
    WriteReal(calories,WIDTH);
    WriteString(" Calories");
    WriteLn
END DisplayEnergy;
```

```
BEGIN  (*Main program*)
  GetIntake(fats, carbohydrates);
  fatskJ := CalcFatsEnergy(fats);
  carbokJ := CalcCarboEnergy(carbohydrates);
  totalkJ := fatskJ + carbokJ;
  calories := ConvertToCalories(totalkJ);
  DisplayEnergy(fatskJ, carbokJ, calories)
END EnergyCalculator.
```

5.7.5   Testing

The test table should include cases such as:

Inputs		Reason	Expected energy outputs			Actual outputs		
Fat	*Carbo*		*Fat*	*Carbo*	*Calories*	*Fat*	*Carbo*	*Calories*
0	0		0	0	0			
10	0		0	1.70E+02	4.05E+01			
0	10		3.80E+02	0	9.05E+01			
10	10		3.80E+02	1.70E+02	1.31E+02			

(The actual form of the energy output in Calories will depend on your implementation of WriteReal.)

Exercise 5.2

Fill in the reasons for the test cases identified in the above test table. Run EnergyCalculator and compare the actual outputs with the expected. What other test cases ought to be included?

Self test 5.2

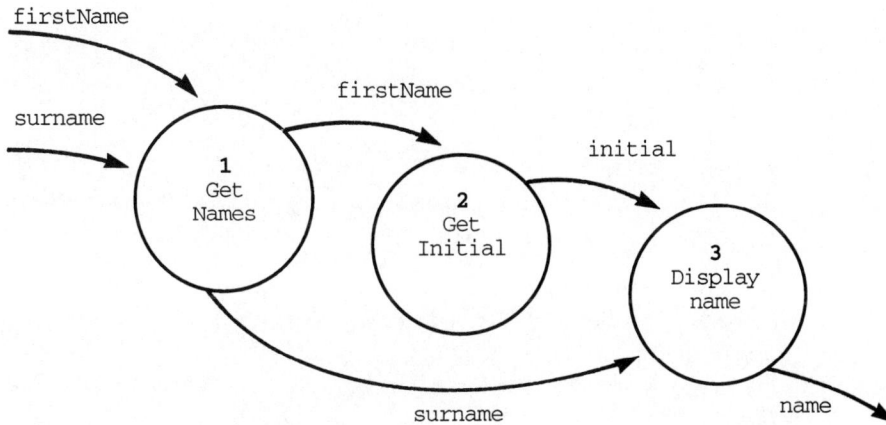

From the level 1 DFD above, decide which one of the following could be a correct procedure heading for GetInitial.

a) PROCEDURE GetInitial(firstName : StringType;
                             VAR initial : CHAR);
b) PROCEDURE GetInitial(VAR firstName : StringType;
                             VAR initial : CHAR);
c) PROCEDURE GetInitial(VAR firstName : StringType;
                             initial : CHAR);
d) PROCEDURE GetInitial(firstName : StringType;
                             initial : CHAR);

Self test 5.3

Which one of the statements below is true?

a) Cohesion and coupling are used to determine the data types used in a program.
b) Modules should have high cohesion and low coupling.
c) Modules should have low cohesion and high coupling.
d) Cohesion and coupling provide a measure of the complexity of modules.

Exercise 5.3

Design, implement and test a program to convert an input time, given in seconds, to hours, minutes and seconds.

6 IF statement and BOOLEAN types

6.1 BOOLEAN data type

6.1.1 BOOLEAN expressions

BOOLEAN is one of the basic Modula-2 data types and BOOLEAN variables can take a value of either TRUE or FALSE.

BOOLEAN expressions compare values to give a BOOLEAN result. For example, the BOOLEAN operator > means greater than, so the BOOLEAN expression;

```
age > 21
```

compares the value of the variable age with 21. If the value of age is greater than 21 the expression evaluates to TRUE, otherwise it evaluates to FALSE.

Similarly,

```
choice = 'a'
```

compares the value of the variable choice with the character 'a'. If the value of choice is equal to 'a' the expression evaluates to TRUE, otherwise it evaluates to FALSE.

A simple BOOLEAN expression has the form:

operand   relational operator   operand

6.1.2 Relational operators

A Modula-2 relational operator may be one of the following:

Modula-2 operator	What it means
=	equal to
<	less than
<=	less than or equal to
>	greater than
>=	greater than or equal to
<>	not equal to
#	not equal to

6.1.3   BOOLEAN operands

Operands in BOOLEAN expressions must be simple data types, such as INTEGER, CARDINAL and CHAR. Literals (such as 21, or 'a') or variables can be used as operands.

Although Modula-2 does not allow strings (i.e. arrays of characters) to be used as operands in BOOLEAN expressions, we can write our own function to provide this facility, as you will see later.

In any expression the operands being compared must be ASSIGNMENT COMPATIBLE. (See Appendix B.)

Self test 6.1

Assuming that variables have been declared, and initialized as follows:

```
ch := 'C';
card := 69;
```

evaluate the following BOOLEAN expressions:

```
a)              ch >= 'D'
b)              ch < CHR(card)
c)              ch = CHR(ORD('D') - 1)
d)              ORD(ch) <= (card -2)
```

6.2   Introducing the IF statement for selection

In computer programs it is often necessary to vary the action to be taken depending on some condition. As an example, here is a very short Modula-2 program, which may display a message depending on an input value:

```
MODULE Ageism1;
(*Purpose: To demonstrate the use of IF
**Uses module: InOut*)
FROM InOut IMPORT WriteLn, ReadCard, WriteCard, WriteString;
VAR
     age : CARDINAL;
BEGIN
     WriteString("How old are you?:");
     ReadCard(age);
     WriteLn;
     IF age > 21 THEN
          WriteString("Old Timer!")
     END (*IF*);
     WriteLn
END Ageism1.
```

Sample output:
```
     How old are you?:22
     Old Timer!
```

If the CARDINAL value input is more than 21 (age > 21), then the message Old Timer! is displayed, but if the value is 21 or less no message is displayed. The condition (age > 21) 'guards' entry to the body of the IF statement.

This program can be modified so that it displays a message in both cases. This is done by introducing an ELSE into the IF statement:

```
MODULE Ageism2;
(*Purpose: To demonstrate the use of IF and ELSE,
** or how to insult everyone
**Uses module: InOut *)
FROM InOut IMPORT WriteLn, ReadCard, WriteCard, WriteString;
VAR
     age : CARDINAL;
BEGIN
     WriteString("How old are you?:");
     ReadCard(age);
     WriteLn;
     IF age > 21 THEN
          WriteString("Old Timer!")
     ELSE
          WriteString("I don't believe that you are only ");
          WriteCard(age,2);
          WriteString(" years old!")
     END (*IF*);
     WriteLn
END Ageism2.
```

Sample output:

```
How old are you?:17
I don't believe that you are only 17 years old!
```

The ELSE means 'in all other cases'. When a value of 21 or less is input to this program, a three part message is displayed on a single line.

Using a third variation of the IF statement it is possible to select particular values for special treatment:

```
MODULE Ageism3;
(*Purpose: To demonstrate the use of IF, ELSIF and ELSE
**Uses module: InOut*)
FROM InOut IMPORT WriteLn, ReadCard, WriteCard, WriteString;
VAR
    age : CARDINAL;
BEGIN
    WriteString("How old are you?:");
    ReadCard(age);
    WriteLn;
    IF age > 21 THEN
        WriteString("Old Timer!")
    ELSIF age <= 3 THEN
        WriteString("Baby Face!")
    ELSIF age = 16 THEN
        WriteString("How Sweet!")
    ELSE
        WriteString("I don't believe that you are only ");
        WriteCard(age,2);
        WriteString(" years old!")
    END (*IF*);
    WriteLn
END Ageism3.
```

Sample output:

```
How old are you?:2
Baby Face!
```

There may be any number of occurrences of ELSIF, but only one ELSE. Only one out of the possible four messages will be displayed.

There are three expressions which act as 'guard' conditions in this last program:

```
age > 21
age <= 3
age = 16
```

These are BOOLEAN expressions which can be either TRUE or FALSE.

The first guard expression found to be TRUE is the one whose statements are used. If none of the guard expressions is TRUE then the ELSE statements are used.

Note that ELSIF is one word, not two, and does not have an E in the middle!

IF statement syntax chart:

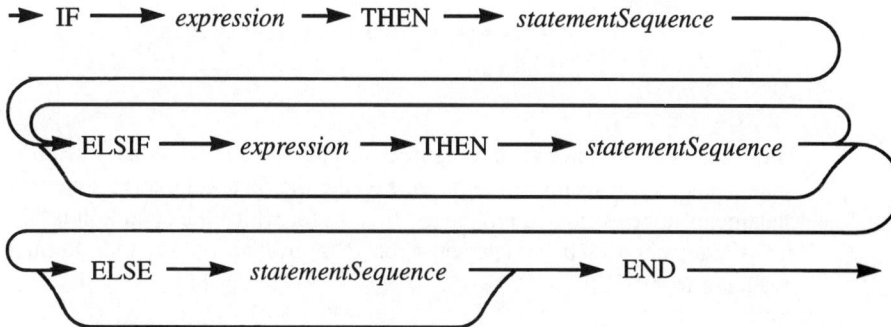

As demonstrated by the Ageism programs, there are three forms in which IF statements can be used:

1.   Ageism1 uses the form:

```
IF (this condition is TRUE) THEN
    execute these statements
END;  (*IF*)
```

This represents a simple yes or no choice; we execute the statements within the IF or we do nothing.

2.   Ageism2 uses the form:

```
IF (this condition is TRUE) THEN
    execute these statements
ELSE
    execute these alternative statements
END;  (*IF*)
```

This time the choice is of an either/or variety; we either execute the first set of statements or we execute the alternative statements. We must do one or the other, and can't do both.

3.   `Ageism3` has the form:

```
IF (this condition is TRUE) THEN
    execute this first set of statements
ELSIF ( this alternative condition is TRUE) THEN
    execute this second set of statements
ELSIF ..... THEN
    .....
    .....
ELSE
    execute these alternative statements
END;   (*IF*)
```

Here, we have a choice from a number of alternatives; we either execute the first set of statements, or the second, etc., or we execute the final alternative statements. The set of statements to be evaluated will be the first set for which the condition is TRUE. Only one set of statements will be selected even if more than one of the alternative conditions evaluates to TRUE.

6.3   BOOLEAN variables and IF statements

6.3.1   Using BOOLEAN operators

Sometimes an IF statement requires that two or more simple BOOLEAN expressions are used together as guard conditions. The simple expressions must be enclosed in parentheses, for example:

```
IF (choice = 'a') AND (age > 50) THEN
    .....
    (*statements to be executed if both conditions are true*)
    .....
END;  (*IF*)
```

Where two or more simple expressions are linked by AND, then all must be TRUE for the result to be TRUE.

```
IF (choice = 'a') OR (choice = 'b') THEN
    .....
    (*statements to be executed if either condition is true*)
    .....
END;  (*IF*)
```

Where two or more simple expressions are linked by OR, if at least one is TRUE then the result is TRUE.

```
IF (age > 21) AND NOT (age >50) THEN
    .....
    (*statements to be executed if expression is true*)
    .....
END;  (*IF*)
```

The NOT operator requires only one operand, which it precedes.

The effect of NOT is to negate the value of its operand. It has a higher precedence than both AND and OR, which means that the above statement will be evaluated like this:

```
IF (age > 21) AND (NOT (age >50)) THEN
    .....
    (*statements to be executed if expression is true*)
    .....
END;  (*IF*)
```

NOT can be a useful operator, but in the above example the programmer's intention is not as clear as it might be. An equivalent but more understandable version of the IF statement would be:

```
IF (age > 21) AND (age <= 50) THEN
    .....
    (*statements to be executed if both conditions are true*)
    .....
END;  (*IF*)
```

It is worth exploring alternative ways of forming complex BOOLEAN expressions because this can help with both clarity and maintainability of programs.

The BOOLEAN operators AND and OR may be used to link several simple expressions together. It is a good idea to use extra brackets, especially if using both AND and OR in the same expression, to make the meaning absolutely clear.

When using BOOLEAN operators the operands must always be BOOLEAN and the result of the operation will also always be BOOLEAN.

BOOLEAN operators:

NOT or ~
>   takes a single operand.
>   If the operand is FALSE this operator returns TRUE.
>   If the operand is TRUE this operator returns FALSE.

AND or &
>   takes two operands.
>   If both operands are TRUE this operator returns TRUE,
>   otherwise it returns FALSE.

OR
>   takes two operands.
>   If either operand is TRUE this operator returns TRUE,
>   otherwise it returns FALSE.

The truth table below shows the effect of these operators using two BOOLEAN variables, **A** and **B**. **T** represents a value of TRUE and **F** a value of FALSE.

A	B	NOT A	A AND B	A OR B
F	F	T	F	F
F	T	T	F	T
T	F	F	F	T
T	T	F	T	T

6.3.2   Precedence of BOOLEAN operators

BOOLEAN expressions are evaluated from left to right and the evaluation stops as soon as the outcome is certain.

NOT	Highest precedence
AND	
OR	
<, >, <=, >=, =, <>	Lowest precedence

Just as with arithmetic expressions, parentheses ( ) can be used to force a desired precedence. It is a good policy to use parentheses whenever they can help to clarify your meaning.

6.3.3   BOOLEAN variables

Instead of using expressions which return BOOLEAN values it is possible to use BOOLEAN variables, for example:

```
MODULE SillyBilly;
(*Purpose: Example using BOOLEAN variables
**Uses module: InOut*)
FROM InOut IMPORT WriteString, WriteLn, ReadCard, WriteCard;
VAR
    found, valid : BOOLEAN;
    inputValue : CARDINAL;
BEGIN
    found := TRUE;
    valid := FALSE;
    WriteString("Give me a number greater than 5: ");
    ReadCard(inputValue);
    valid:=(inputValue > 5);
    IF NOT valid THEN
        WriteLn;
        WriteString("Silly Billy, ");
        WriteCard(inputValue,2);
        WriteString(" is not greater than 5!");
        WriteLn
    ELSE
        WriteString("Thank you!");
        WriteLn
    END (*IF*)
END SillyBilly.
```

TRUE and FALSE are Modula-2 constants; they are not character strings and therefore do not need to be enclosed in quotes.

BOOLEAN variables can be very useful for recording events in a program, which may be tested for later. Variables like valid, used as indicators, are often called flags or switches.

BOOLEAN variables cannot be input or output directly using the facilities in InOut because TRUE and FALSE are internal to the Modula-2 language.

Self test 6.2

Given that A, B, C are BOOLEAN variables, draw truth tables for each of the following expressions to determine which ONE expression is NOT equivalent to the other three:

a)   (A AND B) OR (A AND C)
b)   (A AND (B OR C))
c)   (A OR B) AND (A OR C)
d)   (A AND B AND C) OR (A AND B) OR (A AND C)

Self test 6.3

The following assignment statement gives the BOOLEAN variable notFound a value of TRUE or FALSE depending on the outcome of the BOOLEAN expression:

```
notFound := (match = 'N');
```

Determine which ONE of the following is equivalent to the above statement:

a)
```
IF match = 'Y' THEN
      notFound  := FALSE
ELSE
      notFound := TRUE
END;
```

b)
```
IF match = 'N' THEN
      notFound  :=TRUE
ELSE
      notFound := FALSE
END;
```

c)
```
IF notFound = 'N' THEN
      match   := FALSE
ELSE
      match := TRUE
END;
```

d)
```
IF match = 'N' THEN
      notFound  := FALSE
ELSE
      notFound := TRUE
END;
```

6.4   Case study: *Decisions, decisions*

6.4.1   Requirements

What shall we do today?

At weekends and holidays my family and I like to amuse ourselves in different ways. Sometimes the weather restricts what we can do; sometimes our budget is limited. We don't like queues and crowds, so we tend to avoid going to popular attractions, such as theme parks on public holidays. It is often difficult to reach a majority decision on any proposals as to what we should do on any particular day. How much simpler it would be if we could get a computer to help us make such decisions.

6.4.2   Specification

A decision-making computer program needs to be supplied with a set of relevant facts and a set of rules for the selection of each of the possible options. The rules are then used with the facts to reach a conclusion.

Let's start by drawing up a list of tasks.

The user wants to:
>   obtain a suggestion about what it would be appropriate to do on a particular day.

To satisfy this the computer program must:
>   allow the user to enter some facts about the day,
>   test the facts against a set of rules to determine the most suitable activities and then display the result.

A question and answer format could be used for entering the facts or, if choices are limited, a menu of options may be easier to use.

The program requires the user to input some facts on which to base a decision. For example:

>   What is the weather? Is it sunny, rainy, cloudy or snowy?
>   What is the temperature?
>   How much spending money is available?
>   Is it a public holiday?
>   How many people are to take part in the activity?

Next, the program will analyze the facts and decide which of the activity options is the most suitable, based on the rules provided.

Finally, the program will display its recommendation.

Before we can progress we must identify the rules that we want the program to follow. It could be a very complex set of rules, but it is wise to keep to a simple set of variables and options to begin with and expand later. Based on the above five variable factors and a set of six activity options, including a default (ELSE) choice, let's assume the rules are:

No.	Activity	weather	temp.	money	publicHol?	people
1	Cinema	Not sunny Not snowy	-	>=£4	-	>1
2	Scrabble	Rainy/snowy	-	-	-	>2
3	Theme park	Sunny	>15	>£12	N	>2
4	Zoo	Sunny	>15	>£5	N	>2
5	Bike ride	Sunny	<22	-	-	>1
ELSE						
6	Think of something new!					

If you consider working your way down each set of rules in the table you'll notice that the order is not entirely accidental; for example, note the similarity between theme park and zoo. If these options were reversed then the theme park option would never be chosen. When drawing up a list of choices like this it is important to ensure that all options are achievable.

6.4.3   Design

The problem has been specified; now we must begin to design the program. Firstly, a context diagram to describe the overall system.

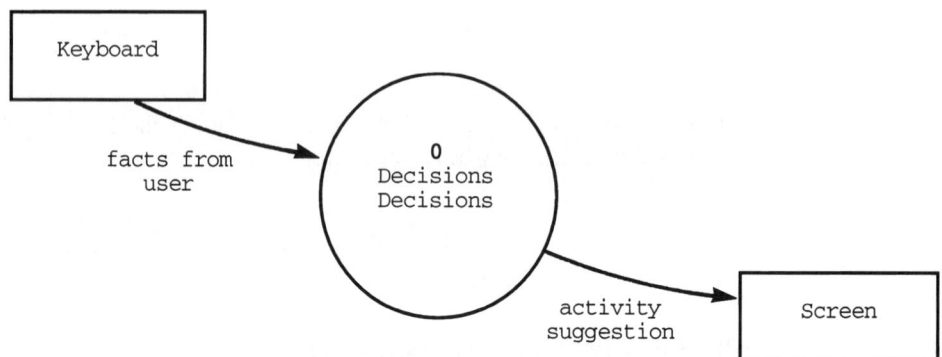

Three stages can be identified in the description of what is required:

```
GetFacts
AnalyzeFacts
DisplaySuggestion
```

These provide the first level of decomposition, (level 1 DFD).

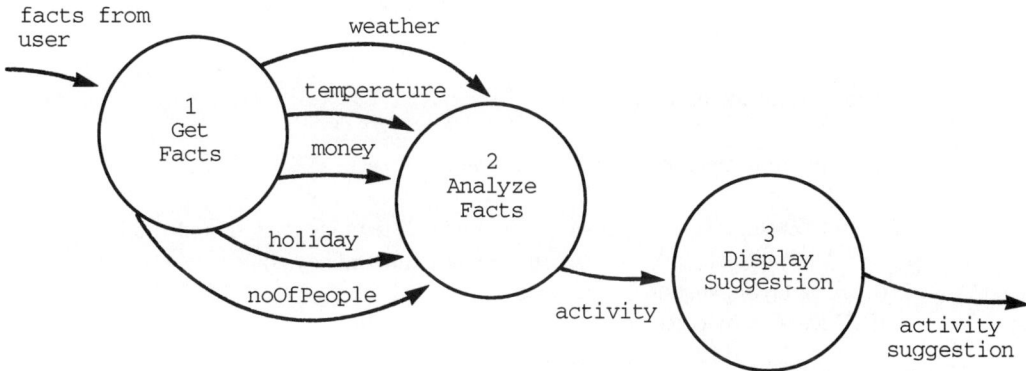

There is no advantage in decomposing any of these processes further, since each constitutes a simple procedure.

The next stage of the design is to draw up the structure chart to bring together the context diagram (level 0 DFD) and level 1 DFD.

As with the SpellCheck example in Chapter 5, it is a simple matter to identify the three main processing regions covering input flows, transform flows and output flows.

GetFacts is the only input process; AnalyzeFacts, the transform process and DisplaySuggestion, the only output process. The executive program is DecisionsDecisions represented by the level 0 box at the top of the structure chart. This is the executive process and represents the main program and each process bubble on the level 1 DFD becomes a box beneath it in the structure chart.

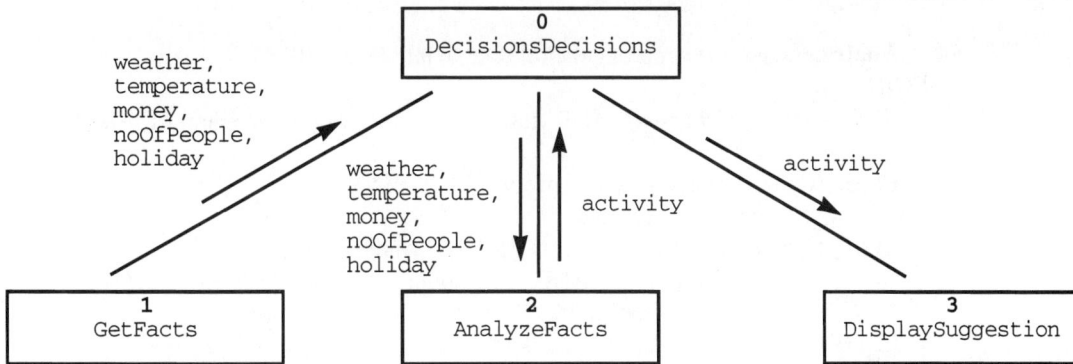

If any level 2 DFD processes were required, these would be placed below the level 1 process which they represent, and so on until all the DFD processes have been incorporated in the structure chart. (We will be looking at an example that requires this when we discuss design further in Chapter 14.)

The arrows indicate the flow of data between the procedures.

The next stage is to describe the internal workings of each of the procedures identified in the structure chart, ensuring that the parameters match the data flows between them.
We can do this in pseudocode before having to worry about the nitty-gritty detail of exact Modula-2 syntax.

The pseudocode becomes:

0   DecisionsDecisions: (*Main program*)
```
BEGIN
     GetFacts                (weather,temperature,money,noOfPeople,holiday)
     AnalyzeFacts            (weather,temperature,money,noOfPeople,holiday,activity)
     DisplaySuggestion       (activity)
END DecisionsDecisions.
```

1   GetFacts:
```
BEGIN
     Ask about the weather
     Read weather
     Ask about the temperature
     Read temperature
     Ask about spending money
     Read money
     Ask whether public holiday
     Read holiday
     Ask about number of people
     Read people
END GetFacts;
```

2   AnalyzeFacts: (*Interpreting the rules table into IF..ELSIFs*)
```
BEGIN
     IF NOT (sunny OR snowy) AND (money >= 4) AND (noOfPeople > 1) THEN
             activity := cinema
     ELSIF (rainy OR snowy) AND (people > 2) THEN
             activity := scrabble
     ELSIF (sunny)AND (temperature > 15) AND (money >12)
                             AND NOT holiday AND (noOfPeople > 2)THEN
             activity := theme park
     ELSIF (sunny) AND (temperature > 15) AND (money >5)
                             AND NOT holiday AND (noOfPeople > 2) THEN
             activity := zoo
     ELSIF (sunny) AND (temperature <22) AND (noOfPeople >1) THEN
             activity := bike ride
     ELSE
             activity := something new
     END IF
END AnalyzeFacts;
```

DisplaySuggestion:
BEGIN
    Display titles
    Depending on choice of activity, display one of
    "cinema", "scrabble", "theme park", "zoo", "bike ride"
                      or "think of something new!"
    New line
END DisplaySuggestion;

If you refer back to the rule resulting in the cinema suggestion, you'll notice that the rules table specified 'not sunny, not snowy'. It can be tempting to link negatives with OR because in normal spoken English it sounds quite correct to say that it is not sunny or snowy when you mean that neither is true. However, the logical representation of this rule can be expressed in two equivalent forms:

    NOT sunny AND NOT snowy
    NOT (sunny OR snowy)

and these are not the same as:

    NOT sunny OR snowy

We can illustrate this using truth tables:

sunny	snowy	NOT sunny	NOT snowy	NOT sunny AND NOT snowy
T	T	F	F	F
T	F	F	T	F
F	T	T	F	F
F	F	T	T	T

sunny	snowy	sunny OR snowy	NOT(sunny OR snowy)
T	T	T	F
T	F	T	F
F	T	T	F
F	F	F	T

sunny	snowy	NOT sunny	NOT sunny OR snowy
T	T	F	T
T	F	F	F
F	T	T	T
F	F	T	T

So the first two expressions give identical results and provide a TRUE value only when both sunny and snowy are FALSE. The third expression gives a different result.

6.4.4   Implementation

The pseudocode design leaves unresolved the matter of how the input facts are to be represented inside the computer.

Modelling our data
Let's see how we can model the data using Modula-2's basic data types.

weather:
The rules allow for four weather values: sunny, rainy, cloudy or snowy.
How do we represent these within our program?

- As string variables?
  Using string variables is possible, but is not ideal, since Modula-2 does not allow expressions such as:
  ```
  IF weather = " rainy" THEN ....
  ```
  although in Chapter 12 we will show you how to write a procedure to carry out this sort of comparison.

- As a CHAR variable?
  Using just the first letter of each of the four weather values could be a way round the above problem, as we could make weather a variable of type CHAR but, unfortunately in this case, we have two words beginning with 's' which makes it difficult to select a suitable unique CHAR value to represent each weather value.

- As BOOLEAN variables?
  We could make each value of weather a BOOLEAN variable, so Sunny could take the value TRUE or FALSE, and so on. However, this would increase the number of variables required and necessitate input via a series of yes/no questions. In this example, as we are assuming only one of Sunny, Rainy, Cloudy or Snowy can be true at any one time, we would also have to provide a means of ensuring that only one of the variables gets assigned the value TRUE.

- As a CARDINAL variable?
  As we have only a limited number of choices, an alternative solution is to use a menu.

  ```
  What is the weather like?
      1   Sunny
      2   Rainy
      3   Cloudy
      4   Snowy

      Answer (range 1 - 4) :
  ```

Using this approach the data type for weather can be a CARDINAL variable or a subrange type [1..4]. However, this does make the internal workings of our program a little cryptic as weather values are coded as numbers.

- As an enumerated type?
  Yet another alternative is to use an enumerated type which allows us to declare our own type with the set of values sunny, rainy, cloudy and snowy.
  We will look at this possibility in Chapter 10.

For the time being the menu alternative seems to provide the most convenient representation, although it does mean that weather will be represented by a number within our program; something we don't like because it will not enhance the clarity of the program code.

Programmers using older languages, which provided a smaller set of basic data types than Modula-2, had to resort to just such techniques as this. We'll cure this particular piece of nastiness later but, as our main objective here is to illustrate the use of the IF statement, we'll stick with this representation for you to think about and for comparison with the revised version discussed in Chapter 10.

temperature:
Temperature can be represented simply by a variable of INTEGER type.

money:
Assuming the value of money is never going to be a negative amount, it can be represented using a variable of CARDINAL type.

noOfPeople:
The number of people can also be represented using a variable of CARDINAL type.

holiday:
A BOOLEAN variable would seem appropriate here; however, BOOLEANs cannot be input or output directly. Also, the user needs to be prompted, using a question of suitable format, perhaps with a yes/no answer, like this:

```
Is it a public holiday today (y or n)?
```

In this case, the input would be to a CHAR variable. (It is desirable to allow the input to be typed using upper or lower case characters.) We can then convert the y/n to a BOOLEAN for clarity of processing inside the program.

activity:
Here we have a similar problem to that of weather; the allowable values being strings of characters. This time we have six possible values:

cinema
scrabble
theme park
zoo
bike ride
something new

The same choices of representation are available as were applicable to weather.

Again, for the sake of simplicity, we'll use the CARDINAL subrange [1..6] with activity 1 being the cinema, 2 scrabble, and so on.

So, the input variables will be:

weather	CARDINAL subrange [1..4]
temperature	INTEGER (whole number, but could be negative)
money	CARDINAL
noOfPeople	CARDINAL
holiday	BOOLEAN derived from Yes/No CHAR input

and output variables:

activity	CARDINAL subrange [1..6]

All that remains to be done is to check the parameter requirements for the procedures

GetFacts has five variable parameters: weather, temperature, money, holiday and noOfPeople.

AnalyzeFacts has five value parameters for input and one variable parameter for output, activity.

DisplaySuggestion has just one value parameter, activity.

The formal parameter declaration in the first two procedures would be slightly neater if we changed the order of the five parameters to put the three cardinal parameters together.

We can now turn our pseudocode into the final program code:

```
MODULE DecisionsDecisions;
(*
**Purpose:What shall we do today?  Decision making program
**Uses module: InOut
*)
FROM InOut IMPORT Read, WriteString, ReadInt, ReadCard,
                                         WriteLn;
VAR
    temperature : INTEGER;
    weather,money,noOfPeople : CARDINAL;
    holiday : BOOLEAN;
    activity : CARDINAL;

PROCEDURE GetFacts (  VAR temperature:INTEGER;
                      VAR holiday:BOOLEAN;
                      VAR weather,money,noOfPeople:CARDINAL);
(*Gets the facts from the user
**Pre: None
**Post: temperature, holiday,weather,money,
**noOfPeople contain values set by the user*)
VAR
    ch, onHoliday : CHAR;
```

```
BEGIN
    WriteString("Decisions, Decisions");
    WriteLn;
    WriteString("What is the weather like?");
    WriteLn;
    WriteString("1   Sunny");
    WriteLn;
    WriteString("2   Rainy");
    WriteLn;
    WriteString("3   Cloudy");
    WriteLn;
    WriteString("4   Snowy");
    WriteLn;
    WriteString("Answer (range 1-4)   ");
    ReadCard(weather);
    WriteString("What is the temperature in Celsius?  ");
    ReadInt(temperature);
    WriteString("How much money can you spend today?  ");
    ReadCard(money);
    WriteString("Is it a public holiday today? (Y/N)   ");
    Read(onHoliday);
    (*Read end of line character generated by pressing
    **the RETURN key *)
    Read(ch);
    IF (onHoliday = 'Y') OR (onHoliday = 'y') THEN
        holiday:= TRUE
    ELSE
        holiday:= FALSE
    END (*IF*);
    WriteString("How many people are there today?  ");
    ReadCard(noOfPeople)
END GetFacts;


PROCEDURE AnalyzeFacts ( temperature:INTEGER;
                         holiday:BOOLEAN;
                         weather,money,noOfPeople:CARDINAL;
                         VAR activity:CARDINAL);
(*Interprets the facts in order to make activity suggestion
**Pre: temperature, holiday,weather,money,
**noOfPeople contain valid values
**Post:  activity contains a number between
**1 and 6 to represent activity suggestion based on
**input values *)
BEGIN
    IF NOT((weather = 1) OR (weather = 4))
                  AND (money >= 4) AND (noOfPeople > 1) THEN
        activity := 1 (*cinema*)
    ELSIF ((weather = 2) OR (weather = 4))
                  AND (noOfPeople > 2) THEN
        activity := 2 (*scrabble*)
    ELSIF  (weather = 1)
                  AND (temperature > 15)
                  AND (money > 12) AND NOT holiday
                  AND (noOfPeople > 2) THEN
        activity := 3 (*theme park*)
```

```
        ELSIF   (weather = 1)
                    AND (temperature > 15)
                    AND (money > 5) AND NOT holiday
                    AND (noOfPeople > 2) THEN
            activity := 4  (*zoo*)
        ELSIF   (weather = 1)
                    AND (temperature <22)
                    AND (noOfPeople > 1) THEN
            activity := 5 (*bike ride*)
        ELSE
            activity := 6 (*something new*)
        END (*IF*)
    END AnalyzeFacts;

    PROCEDURE DisplaySuggestion (activity : CARDINAL);
    (*Displays an activity suggestion
    **Pre: activity contains a valid value
    **Post:  None *)
    BEGIN
        WriteLn;
        WriteString("Your best option today is to ");
        IF activity = 1 THEN
            WriteString("go to the cinema")
        ELSIF activity = 2 THEN
            WriteString ("play scrabble")
        ELSIF activity = 3 THEN
            WriteString ("go to a theme park")
        ELSIF activity = 4 THEN
            WriteString ("visit the zoo")
        ELSIF activity = 5 THEN
            WriteString ("go on a cycle ride")
        ELSE
            WriteString ("think of something new!")
        END (*IF*);
        WriteLn
    END DisplaySuggestion;

    BEGIN (*Main DecisionsDecisions program*)
        GetFacts(temperature,holiday,weather,money,noOfPeople);
        AnalyzeFacts(temperature,holiday,weather,money,
                                        noOfPeople,activity);
        DisplaySuggestion(activity)
    END DecisionsDecisions.
```

6.4.5   Testing

How can we be sure that our program works?

A source file that compiles is free of syntax errors. But this is no guarantee of a working program; there may still be semantic errors.

The introduction of conditions in the form of IF statements increases the complexity of a program. Indeed, counting the simple conditions is one way of quantifying the complexity of a program. As the complexity increases so does the probability of introducing errors.

Subjecting programs to carefully designed tests and thorough evaluation of the results can increase our confidence that a program performs as intended.

During testing we should aim for every part of every instruction in the program to be executed at least once. For the parts of the program which are optional a special set of input data may be needed which gives rise to the appropriate set of conditions to force the execution of certain instructions.

In order to claim that a program is 100% tested the programmer would need to prepare test data which provides every possible value and combination of values of input data and every set of conditions which could arise inside the program to give every different variation on the output side. This is sometimes called exhaustive testing, which is an apt description because it not only exhausts all program possibilities but is very likely to exhaust the tester! To provide some measure of what that would mean in practice consider a very small part of the DecisionsDecisions program we have just designed.

```
......
......
ELSIF (weather=1) AND (temperature>15)
      AND (money>5) AND NOT holiday AND (noOfPeople>2) THEN
   activity := 4;
......
......
```

If we provide a complete set of test data to test these conditions we would need to set up:

input	values	number of cases
weather	less than 1,	
	1,	
	2 or 3,	
	4	
	greater than 4	5
temperature	less than 15,	
	15,	
	greater than 15	3
money	less than 5,	
	5,	
	greater than 5	3
holiday	y,	
	n,	
	other	3
noOfPeople	less than 2,	
	2,	
	greater than 2	3

The total number of tests required to exhaust all possible combinations is therefore:

$5 \times 3 \times 3 \times 3 \times 3 = 405$

Each condition would need to be methodically logged in a table to display the findings, as described in Chapter 4. For example:

Test table:

Test values	Reason for test	Expected outcome	Actual outcome	Resolution of result
weather=1 temperature=16 money=6 holiday='n' people=4	testing zoo condition	choice is zoo visit	zoo test	successful
weather=1	....	....	....	....

Apart from small, trivial programs it is not usually practical to test for every possible outcome. It is, however, possible to test for a number of specific types of error which often occur.

If a set of test data can be preserved (e.g. by using a test harness as described in Chapter 5) then it can be used again to test the program after any modifications.

Self test 6.4

Given that A and B are BOOLEAN variables, which one of the following expressions is equivalent to;

```
A<>B
```

a)   (A AND B) OR (NOT B AND NOT A)
b)   NOT (A OR B)
c)   NOT A OR NOT B
d)   (A AND NOT B) OR (B AND NOT A)

Exercise 6.1

Draw up a set of test values to test the theme park conditions in DecisionsDecisions.

Exercise 6.2

a)   Design your own set of conditions for a decision making program based on choosing a holiday destination.

b)   Following a similar format to DecisionsDecisions, implement your program.

c)   Design suitable test data for this program.

d)   Carry out the testing of your program and complete a test table according to the format shown above.

Exercise 6.3

The average daily energy requirement for an adult is about 2600 Calories. Modify the CalculateEnergy program, designed in Chapter 5, so that it informs the user when intake of fats and carbohydrates is insufficient.

7 FOR statement and ARRAY types

7.1 Iteration

The Modula-2 programs encountered so far have had a simple structure and the only way to repeat a program several times has been to re-run it. This is somewhat limiting as computers are especially good at repetitive tasks and most computer programs involve repetition of at least part of the code.

In order to control iteration (or repetition) within a programming language, there must be three components present:

- a means of determining when iteration is to begin,

- a means of indicating which statements are to be included in the iteration,

- a way of determining when iteration will stop.

7.1.1 GOTO nowhere

If you have done some programming before you may be tempted to introduce a four-letter word at this point: GOTO. However, in your well designed and constructed Modula-2 software there is no need for such language!

GOTO is used by some programming languages to allow jumps to be made from one part of a program to another. This can result in a tangled web of links which make a program very difficult to understand and impossible to verify. In fact, such are the perils of an abundance of GOTOs that they are not allowed at all in Modula-2. The language provides enough constructs to ensure that GOTO is never required.

7.1.2 Program statements for iteration

Repetition, iteration or looping in well-structured programs can be achieved in several different ways. Modula-2 provides four different statements to control iteration:

```
FOR.....DO.....END
WHILE......DO.....END
REPEAT.....UNTIL
LOOP.....END
```

We'll start by looking at the FOR statement. The other three are covered in detail in Chapter 8.

7.2   The FOR statement

7.2.1   Introducing the FOR statement

In Modula-2, as in several other programming languages, the FOR statement is used to repeat an action or group of actions a pre-determined number of times.
Here is the syntax chart.
FOR statement syntax chart:

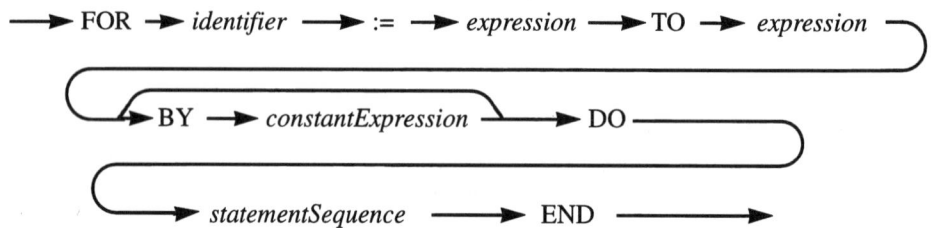

A good example of this kind of action is illustrated by an elderly relative who was a firm believer in the maxim that for good digestion every mouthful of food should be chewed exactly 25 times. He stuck so rigidly to this principle that by the time he was half-way through the first course the rest of us would have demolished our meal, burped politely and started the washing up. No one dared speak to him during meals because, apart from slowing him down even further, he was very likely to lose count!

In Modula-2 we could describe the processing of each mouthful as:

```
FOR chewCount := 1 TO 25 DO
    MasticateFoodOnce
END;
```

This is a case where an action is being repeated a specified number of times. The process is iterative and, in this case, because the number of repetitions required is known before the iterative process is started, it is a process of **definite iteration**. This is in contrast to **indefinite iteration** which would describe the way we, and we suspect you, chew food. When food enters our mouths we don't know how many chews we are going to apply; we simply mash it between our teeth until it is in a swallowable consistency and is unlikely to qualify us as candidates for the Heimlich manoeuvre!

The FOR statement is most definitely just for definite iteration.

Remember we need:
- a way to start the iteration,
- a way of showing the program statements that are to be repeated and
- a way of making the repetition stop.

The keyword FOR is the signal that iteration is about to begin.

It is clear which statements are to be iterated because they are enclosed between the FOR and the corresponding END.

As the word END is used to terminate other iterative loops it is a good idea to put a (*FOR*) comment after END to indicate to which statement it belongs. It is also good style to indent all the statements inside the FOR statement, as shown in the examples in this chapter.

FOR statements maintain a counter called the control variable. This control variable is set to a start value when the loop begins and its value is modified on each cycle or 'pass' of the loop according to an increment. The iteration stops when a preset limit value is reached. The value of the control variable is compared to the limiting value BEFORE each 'pass' of the loop, including the first, to test whether more cycles are required or the looping should stop.

The simplest case is where no increment is specified, e.g.

```
FOR count:= 1 to limit DO
    (*repeated statements*)
END
```

In this case an increment value of 1 is assumed and iteration will stop when count>limit. If this happens to be true before the first cycle, then the FOR loop is by-passed altogether.

At the end of each iteration the control variable is incremented, then the next pass begins with the exit test, which compares the value in the control variable with the value of the limit.

When the exit condition becomes true, iteration stops and the program continues with the statement immediately after the END of the FOR loop.

The short program Count will prompt the user for a CARDINAL number then list on the screen (or standard output device) all the cardinal numbers from 1 up to the number input.

```
MODULE Count;
(*Purpose: To demonstrate FOR by counting upwards
**Uses module: InOut*)
FROM InOut  IMPORT WriteString,WriteLn, ReadCard,WriteCard;
VAR
    number, limit : CARDINAL;
BEGIN
    WriteString("Please enter a CARDINAL number ");
    ReadCard(limit);
    WriteLn;
    FOR number:=1 TO limit DO
        WriteCard(number,1);
        WriteLn
    END (*FOR*)
END Count.
```

Output:

```
Please enter a CARDINAL number  6
1
2
3
4
5
6
```

The following multiplication table program has a FOR statement which always repeats the same number of times. However the output is varied according to a single CARDINAL value, which is input before the FOR statement.

```
MODULE TimesTable;
(*Purpose: To generate a times table
**Uses module: InOut*)
FROM InOut  IMPORT WriteString,WriteLn,ReadCard,WriteCard;
VAR
    number,table : CARDINAL;

BEGIN
    WriteString("Please enter the times table required: ");
    ReadCard(table);
    WriteLn;
    WriteLn;
    FOR number:=1 TO 12 DO
        WriteCard(table,1);
        WriteString(" x ");
        WriteCard(number,1);
        WriteString(" = ");
        WriteCard(table*number,1);
        WriteLn
    END;
END TimesTable.
```

Output:

```
Please enter the times table required:   5

5 x 1 = 5
5 x 2 = 10
5 x 3 = 15
5 x 4 = 20
5 x 5 = 25
5 x 6 = 30
5 x 7 = 35
5 x 8 = 40
5 x 9 = 45
5 x 10 = 50
5 x 11 = 55
5 x 12 = 60
```

An increment value of 1 has been used by default in all the FOR statements so far in this chapter. However, the FOR statement syntax does allow the programmer to specify a different increment or step value by using the format:

```
FOR control variable := start TO limit BY increment DO
    (*repeated statements*)
END; (*FOR*)
```

where the italics indicate variables/values to be substituted as required, for example:

```
FOR count:= 1 TO 10 BY 2 DO
    (*repeated statements*)
END; (*FOR*)
```

This time the control variable count is stepped up by 2 after each pass, as follows:

pass number	count value
1	1
2	3
3	5
4	7
5	9

To commence a sixth pass, count would need to become 11, so the exit condition is true since (count>10), and the iteration stops.

7.2.2   Counting backwards

Sometimes it is necessary to count downward instead of upwards.

Compilers are designed to recognize this by the presence of a negative increment value, for example:

```
FOR number := 10 TO 2 BY -1 DO
    (*repeated statements*)
END; (*FOR*)
```

number takes each of the values 10, 9, 8, 7, 6, 5, 4, 3 and 2 in turn. The iteration stops when number becomes less than 2 (i.e. number < 2).

Here is this FOR statement in action:

```
MODULE RollOver;
(*Purpose: To demonstrate FOR by counting downward
**Uses module: InOut*)
FROM InOut  IMPORT WriteString,WriteLn,WriteCard;
VAR
    number : CARDINAL;

    PROCEDURE Verse(number:CARDINAL);
    BEGIN
        WriteString("There were ");
        WriteCard(number,1);
        WriteString(" in the bed");
        WriteLn;
        WriteString("And the little one said;");
        WriteLn;
        WriteString("'Roll over, roll over'");
        WriteLn;
        WriteString("They all rolled over; one fell out");
        WriteLn
    END Verse;

BEGIN
    FOR number:=10 TO 2 BY -1 DO
        Verse(number)
    END; (*FOR*)
    WriteString("There was 1 in the bed");
    WriteLn;
    WriteString("And the little one said;");
    WriteLn;
    WriteString("'zzzzzzzzzz....'");
    WriteLn
END RollOver.
```

Output:

```
There were 10 in the bed
And the little one said;
'Roll over, roll over'
They all rolled over; one fell out
There were 9 in the bed
And the little one said;
'Roll over, roll over'
They all rolled over; one fell out
There were 8 in the bed
And the little one said;
'Roll over, roll over'
They all rolled over; one fell out
. . . . .
. . . . .
. . . . .
. . . . .
There were 2 in the bed
And the little one said;
'Roll over, roll over'
They all rolled over; one fell out
There was 1 in the bed
And the little one said;
'zzzzzzzzzz....'
```

7.2.3   Testing FOR loops

Considering how to test the program Count (see Section 7.2.1) raises some interesting questions. The program requires a single CARDINAL value to operate successfully so this is one type of data value you must use to test it.

What would happen if the value 1 was entered? What about zero?
These are special cases called boundary values, just inside or outside the range of values which the program is designed to use and is described in Chapter 5.
A programmer needs to be clear how the program behaves if these values are encountered.
The value 1 should cause a single iteration, with the number 1 displayed. The value zero should result in zero iterations, i.e. the exit condition is true the first time it is tested so the loop is bypassed with no output.

Test data should also include invalid values, such as negative numbers and non-numeric characters. You should be able to answer the question: What will happen to your program if invalid data values are entered?

7.2.4 Things not to do with a FOR in Modula-2

1. The control variable must be local to the part of the program where the FOR statement resides. Only if the FOR statement is in the main program should a global variable be used to control it.

   Modula-2 does not allow a formal parameter to be used to control a FOR statement. When you try to compile your program a syntax error should warn you that you have done this. Should you ever wish to do so, then simply define a local variable of the same data type and transfer the value to or from the parameter using an assignment statement.

2. It is illegal to attempt to make an assignment to the control variable within the FOR loop, as in the following program extract:

```
start:=1;
limit:=10;
FOR num:=start TO limit DO
     num:=8;
     WriteCard(num,1);
     WriteLn
END; (*FOR*)
```

3. It is illegal to attempt to make an assignment to the start value within the FOR loop:

```
start:=1;
limit:=10;
FOR num:=start TO limit DO
     start:=8;
     WriteCard(num,1);
     WriteLn
END; (*FOR*)
```

4. It is illegal to attempt to make an assignment to the limit value within the FOR loop:

```
start:=1;
limit:=10;
FOR num:=start TO limit DO
     limit:=4;
     WriteCard(num,1);
     WriteLn
END; (*FOR*)
```

The above examples can be tempting if you feel you want to cut short the number of iterations made by the loop. If this is the case, you should be using a different kind of loop than a FOR loop. (See Chapter 8.) Remember that a FOR loop is designed to deal with definite iteration where the number of cycles is known when the loop is started.

5.   The value of the control variable after the loop has terminated is undefined. Your
     compiler may not object to this, but don't be fooled.

```
start:=1;
limit:=10;
FOR num:=start TO limit DO
    WriteCard(num,1);
    WriteLn
END;  (*FOR*)
WriteCard(num,1);
```

The value given could be the limit value, or the limit value +1, or anything at all.
We have one compiler that gives the limit value and another that gives (limit+1). In
fact, it needn't be either of these values; it could be anything, so should not be used
in this way. Sometimes it may work as you expect, but other times the results may
be disastrous.

Self test 7.1

What would be the output from the following program segment?

```
limit := 20;
increment:=3;
bottom:=2;
FOR count := limit TO bottom BY increment DO
    WriteCard (count, 3)
END;   (*FOR*)
```

Self test 7.2

Given the FOR statement header:
    FOR counterVariable := initialValue TO limit DO
which of the following statements is not true?

a)   counterVariable cannot be a parameter.
b)   It is an error to make an assignment to counterVariable from
     within the loop.
c)   counterVariable is equal to limit on exit from the loop.
d)   initialValue and limit cannot be REAL.

Self test 7.3

Given the FOR statement header:
    FOR letter:= 'H' TO 'E' BY -2 DO
describe the sequence of values that will be generated in letter.

7.3   ARRAY types

7.3.1   Structured types

Basic types, such as INTEGER, CARDINAL, BOOLEAN and REAL have values that are single items of data and are said to be unstructured types. In practice, if we are to get a computer to do useful work for us we don't want to be limited to using only the simple data types we have discussed so far. 'Real world' tasks often involve handling more complex data, perhaps in the form of lists or tables. To handle such arrangements of data most programming languages provide structured data types. These structured types enable us to model more closely the domain of the task for which we are using the computer. They provide greater scope for us to abstract ourselves from concern about exactly HOW things will be handled inside the computer, allowing us to concentrate on WHAT we want done.

The ARRAY type is a structured type and an ARRAY variable can contain a list of components where all components are of the same type. So we could set up an array of CHAR values (i.e. a character string), an array of REALs, an array of INTEGERs, etc. or even, as you will see later in the chapter, an array of arrays.

7.3.2   One-dimensional arrays

First, let's suppose we are designing a program which needs to input five integer values, and perform some calculation using all five numbers before returning an integer result.

It is not difficult to think of six unique names for our variables: five for input and one for output. The program is a bit repetitive, but not too difficult to write:

```
MODULE FiveInputs;
FROM InOut IMPORT ReadInt, WriteInt, WriteLn;
VAR n1,n2,n3,n4,n5,result:INTEGER;

PROCEDURE ReadValues(VAR n1,n2,n3,n4,n5:INTEGER);
BEGIN
    ReadInt(n1);
    ReadInt(n2);
    ReadInt(n3);
    ReadInt(n4);
    ReadInt(n5)
END ReadValues;

PROCEDURE CalculateResult(   n1,n2,n3,n4,n5:INTEGER;
                             VAR result:INTEGER);
BEGIN
    (* The formula would be placed here*)
END CalculateResult;

PROCEDURE WriteResult(result:INTEGER);
BEGIN
    WriteInt(result,4)
END WriteResult;
```

```
BEGIN (*Main Program*)
    ReadValues(n1,n2,n3,n4,n5);
    CalculateResult(n1,n2,n3,n4,n5,result);
    WriteResult(result)
END FiveInputs.
```

Now, suppose we wish to extend this problem to deal with 20 values. We need to define 21 integer variables, all with unique names. ReadValues becomes a list of 20 similar statements and the procedure parameter lists are ridiculously long.
There just has to be a better way of doing this!

It would be helpful if ReadValues had one ReadInt statement enclosed in a FOR statement. It could then be repeated 20, 100 or even 1000 times, as required. The only problem is how to tell Modula-2 to change the variable name on each pass of the FOR loop, so that we end up with the correct number of distinct values.

As you've probably guessed, using an array can provide a neater solution to this problem. A good way to visualize an array is as a numbered row of pigeon holes (or left luggage lockers).

Each can contain an item. In an array, all items must be of the same data type.

For our example, an array of 20 integers could be declared in Modula-2 as follows:

```
VAR
    num : ARRAY [1..20] OF INTEGER;
```

num is the identifier we have chosen to represent the whole array.
[1..20] are the **array bounds**. The range specifies how many components the array num can contain. In this case, the bounds are a subrange of type CARDINAL and 20 is the maximum number of components the array can contain.
The OF INTEGER part specifies what the types of the components are to be. (In this case it's INTEGER, but we could just have easily used CHAR, CARDINAL, REAL, etc.)

Individual components of arrays can be accessed using an index (or subscript) inside square brackets.

For example, we can assign values to the array variable num:

```
num[1] := 56;
num[2] := 14;
....
....
num[20]:= 82;
```

or, more generally, num[count] where count would be a variable of CARDINAL type. So, a FOR statement like this could be used to input 20 integer values into the array:

```
limit:=20;
FOR count := 1 TO limit DO
    ReadInt(n[count])
END; (*FOR*)
```

In the declaration:

```
VAR
    num : ARRAY [1..20] OF INTEGER;
```

num's type is an ARRAY but it hasn't actually got a name; it's an **anonymous type**, in the same way that the subranges you met in Chapter 2 were anonymous types.

We could have used a TYPE declaration to give it an identifying name before declaring the variable.

```
TYPE
    ArrayType = ARRAY [1..20] OF INTEGER;

VAR
    num : ArrayType;
```

Also, array bounds are not restricted to subranges of CARDINAL type. They can be any ordinal type that has well defined limits including CHAR, BOOLEAN, an enumerated type, or a subrange of CHAR, INTEGER or CARDINAL. (Enumerated types will be covered in Chapter 10.)

```
TYPE
    CharIndexA = ARRAY CHAR OF REAL;
    IntIndexA = ARRAY [-27..36] OF CHAR;
    CharIndexB = ARRAY ['a'..'z'] OF INTEGER;
```

are all legal type declarations, however, these are NOT:

```
TYPE
    IntIndexB = ARRAY INTEGER OF CHAR;
    RealIndexA = ARRAY REAL OF CHAR;
    RealIndexB = ARRAY [1.4..6.7] OF CHAR;
```

`IntIndexB` is not allowed because, although an INTEGER is an ordinal type, the bound limits are not well defined because the maximum and minimum INTEGER values depend on your computer/compiler combination. The situation is similar for CARDINAL as, although it has a fixed lower limit of 0, it has no fixed upper limit.
`RealIndexA` and `RealIndexB` are both illegal as REAL is not an ordinal type.

The index or subscript used to reference an element of an array can be a literal value, a variable, or an expression, but it must be of the correct type and within the bounds.

You can make use of constants rather than literal values when declaring array bounds. This approach has definite advantages when maintaining program code. For example, suppose we decided to change the length of an array used by a program; all we would need to do is change one line to set the constant to its new value. If we used a literal value we would need to examine the entire program, changing each occurrence of the upper array bound to the new value. It would be easy to miss one or more instances of the value in a long program.

7.3.3   Compatibility

Consider these type and variable declarations:

```
TYPE
    RealArray = ARRAY [1..4] OF REAL;
VAR
    hisArray : RealArray;
    herArray : RealArray;
    myArray, yourArray : ARRAY [1..4] OF REAL;
    ourArray : ARRAY [1..4] OF REAL;
```

`hisArray`, `herArray`, `myArray`, `yourArray` and `ourArray` are all arrays of four REAL elements, but Modula-2 does not regard them as all of the SAME type.

`hisArray` and `herArray` are the SAME type as each other because they are declared using the same type name.
`myArray` and `yourArray` are the SAME type as each other because they are declared together as being of the SAME anonymous type.
None of the others are the SAME. (See Appendix B.)

Modula-2 allows whole arrays to be assigned to one another provided they are both of the SAME type, so:

```
hisArray := herArray;
```

will assign all components of `herArray` to `hisArray`.

The assignment:

```
myArray := ourArray;
```

is not allowed, as these arrays are not of the SAME type.

Whole arrays can also be passed as parameters, again provided the formal and actual array parameters are of the SAME type.
So given the procedure heading:

PROCEDURE Display(theArray : RealArray);

the call:

```
Display(hisArray);
```

is legal, but the call:

```
Display(yourArray);
```

is not.

Note that in the case of whole arrays there is no distinction between SAME, COMPATIBLE and ASSIGNMENT COMPATIBLE. For compatibility, types must be the SAME.

7.3.4   Open array parameters

One difficulty with the above Display procedure is the fact that, with a named formal parameter of type RealArray, which, remember, has a base type of ARRAY [1..4] OF REAL, Display can only accept actual parameters that have also been declared as type RealArray and must, therefore, have four components.
No such restriction exists for the WriteString procedure that can imported from the InOut library module. Calls to WriteString require an actual parameter which is an array of characters (i.e. a string). The library procedure doesn't know how long the strings you provide will be; it must cope with whatever you send it.
Modula-2 provides **open array parameters** to allow you to declare formal parameters without specifying the array size. Using an open array parameter the procedure Display can be written to cope with varying array sizes

```
PROCEDURE Display(TheArray : ARRAY OF REAL);
```

Notice that the array bounds are not specified. This formal parameter will accept, as corresponding actual parameter, any array of REALs no matter what size.

Three points to beware of:

1. This boundless form of array declaration cannot be used anywhere else but within formal parameter lists, so you won't get away with declaring variables of type ARRAY OF CHAR without including the bounds. You must include array bounds when you declare **actual** array parameters.

2. Open array parameters can be used for single-dimensional arrays only, although future language revisions may extend the facility to multi-dimensional arrays;

3. The index type of an open array parameter is always a subrange of CARDINAL with a lower bound of 0, even if the bounds of the corresponding actual parameter were of a different type. So even though your original array may be indexed with letters of the alphabet, ['a'..'z'] (e.g. list['b']) if it is passed to a procedure via an open array parameter the index type and range is lost and the array elements must be accessed with CARDINAL indices, (e.g. list[1]).

7.3.5   The HIGH function

Within a procedure we may well want to know the bounds of an array that has been passed to it as an open array parameter. The lower bound is always 0, but as the range is lost how do we know what the upper bound is to be?
Modula-2 provides a built-in function called HIGH to enable us to obtain this information.

Here's an example to illustrate:

```
PROCEDURE Display (theArray : ARRAY OF CHAR);
VAR
    index : CARDINAL;
BEGIN
    FOR index := 0 TO HIGH(theArray) DO
        Write(theArray[index])
    END (*FOR*)
END Display;
```

HIGH(theArray) returns the upper bound of the array theArray. This is not quite the same as the length of the array as the lower bound is 0. The length is actually HIGH(theArray)+1
Note that you can only successfully apply the function HIGH to single-dimensional arrays that have been passed via an open array parameter.

7.3.6   **String types**

A 'string' variable is a special case of an ARRAY type. Each element of a string array is a CHAR variable.
The declaration,

```
VAR
     name : ARRAY [0..5] OF CHAR;
```

allocates memory space for six characters and, as with any array, the individual elements can be referred to by qualifying the variable identifier using a subscript or index. Thus, name[0] represents the first character of the 'string' contained in name.

A string is a special type of ARRAY because it is often considered as a single variable. Variables of string type are useful because, as well as using them as parameters for InOut procedures, we can make direct assignments to them. The length of the literal string being assigned need not match the array length exactly provided the array is big enough. The array is filled from the left-most element (name[0]) so, if the number of characters stored is less than the maximum length, then there will be some 'empty' elements at the right-hand end. A special terminator character, null or 0C in octal (base 8), is placed in the first empty element.
A string assignment statement handles placement of the terminating character automatically but, if you are loading or reading a string array one component at a time, you will need to insert or check for the terminating 0C.
Given the variable declaration:

```
VAR
     name : ARRAY [0..5] OF CHAR;
```

and the assignment:

```
name := "Pamela";
```

	0	1	2	3	4	5
name	P	a	m	e	l	a

the literal string has six characters and will completely fill the array, however;

```
name := "Ian";
```

	0	1	2	3	4	5
name	I	a	n	0C		

will cause the terminator to be inserted as character name[3] while the contents of name[4] and name[5] remain undefined.

In his book, *Programming in Modula-2*, N. Wirth, the designer of Modula-2, states that string types should have a lower index bound of 0. However, what is not clear is whether this is to be regarded as a strict rule or simply as a convention. Consequently, some Modula-2 compilers may allow other lower bounds, while others may not. We recommend that you stay on the safe side and when you want an array to behave as a string use a lower bound of 0.

Wirth also states that an open array parameter of type ARRAY OF CHAR should also accept actual parameters of type CHAR, although earlier editions of his book did not contain this ruling and, consequently, some older compilers may not treat single character strings as compatible with type CHAR.

String variables can be assigned to one another provided they are of the SAME type. (See Appendix B.)

7.3.7   Multi-dimensional arrays

Take a look at the following program, Marks.

```
MODULE Marks;
(*Purpose: To calculate student marks
**Uses module: InOut*)
FROM InOut IMPORT WriteString, WriteLn, WriteCard, ReadCard;
CONST
    LIMIT=10;
TYPE
    MarksArray=ARRAY [1..LIMIT] OF CARDINAL;

(*MarksArray has been declared at the beginning of the
**program, as a global, user-defined data type.  It may
**be used throughout the program, in place of
**ARRAY [1..Max] OF CARDINAL*)
VAR
    marks1,marks2,marks3,totals:MarksArray;

    PROCEDURE ReadMarks (VAR marks : MarksArray);
    (*Gets the marks from the user
    **Pre-conditions: None
    **Post-conditions: marks contains an array of
    **LIMIT marks*)
    VAR
        count : CARDINAL;
    BEGIN
        FOR count:= 1 TO LIMIT DO
            WriteString("Please Enter Mark ");
            WriteCard(count,1);
            WriteString("  ");
            ReadCard(marks[count]);
            WriteLn
        END (*FOR*)
    END ReadMarks;
```

```
PROCEDURE TotalMarks (    marks1, marks2, marks3:MarksArray;
                          VAR totals:MarksArray);
(*Calculates mark totals
**Pre-conditions: marks1,marks2,marks3 each contains
**an array of LIMIT marks
**Post-conditions: totals contains an array of LIMIT
**totals calculated by adding the corresponding
**marks from marks1,marks2 and marks3*)
VAR count:CARDINAL;
BEGIN
    FOR count:= 1 TO LIMIT DO
        totals[count]:=marks1[count]
                          +marks2[count]+marks3[count]
    END (*FOR*)
END TotalMarks;

PROCEDURE WriteTotals(totals:MarksArray);
(*Displays the elements in the array of totals
**Pre-conditions: totals contains an array of LIMIT marks
**Post-conditions: None*)

VAR
    count:CARDINAL;
BEGIN
    WriteString("Total marks");
    WriteLn;
    FOR count:=1 TO LIMIT DO
        WriteCard(totals[count],1);
        WriteLn
    END (*FOR*)
END WriteTotals;

BEGIN(*Main Program*)
    WriteString("Please enter marks for first assignment");
    WriteLn;
    ReadMarks(marks1);
    WriteString("Please enter marks for second assignment");
    WriteLn;
    ReadMarks(marks2);
    WriteString("Please enter marks for third assignment");
    WriteLn;
    ReadMarks(marks3);
    TotalMarks(marks1,marks2,marks3,totals);
    WriteTotals(totals)
END Marks.
```

In the program Marks there were three separate single-dimensional arrays, but this is not very convenient when the data is to be displayed in tabular form.

Student	Mark 1	Mark 2	Mark 3	Total
1	30	50	60	140
2	50	35	32	117
3	46	33	62	141
etc..				

Here is one way of displaying the table:

```
PROCEDURE DisplayMarks(marks1,marks2,marks3,
                                totals:MarksArray);
VAR
    count : CARDINAL;
BEGIN
    WriteString("Student  Mark 1   Mark 2   Mark 3   Total");
    WriteLn;
    FOR count := 1 TO LIMIT DO
        WriteCard(count,4);
        WriteCard(marks1[count],10);
        WriteCard(marks2[count],9);
        WriteCard(marks3[count],9);
        WriteCard(totals[count],9);
        WriteLn
    END (*FOR*)
END DisplayMarks;
```

However, there is a neater solution, suggested by the output format, which results in a clearer, more adaptable method of programming. This is to use a tabular or two-dimensional storage arrangement. Each 'element' of the data has a row number and a column number. For example, the third student's marks are on row 3; mark 2 for student 3 is in the element at the intersection of row 3 and column 2.

In Modula-2 a two-dimensional array can be declared as follows:

```
CONST
    MARKS = 4;          (*Number of marks in one row*)
    STUDENTS = 6;       (*Number of students in list*)
TYPE
    MarksType = ARRAY [1..MARKS] OF CARDINAL;
    MarksArrayType = ARRAY [1..STUDENTS] OF MarksType;
VAR
    marksArray : MarksArrayType;
```

marksArray is, in fact, an array of arrays. To access a particular element, two CARDINAL index values are required to identify the row number and column number. For example, marksArray[3,2] would address the second mark for the third student. (Individual elements can also be accessed using an alternative form of notation; marksArray[3][2] .)

To achieve a general traversal of the array (i.e. to access every element in turn) both the row and column indexes would need to be varied. For a two-dimensional array this can be achieved by 'nesting' one FOR loop inside another:

```
FOR row:= 1 TO STUDENTS DO
    WriteCard(row,3);
    FOR column:= 1 TO MARKS DO
        WriteCard(marksArray[row,column],5)
    END(*FOR column*);
    WriteLn
END (*FOR row*)
```

The outer FOR loop varies the `row` number and the inner loop varies the `column` number. The statement of the inner loop is executed once for each element of the array, i.e. (STUDENTS * MARKS) times.

When nesting loops, the inner loop must be completely contained within the outer loop. In fact,

```
FOR row := 1 TO STUDENTS DO
    FOR column := 1 TO MARKS DO
        ........
END (*row*)
    END; (*col*)
```

will treat the first END as the end of the inner loop (i.e. col) and the second END as the end of the outer loop (i.e. row).

It is possible to construct arrays with more than two dimensions. In fact, a two-dimensional array of string variables can also be thought of as a three-dimensional array of CHAR.

```
CONST
    ROWS = 5;
    COLUMNS = 6;
    LIMIT = 20;

TYPE
    NameType = ARRAY[0..LIMIT] OF CHAR;
    NameArrayType = ARRAY[1..ROWS],[1..COLUMNS] OF NameType;

VAR
    nameArray : NameArrayType;
```

Note the alternative way that `NameArrayType` has been defined, compared to `MarksArrayType` in the previous example.
`MarksArrayType` could have been declared:

```
MarksArrayType = ARRAY [1..STUDENTS],[1..MARKS] OF CARDINAL;
```

Either method is fine, but the former may be preferable if individual rows or columns are to be handled separately.

It is possible to traverse `nameArray`, character by character, using three indices and three nested FOR loops:

```
FOR row:=1 TO ROWS DO
    FOR column:=1 TO COLUMNS DO
        FOR char:=1 TO LIMIT DO
            Write(nameArray[row, column, ch]);
            Write(" ")
        END (*FOR ch*)
    END (*FOR column*);
    WriteLn
END (*FOR row*)
```

Exercise 7.1

Write a program that uses nested FOR loops to transpose the student mark table (see Section 7.3.7), without redefining the array.

i.e. students are displayed in columns and marks in rows.

7.3.8   Case study: *Square-bashing*

Drill-Sergeant Arbuthnott is in charge of a squad of 25 recruits. By an extraordinary chance his surname, as well as those of the members of his squad, all begin with a different initial letter.

Arbuthnott is extremely up to date; he uses a computer to plan his squad's square-bashing manoeuvres. He has set up the Modula-2 declarations to represent his squad as a 5x5 array of initials:

```
CONST
    SQSIZE = 5;
TYPE
    SquadArray = ARRAY [1..SQSIZE],[1..SQSIZE] OF CHAR;
VAR
    squad : SquadArray;
```

He has written two procedures: one to set up the squad members in their start position:

```
PROCEDURE SetUp(VAR squad : SquadArray);
VAR
    row, col : CARDINAL;
BEGIN
    FOR row:=1 TO SQSIZE DO
        FOR col:=1 TO SQSIZE DO
            squad[row, col]:=CHR(ORD('A')+SQSIZE*(row-1)+col);
        END  (*FOR*)
    END (*FOR*)
END SetUp;
```

and the other to display his squad:

```
PROCEDURE DisplaySq(squad : SquadArray);
VAR
    row, col : CARDINAL;
BEGIN
    FOR row:=1 TO SQSIZE DO
        FOR col:=1 TO SQSIZE DO
            Write(squad[row, col]);
        END;  (*FOR*)
        WriteLn;
    END (*FOR*)
END DisplaySq;
```

So the main program:

```
BEGIN  (*SquareBash*)
   SetUp(squad);
   DisplaySq(squad)
END SquareBash.
```

results in:

B	C	D	E	F
G	H	I	J	K
L	M	N	O	P
Q	R	S	T	U
V	W	X	Y	Z

Exercise 7.2

Arbuthnott is currently puzzling over how to write a procedure that takes the start array and rotates the squad by 180°, giving:

Z	Y	X	W	V
U	T	S	R	Q
P	O	N	M	L
K	J	I	H	G
F	E	D	C	B

His first attempt involves using a second array :

```
PROCEDURE RotateSquad(    oldSq : SquadArray;
                          VAR newSq : SquadArray);
VAR
    row, col : CARDINAL;
BEGIN
    FOR row:=1 TO SQSIZE DO
        FOR col:=1 TO SQSIZE DO
            newSq[row,col]:=oldSq[SQSIZE+1-row,SQSIZE+1-col];
        END  (*FOR*)
    END (*FOR*)
END RotateSquad;
```

Then he comes up with a procedure:

```
PROCEDURE RotateSquad(VAR squad : SquadArray);
```

that does the rotation using only one array. Can you?

Self test 7.4

What is the value of count at the end of the following program segment?

```
count:=0;
FOR i := 15 TO 1 BY -2 DO
    FOR j:= 1 TO i DO
        count:=count+1
    END(*j*)
END(*i*)
```


Self test 7.5

Given the declarations below:

```
TYPE
    Str = ARRAY[0..20] OF CHAR;
    Tbl = ARRAY["A".."E"],[1..5] OF Str;
VAR
    table : Tbl;
```

which of the following statements are valid?

a)   ReadString(table["B",4]);
b)   ReadString(table[6,"C"]);
c)   ReadString(table["E"]);
d)   ReadString(table[0,"A",2]);
e)   Read(table["A",2,19]);

Exercise 7.3

Design and write a program which inputs a word, decides whether it is a palindrome (i.e. reads the same forwards and backwards) and outputs the result.

Exercise 7.4

Design and write a program which inputs an entire string of text (single line, no spaces) then outputs it character by character according to the following rules:

    instead of * output a space
    instead of & output a new line (WriteLn)
    instead of @ output four spaces
    convert all lower case alphabetic characters to capitals
    output all other characters unchanged

Try the following input string:

Program*Design&&1.@Conceive&2.@Design&3.@Code&4.@Debug&5.@Test&

Your program should produce a table like this:

```
Program Design

1.  Conceive
2.  Design
3.  Code
4.  Debug
5.  Test
```

8   WHILE, REPEAT and LOOP statements

8.1   Indefinite iteration

The FOR statement, discussed in the previous chapter, is a powerful means of program control. It enables us to use repetition in programs and it greatly facilities the manipulation of arrays. The FOR loop provides **definite iteration**; that is to say, it can only be used when the number of iterations can be determined before the loop starts. However, there are some types of iteration that cannot be achieved using FOR.

Imagine a program that is required to redisplay a menu until the user decides to quit, or to read in characters repeatedly until it detects a termination character. In these situations there is no way of knowing in advance how many iterations will be required so a FOR statement is not going to help us.

To handle such cases Modula-2 also provides three types of **indefinite iterative** control statements: WHILE, REPEAT and LOOP.

WHILE and REPEAT are found in most high level programming languages, whereas LOOP is an alternative provided by some. There are differences in the circumstances under which the WHILE and REPEAT statements are most convenient to use.

The LOOP statement is, in fact, the most versatile of the three, able to produce the same effect as the others and, in some situations, it is much less awkward to use.

You may recall from our discussion in Chapter 7 that iteration has to be controlled and must contain three important elements:

- a means of determining when iteration is to begin,
- a means of indicating which statements are to be included in the iteration,
- a way of determining when iteration will stop.

Unlike FOR, none of these iterative statements has an built-in counter so, unless you want the iteration to continue forever, you must remember to include a mechanism for terminating the loop yourself.

Any iterative sections of program code that are not to repeat forever, must contain a variable whose value can change during an iteration to determine when repetition is to end. This variable is known as the **loop variant**.

8.2   The WHILE statement

```
WHILE condition is TRUE DO
   ....
END (*WHILE*)
```

The first thing that happens when entering a WHILE loop is that there is a test for the entry condition. The first line contains a relational expression determining the condition for entering or continuing the iteration. As this test takes place before the loop is entered for the first time, WHILE can be used in cases where zero iterations are a possibility. If the relational expression returns FALSE then the program continues at the statement following the END (*WHILE*), otherwise the loop statements are executed and the test is repeated. The relational expression acts as a 'guard' that permits or prohibits entry to the body of the loop.

The following example module is designed to simulate the action of a central heating thermostat. The user enters the thermostat temperature setting and the current room temperature. The program uses a WHILE loop to increase the temperature up to the required value.

```
MODULE Thermostat1;
(*Purpose: To demonstrate WHILE by simulating a thermostat
**Uses module: InOut*)
FROM InOut IMPORT WriteString,WriteLn,ReadInt,WriteInt;
VAR
    setting,temp:INTEGER;
BEGIN
    WriteString("Enter thermostat setting ");
    ReadInt(setting);
    WriteLn;
    WriteString("Enter current temperature ");
    ReadInt(temp);
    WriteLn;
    WHILE (temp <= setting) DO
        WriteInt(temp,1);
        WriteLn;
        temp:=temp+1
    END (*WHILE*)
END Thermostat1.
```

WHILE syntax chart:

→ WHILE ⟶ *expression* ⟶ DO ➤ *statementSequence* ⟶ END →

8.2.1   Sentinel values

Imagine we wanted to read in a stream of input values. If we don't know in advance exactly how many values to be read, how do we know when to stop? A common technique is to use what is called a sentinel value; a value which cannot possibly be a normal valid input value, but can be used to signal the end of the input stream. In practice, when reading in text characters, the sentinel value is the EOL (end-of-line) or the EOF (end-of-file) character, but could be whatever we choose. If, for example, we are reading in a stream of values representing people's ages we could use 999 as the sentinel, based on the reasonable assumption that nobody's real age will be 999.
As the WHILE loop condition is checked before the loop is entered we need to have a value to test before entering the loop. To do this we need to read the first value on the input stream prior to entering the loop to provide an input value for the first test.

The following procedure demonstrates a WHILE loop in action reading a series of integer numbers from the keyboard. The sentinel value is 999 which, when entered, should terminate the loop. Notice that the loop will also terminate when 10 numbers have been input if no 999 is read beforehand, i.e. numbers will be read in and stored in the array list until either a 999 is detected or 10 numbers have been read.

```
PROCEDURE ReadNumArray(VAR numArray : ARRAY OF INTEGER);
VAR
    count:CARDINAL;
    num : INTEGER;
BEGIN
    count:=0;
    ReadInt(num);(*Read num number ahead of WHILE loop*)
    WHILE ((num<>999) AND (count < 10)) DO
        numArray[count] := num;
        count:=count+1;
        ReadInt(num)
    END (*WHILE*);
    (*Continue from here on exit*)
END ReadNumArray;
```

8.3   The REPEAT statement

```
REPEAT
    ....
UNTIL condition is TRUE
```

In contrast to the WHILE loop, which tests for an exit condition at the beginning of the loop, the exit condition in a REPEAT loop is checked at the end. If the relational expression returns TRUE then the exit condition has been reached and the program continues from the statement after UNTIL..., otherwise the loop statements are executed again.
The exit condition is at the end, with the consequence that initial entry to the body of the loop is 'unguarded'. The statements within the loop will always be executed at least once.

Here's the Thermostat program again; this time written using a REPEAT loop.

```
MODULE Thermostat2;
(*Purpose: To demonstrate REPEAT by simulating a thermostat
**Uses module: InOut*)
FROM InOut IMPORT WriteString,WriteLn,ReadInt,WriteInt;
VAR
    setting,temp:INTEGER;
BEGIN
    WriteString("Enter thermostat setting ");
    ReadInt(setting);
    WriteLn;
    WriteString("Enter current temperature ");
    ReadInt(temp);
    WriteLn;
    REPEAT
        WriteInt(temp,1);
        WriteLn;
        temp:=temp+1
    UNTIL (temp>setting)
END Thermostat2.
```

Offering the user a number of menu choices is an application for which a REPEAT loop is convenient. The minimum looping requirement is for the menu to be displayed once for Quit to be chosen.

```
PROCEDURE Menu;
VAR
    choice, ch :CHAR;
    score:INTEGER;
BEGIN
    score:=0;
    REPEAT
        WriteLn;
        WriteString("Super Brain Quiz");
        WriteLn;
        WriteString("A. Category A Questions - Calculus");
        WriteLn;
        WriteString("B. Category B Questions - Trigonometry");
        WriteLn;
        WriteString("C. Category C Questions - Arithmetic");
        WriteLn;
        WriteString("Q. Quit");
        WriteLn;
        WriteString("Which category of questions? :");
        Read(choice);
        Read(ch);   (*Read the carriage return if necessary*)
        choice:=CAP(choice);
        IF (choice >="A") AND (choice<="C") THEN
            ProcessChoice(choice, score)
        END (*IF*)
    UNTIL choice = "Q";
    (*processing continues here after Quit chosen*)
    WriteString("Total Score is ");
    WriteInt(score,2);
    WriteLn
END Menu;
```

Note that after Quit is chosen no further processing is required inside the loop and we don't want to call ProcessChoice. We have chosen to use an IF statement to avoid calling ProcessChoice the last time.

REPEAT syntax chart:

➤ REPEAT ⟶ *statementSequence* ⟶ UNTIL ⟶ *expression* ⟶

Exercise 8.1

The following procedure, ReadCapLine, is intended to read characters from the standard input device, probably the keyboard. The sentinel value is a semi-colon ';' which, when entered, should terminate the loop.

```
PROCEDURE ReadCapLine(VAR line : ARRAY OF CHAR);
VAR
    count:CARDINAL;
    ch : CHAR;
BEGIN
    count:=0;
    (*Read first character ahead of WHILE loop*)
    Read(line[count]);
    (*Read character generated by pressing ENTER key*)
    Read(ch);
    WHILE ((line[count]<>";") AND (count < 50)) DO
        line[count] := CAP(line[count]);
        count:=count+1;
        Read(line[count]);
        (*Read character generated by pressing ENTER key*)
        Read(ch)
    END (*WHILE*);
    (*Continue from here on exit*)
END ReadCapLine;
```

There is a semantic error in this procedure. See if you can find and correct it.
(Hint: What if there was no ';' and the 51st character was lower case? If you still can't see it, try running it and see what happens. You will need to write an output routine to see the result.)

Exercise 8.2

Rewrite ReadCapLine using a REPEAT loop. Make a note of any problems you encounter and how you solve them.

Exercise 8.3

Rewrite Menu using a WHILE loop. Again, note down your problems and solutions.

Comment on Exercises 8.2 and 8.3

If you didn't find any problems when you tried Exercises 8.2 and 8.3, then your procedures may contain bugs. What happens if the first character to ReadCapLine is a semi-colon ';' ? Can your REPEAT version cope? How did you get around the problem of the first value of choice in your WHILE loop Menu? Did you need extra statements, like the read ahead, or did you set up a dummy value?

8.4   The LOOP statement

REPEAT and WHILE loops are found in many programming languages, whereas the LOOP statement is less common. The LOOP statement can do the same jobs as WHILE and REPEAT but is intended to provide greater flexibility in constructing loops.

```
LOOP
    .....
    (**)IF condition is TRUE THEN EXIT END;
    .....
END (*LOOP*)
```

When the exit condition is met, all the remaining statements within the loop are skipped. The EXIT statement can be placed at the beginning of the loop to act like a WHILE statement; at the end of the loop to act like REPEAT, or anywhere you wish inside the loop. The empty comment (**) is a useful way of making the exit condition statement stand out. The END following EXIT signifies the end of the IF statement. Also, notice that in line with common practice we have not indented the IF statement as we would normally.

Here's that Thermostat program yet again; this time written using a LOOP statement.

```
MODULE Thermostat3;
(*Purpose: To demonstrate LOOP by simulating a thermostat
**Uses module: InOut*)
FROM InOut IMPORT WriteString,WriteLn,ReadInt,WriteInt;
VAR
    setting,temp:INTEGER;
BEGIN
    WriteString("Enter thermostat setting ");
    ReadInt(setting);
    WriteLn;
    WriteString("Enter current temperature ");
    ReadInt(temp);
    WriteLn;
    LOOP
        WriteInt(temp,1);
        WriteLn;
        temp:=temp+1;
        (**)IF (temp>setting) THEN EXIT END
    END (*LOOP*)
END Thermostat3.
```

Self test 8.1

The way we have used the exit condition in Thermostat3 is equivalent to;

a) a REPEAT statement OR
b) a WHILE statement OR
c) neither?

Here's the `ReadCapLine` procedure from the Exercise 8.1; this time re-written to use a LOOP statement instead of a WHILE.

```
PROCEDURE ReadCapLine (VAR line:ARRAY OF CHAR);
VAR
    count:CARDINAL;
    ch : CHAR;
BEGIN
    count:=0;
    LOOP
        Read(line[count]);
        Read(ch);   (*Read RETURN character if necessary*)
        line[count]:=CAP(line[count]);
        (**)IF ((line[count]=";") OR (count >= 50)) THEN
                EXIT END;
        count:=count+1
    END (*LOOP*);
    (*Continue from here on exit*)
END ReadCapLine;
```

Notice that no read ahead is required. Also, the exit condition is true if the first character input is ';'.

Here's the `Menu` procedure again. This time rewritten to use a LOOP statement instead of a REPEAT.

```
PROCEDURE Menu;
VAR
    choice, ch : CHAR;
    score:  INTEGER;
BEGIN
    score:=0;
    LOOP
        WriteLn;
        WriteString("Super Brain Quiz");
        WriteLn;
        WriteString("A. Category A Questions - Calculus");
        WriteLn;
        WriteString("B. Category B Questions - Trigonometry");
        WriteLn;
        WriteString("C. Category C Questions - Arithmetic");
        WriteLn;
        WriteString("Q. Quit");
        WriteLn;
        WriteString("Which is your choice of topic? :");
        Read(choice);
        Read(ch);   (*Read carriage return if necessary*)
        choice:=CAP(choice);
        (**)IF (choice = "Q") THEN EXIT END;
        IF (choice>="A") AND (choice<="C") THEN
            ProcessChoice(choice, score)
        END
    END; (*LOOP*)
    (*processing continues here after Quit chosen*)
    WriteString("Total Score is ");
    WriteInt(score,2);
    WriteLn
END Menu;
```

LOOP syntax chart:

➤ LOOP ———➤ *statementSequence* ————➤ END ————➤

8.4.1   Making a stylish EXIT

The LOOP statement gives the programmer the freedom to place an exit condition between the LOOP and the END, wherever it seems most appropriate.

In fact, in this respect, Modula-2 allows programmers more freedom than may be good for their programs. There is nothing to stop a programmer from including a number of EXIT statements within a single LOOP, or indeed leaving it out altogether.

While omitting the EXIT statement may be justified occasionally, such as in some continuous process control programs, one of the ways we can contribute to the clarity and maintainability of our programs is to ensure that, like the channel tunnel, all such segments of code have just one entry point and one exit point.

This is a good principle to follow even if the rules of Modula-2 don't always require it, so let's override the language boundaries on this point and introduce a tighter set of rules to follow when using LOOPs.

(Typically, the LOOP exit condition will be tested using an IF statement, as in our examples.)

Our rules on LOOP EXIT statements should, perhaps, be:

1. there must be just one EXIT statement in a LOOP;
2. the EXIT should be placed where it is clearly visible, not deeply nested in a complex piece of program code;
3. the exit condition should be as simple as possible;
4. the EXIT statement should be commented, or marked with a dummy comment (**).

There is a strong argument that it is only possible to make a stylish exit from a LOOP statement if the exit condition is the first statement within the loop body (i.e. if it is equivalent to a WHILE statement). If a program's correctness is to be verified formally, repetitive code segments should be guarded at the beginning. If the guard conditions are not satisfied, the loop body should never be entered. For more information on this we suggest you read the work of E. Dijkstra, on formal methods.

8.5   HALT

Modula-2 provides a parameterless function called HALT that causes a program to stop immediately. It should be used only in circumstances in which it would be impossible for the program to continue correctly.

8.6   Infinite loops

In normal circumstances loops need exit conditions which can become true in the course of the iteration. If, by accident, a condition is included which cannot be met during the loop processing then the loop will not end and the program will need to be interrupted and terminated in an abnormal way. It is wise to adopt a belt and braces attitude to the exit condition, such as our decision to include an upper limit to the character count in ReadCapLine in addition to the sentinel ';'. (See Exercise 8.1)

There are some applications and special cases in advanced Modula-2 programming when infinite iteration may be a deliberate policy, such as the continuous monitoring of an industrial process or sensor.

8.7   Nested loops

As with FOR statements, WHILE, REPEAT and LOOP statements can be nested inside one another, but be careful; nesting can make your code very difficult to understand.

If you nest a LOOP statement within another LOOP statement, the inner EXIT statement terminates only the inner loop.

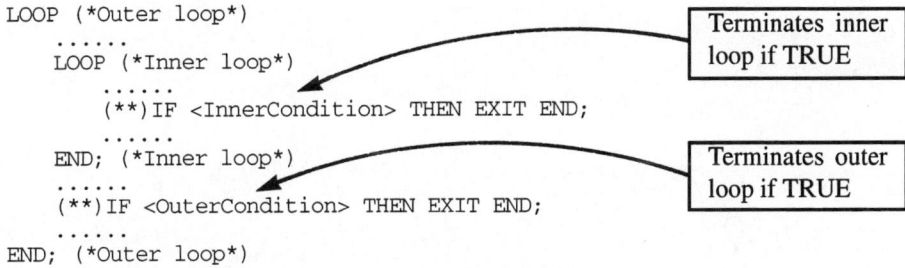

```
LOOP (*Outer loop*)
    ......
    LOOP (*Inner loop*)
       ......
       (**)IF <InnerCondition> THEN EXIT END;
       ......
    END; (*Inner loop*)
    ......
    (**)IF <OuterCondition> THEN EXIT END;
    ......
END; (*Outer loop*)
```

> Terminates inner loop if TRUE

> Terminates outer loop if TRUE

However, if you have, for example, a WHILE statement nested within a LOOP statement, the EXIT statement appearing within the WHILE loop will terminate both loops.

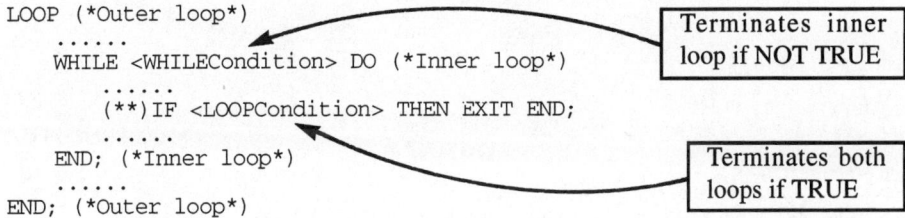

```
LOOP (*Outer loop*)
    ......
    WHILE <WHILECondition> DO (*Inner loop*)
       ......
       (**)IF <LOOPCondition> THEN EXIT END;
       ......
    END; (*Inner loop*)
    ......
END; (*Outer loop*)
```

> Terminates inner loop if NOT TRUE

> Terminates both loops if TRUE

Exercise 8.4

One method of calculating the square root of a number is to use an iterative approach, taking an initial guess, then refining it progressively closer to the correct value.

Make a first guess (other than zero) then apply the following formula;

```
nextGuess := ((number / lastGuess) + lastGuess) / 2.0;
```

repeatedly until the difference between successive approximations becomes sufficiently small, say, no bigger than 1.0E-09.

Write a function procedure to calculate the square root of a number using this iterative technique.

9   Handling text files

Programs need data. For example, our `DecisionsDecisions` program in Chapter 6 required data in the form of rules on which to base a decision about the day's activity. Since it would not be practical for the user of the program to type in this data each time the program is run, we included that data with the source code as an integral part of the program.

This is one example of a program which could be made more flexible and reusable by separating the data from the program. If the data could be stored in a data file to be read by the program, an alteration to the rules would require a simple change to the data file without any necessity to recompile the program.

Sometimes it is wholly impractical to incorporate data within the program source code. For example, the program associated with a supermarket bar code reader would require a description and price of every type of product on sale in the store. It certainly would not be practical to incorporate this within the program itself. Nor would it make sense to key it in each time the program is run.

The best way to deal with large amounts of data is to use data files.

You use files each time you create, compile and run a program. To your computer system, a data file is the same as any other file. It has a name by which it can be identified and is located on a storage device, probably a disk. You can decide what to call your files, but there may be restrictions imposed by your computer system on the length and the characters that can be used in file names.

As you have no doubt discovered, you need to choose file names wisely so you will remember which files are which and to ensure that you do not inadvertently overwrite existing files. Never use the same name as the program for your data file or you will be in danger of overwriting your program file. A sensible scheme is to use an extension such as `.dat` to distinguish then from other kinds of files.

9.1 Redirecting input and output

Most programs need to communicate with the user at some point, using a standard input device and a standard output device. Modula-2 allows you to change the standard device settings during the course of the program so, for example, input could be taken from a file rather than the keyboard. Facilities for accomplishing this can be found in the InOut library module.

9.1.1 The variable Done

```
VAR
     Done : BOOLEAN;
```

If a successful call is made to one of InOut's input or output facilities, then the variable Done is set to TRUE, otherwise it is FALSE.

It indicates whether a file has been opened, read from or written to, successfully and is particularly useful for detecting the end of a file to determine when input is finished. When input is complete, a further read will be unsuccessfully and Done set to FALSE.

Done can be imported into your program from InOut and used in a similar way to any other BOOLEAN variable. However, its value is set by the system and you should not try to assign a value to it directly.

9.1.2 The procedure OpenInput

```
PROCEDURE OpenInput(defext : ARRAY OF CHAR);
```

OpenInput replaces the standard input device with the named data file. The parameter defext represents a default file name extension, e.g. OpenInput("dat").

OpenInput displays a prompt: in>

The user types the file name in full if OpenInput has been given no parameter, otherwise the user types in the file name followed by . and the program adds the extension.

This becomes the input file. The file must exist and be accessible to the program at run time. The effect of this command is to disable the standard input device and set the reading position to the start of the named data file. Any input commands received after this statement take data from the data file.

For example:
```
OpenInput("dat");
```
prompts the user at run time:
```
in>
```
If the user then types:
```
stock.
```
this opens for input a file called stock.dat, which must be located in the current working directory. If the procedure is successful then the InOut variable Done will contain the BOOLEAN value TRUE.

Note: Many compilers implement OpenInput differently, so you will need to check your manual.

9.1.3   The procedure `OpenOutput`

```
PROCEDURE OpenOutput(defext : ARRAY OF CHAR);
```

`OpenOutput` replaces the standard output device with the named data file. As with `OpenInput`, the parameter `defext` represents a default file name extension, e.g. `OpenOutput("dat")`.

`OpenOutput` displays a prompt:
```
out>
```
In a similar fashion to `OpenInput`, the user types the filename in full if `OpenOutput` has been given no parameter, or else the user types in the filename followed by . and the program adds the extension.

This becomes the output file. If the file does not exist then an empty data file with the given name is created and opened for output. If the file does exist then it is effectively wiped clean, losing all previous data when it is opened for output. The standard output device is disabled after this statement has been executed. Any data transferred using an output command will be written to the data file.

`OpenOutput` replaces the standard output device with the named file.

For example:
```
OpenOutput("dat");
```
prompts the user at run time: `out>`

If the user then types:
```
personnel.
```
this either opens an existing file called `personnel.dat` for output, losing the previous contents of the file, or, if no file with this name exists, a new file with this name is created in the current working directory and opened for output. The value of the variable `Done` following a call to this procedure indicates whether the file was successfully opened or not.

Note: Many compilers implement `OpenOutput` differently, so you will need to check your manual.

9.1.4   The procedure `CloseInput`

```
PROCEDURE CloseInput;
```

`CloseInput` cancels the redirection and reinstates the standard input. Any subsequent `OpenInput` command involving the same file will set the reading position back to the beginning of the file. `CloseInput` has no arguments.

9.1.5   The procedure `CloseOutput`

```
PROCEDURE CloseOutput;
```

`CloseOutput` cancels the redirection and reinstates the standard output. Any subsequent `OpenOutput` for the same file will set the writing position back to the start of the file, thus erasing all previous data from the file. `CloseOutput` has no arguments.

9.1.6   Limitations of redirection

Using redirection to read and write data files has certain limitations. In particular, it is only possible to have one input and one output file open at any time. If it is impossible to organize a program design with this limitation then redirection cannot be used.

Another problem is that it is not possible to have a two-way communication with the user of the program while redirection is in effect. This factor is significant when deciding the order of events in a program which needs to make use of files in this way. When the file is small enough the solution may be to read the whole file into an array in memory at the beginning of the program and/or build up the output data in an array in memory and write it all out at the end of the program. This means that the standard input and output are available throughout the main part of the program. However, when processing large data files, redirection might not be the best method.

Among the library modules supplied with your compiler you should find one called FileSystem. This provides facilities for more sophisticated file handling, but details vary between systems so we do not propose to explore it further now.

However, remember what we said earlier - EXPERIMENT!

9.1.7   Using redirection to copy a file

The following short example program uses input/output redirection to copy the contents of one file to another.

```
MODULE Copy;
(*Purpose: To copy the contents of a file
**Uses module: InOut*)
FROM InOut IMPORT OpenInput, OpenOutput, CloseInput, CloseOutput,
Done, Read, Write;
VAR
    ch : CHAR;
BEGIN
    (*Open a file for input. *)
    (*You may need to alter this line; see Section 9.1.2*)
    OpenInput("txt");
    (*Open a file for output*)
    (*You may need to alter this line; see Section 9.1.3*)
    OpenOutput("txt");
    (*Read the first character before entering the loop*)
    Read(ch);
    WHILE Done DO (*Loop while Read(ch) is successful*)
        Write(ch);
        Read(ch)
    END; (*WHILE*)
    CloseInput;
    CloseOutput
END Copy.
```

(When reading a file, some programmers find a LOOP statement more intuitive, as it avoids the need to read ahead of the loop. However, as explained in Chapter 8, there are other arguments against widespread use of the LOOP statement.)

9.1.8   The constant EOL

EOL represents the end of line character. Wirth specifies it as the record separator character, ASCII value 36C (octal). However, its actual value may differ between systems. This does not usually present a problem because EOL is exported as a constant by the InOut module and you do not need to know its actual value to use it in your programs. Its type is CHAR so it can be used with InOut's Read and Write procedures as well as be assigned to a variable of type CHAR.

As the following example demonstrates, the call Write(EOL) has the same effect as WriteLn.

```
MODULE EndOfLine;
(*Purpose: To demonstrate equivalence of Write(EOL)
**to WriteLn
**Uses module: InOut *)
FROM InOut IMPORT EOL, WriteString, Write,WriteLn;
BEGIN
    WriteString("This line is broken by ");
    Write(EOL);
    WriteLn;
    Write(EOL);
    WriteString("three end of line characters")
END EndOfLine.
```

9.1.9   ReadString and WriteString

The ReadString and WriteString procedures are both exported by the module InOut to handle input and output of strings of characters. Both are provided for convenience as similar action can be produced using InOut's Read and Write procedures to handle strings one character at a time.

Here's a version of WriteString using Write. We've called it MyWriteString.

```
PROCEDURE MyWriteString( s : ARRAY OF CHAR);
CONST
    NULL = 0C;
VAR
    index : CARDINAL;
BEGIN
    index := 0;
    WHILE ((index<=HIGH(s)) AND (s[index]<>NULL)) DO
        Write(s[index]);
        INC(index)
    END (*WHILE*)
END MyWriteString;
```

Simulating `ReadString` using `Read` is a little more complicated as `ReadString` allows the user to correct typing errors using the backspace key. `ReadString` ignores leading blanks and terminates the input when it meets a control character or a non-leading space. Here's our version, which is partly acceptable, (see Exercise 9.1):

```
PROCEDURE MyReadString(VAR s : ARRAY OF CHAR);
CONST
    NULL = 0C;        (*null character*)
    BS = 10C;         (*back space*)
    SPACE = 40C;      (*space character*)
    DEL = 177C;       (*delete*)
VAR
    index : CARDINAL;
    ch : CHAR;
    finish : BOOLEAN;
BEGIN
    index := 0;
    finish := FALSE;
    REPEAT
        Read(ch);
        IF ch = BS THEN
            IF index>0 THEN
                DEC(index)
            END
        ELSIF ((ch>=NULL) AND (ch<=SPACE)) OR (ch=DEL) THEN
            IF index<=HIGH(s) THEN
                s[index]:=NULL;
                finish := TRUE
            END
        ELSE
            s[index] := ch;
            INC(index)
        END; (*IF*)
    UNTIL finish OR (index>HIGH(s))
END MyReadString;
```

Exercise 9.1

Actually, `MyReadString` does not quite exactly match the action of `ReadString`. Carry out some tests to find the differences and see if you can amend `MyReadString` to provide a closer simulation.

9.1.10   The variable `termCH`

If `InOut`'s `ReadString` is terminated using a space or control character, this character is not returned as part of the input string. However, its value is stored in an `InOut` variable called `termCH` which can be imported from `InOut` if required.

9.1.11   Using redirection of output

When redirecting output to a file you need to write a delimiting character after every value you output, otherwise it will be difficult to write a program which can read the file you have created. The delimiter could be a space or an end of line character, i.e. Write(" ") or WriteLn.

Self test 9.1

Describe what the following program segment does:

```
OpenInput("dat");
count := 0;
Read(name[count]);
WHILE (NOT InOut.Done) AND (count  < 100) DO
    IF name[count] = EOL THEN
        WriteLn
    ELSE
        Write(name[count])
    END (*IF*);
    INC(count);
    Read(name[count])
END (*WHILE*)
WriteLn;
CloseInput;
```

9.2   Case study: *Supermarket bar code reader*

9.2.1   Requirements / specification

A program is required which will simulate the operation of a bar code reader at a supermarket checkout. A bar code contains a stock code uniquely identifying an item and providing a key to the stock file, which holds the current price of the item. The stock file contains an entry for each item on sale in the supermarket.

For each stock item the file will contain three values:

stockCode	CARDINAL
stockName	up to 40 characters, no spaces
unitPrice in pence	CARDINAL

The main purpose of the program is to input a stockCode value, match to the stock file, and output the stockName and price. If there is no match for the stockCode then the message 'no match found' will be output instead. A keyboard can be used as the input device to simulate the bar code reader.

stockName and price are to be used on the receipt.

9.2.2   The stock file

You can create a stock file using a wordprocessor or a text editor. Each value must be delimited by at least one space or put on a new line. For this reason, no spaces may be included in values, but an underline or hyphen may be used to separate words in the stock names.

The file could look something like this:

```
4192  Heinz_beans_and_burgerbites          22
4444  Heinz_spaghetti_in_tomato_sauce      19
5151  Heinz_spaghetti_with_sausages        21
.....and so on.
```

This format of a line per item makes mistakes more apparent but, if you prefer, it will work perfectly well formatted like this:

```
4192
Heinz_beans_and_burgerbites
22
4444
Heinz_spaghetti_in_tomato_sauce
19
.....and so on.
```

We have used abbreviated, but genuine, European Article Number stock codes here, from cans in the food cupboard. However, for our purpose, any numbers will do provided that none are duplicated.

9.2.3   Design

Context diagram (Level 0 DFD):

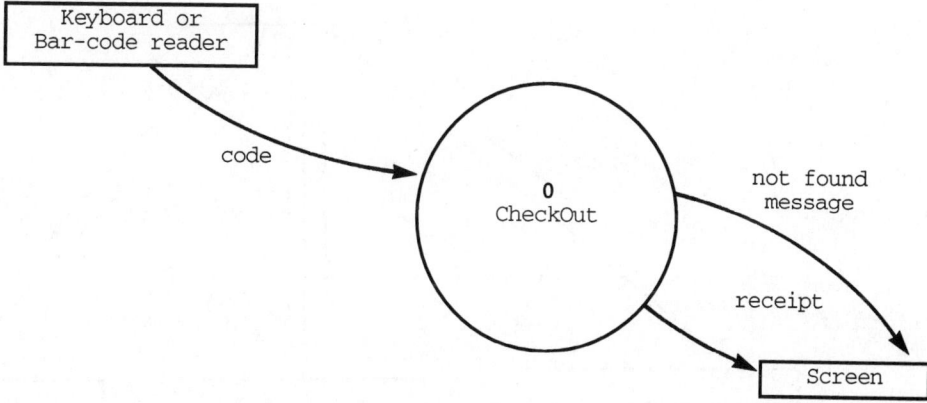

The level 1 DFD:

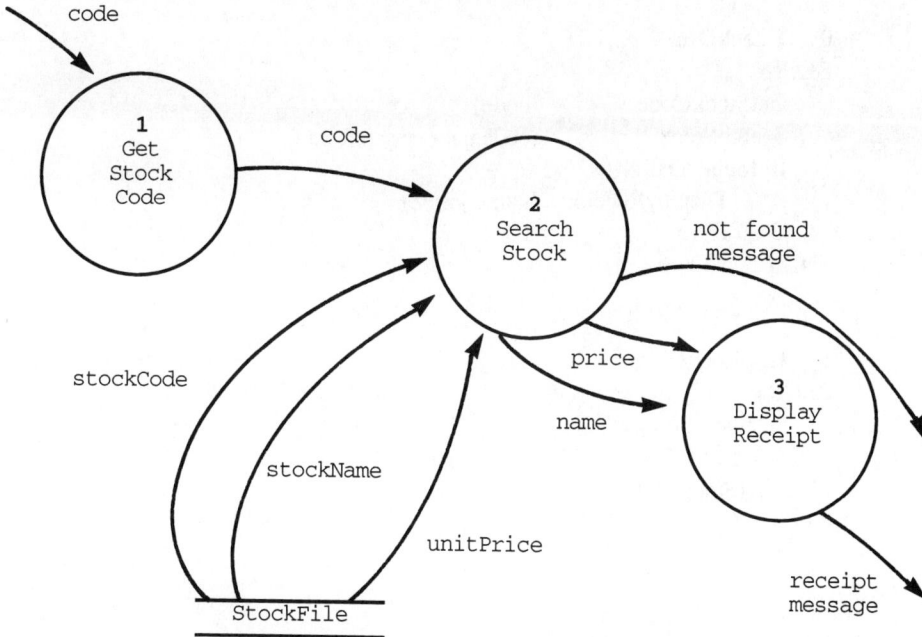

The structure chart becomes:

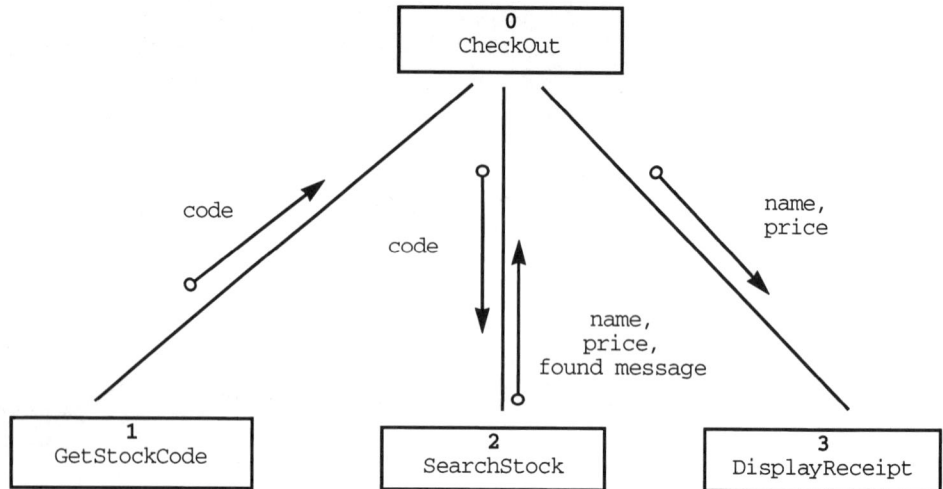

The pseudocode:

0   CheckOut:
BEGIN
    GetStockCode   (code)
    SearchStock   (code,name,price,found)
    IF found THEN
        DisplayReceipt   (name, price)
    END IF
END CheckOut.

1   GetStockCode:
BEGIN
    Display Prompt
    Input stockCode
END GetStockCode;

SearchStock is a little more difficult. We need to read the first code number from the file and then check if this is the one we are looking for. If it is, we need look no further, i.e. the loop can be skipped. If, on the other hand, the code is not the one that we seek, we still need to read its stock name and unit price in order to remove them from the input stream, before reading and checking the next stock code. While unread entries remain in the file and we have not found the code, we need to repeat this process. After the loop ends, we check if the appropriate code has been found and, if so, we read the corresponding stock name and unit price.

2   SearchStock:
```
BEGIN
    found:=FALSE
    Open stock file
    Read the stockCode
    IF code=stockCode THEN
        found:=TRUE
    END IF
    WHILE read is successful (i.e. not end of file) AND not found DO
        Read the stockName and unitPrice
        Read the next stockCode
        IF code=stockCode THEN
            found:=TRUE
        END IF
    END WHILE
    IF found THEN
        Read the stockName
        Read the unitPrice
    END IF
    Close stock file
END SearchStock;
```

3   DisplayReceipt:
```
BEGIN
    Output name
    Output price
END DisplayReceipt;
```

9.2.4   Implementation

```
MODULE CheckOut;
(*Purpose: Program to simulate the operation of a
**bar-code reader at a supermarket check-out
**Uses module: InOut
*)
FROM InOut IMPORT   ReadCard, ReadString, Read, OpenInput,
            CloseInput, Done,WriteLn, WriteCard, WriteString;
TYPE
    NameArray=ARRAY [0..40] OF CHAR;
VAR
    name:NameArray;
    code,price:CARDINAL;
    found :BOOLEAN;


PROCEDURE GetStockCode (VAR code : CARDINAL);
(*Gets a code number for user acting as bar code reader
**Pre: None
**Post: code contains a CARDINAL number
*)
BEGIN
    WriteString("Enter the stock code ");
    ReadCard(code);
    WriteLn
    (* it is tempting to simplify the program by removing
    **this procedure  but it is an advantage to
    ** have this as a separate procedure to allow for some
    ** validation to be added later *)
END GetStockCode;


PROCEDURE SearchStock (   code : CARDINAL;
                          VAR stockName : NameArray;
                          VAR unitPrice :CARDINAL;
                          VAR found : BOOLEAN);
(*Searches a file for a stock code and retrieves name
**and price
**Pre: code contains a CARDINAL number
**Post: if found is TRUE, name and price contain
**the item information corresponding to code.  If found
**is FALSE, the contents of name and price are undefined
*)
VAR
    stockCode : CARDINAL;
    space : CHAR;
BEGIN
    found:=FALSE;
    (*You may need to alter this line; see Section 9.1.2*)
    OpenInput("dat");
    ReadCard(stockCode);
    IF code=stockCode THEN
        found:=TRUE
    END;   (*IF*)
    WHILE Done AND NOT found DO
        ReadString(stockName);
        (*No need to read the space before the name
        **as ReadString skips it*)
        Read(space);  (*Read the space separator*)
```

```
                ReadCard(unitPrice);
                ReadCard(stockCode);
                IF code=stockCode THEN
                    found:=TRUE
                END
        END; (*WHILE*)
        IF found THEN
            ReadString(stockName);
            ReadCard(unitPrice)
        END;
        CloseInput
END SearchStock;

PROCEDURE DisplayReceipt (   name:NameArray;
                            price : CARDINAL);
(*Displays name and price information
**Pre: name and price contain assigned values
**Post: None
*)
BEGIN
    WriteString(name);
    WriteString("      ");
    WriteCard (price,2);
    WriteString("pence");
    WriteLn
END DisplayReceipt;

BEGIN (* MAIN PROGRAM *)
    GetStockCode(code);
    SearchStock(code, name, price, found);
    IF found THEN
        DisplayReceipt(name, price)
    ELSE
        WriteString("no match found");
        WriteLn
    END(*IF*)
END CheckOut.
```

Exercise 9.2

Design and write a program which will read details of up to 100 stock items. Input from the keyboard and create a stock file (name to be determined at run time) which can be read by your program CheckOut. You will need to store the input details in memory until all items have been read, then create the file at the end of the program. Your program needs to provide a means by which the user can signal that all items have been entered.

Exercise 9.3

Finish the design for the program SpellCheck from Chapter 5, then write the program according to the specification below. For testing, use a text editor to set up a dictionary file containing about 50 words.

The program should repeat the sequence of prompting the user to input a word, reading the word, checking it against the dictionary and reporting on whether a match was found, until the user chooses to quit.
An additional feature which you could include is to validate each character of the input word and reject the word if any non-alphabetic characters are present.

9.3   Case study: *The Unix wc utility*

If you have used a computer running the Unix operating system, you may have come across a utility program named wc. wc is a program which counts characters, words and lines of text in an input file.

To provide another illustration of an application using input/output redirection, let's design and implement a Modula-2 version of wc. In stating the requirements for our program we'll make some assumptions about exactly what will count as a word.

9.3.1   Requirements / specification

The wc program is to allow input of a text file and is to count the number of characters, words and lines in the file. Blank lines should be included in the line count.

Numbers written as figures (e.g. 321) are not to be counted as words and end of line characters must not be included in the character total.

Hyphenated words will be counted as a single word, as will words containing an apostrophe.

A space is to count as a character.

9.3.2   Design

Counting characters should not be too difficult to implement as we simply require a program similar to the Copy program listed in Section 9.1.7, but with a counter variable included. Similarly, counting lines should not present too many problems as we can count the EOL characters. However, a trickier design decision is how to detect complete words in order to count them. One approach to this would be to count words input from the keyboard by looking for the spaces between them. Another method, if we don't wish to count number figures as words, might be to say that when we find an alphabetic character in the input stream we are in a word and when we find a non-alphabetic character we are not in a word.

Context diagram (level 0 DFD):

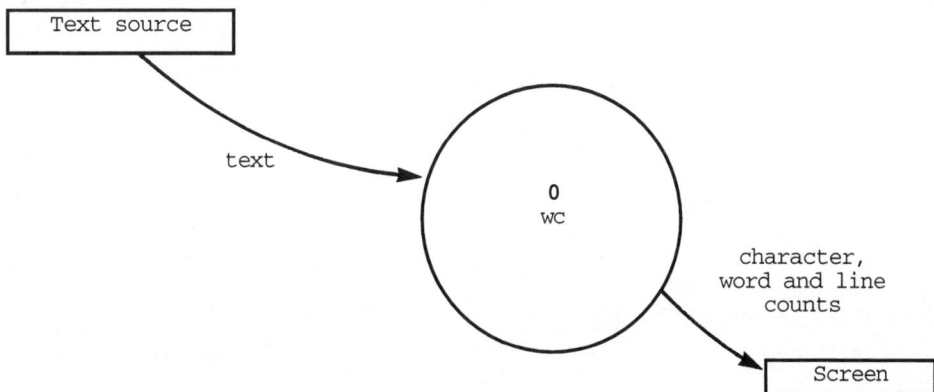

The level 1 DFD (assuming that the source is to be a text file):

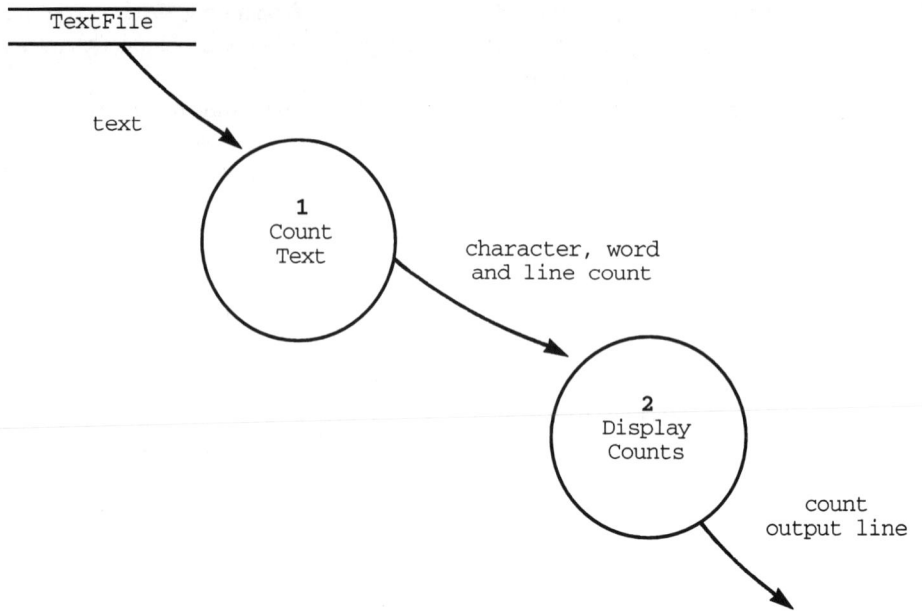

```
 _____
| TextFile       |
|_____|
         \
          \  text
           \
            ↘
              ⭕
             1
           Count
            Text            character, word
                            and line count
                                    ↘
                                       ⭕
                                      2
                                   Display
                                   Counts
                                              count
                                              output line
                                                    ↘
```

The structure chart for wc becomes:

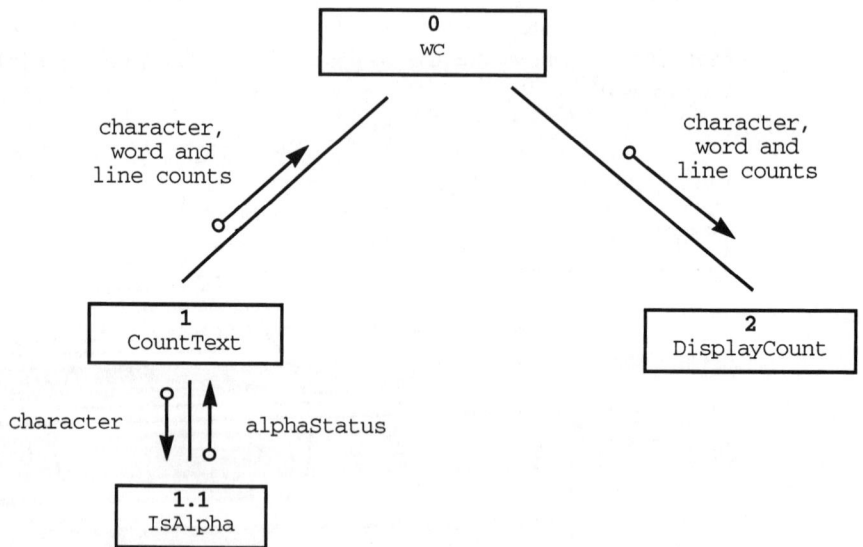

```
                        ┌──────────────┐
                        │      0       │
                        │      WC      │
                        └──────────────┘
                        /              \
        character,     /                \    character,
        word and      /                  \   word and
        line counts  ↗                    ↘  line counts
                    /                        \
          ┌──────────────┐          ┌──────────────┐
          │      1       │          │      2       │
          │  CountText   │          │ DisplayCount │
          └──────────────┘          └──────────────┘
                 ↓↑
       character    alphaStatus
                 │
          ┌──────────────┐
          │     1.1      │
          │   IsAlpha    │
          └──────────────┘
```

and the pseudocode:

0   wc:
BEGIN
    CountText   (character, word and line counts)
    DisplayCount   (character, word and line counts)
END wc.

If all goes well and these are to become our procedures:

1   CountText:
BEGIN
    Set counters to 0
    Openfile
    Read a character
    WHILE not the end of the file DO
        Now In Word if character is alphabetic
        Now In Line if character is not EOL
        IF last character was not in a Word AND current character is THEN
            Add 1 to wordCount
        END IF
        IF last character was not in a line AND current character is THEN
            Add 1 to lineCount
        END IF
        Read the next character
    END WHILE
    Closefile
END CountText;

2   DisplayCount:
BEGIN
    Output charCount, wordCount, lineCount
END DisplayCount;

OpenFile and CloseFile can be implemented using InOut.OpenInput and InOut.CloseInput, so there is no need to refine these further. Looking through the CountText pseudocode it is apparent that we need a function to check if a character is alphabetic. DisplayCount can be implemented with no further refinement.

1.1 IsAlpha:
BEGIN
    IF ch is in range A-Z or a-z THEN
        RETURN TRUE
    ELSE
        RETURN FALSE
    END IF
END IsAlpha;

9.3.3   Implementation

Our implementation is called wc and is listed on the following pages.

Notice that, instead of using IF/ELSE statements to set nowInLine and nowInWord, thus:

```
IF IsAlpha(Ch) THEN
    NowInWord:=TRUE
ELSE
    NowInWord:=FALSE
END; (*IF*)
```

We have used the compact equivalent:

```
nowInWord := IsAlpha(Ch);
```

because we find it more elegant. However, it is arguably less clear than the IF/ELSE alternative until you get used to it.

```
MODULE wc;
(*
**Purpose: wc program module counts the number of
**characters, words and lines in a text file.
**Uses module:  InOut
*)
FROM InOut IMPORT OpenInput,CloseInput,Read,
              WriteLn,WriteString,WriteCard,EOL,Done;
VAR
    charCount,lineCount,wordCount : CARDINAL;


PROCEDURE CountText( VAR charCount,wordCount,
                         lineCount:CARDINAL);
(*Pre: None
**Post: No. of characters is returned in CharCount
**      Number of words is returned in WordCount
**      Number of lines is returned in LineCount*)
VAR
    ch:  CHAR;
    wasInLine,wasInWord,nowInLine,nowInWord:BOOLEAN;


    PROCEDURE IsAlpha(Ch:CHAR):BOOLEAN;
    (*Pre: ch can be any character from character set
    **Post:  TRUE if ch is an alphabetic character,
    **otherwise FALSE *)
    BEGIN
        IF ((CAP(ch)>="A") AND (CAP(ch)<="Z")) THEN
            RETURN TRUE
        ELSE
            RETURN FALSE
        END
    END IsAlpha;


BEGIN  (*CountText*)
    charCount:=0;
    lineCount:=0;
    wordCount:=0;
    wasInWord:=FALSE;
    wasInLine:=FALSE;
    nowInLine:=FALSE;
    (*Open the file*)
    (*You may need to alter this line; see Section 9.1.2*)
    OpenInput ("txt");
    IF NOT Done THEN   (*the OpenInput call failed*)
        WriteString ("Could not open file - - sorry.");
        WriteLn
    ELSE
        Read (ch);
        WHILE Done DO
        (*until we run out of characters to read*)
            nowInWord := IsAlpha(ch);
            nowInLine := (ch<>EOL);
            (*Count words*)
            IF NOT wasInWord AND nowInWord THEN
                wordCount:=wordCount+1
            END; (*IF*)
```

```
            (*Count lines*)
            IF NOT wasInLine AND nowInLine THEN
                lineCount:=lineCount+1
            END; (*IF*)

            (*Count characters*)
            IF nowInLine THEN
                charCount:=charCount+1
            END; (*IF*)
            wasInWord:=nowInWord;
            wasInLine:=nowInLine;
            Read(ch) (*Read the next character*)
        END; (*WHILE*)
        CloseInput
    END (*IF*)
  END CountText;

PROCEDURE DisplayCount(charCount,wordCount,lineCount:CARDINAL);
(*Pre: Number of characters is in charCount
**      Number of words is in wordCount
**      Number of lines is in lineCount
**Post: None*)
BEGIN
    WriteLn;
    WriteString("Number of Characters:  ");
    WriteCard(charCount,1);
    WriteLn;
    WriteString("Number of Words:  ");
    WriteCard(wordCount,1);
    WriteLn;
    WriteString("Number of Lines:  ");
    WriteCard(lineCount,1);
    WriteLn
END DisplayCount;


BEGIN (*Main wc program*)
    CountText(charCount,wordCount,lineCount);
    DisplayCount(charCount, wordCount,lineCount)
END wc.
```

9.3.4 Testing

It seems that there's just one more job to be done to complete the program. That is to test wc. Any problems found will necessitate an iterative process of design modification, recoding and retesting until all is well.

In fact, you will find that all is not entirely well with wc. We liked the initial idea of determining the start of a word with an alphabetic character and see no reason not to retain it, but suspect there may be some problems due to trying to detect the end of words by simply looking for a non-alphabetic character. For this and other reasons wc needs proper testing.

Exercise 9.4

Construct a test table and put wc through its paces, not forgetting to include blank lines, apostrophes and hyphens in your tests.
In the light of your findings, modify wc as necessary.

10 CASE statement and enumerated types

10.1 The CASE statement

When a program is to make a decision from a number of alterative options an IF
statement of the following form can be used:

```
IF condition1 is TRUE THEN
    .....
ELSIF condition2 is TRUE THEN
    ....
ELSIF conditionN is TRUE THEN
    .....
ELSE
    .....
END; (*IF*)
```

There are occasions, however, when this type of statement can produce code which is
difficult to follow and inefficient to run, because of the number of different conditions
involved.

As an alternative, Modula-2 provides the CASE statement, which can be used when a
selection is to be made from a list of choices and the choice is dependent on the value of
a particular variable.

Here is an illustration to demonstrate the use of CASE statements.

10.1.1 Case study: *'Soundex' using the CASE statement*

Imagine an automated telephone directory which allows you to type in a name, searches
for it in the directory and, if found, displays the corresponding phone number. You
might not always know the exact spelling of the name you wish to find, so a useful
feature to include in such a system would be the facility to cope with mis-spelled names.
For example, you may be searching for Stephens but mistakenly believe the spelling is
Stevens. 'Soundex' is a method of encoding names into sequences of digits in such a
way that slight spelling variations are unlikely to affect the code produced. The basis of
the encoding is the following series of character groupings:

group 0:   A, E, I, O, U, H, W, Y
group 1:   B, F, P, V
group 2:   C, G, J, K, Q, S, X, Z
group 3:   D, T
group 4:   L
group 5:   M, N
group 6:   R

The characters in a name are first encoded as digits according to grouping, so:
STEPHENS becomes 23010052, and STEVENS becomes 2301052

Consecutive, similar digits are then replaced by a single digit and, finally, all 0s are removed, thus:
STEPHENS becomes 23152, and STEVENS becomes 23152.

The codes match and both names will be returned using either spelling.

As an example of using a CASE statement to make a selection based on a CARDINAL value, the following program uses a CASE statement to display the letters belonging to any input 'Soundex' group number.

```
MODULE SoundexGroups;

FROM InOut IMPORT WriteString, WriteLn, ReadCard;
VAR
    group : CARDINAL;
BEGIN
    WriteString("Please enter group number ");
    ReadCard(group);
    CASE group OF
        0 : WriteString(" A, E, I, O, U, H, W, Y ");
            WriteLn
    |   1 : WriteString(" B, F, P, V ");
            WriteLn
    |   2 : WriteString(" C, G, J, K, Q, S, X, Z ");
            WriteLn
    |   3 : WriteString(" D, T ");
            WriteLn
    |   4 : WriteString(" L ");
            WriteLn
    |   5 : WriteString(" M, N ");
            WriteLn
    |   6 : WriteString(" R ");
            WriteLn
        ELSE
            WriteString("No such grouping");
            WriteLn
    END (*CASE*)
END SoundexGroups.
```

The CASE statement begins by evaluating an expression, or a controlling variable, which must be of ordinal type. In the SoundexGroups example this controlling variable is group which is of CARDINAL type.

All possible values (in this case 1,2,3,4,5, and 6) are listed as CASE labels, together with the statements to be executed for each label. The ELSE is included to mean 'in all other cases'. On execution of a CASE statement ONE of the alternative cases must be true, so it is advisable to include the ELSE. A run-time error can occur if a value is encountered which is not among the list of alternatives.

The symbol, |, can be thought of as representing **or** and is used to separate the statements associated with one label from the next.

The actions associated with a particular CASE label may be described using one or more program statements.

The procedure at the heart of the 'Soundex' encoding would need to accept a name as an input parameter and return the appropriate code. (The code can be handled most conveniently if, like the name, it is an ARRAY OF CHAR rather than of CARDINAL type.)

The following module contains a procedure, Encode, designed to carry out the 'Soundex' encoding using a CASE statement.

```
MODULE Soundex;
FROM InOut IMPORT ReadString,WriteString, WriteLn;
CONST
    NULL = 0C; (*Null character to terminate a string*)
VAR
    name,code:ARRAY [0..20] OF CHAR;

PROCEDURE Length(str : ARRAY OF CHAR) : CARDINAL;
(*Returns the length of the string str
**Pre: str contains a string of characters
**Post: returns the length of the string*)
VAR
    index : CARDINAL;
BEGIN
    index := 0;
    WHILE (index<=HIGH(str)) AND (str[index]<>NULL) DO
        INC(index)
    END;
    RETURN index
END Length;

PROCEDURE Encode(name : ARRAY OF CHAR;
                        VAR code : ARRAY OF CHAR);
(*Returns the coded representation of a name
**Pre: name contains a string of characters
**Post: code contains the coded representation
**of name*)
VAR
    lastLetter:CHAR;
    letter,count:CARDINAL;
BEGIN
(*lastLetter keeps track of previous characters to identify
**duplicates to be removed. It is initialized to null*)
    lastLetter:=NULL;

(*Initialize counter to count digits in the code*)
    count:=0;

(*For each letter in the name*)
    FOR letter:=0 TO Length(name) DO
        CASE CAP(name[letter]) OF
    (*Convert the letter to the group code*)
            'A','E','I','O','U','H','W','Y' : code[count]:='0'
        |   'B','F','P','V'                 : code[count]:='1'
        |   'C','G','J','K','Q','S','X','Z' : code[count]:='2'
        |   'D','T'                         : code[count]:='3'
        |   'L'                             : code[count]:='4'
        |   'M','N'                         : code[count]:='5'
        |   'R'                             : code[count]:='6'
        ELSE
            (*Included to catch other possible values but
            **does nothing with them*)
        END; (*CASE*)
```

```
              IF (code[count]=lastLetter) OR (code[count]='0') THEN
                 lastLetter:=code[count];  (*Update lastLetter*)
                 DEC(count)                (*and remove repeated
                                           **characters*)
              ELSE
                 lastLetter:=code[count]   (*Update lastLetter*)
              END; (*IF*)
              INC(count);                (*Increment code digit count*)
              code[count]:=NULL;     (*Terminate code array with null*)
           END (*FOR*)
        END Encode;

        BEGIN  (*Main program*)
           WriteString("Please type in a name");
           WriteLn;
           ReadString(name);
           Encode(name,code);
           WriteString(code);
           WriteLn
        END Soundex.
```

Notice how the CASE statement labels make it very clear which values are being used for selection. The equivalent IF statement would be very unwieldy indeed:

```
IF (name[letter]='A') OR (name[letter]='E')
      OR (name[letter]='I') OR (name[letter]='O')
      OR (name[letter]='U') OR (name[letter]='H')
      OR (name[letter]='W') OR (name[letter]='Y') THEN
   code[count] := '0'
ELSIF (name[letter]='B') OR (name[letter]='F')
      OR (name[letter]='P') OR (name[letter]='V') THEN
   code[count] := '1'
ELSIF .................
```

PHEW! See what we mean?

It would be useful to allow names to be input to Soundex using both upper and lower case letters. One way to do this is to construct the CASE labels to include the lower case characters also; i.e.

```
CASE name[letter] OF
   'A','E','I','O','U','H','W','Y',
           'a','e','i','o','u','h','w','y' : code[count]:='0'
   .......
```

Alternatively, we could use the CAP function to convert all characters to upper case first; i.e.

```
CASE CAP(name[letter]) OF
   'A','E','I','O','U','H','W','Y' : code[count]:='0'
   .......
```

Unfortunately, these CASE labels are rather long.

When label values are consecutive it is possible to show them as a range of values. FOR example, you may remember the wc program in Chapter 9, which made use of a function procedure, IsAlpha, designed to check for a character to determine whether it is alphabetic.

```
PROCEDURE IsAlpha(ch:CHAR):BOOLEAN;
BEGIN
    IF ((CAP(ch)>="A") AND (CAP(ch)<="Z")) THEN
        RETURN TRUE
    ELSE
        RETURN FALSE
    END (*IF*)
END IsAlpha;
```

This function can be written more clearly using a CASE statement:

```
PROCEDURE IsAlpha(ch:CHAR):BOOLEAN;
BEGIN
    CASE CAP(ch) OF
        "A".."Z" : RETURN TRUE
    ELSE
        RETURN FALSE
    END (*CASE*)
END IsAlpha;
```

or as;

```
PROCEDURE IsAlpha(ch:CHAR):BOOLEAN;
BEGIN
    CASE ch OF
        "A".."Z","a".."z" : RETURN TRUE
    ELSE
        RETURN FALSE
    END (*CASE*)
END IsAlpha;
```

which explicitly lists the lower case letters in the CASE label rather than convert them to upper case.

As with other Modula-2 control structures, CASE statements can be nested. For an example, see Section 10.2.6.

CASE statement syntax chart:

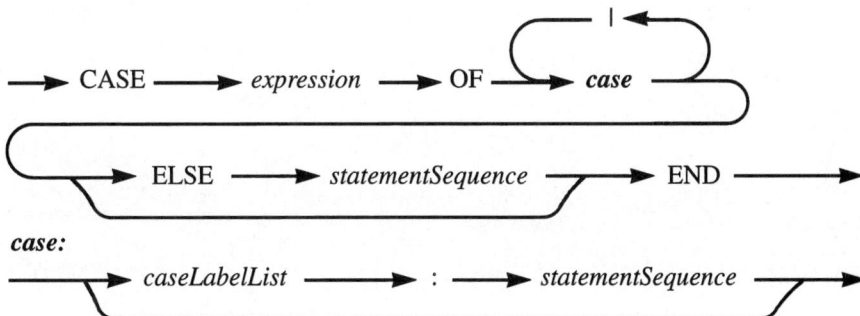

case:

10.2   **Enumerated types**

Enumerated types allow a programmer to declare types that can make the description of values within a program relate more closely to natural language. To illustrate, let's take a fresh look the `DecisionsDecisions` program in Chapter 6, which used a complex set of rules to reach a decision.

Here is the rules table again:

No.	Activity	weather	temp.	money	publicHol?	people
1	Cinema	Not sunny Not snowy	-	>=£4	-	>1
2	Scrabble	Rainy/snowy	-	-	-	>2
3	Theme park	Sunny	>15	>£12	N	>2
4	Zoo	Sunny	>15	>£5	N	>2
5	Bike ride	Sunny	<22	-	-	>1
ELSE						
6	Think of something new!					

There were some problems in determining the best way to represent the weather. In Chapter 6 we compromised by using a menu, represented internally by a subrange of CARDINAL variable.

Rather than symbolizing things for the computer's sake it would be better if we could use a representation more convenient for humans. What would have been preferable is to have defined weather like this:

```
TYPE
    WeatherType=(Sunny, Cloudy, Rainy, Snowy);
VAR
    weather:WeatherType;
```

This allows the variable `weather` to take any of the values: `Sunny`, `Cloudy`, `Rainy` or `Snowy`. This is a much clearer, more natural way of representing things.

`WeatherType` is, in fact, an example of an enumerated type.

Our dictionary defines enumerate as; to mention in order, or to go through a list of items. This is exactly what is done when declaring enumerated types.

Variables of enumerated type may hold any one of the values enumerated in the type declaration.

10.2.1 Using variables of enumerated type

Variables of enumerated type can be used in assignment statements, such as:

```
weather:= Sunny;
```

(Sunny is not a literal string, although it looks similar, so no quotes are required to delimit it.)

Variables of enumerated type can also be used in relational expressions, such as:

```
IF (weather=Cloudy) AND NOT holiday THEN
     choice:=6
END (*IF*)
```

and as parameters:

```
PROCEDURE GetFacts(VAR weather:WeatherType;
                   VAR temperature:INTEGER;
                   VAR holiday: BOOLEAN;
                   VAR money, noOfPeople:CARDINAL);
```

10.2.2 Input and output of enumerated values

Something which may be tempting, but will not work with an enumerated type variable, is to try and print out its value using a standard InOut procedure, such as WriteString. In common with BOOLEAN type, it is not possible to input or to output values of enumerated type directly, using the facilities provided by InOut.
So,

```
WriteString(weather)
```
is illegal and

```
ReadString(weather)
```
is also illegal.

It is, therefore, often necessary to perform a conversion between string input, which can be via ReadString, and the equivalent enumerated type value.
On output an enumerated type value is usually replaced by the equivalent string variable, which can then be output using WriteString. The CASE statement is an ideal tool for this purpose.
For example,

```
CASE weather OF
      Sunny : WriteString("Sunny")
   |  Cloudy : WriteString("Cloudy")
   |  Rainy : WriteString("Rainy")
   |  Snowy : WriteString("Snowy")
ELSE
END; (*CASE*)
```

10.2.3 Case study: *Decisions/Decisions revisited*

We are now in a position to re-write our DecisionsDecisions program from Chapter 6; this time making use of enumerated types.

We will start you off then leave it to you to complete the job as an exercise.

Two new data types can be declared:

```
TYPE
    WeatherType=(Sunny,Cloudy,Rainy,Snowy);
    ActivityType=(Cinema,Scrabble,ThemePark,Zoo,
                                    BikeRide,Think);
```

with variables:

```
VAR
    weather : WeatherType;
    activity : ActivityType;
```

and a new procedure for input:

```
PROCEDURE GetWeather (VAR weather:WeatherType);
VAR
     inWeather : CARDINAL;
BEGIN
    WriteLn;
    WriteString("What is the weather like?");
    WriteLn;
    WriteString("1.      Sunny");
    WriteLn;
    WriteString("2.      Cloudy");
    WriteLn;
    WriteString("3.      Rainy");
    WriteLn;
    WriteString("4.      Snowy");
    WriteLn;
    WriteString("[1-4] : ");
    ReadCard(inWeather);
    CASE inWeather OF
            1: weather := Sunny
        |   2: weather := Cloudy
        |   3: weather := Rainy
        |   4: weather := Snowy
    ELSE
        WriteString("Not a valid choice; assumed Sunny");
        weather := Sunny
    END (*CASE*)
END GetWeather;
```

The statements in GetFacts concerned with inputing the weather could be replaced by a procedure call to GetWeather.

AnalyzeFacts could also make good use of enumerated types.

```
PROCEDURE AnalyzeFacts (weather:WeatherType;
                        temperature:INTEGER;
                        holiday: BOOLEAN;
                        money, noOfPeople:CARDINAL;
                        VAR activity:ActivityType);
BEGIN
    IF ((weather <> Sunny) AND (weather <> Snowy))
            AND (money >= 4) AND (noOfPeople > 1) THEN
        activity:=Cinema
    ELSIF ((weather=Rainy) OR (weather=Snowy))
            AND (noOfPeople > 2) THEN
        activity:=Scrabble
    ELSIF   (weather=Sunny)
            AND (temperature > 15) AND (money > 12)
            AND NOT holiday AND (noOfPeople > 2) THEN
        activity:=ThemePark
    ELSIF   (weather=Sunny)
            AND (temperature > 15) AND (money > 5)
            AND NOT holiday AND (noOfPeople > 2) THEN
        activity:=Zoo
    ELSIF   (weather=Sunny)
            AND (temperature<22) AND (noOfPeople>1) THEN
        activity:= BikeRide
    ELSE
        activity:=Think
    END (*IF*)
END AnalyzeFacts;
```

The output procedure would also need to be changed.

```
PROCEDURE DisplaySuggestion (activity:ActivityType);
BEGIN
    WriteLn;
    WriteString("The suggestion is that you should ");
    CASE activity OF
            Cinema : WriteString("go to the cinema")
        |   Scrabble : WriteString("play scrabble")
        |   ThemePark : WriteString("go to a theme park")
        |   Zoo : WriteString("go to the zoo")
        |   BikeRide : WriteString ("go for a bicycle ride")
    ELSE
        WriteString("think of something new!")
    END (*CASE*);
    WriteLn
END DisplaySuggestion;
```

Don't be discouraged from using enumerated types because of the necessity to convert for input and output. This is a small price to pay for having code which is more maintainable and easier to understand.

Exercise 10.1

Now over to you to complete the re-write of DecisionsDecisions making use of CASE and enumerated types.

10.2.4   Further properties of enumerated types

No value can belong to more than one enumerated type, as this would cause ambiguity. So the joint declarations of:

```
TYPE
    Friends=(John,Paul,Mary,Tim);
    Family=(Tony,Susan,John,Jane);
```

are illegal because type of John is unclear.

Although it is not significant in the above example, enumerated types are ordinal types. That means that the order in which you specify the values determines the respective ordinal numbers and sequencing. Using the declarations:

```
TYPE
    WeatherType=(Sunny, Cloudy, Rainy, Snowy);
VAR
    weather:WeatherType;
```

Sunny has ordinal position 0, Cloudy 1, Rainy 2 and Snowy 3, so our program could, if required, loop through each possible value for weather using a FOR statement:

```
FOR weather:=Sunny TO Cloudy DO
    .....
    .....
END;  (*FOR*)
```

An enumerated type can also be used in a relational expression, so

```
weather > Cloudy
```

would be valid.

If the value of weather was Rainy or Snowy, then the expression would be TRUE; if Sunny or Cloudy, then it would be FALSE.
There are some applications where this may be of use, for example:

```
TYPE
    DayType=(Mon, Tue, Wed, Thu, Fri, Sat, Sun);
VAR
    today, tomorrow, restDay, payDay : DayType;
```

In this example the sequence of the values is important. You could use ordinal position to determine that if today is Wed, then tomorrow will be Thu, although you would have to arrange to handle the wrap-around at the end of the week when today is ordinal position 6. We'll show you how this can be done in a moment. (See Section 10.2.5.)

It is also legal to use an enumerated type to specify the bounds of an array. For example;

```
VAR
    age : ARRAY Friends OF CARDINAL;
```

The elements of `age` could then be accessed:

```
age[John]:=19;
age[Paul]:=18;
age[Mary]:=19;
age[Tim]:=20;
```

10.2.5   Standard functions and procedures with enumerated types

Modula-2 includes some built-in functions for making use of the ordinal positions of values of enumerated type.

Here are some functions that can be used with values or variables of enumerated type, with example argument(s) based on the declarations in Section 10.2.4.

Function	Action
ORD(Wed)	Returns the value 2, ORD(Mon) returns zero.
VAL(DayType,5)	Inverse of ORD, returns Sat
MAX(DayType)	Returns maximum value, Sun
MIN(DayType)	Returns minimum value, Mon

Procedure	Action
INC(today)	Increments to the next ordinal value.
DEC(today)	Decrements to the previous ordinal value.

If `today` has the value Sun, then `INC(today)` is illegal. Some compilers may not help you by pointing out the error, so be careful. The same is true if you call `DEC(today)` when `today` has the value Mon.

Here's an example of how to get around this problem:

```
IF today =MAX(DayType) THEN
    today := MIN(DayType)
ELSE
    INC(today)
END (*IF*);
```

10.2.6   Nesting of CASE statements

There are occasions where more than one variable is required to reach a decision, for example, using the declarations:

```
TYPE
    Months=(Jan,Feb,Mar,Apr,May,Jun,Jul,Aug,Sep,Oct,Nov,Dec);
VAR
    thisMonth:Months;
    maxDays, thisYear:CARDINAL;
```

We can determine how many days there are in `thisMonth` as follows:

```
CASE thisMonth OF
    Sep,Apr,Jun,Nov : maxDays:=30
|   Feb :   CASE thisYear MOD 4 OF
                0 :     CASE thisYear = 2000 OF
                            TRUE : maxDays:=28
                        ELSE
                            maxDays:=29
                            (*leap year*)
                        END (*CASE thisYear*)
            ELSE
                maxDays:=28
            END (*CASE thisYear MOD 4*)
ELSE
    maxDays:=31
END (*CASE thisMonth*);
```

Exercise 10.2

In order to provide an illustration of nested CASE statements, the above example is somewhat contrived. It is not the simplest way to achieve the desired result and is, in fact, a situation where IF statements would be clearer than using CASE.

Write and test a function procedure that takes the name of a month and the year as input parameters and returns the number of days in the month,

(i)   using CASE statements and

(ii)   using IF statements.

10.3   Subrange type

In Section 2.6.3 we introduced the possibility of declaring subrange types. To recap briefly: a subrange is a sequence of consecutive values, chosen from an ordinal type, such as CARDINAL, INTEGER or CHAR. A subrange is specified, inside square brackets, using a lower and an upper limit. These limits must be specified using constants.

It is also possible to declare a type that is a subrange of an enumerated type.

```
TYPE
    Dates = [1..31]
    Months=(Jan,Feb,Mar,Apr,May,Jun,Jul,Aug,Sep,Oct,Nov,Dec);
    SummerMonths = [Jun..Aug];
```

Given the above declarations:
- variables of subrange type Dates can only take values between 1 and 31 inclusive,
- variables of enumerated type Months can take any of the values Jan, Feb, Mar, Apr, May, Jun, Jul, Aug, Sep, Oct, Nov, Dec,
- variables of type SummerMonths can only take values Jun, Jul, Aug,
- variables of subrange type can be used in any way the parent type could be used, provided the range bounds are not exceeded.

When being used as a formal parameter the type must be specified using a name, e.g.

```
PROCEDURE (VAR Birthday:Dates) is legal
PROCEDURE (VAR Birthday:[1..31]) is illegal
```

and the actual calling parameter must be of the SAME named type. (See Appendix B.)

Self test 10.1

Given the input values:
    73 70 29 35 42 129 62 40 36 1 23 999 12
find the value of count on exit from the loop in the program segment below:

```
count:=0;
LOOP
    ReadCard (value);
    (**) IF value = 999 THEN EXIT END;
    CASE value OF
        70..100   : INC(count,3)
    |   60..69    : INC(count,2)
    |   40..59    : INC(count,1)
    |   0..34     : DEC(count)
    ELSE
    END (*CASE*);
END(*LOOP*);
WriteCard (count,3);
```

Self test 10.2

Given the following definitions:

```
TYPE
    DayType = (Sun,Mon,Tues,Wed,Thur,Fri,Sat);
VAR
    day, payday, restday:DayType;
```

which of the following are valid statements?

a) payday:=Fri;
b) payday:=INC(restday);
c) FOR day:= Sun TO Sat DO END (*FOR*);
d) InOut.WriteString(payday);

Self test 10.3

Which of the following are legal subrange type definitions?

a) TYPE Array=ARRAY [6..10] OF REAL;
b) TYPE Line=ARRAY [1,2,3,4] OF CHAR;
c) TYPE List=ARRAY [CARDINAL] OF CHAR;
d) TYPE Marks=ARRAY [1.0..5.0] OF REAL;
e) TYPE Range=[5.2..6.5];
f) TYPE Letters=["p","q","r"];
g) TYPE WeekEnd=[Fri..Sun];
h) TYPE Evens=[2,4,6,8];

Self test 10.4

Which of the following could appear as a legal CASE labels in a Modula-2 program?

a) Fred
b) "x"
c) 1.0
d) 77
e) 'P'
f) "Monday"
g) TRUE

10.4   Case study: *Doctor's dilemma*

10.4.1   Requirements / specification

A patient suffering from selective amnesia can remember everything except names. He goes to see a hospital consultant about the problem but, afterwards, when phoning to arrange a follow-up appointment, he cannot remember the consultant's name. Fortunately, the appointments clerk can identify every consultant when given simple yes/no answers to four questions concerning their description.

The characteristics of the 12 hospital consultants can be represented in a table:

Consultant	Glasses	Male	Tall	Curly
IanTravenus	T	T	F	T
MattErnity	F	T	T	T
PaulPitate	F	T	F	T
CathyTerr	F	F	F	T
SueCher	T	F	F	T
DiAlisis	F	F	T	T
LeeShun	F	T	F	F
RexRay	T	T	F	F
ArthurPeadic	T	T	T	T
GerryHattrick	F	T	T	F
AnnaSetic	T	F	T	T
EmmaRoid	F	F	T	F

T represents TRUE, i.e. the consultant possesses this characteristic; **F** represents FALSE, i.e. the consultant does not possess the characteristic.

The requirement is to write a program to ask the patient four questions, each demanding a yes/no answer, in order to obtain a description and hence to identify the consultant the forgetful patient saw originally.

The descriptions of the consultants are to be sorted in a text file with the format:

```
TTFT    IanTravenus
FTTT    MattErnity
FTFT    PaulPitate
FFFT    CathyTerr
TFFT    SueCher
FFTT    DiAlisis
FTFF    LeeShun
TTFF    RexRay
TTTT    ArthurPeadic
FTTF    GerryHattrick
TFTT    AnnaSetic
FFTF    EmmaRoid
```

10.4.2   Design

First the context diagram; (the level 0 DFD).

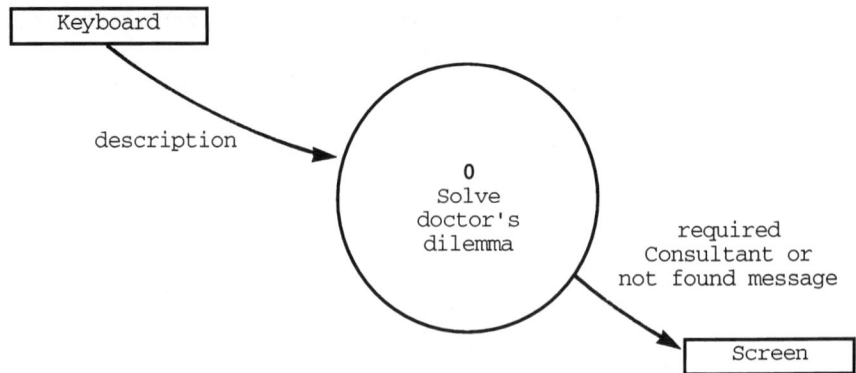

Next, refine the main process to give the level 1 DFD.

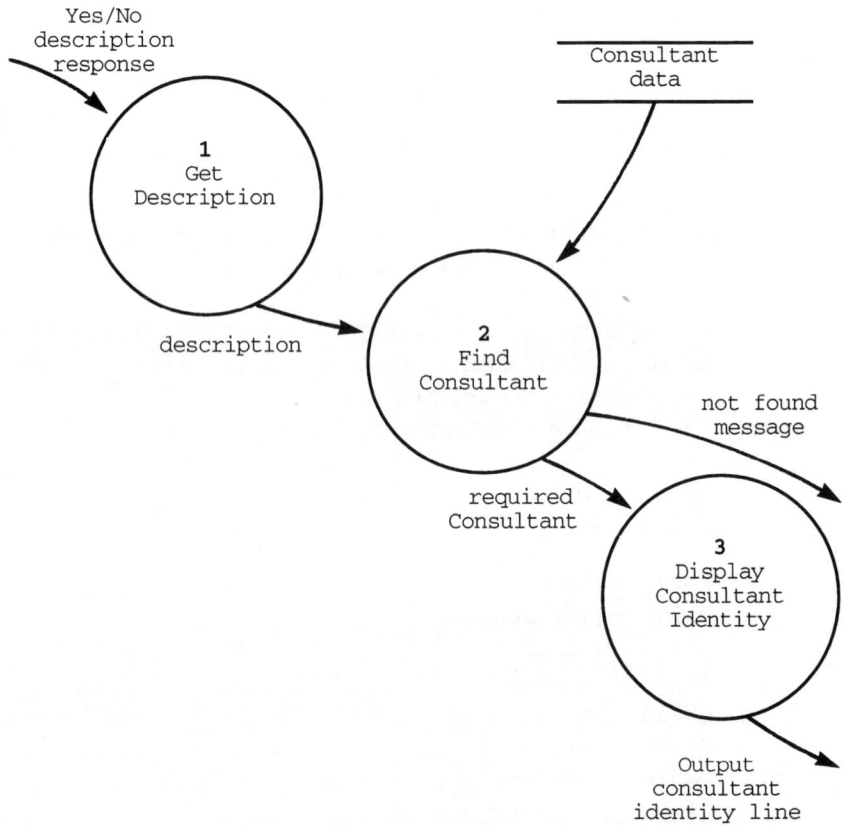

From the data flow diagrams, derive the structure chart.

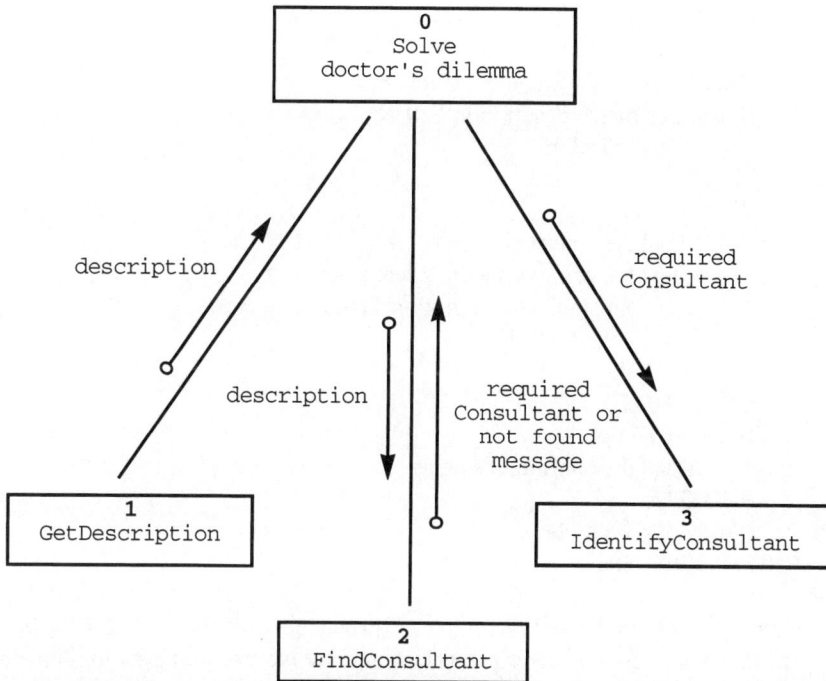

Our top level pseudocode solution becomes:

0   DoctorsDilemma:
BEGIN
    GetDescription   (description)
    FindConsultant   (description, requiredConsultant, found)
    IF found THEN
        IdentifyConsultant   (requiredConsultant)
    ELSE
        display "not found" message
    END IF
END ConsultantMystery.

and the procedures:

1   GetDescription:
BEGIN
    FOR each characteristic
        Ask if consultant had the characteristic and obtain yes/no answer
    END FOR
END GetDescription;

2   FindConsultant:
BEGIN
    found:=FALSE
    Open consultant file
    Read the first consultant's features from file
    IF features match description THEN
        found:=TRUE
    END IF
    WHILE read is successful (i.e. not end of file) AND not found DO
        Read the consultant name
        Read the next consultant's features
        IF features match description THEN
            found:=TRUE
        END IF
    END WHILE
    IF found THEN
        Read the consultant's name
    END IF
    Close consultant file
END FindConsultant;

Compare this with the `SearchStock` procedure in Section 9.2.4; it is very similar. However, in this case it is not yet clear how we are going to implement the task of checking whether the features read from the file match the the description, so a further level of sub-division seems appropriate.
Rather than looking for four matching features, `CheckMatch` starts by assuming that there IS a match. If any characteristic does NOT match, then `match` is altered to FALSE.

2.1   CheckMatch:
BEGIN
    Initially, assume a match has been found, i.e. match := TRUE
    FOR each feature DO
        IF feature does not match description THEN
            match:=FALSE
        END IF
    END FOR
    RETURN match
END CheckMatch;

We should now go back and amend the DFD and structure chart in the light of this addition.
The final procedure, `IdentifyConsultant`, is very straightforward.

3   IdentifyConsultant:
BEGIN
    Display Consultant name
END IdentifyConsultant;

10.4.3   Implementation

Here are the type specifications, constant and variable declarations, and the main program body.

Notice we have used an enumerated type to describe the consultants' characteristics. This enumerated type is then used as the array bounds to declare a two-dimensional array of BOOLEAN values representing the consultant description.

```
TYPE
    NameType = ARRAY [0..15] OF CHAR;
    CharacteristicType=(Glasses,Male,Tall,Curly);
    CharacteristicArray=ARRAY CharacteristicType OF BOOLEAN;
VAR
    name : NameType;
    found : BOOLEAN;
    description:CharacteristicArray;


BEGIN   (*Main body of DoctorsDilemma*)
    GetDescription(description);
    FindConsultant(description,name,found);
    IF found THEN
        IdentifyConsultant(name)
    ELSE
        WriteString("Nobody matches this description")

    END
END DoctorsDilemma.
```

The function procedure, CheckMatch, looks for a mismatch between the description and a consultant's features using the relational expression:

```
decription[feature]<>(characteristics[ORD(feature)]='T')
```

feature is of type CharacteristicType, so, on the left hand side of the expression:

```
decription[feature]
```

represents a BOOLEAN value.

On the right hand side of the expression ORD(feature) returns an index to the characteristics array read from the file, so characteristics[ORD(feature)] represents a CHAR value; either 'T' or 'F'.

If the value is 'T',

```
characteristics[ORD(feature)]='T'
```

evaluates to TRUE, otherwise it evaluates to FALSE.

The program implementation follows:

```
MODULE DoctorsDilemma;
(*
**Purpose: To identify a consultant from a description
**Uses module: InOut
*)
FROM InOut IMPORT WriteString, WriteLn,OpenInput,
                      Done,ReadString,CloseInput,Read;
TYPE
    NameType = ARRAY [0..15] OF CHAR;
    CharacteristicType=(Glasses,Male,Tall,Curly);
    CharacteristicArray=ARRAY CharacteristicType OF BOOLEAN;
VAR
    name : NameType;
    found : BOOLEAN;
    description:CharacteristicArray;


PROCEDURE GetDescription(VAR description:CharacteristicArray);
(*Gets a consultant description from the user
**Pre: None
**Post: description contains an array of
**BOOLEAN values*)
VAR
    yesNo : CHAR;
    feature:CharacteristicType;
    term : CHAR;
BEGIN
    FOR feature:=Glasses TO Curly DO
        description[feature]:=FALSE;
        WriteString("Was the consultant ");
        CASE feature OF
                Glasses : WriteString("wearing glasses?")
            |   Male : WriteString("male?")
            |   Tall : WriteString("tall?")
            |   Curly : WriteString("curly haired?")
            ELSE
        END; (*CASE*)
        WriteString("  (Y/N)?");
        WriteLn;
        Read(yesNo);
        Read(term);   (*Read end of line character*)
        WriteLn;
        IF (CAP(yesNo)="Y") THEN
            description[feature]:=TRUE
        END (*IF yesNo *)
    END (*FOR*)
END GetDescription;
```

```
PROCEDURE FindConsultant(description:CharacteristicArray;
                         VAR requiredConsultant : NameType;
                         VAR found:BOOLEAN);
(*Seeks to find a consultant whose characteristics match
**the description using the consultant's file
**Pre: decription contains an array of 4 BOOLEAN values
**Post: if found is TRUE, requiredConsultant contains
**the name of the consultant matching the description,
**otherwise the contents of requiredConsultant is
**undefined*)
VAR
    characteristics : ARRAY[0..3] OF CHAR;
    consultant : NameType;
    match:BOOLEAN;

    PROCEDURE CheckMatch(characteristics : ARRAY OF CHAR;
                 description:CharacteristicArray):BOOLEAN;
    (*Checks for a match between description and
    **characteristics
    **Pre: characteristics contains an array
    **of 4 characteristics represented by 'T' and 'F'
    **description contains an array of 4 BOOLEAN values
    **Post: CheckMatch returns TRUE if a match
    **is found, otherwise returns FALSE*)
    VAR
        feature:CharacteristicType;
        match:BOOLEAN;
    BEGIN
        match:=TRUE;
        FOR feature:=Glasses TO Curly DO
            IF description[feature]<>
                       (characteristics[ORD(feature)]='T') THEN
                match:=FALSE
            END (*IF*)
        END; (*FOR*)
        RETURN match
    END CheckMatch;

BEGIN  (*FindConsultant*)
    found:=FALSE;
    (*You may need to alter this line; see Section 9.1.2*)
    OpenInput("dat");
    ReadString(characteristics);
    IF CheckMatch(characteristics,description) THEN
        found:=TRUE
    END; (*IF*)
    WHILE Done AND NOT found DO
        ReadString(consultant);
        ReadString(characteristics);
        IF CheckMatch(characteristics,description) THEN
            found:=TRUE
        END; (*IF*)
    END; (*WHILE*)
    IF found THEN
        ReadString(requiredConsultant)
    END; (*IF*)
    CloseInput
END FindConsultant;
```

```
PROCEDURE IdentifyConsultant(name : NameType);
(*Displays a consultant's name
**Pre: name contains an array of characters
**Post: None*)
BEGIN
    WriteString("The consultant is ");
    WriteString(name);
    WriteLn
END IdentifyConsultant;


BEGIN  (*Main body of DoctorsDilemma*)
    GetDescription(description);
    FindConsultant(description,name,found);
    IF found THEN
        IdentifyConsultant(name)
    ELSE
        WriteString("Nobody matches this description")

    END
END DoctorsDilemma.
```

10.4.4   Testing

First, let's look at the program as a black box, i.e. concentrating on inputs and output, without concerning ourselves with the program's internal workings.

Besides the file, there are four inputs to the program, each in the form of a yes/no answer. So, our test data should scrutinize each of these four values independently, looking at the following cases:

Valid answers:	Y, N, y, n
Possible invalid answers:	X ,a, 2, *

We need to ensure that the program meets the specification, in that a given input will produce the appropriate matching output. We should, therefore, as a minimum, test with a set of values for which we expect to find a match, e.g. N, N, Y, Y for DiAlisis, as well as with a non-matching set of input values, e.g. N, N, N, N. In addition, tests should be included to ensure that the first and last values, in the table of doctors, is processed correctly, i.e. Y, Y, N, Y for IanTravenus and N, N, Y, N for EmmaRoid.

Sometimes our testing may also need to look more closely at how the program works, i.e. white box testing. For example, we might feel it is appropriate to include a test to ensure that the input values are not transposed, e.g. that N N, Y, Y is not read as Y, Y, N, N. Although, in this case such a test is probably unnecessary provided the black box test results are satisfactory.

Exercise   10.3

Complete a test table for `DoctorsDilemma`, based on the test cases discussed above and perform the testing on the program.

Exercise   10.4

This is a picture of the new and very tall, Doctor CyKeyatric, who has just joined the staff. Carry out any modifications required in order to include Cy's details in the list of doctors. Re-test the program to make sure that it still works.

Exercise 10.5

Using a variable of enumerated type to represent months of the year, write a program that allows you to input a date of birth (day and month) and then outputs the corresponding astrological star sign.

Aquarius	20 Jan - 17 Feb	Leo	23 Jul - 22 Aug
Pisces	18 Feb - 19 Mar	Virgo	23 Aug - 22 Sep
Aries	20 Mar - 19 Apr	Libra	23 Sep - 22 Oct
Taurus	20 Apr - 20 May	Scorpio	23 Oct - 21 Nov
Gemini	21 May - 20 Jun	Sagittarius	22 Nov - 21 Dec
Cancer	21 Jun - 22 Jul	Capricorn	22 Dec - 10 Jan

11 RECORD and SET types

11.1 RECORD type

Structured types allow variables to represent collections of data items. The ARRAY type is one structured type we have already discussed but, useful as arrays can be, they have a significant restriction; they can be used only to hold data items of a single type. This restriction can be overcome by using RECORD types, which may consist of components having a variety of types. The components of a record are generally referred to as fields.

A RECORD type declaration has the form:

```
TYPE
    RecordType =   RECORD
                       fieldA, fieldB : someTYPE;
                       fieldC : anotherTYPE
                   END;
```

and variables can be declared:

```
VAR
    firstRecord, secondRecord : RecordType;
```

Within your programs you can identify a particular field by giving the record variable identifier name, followed by a dot, then the identifier of the field.
For example:

```
    firstRecord.fieldA
```

refers to `fieldA` of `firstRecord`.

The field types within a record can be any type, including arrays and other records and, as you'll see shortly, a record can be used even as the component type of an array.

11.1.1 The WITH statement

The WITH statement can be used instead of the dot notation.

```
WITH firstRecord DO
    fieldA:= value
END;
```

To avoid ambiguity, WITH may be used only for one RECORD variable at a time. This means that WITH statements cannot be nested.

11.1.2   Case study: *Bar code reader revisited*

In Chapter 9 we used, as an example, a supermarket bar code reader that needed to reference a stock file in order to produce a receipt. Unfortunately, each receipt was limited to a single item. We can now create a program that is more practical. First, we need to revise the requirement.

The requirement is to write a program to produce a supermarket customer's till receipt by inputing the stock codes of items in the customer's trolley (as though read by a bar code reader) and inputing the corresponding item quantities. The program should then look each code up in a stock file to obtain the product name and its unit price. When item input is complete the program should input the amount of money tendered by the customer in payment, before finally producing a till receipt with calculated totals and the change due, as shown in the following example:

```
┌──────────────────────────────────────┐
│           S U P E R C U T S           │
│                                        │
│        COVENTRY CITY BRANCH            │
│                                        │
│   ********************************     │
│                                        │
│   WHITE_BREAD       1      0.64        │
│   JELLY             2      0.58        │
│   RED_SALMON        1      1.25        │
│   BKD_BEANS_X_4     2      2.28        │
│                                        │
│   TOTAL                    4.75        │
│   ITEMS             6                  │
│   CASH                    10.00        │
│   CHANGE DUE               5.25        │
│                                        │
│   ********************************     │
│                                        │
│           THANK YOU                    │
│        FOR SHOPPING AT                 │
│           SUPERCUTS                    │
└──────────────────────────────────────┘
```

The stock file required is similar to the stock file used in Chapter 9, except this time unit prices are to be more realistically held as REAL values rather than CARDINAL. Thus, each stock item consists of:

```
stockCode
stockName
unitPrice
```

These components or fields make up a stock record and we can declare this in a Modula-2 program as follows:

```
TYPE
    StringArray [0..15] OF CHAR;
    (*We have reduced the number of characters allowed for
    ** stock names so that they will fit on a receipt*)

    StockType =   RECORD
                        stockCode:CARDINAL;
                        stockName:StringArray;
                        unitPrice:REAL;
                  END (*StockType*)
```

This arrangement allows each unit of data, no matter how complex, to be stored as a RECORD.

We can declare variables to be of StockType:

```
VAR
    stockRecord : StockType;
```

To input data from standard input into a single record:

Provided that we have imported ReadCard, ReadString and ReadReal, the following sequence of statements will input values from the standard input to each of the fields of stockRecord.
The RECORD variable identifier is used to prefix (or qualify) the individual field identifiers;

```
ReadCard(stockRecord.stockCode);
ReadString(stockRecord.stockName);
ReadReal(stockRecord.unitPrice);
```

As you can see, the identifiers can become rather long when using records. An alternative way to handle these is to use a WITH statement as follows:

```
WITH stockRecord DO
    ReadCard(stockCode);
    ReadString(stockName);
    ReadReal(unitPrice);
END (*WITH*)
```

Once declared we can, if required, use a RECORD type in an ARRAY declaration. This is, in fact, exactly what we will need.

To implement the complete till receipt program using redirection of standard input and output there must be careful planning of the different stages. This is to ensure that the keyboard and screen are available for the data entry phase when the checkout bar code reading activities are simulated and that access can also be made to the stock file. The creation of the till receipt must be deferred until all items of shopping have been dealt with and then produced at the end of the run.

Take a closer look at the sample till receipt.

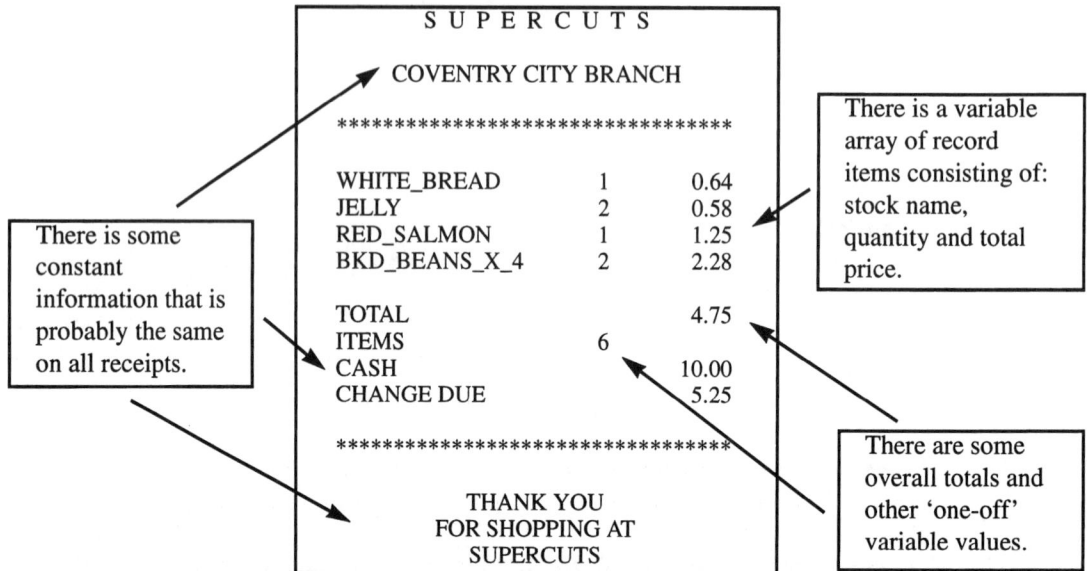

A sensible way to deal with the till receipt is to store the details required to create each item line until all of a customer's shopping has been processed.

Each set of details can be formatted as a record. We can then use an array of records to represent all of the items to appear on the receipt. However, using an array does mean that we will have to impose a maximum number of items on a till receipt.

Let's assume for the sake of convenience that, in our example, a single till receipt may contain a maximum of 50 items. We can declare an array of records in which to assemble the data for a receipt:

```
CONST
    MAXREC=50;

TYPE
    ReceiptType = RECORD
                     stockName:StringArray;
                     quantity:CARDINAL;
                     itemTotal : REAL;·
                  END;

    ReceiptArrayType = ARRAY [1..MAXREC] OF ReceiptType;
```

Now that we have a data type which is an array of records, we can declare variables:

```
VAR
    receiptArray:ReceiptArrayType;
    receipt : ReceiptType;
```

So `receiptArray` represents an array of 50 records and `receipt` represents a single receipt record.

We will also need variables for the total bill, the total number of items purchased, the cash tendered and the change due.

```
VAR
    index, noOfItems : CARDINAL;
    totalBill, cashTendered, changeDue : REAL;
```

To assign values to fields in an array of records:

To access an element of the array of records, `receiptArray`, we need to specify an array index. Thus, we could assign values to the fields of the fifth record in `receiptArray` as follows:

```
receiptArray[5].stockName:= "JELLY";
receiptArray[5].quantity:= 2;
receiptArray[5].itemTotal:=0.58;
```

Records can be passed as parameters, provided that the formal and corresponding actual parameters are of the SAME type.
The following procedure updates an element of `receiptArray` with information derived from `stockRecord` and the item quantity. `index` is used to indicate which element of `receiptArray` is to be updated.

```
PROCEDURE AddReceiptItem(VAR receiptArray : ReceiptArrayType;
                         index, noOfItems : CARDINAL;
                         stockRecord : StockType);
BEGIN
    WITH receiptArray[index] DO
        stockName := stockRecord.stockName;
        quantity := noOfItems;
        itemTotal := FLOAT(noOfItems)*stockRecord.unitPrice
    END (*WITH*)
END AddReceiptItem;
```

A call to this procedure would be of the form:

```
AddReceiptItem(receiptArray,index,noOfItems,stockRecord);
```

Note that there is no conflict created by using the identifier `stockName` in both `stockRecord` and `receiptArray` because each is qualified by the record identifier.

Alternatively, rather than passing the whole array of records, the procedure could have been written:

```
PROCEDURE AddReceiptItem(VAR receipt : ReceiptType;
                             noOfItems : CARDINAL;
                             stockRecord : StockType);
BEGIN
    WITH receipt DO
        stockName := stockRecord.stockName;
        quantity := noOfItems;
        itemTotal := FLOAT(noOfItems) * stockRecord.unitPrice
    END (*WITH*)
END AddReceiptItem;
```

A call to this procedure would be of the form:

```
AddReceiptItem(receiptArray[index],noOfItems,stockRecord);
```

where a single element of `receiptArray` is used as an actual parameter.

11.1.3   Assignment to variables of RECORD type

Modula-2 permits whole records to be passed between record variables, provided they are of the SAME type.
For example:

```
receiptArray[item]:=receipt;
```

assigns, field to field, the complete record, `receipt`, to the record specified by `item` within the array of records, `receiptArray`.

Exercise 11.1

You should now have enough information to enable you to implement the bar code reader simulator using records. You will need to set up a stock file independently of this program. The easiest way is to create it as a text file, using a text editor, or modify the file you created for Chapter 9. Make sure that every record matches exactly the format expected by your program.

You will also need to find a way for the user to indicate when all items have been input. You may decide to use a sentinel value (perhaps a zero stock code could be used to mean end of data) or you could have a 'Do you want to continue? ' question after each item.

The till receipt should be output to a file, so that it can be printed later, or output directly to a printer if one is available.

Be sure to test your program.

11.1.4   Variant records

Just when you think you have finished with the bar code reader problem a new till receipt surfaces:

```
┌─────────────────────────────────────┐
│        S U P E R C U T S             │
│                                      │
│       COVENTRY CITY BRANCH           │
│                                      │
│  ********************************    │
│                                      │
│  6_BROWN_ROLLS      1      0.69      │
│  SOYA_MARG          3      1.65      │
│  COX_APPLES      L                   │
│  0.86kg @ £0.87/kg  1      0.75      │
│  LEMONADE_2X2LT     2      1.78      │
│                                      │
│  TOTAL                     4.87      │
│  ITEMS              6                │
│  CASH                     10.00      │
│  CHANGE DUE                5.13      │
│                                      │
│  ********************************    │
│                                      │
│        THANK YOU                     │
│     FOR SHOPPING AT                  │
│        SUPERCUTS                     │
└─────────────────────────────────────┘
```

It transpires that not all till receipt items conform to the format that we have used. The supermarket has a number of products, for example fruit and vegetables, which are sold loose, put into bags by the customer, then weighed and priced at the checkout. Weighed items require a different set of data to be stored than do the normal items. We must revise the record definition to take this into account.

We could use a code letter in the stock file to indicate the type of each item. For example, itemType could be the character L to represent loose items, B for bakery, and so forth. So normal items will require file entries of the form:

```
stockCode
stockName
itemType    (*when itemType is not L, i.e. not loose items*)
unitPrice
```

e.g.

```
2137
6_BROWN_ROLLS
B
0.69
```

while loose items require:

```
stockCode
stockName
itemType   (*when itemType is L, i.e. loose items*)
unitOfMeasure
unitPrice
```

e.g.

1473
COX_APPLES
L
kg
0.87

The problem is, we now have a file containing two variants of the record structure. Fortunately, Modula-2 has a special type of record format for just such a situation, called a variant record.

Variant records may have some fields which differ between records. A special field, called a **tag** field, is used to contain a value indicating which record variation is to apply and a CASE statement is used to describe the variant part of the record.

In our example, itemType is the tag field and the record structure for an item in the stock file would become:

```
TYPE
    UnitType = ARRAY [0..5] OF CHAR;

    StockType =    RECORD
                        stockCode : CARDINAL;
                        stockName: StringArray;
                        CASE itemType: CHAR OF
                            'L' :   unitOfMeasure:UnitType
                        ELSE
                            (*nothing*)
                        END; (*CASE*)
                        unitPrice : REAL
                    END (*StockType*);
```

Assuming, as before, we declare a variable to be of StockType:

```
VAR
    stockRecord : StockType;
```

We can read into the record, stockType, either variant of the record, depending on the value in the tag field. However, Modula-2 does not allow a tag field to be used as an actual variable parameter, so we must first read into a local variable.

```
PROCEDURE ReadVariantStock(VAR stockRecord : StockType);
VAR
    item : CHAR;
BEGIN
    WITH stockRecord DO
        ReadCard(stockCode);
        ReadString(stockName);
        Read(item);
        itemType:=item;
        CASE itemType OF
            'L' : ReadString(unitOfMeasure)
        ELSE
                (*nothing*)
        END; (*CASE*)
        ReadReal(unitPrice);
    END (*WITH*)
END ReadVariantStock;
```

The declarations required to set up an array of variant record type to handle items on a till receipt will become:

```
CONST
    MAXREC=50;

TYPE
    StringArray = ARRAY [0..15] OF CHAR;

    UnitType = ARRAY [0..5] OF CHAR;

    ReceiptType = RECORD
                    stockName: StringArray;
                    CASE itemType: CHAR OF
                    (*loose produce sold by weight*)
                    'L' :   weight,unitPrice : REAL;
                            unitOfMeasure: UnitType
                    ELSE
                        quantity : CARDINAL (*Normal items*)
                    END; (*CASE*)
                    itemTotal : REAL
                END (*ReceiptType*);

    ReceiptArrayType = ARRAY [1..MAXREC] OF ReceiptType;
```

and the variable declarations:

```
VAR
    receiptArray:ReceiptArrayType;
    receipt : ReceiptType;
```

The procedure to add an item record to a receipt becomes:

```
PROCEDURE AddReceiptItem(VAR receipt : ReceiptType;
                             itemType : CHAR;
                             wt:REAL; noOfItems:CARDINAL;
                             stockRecord : StockType);
BEGIN
    WITH receipt DO
        stockName := stockRecord.stockName;
        CASE itemType OF
            'L' :   weight:=wt;
                    unitOfMeasure:=stockRecord.unitOfMeasure;
                    itemTotal := wt * stockRecord.unitPrice
        ELSE
            quantity := noOfItems; (*Normal items*)
            itemTotal := FLOAT(noOfItems)
                                    * stockRecord.unitPrice
        END; (*CASE*)
    END (*WITH*)
END AddReceiptItem;
```

Exercise 11.2

Modify the bar code reader program by including variant records to allow for weighed goods, as described in the notes above.

Exercise 11.3

a) Describe the changes that you would make to the bar code reader, variant record program, to allow for a multi-buy discount scheme, whereby selected items of stock are designated as 'three for the price of two.'

b) Implement these changes and re-test the program.

11.2   SET types

A set is an unordered group of unduplicated values of the same 'base type' which should usually be CARDINAL or an enumerated type.

Here are a couple of examples:

NumberSetType:

```
TYPE
    NumberType=[1..10];
    NumberSetType=SET OF NumberType;

CONST
    EVENS=NumberSetType{2,4,4,6,8,10};
    PRIMES=NumberSetType{1,2,3,5,7};

VAR
    chosenNumbers, specialNumbers : NumberSetType;
```

`NumberType` is a subrange of CARDINAL, which is used as the base type for `NumberSetType`. `EVENS` and `PRIMES` are SET constants of the same type.

SetOfMammals:

```
TYPE
    Mammals=(Cat,Dog,Hamster,Rabbit,Rat,Fox,Badger,
                                    Hedgehog,Pig,Cow);
    SetOfMammals=SET OF Mammals;

CONST
    EMPTYPEN=SetOfMammals{};

VAR
    domesticated, wild, farm : SetOfMammals;
```

`Mammals` is an enumerated base type used in `SetOfMammals`. Variables, such as `domesticated` and `wild`, may contain only values taken from the universal set, `Mammals`. The constant, `EMPTYPEN`, is a special set with no elements, aptly named the empty set.

The minimum requirement for every Modula-2 compiler is to allow the following base types for sets. (You can have sets of any of these types.)

    Enumerated types
    Subranges of enumerated types
    Subranges of CARDINAL

For any particular SET type, the elements of the base type form the universal set. Some compilers restrict the number of elements in the universal set. This is because a variable of SET type is represented inside the computer by using one binary digit (or bit) for each member of the universal set.

SET variables or constants of a particular base type are all the same size, with a pattern of zeros and ones indicating which elements are present and which are absent. As a programmer you do not need to know this in order to use SET types, but an understanding will help you to appreciate the restrictions. The number of bits per computer-word is dependent on the type of computer you are using (typically 16 or 32). Some compilers limit the number of elements in a base type to the number of bits per computer-word, others set a maximum number of computer words that can be used to represent a set. If you want to make use of SET types in your programming then it is advisable to investigate what restrictions your compiler imposes on set base types. In addition, many compilers allow SET OF CHAR, but others do not, so don't take this for granted.

11.2.1   Set assignment

There are several different ways that a value can be assigned to a SET variable, for example by listing the elements to be included in the set:

```
domesticated := SetOfMammals{Cat, Dog, Hamster, Rabbit, Rat};
```

using a subrange of the universal set:

```
wild := SetOfMammals{Rat..Badger};
```

assignment between two ASSIGNMENT COMPATIBLE sets:

```
specialNumbers := PRIMES;
```

initializing an empty set:

```
chosenNumbers := NumberSetType{};
```

11.2.2   Set operations

You may have come across the use of sets in mathematics. If so, you may remember the set operations, such as union and intersection and, perhaps, Venn diagrams. Modula-2 has four basic set operators for manipulating sets, which are described below with the help of Venn diagrams.

Symbol	Meaning
+	union
−	difference
*	intersection
/	symmetric difference

In a Venn diagram, circles are used to represent distinct sets of values. Where circles overlap, this represents values that each set shares in common with the other.

If A and B are sets then the following Venn diagrams illustrate the effect of set operators.

Union (A + B)

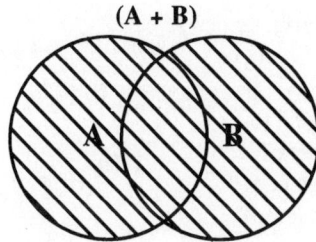

Creates a set containing all of the elements of A and all of the elements of B, without duplicates.

e.g.
(domesticated + wild) gives {Cat, Dog, Hamster, Rabbit, Rat, Fox, Badger, Hedgehog}

Difference (A – B)

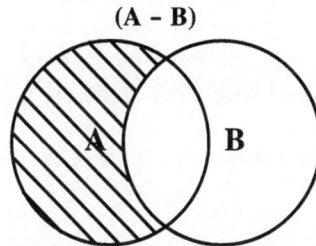

Creates a set containing the elements that A minus all of the elements shared in common with B.

e.g.
(domesticated – wild) gives {Cat, Dog, Hamster}

Intersection (A * B)

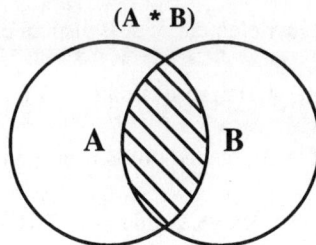

Creates a set containing all of the elements that A shares in common with B.

e.g.
(domesticated * wild) gives {Rabbit, Rat}

Symmetric Difference (A / B)

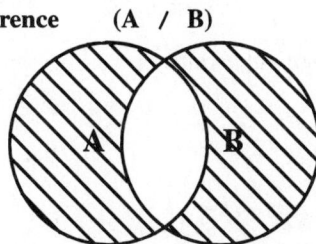

Creates a set containing all of the elements of A and B minus any elements shared in common.

e.g.
(domesticated / wild) gives {Cat, Dog, Hamster, Fox, Badger, Hedgehog}

11.2.3   Relational operators

There are five relational operators used for comparing sets.
Each produces a BOOLEAN result.

Operator	Meaning
=	equal to
<> or #	not equal to
<=	a subset of
>=	a superset of
IN	a member of

11.2.4   Set equality

For two sets to be equal they must have exactly the same elements.
The order of the elements does not matter, therefore {Cat, Pig, Rat} is identical to {Pig, Cat, Rat}.
If two sets differ in either the number of elements or in the values of the elements then they are not equal.

11.2.5   Subsets and supersets

Set A is a subset of set B if every element of A is also an element of B, e.g.

{ Cat, Dog} <= {Cat, Dog, Rabbit} evaluates to TRUE.

Set A is a superset of set B if every element of B is also an element of A, e.g.

{Cat, Dog, Rabbit} >= {Cat, Dog} evaluates to TRUE.

11.2.6   Set membership

IN is used to test whether a particular value of the base type is an element of a set, e.g.
```
   Cat IN domesticated
```

evaluates to TRUE, and

```
   9 IN PRIMES
```

evaluates to FALSE.

A variable of type Mammal could be used in such a comparison, e.g.

```
VAR
    pet : Mammal;

BEGIN....

(*assignment to pet
**somewhere in here*)

    IF pet IN wild THEN
        GiveAdvice
    END (*IF*);

...etc.
```

11.2.7   Standard procedures using sets

There are two procedures provided by Modula-2, INCL and EXCL, which enable elements to be added and removed from sets.

INCL adds an element to a set, e.g.

```
INCL(wild, pig);
```

results in the set, wild, containing

```
{Rat..Badger, Pig}
```

EXCL removes an element from a set, e.g.

```
EXCL (domesticated, Rat);
```

results in the set domesticated containing

```
{Cat, Dog, Hamster, Rabbit}
```

In both INCL and EXCL an expression which is type-compatible with the base type of the set may be used in place of the second parameter, e.g.

```
INCL (domesticated, pet);
```

results in the value of the variable pet being added to the set domesticated.

11.2.8   Case study: *Noughts and crosses using SET type*

There is a particular type of problem where the use of sets provides a neat and efficient solution. Such problems incorporate complex decision making which can be implemented in the form of pattern matching algorithms, using SET types. Here is our version of noughts and crosses (or Tic-tac-toe) which uses sets to provide an efficient way of detecting a winning line, i.e. three noughts or three crosses in a row on the 3 x 3 playing grid.

```
MODULE SetOxo;
(*Purpose: To allow two players to play noughts and crosses
**Uses: InOut
*)
FROM InOut IMPORT Read,ReadCard,WriteCard,
                                WriteLn,WriteString;
CONST
    WINWAYS=8;
    SQUARES=9;
TYPE
    SetOfSquares = SET OF [1..SQUARES];
    PlayerType=(e,X,O);
    WinSets=ARRAY [1..WINWAYS] OF SetOfSquares;
    PlayerSets=ARRAY [X..O] OF SetOfSquares;
CONST
    GRID=SetOfSquares{1,2,3,4,5,6,7,8,9};
VAR
    set:PlayerSets;
    freeSet : SetOfSquares;
    allWinSet:WinSets;
    player,winner:PlayerType;
    draw:BOOLEAN;
    reply,ch:CHAR;

PROCEDURE IntroGame;
(*Introduces the game
**Pre: None
**Post: None*)
BEGIN
    WriteString("Tic-Tac-Toe");
    WriteLn;
    WriteString("-----------");
    WriteLn;
    WriteLn
END IntroGame;

PROCEDURE InitPlayers(VAR set:PlayerSets; VAR
freeSet:SetOfSquares);
(*Initializes the player sets to empty and
**free square set to whole grid
**Pre: None
**Post:set of X occupied squares, set[X], initialized
** to empty
** set of O occupied squares, set[O], initialized to empty
** the freeSet is initialized to the whole grid*)
BEGIN
    set[X]:=SetOfSquares{};
    set[O]:=SetOfSquares{};
    freeSet:=GRID;
END InitPlayers;
```

```
PROCEDURE InitWinSets(VAR allWinSet:WinSets);
(*Initializes an array of possible winning sets
**Pre: None
**Post: the array of sets, allWinSets is initialized to the **
array of 8 possible winning sets*)
BEGIN
    allWinSet[1]:=SetOfSquares{1,2,3};
    allWinSet[2]:=SetOfSquares{4,5,6};
    allWinSet[3]:=SetOfSquares{7,8,9};
    allWinSet[4]:=SetOfSquares{1,4,7};
    allWinSet[5]:=SetOfSquares{2,5,8};
    allWinSet[6]:=SetOfSquares{3,6,9};
    allWinSet[7]:=SetOfSquares{1,5,9};
    allWinSet[8]:=SetOfSquares{3,5,7}
END InitWinSets;

PROCEDURE GetFreeSet(set:PlayerSets):SetOfSquares;
(*Updates the set of unoccupied squares
**Pre: set contains the set of squares occupied by X
**and the set of squares occupied by O
**Post: returns the set of free squares, i.e. squares not
**occupied by X or O*)
BEGIN
    RETURN (GRID - (set[X]+set[O]))
END GetFreeSet;

PROCEDURE CheckWinner(set:PlayerSets; allWinSet:WinSets;
            VAR winner:PlayerType;VAR draw:BOOLEAN);
(*Check if game is finished and determine the result
**Pre: set contains the set of squares occupied by X
**and the set of squares occupied by O,
**allWinSets contains an array of winning sets
**Post: winner contains the player whose occupied set
**includes a winning set, otherwise winner contains e.
**draw is TRUE if winner is e and there are no
**unoccupied squares, otherwise draw is FALSE*)
VAR
    i:CARDINAL;
BEGIN
    winner:=e;
    draw:=FALSE;
    FOR i:=1 TO WINWAYS DO
        IF allWinSet[i]<=set[X] THEN
            winner:=X;
        ELSIF allWinSet[i]<=set[O] THEN
            winner:=O
        ELSIF
            set[X]+set[O]=GRID THEN
            draw:=TRUE
        END (*IF*)
    END (*FOR*)
END CheckWinner;
```

```
PROCEDURE DisplayPlayers(set:PlayerSets);
(*Displays the grid showing current player positions
**Pre: set contains the set of squares occupied by X
**and the set of squares occupied by O
**Post: None*)
VAR
    square:CARDINAL;
BEGIN
    FOR square:=1 TO SQUARES DO
        IF square IN set[X] THEN
            WriteString(" X ");
        ELSIF square IN set[O] THEN
            WriteString(" O ")
        ELSE
            WriteString(" - ")
        END; (*IF*)
        IF (square MOD 3)=0 THEN
            WriteLn
        END (*IF*)
    END; (*FOR*)
    WriteLn
END DisplayPlayers;

PROCEDURE ProcessMove(player:PlayerType;
                      VAR set:PlayerSets;
                      VAR freeSet :SetOfSquares);
(*Processes a move for the current player
**Pre: player contains the current player X or O
**set contains the current set of squares occupied by X
**and the current set of squares occupied by O
**Post: set contains the updated set of squares occupied by X
**and the updated set of squares occupied by O and
**freeSet contains the updated set of unoccupied squares*)
VAR
    pos:CARDINAL;
BEGIN
    freeSet:=GetFreeSet(set);
    REPEAT
        WriteString("Please enter move 1-9 ");
        ReadCard(pos);
    UNTIL ((pos>=1) AND (pos<=SQUARES) AND (pos IN freeSet));
    (*Add new position to player set*)
    INCL(set[player],pos)
END ProcessMove;

PROCEDURE DisplayResult(winner:PlayerType);
(*Displays the result of a game
**Pre: winner contains the player whose occupied set
**includes a winning set, otherwise winner contains e.
**If winner contains e, a draw is assumed
**Post: None*)
BEGIN
    WriteString("The result is ");
    IF winner=X THEN
        WriteString("X has won")
    ELSIF winner=O THEN
        WriteString("O has won")
    ELSE
        WriteString("a draw")
    END; (*IF*)
    WriteLn
END DisplayResult;
```

```
BEGIN (*Main noughts and crosses program*)
    REPEAT (*Play games until user wants to stop*)
        (*Introduce game and initialize player sets to empty
        **and the set of free squares to the whole grid*)
        IntroGame;
        InitPlayers(set,freeSet);
        (*Initialize an array of winning sets*)
        InitWinSets(allWinSet);
        (* Play the Game - X starts*)
        player:=X;
        (*Loop, alternately processing moves for X and O
        **until a win or a draw*)
        LOOP
            ProcessMove(player,set,freeSet);
            CheckWinner(set,allWinSet,winner,draw);
            DisplayPlayers(set);
            (**)IF ((winner=X) OR (winner=O) OR draw) THEN
                                                    EXIT END;
            (*Players take alternate turns*)
            IF player=X THEN
                player:=O
            ELSE
                player:=X
            END (*IF*)
        END; (*LOOP*)
        (*Display the result*)
        DisplayResult(winner);
        (*Play again??*)
        Read(ch);
        WriteString("Play again (Y/N)? ");
        Read(reply);
        Read(ch); (*Read RETURN character*)
        reply:=CAP(reply);
    UNTIL (reply='N')
END SetOxo.
```

In this program the user must enter the moves for both of the players. Exercise 11.5 invites you to write an extended version in which the computer will play against you.

Exercise 11.4

Design and write a program which takes in the name of an animal (as a string variable) converts it to the equivalent enumerated type value, then decides and outputs what category of animal it is.

Your program should use an enumerated type to contain the names of all the animals and sets to represent some different categories, e.g.

    insects
    spiders
    birds
    reptiles
    mammals

After validation and conversion of the input value, use the IN operator to test for set membership.

Any names not recognized should produce a suitable 'don't know' message.

Exercise 11.5

Here is a pattern matching problem for you to tackle, this time based on the Supermarket bar code reader program discussed earlier in the chapter.

The management has devised a brilliant scheme to coerce customers into spending more money. A discount of 10% on the total amount spent is being offered to customers who include at least one purchase from each of five departments within the store on a single shopping receipt. The catch is that the five departments will be chosen each day from all the in-store departments and the customer is not told which departments they are.

The discount will appear automatically on the till receipt and the amount due will be adjusted accordingly.

The solution should be implemented by declaring an enumerated type consisting of the department names. This, in turn, forms the base type and universal set for a SET OF departments. The department number for each sales item can be included in the stock record as a CARDINAL value. Here is the full list of department names and corresponding numbers:

Department Name	deptNo
Bakery	1
Butcher	2
Clothing	3
Delicatessen	4
Fishmonger	5
GreenGrocery	6
Grocery	7
Hardware	8
Newsagent	9
SoftFurnishing	10
Tobacconist	11
WinesAndSprirts	12

Two set variables are required:

- `discountSet`, which is assigned the five target department names at the start of each day (for ease of implementation these can be hard-coded with a simple assignment statement) and
- `customerSet`, which is initialized to the empty set at the start of each till receipt.

For each item of shopping `deptNo` is passed to a new procedure which evaluates it and adds the corresponding department name to `customerSet`.

After the last item of shopping has been processed a sub-total is to be printed on the receipt, then `customerSet` is compared to `discountSet`. To qualify for the 10% discount, `customerSet` must be a superset (>=) of `discountSet`. If this is the case, discount is set to 10% of the sub-total, otherwise discount is set to zero. The discount value is to be printed below the sub-total. The till receipt total is calculated by subtracting the discount value from the sub-total. This is printed below the discount value. The payment details are then printed as before.

Suggested tasks:

a) Design the changes to the till receipt program and implement them as described.
b) Devise a strategy to test the modified program.
c) Carry out the testing and draw up a test table to display the results.

Exercise 11.6

The Noughts and Crosses program, described in this chapter, does not use the computer's potential to act as one of the players.   It is quite a challenging exercise to extend the program so that the computer plays, and never loses.
The computer must have a playing strategy something like the following:

> If possible, move to win this go
> else move to stop a human win on next move
> else move to the square giving best chance of win
> else move to any available free square.

The computer can determine the square offering its best chance of a win by checking which square occurs most frequently in its set of possible ways to win.
However, you will need to ensure that it is programmed not to move in a way that will give the human player two ways to win after his/her next move. For example, imagine that the computer is playing O and current situation is:

```
    X    -    -
    -    O    -
    -    -    X
```

If O moves to position 3,

```
    X    -    O
    -    O    -
    -    -    X
```

then the human will move to position 7 and eventually win.

12 Using modules

12.1 Library modules

By now you'll be quite used to the idea of importing pre-written library procedures into your programs. All Modula-2 systems provide a library of modules from which you can import constants, types, variables or procedures. A few of these modules are fairly standard and found with almost all Modula-2 systems. However, the overall suite of library facilities can and does vary between systems.

If you have been working through the examples in this book you'll be familiar with the InOut library module and have imported its facilities into your own programs; in fact, it is unlikely that you have a single program without it. Almost all your programs are likely to have used the InOut procedures WriteString and WriteLn. If you have tried the file redirection exercises in Chapter 9 you will also have imported the variable Done and the constant EOL from InOut.

Sometimes you may find that there are aspects of the library facilities you would like to change. For example, ReadString allows you to input a string of characters but terminates when you enter a space, so you cannot use it to read in a complete line of characters. Also, you may feel there is some other useful facility you would like to have available. A good example of this is the fact that not all Modula-2 systems provide a procedure in the RealInOut library module to allow output of a REAL number in fixed point format.

One of the great advantages of Modula-2 over its predecessor, Pascal, is that the library facilities provided with the system are not part of the language definition; you are free to write modules to suit your own particular requirements. So you can, if you wish, write your own input/output module tailored exactly to your specification.

12.2 Writing your own input/output module

As its name indicates, modules are a concept at the core of the Modula-2 language but, before discussing their importance more fully, let me give you a practical example with our own module to provide some more convenient input and output facilities.
Here are a couple of features we think it would be useful to include, but you can add some more of your own if you wish.

Procedure 1.
> A single procedure to output a string of characters, followed by a new line.
> (Using InOut's procedures to accomplish this necessitates a call to
> WriteString followed by a call to WriteLn.)

Procedure 2.

A procedure to allow input of strings of characters, terminated by an EOL character rather than by a space as with InOut's ReadString.

(This would be a very useful facility, but is not included in Wirth's 'standard' library.)

Library modules can themselves import from other library modules so we'll make life easier by making use of the existing InOut facilities when writing the two procedures we require.

Procedure 1:   Let's call it WriteStringLn;

```
PROCEDURE WriteStringLn(s : ARRAY OF CHAR);
BEGIN
   WriteString(s);
   WriteLn
END WriteStringLn;
```

Procedure 2:   Let's call it ReadLine;

```
PROCEDURE ReadLine(VAR s:ARRAY OF CHAR);
CONST
    NULL=0C;
VAR
    ch:CHAR;
    index:CARDINAL;
BEGIN
    index:=0;
    Read(ch);
    WHILE ((ch<>EOL) AND Done) DO
        s[index]:=ch;
        INC(index);
        (*Place the end of string
        **marker after last character*)
        s[index]:=NULL;
        Read(ch)
    END
END ReadLine;
```

12.2.1   Introducing definition and implementation modules

Library modules consist of two parts: a definition part and an implementation part. These two parts are written as a pair of modules: a definition module and a corresponding implementation module. The definition module contains information about the facilities exported by the module and usable by other program parts, while the implementation module contains the code detail. When making use of facilities provided by library modules we have only to know what the definition part contains to determine how to use them. We don't have to worry about the implementation detail, which can remain hidden within the implementation module. If you look through the manual provided with your Modula-2 system you will see that you are given only the definition module descriptions of library modules; the implementation source code is not usually available to you.

We've called our example I/O module MyIO.

Here's its DEFINITION MODULE which should be saved as MyIO.def:

```
DEFINITION MODULE MyIO;

PROCEDURE WriteStringLn(s : ARRAY OF CHAR);

PROCEDURE ReadLine(VAR s:ARRAY OF CHAR);

END MyIO.
```

Notice that the definition module contains just the procedure headings, which is all the information required by anyone wanting to use MyIO's facilities.

Here's the corresponding IMPLEMENTATION MODULE, which contains the full procedure coding and should be saved as MyIO.mod:

```
IMPLEMENTATION MODULE MyIO;
FROM InOut IMPORT WriteString, WriteLn, Read, Done,EOL;

PROCEDURE WriteStringLn(s : ARRAY OF CHAR);
BEGIN
    WriteString(s);
    WriteLn
END WriteStringLn;

PROCEDURE ReadLine(VAR s:ARRAY OF CHAR);
CONST
    NULL=0C;
VAR
    ch:CHAR;
    index:CARDINAL;
BEGIN
    index:=0;
    Read(ch);
    WHILE ((ch<>EOL) AND Done) DO
        s[index]:=ch;
        INC(index);
        s[index]:=NULL;
        Read(ch)
    END
END ReadLine;

END MyIO.
```

Separate compilation of the DEFINITION MODULE and the IMPLEMENTATION MODULE is usually required, in which case the DEFINITION MODULE must be compiled BEFORE it is possible to compile the IMPLEMENTATION MODULE.

12.2.2   Program modules

We have written the MyIO module to provide facilities to other program modules; neither the definition nor the implementation modules can be run independently. The procedures must be imported into a program module, such as the following:

```
MODULE TryMyIO;

FROM MyIO IMPORT WriteStringLn, ReadLine;

VAR
    s : ARRAY [0..100] OF CHAR;
BEGIN
    WriteStringLn("Please type in a line of text ");
    ReadLine(s);
    WriteStringLn("The text was: ");
    WriteStringLn(s)
END TryMyIO.
```

The TryMyIO module is a program module, just as all the previous programs in this book have been program modules. This can be saved as TryMyIO.mod.

A complete Modula-2 program can consist of as many definition and implementation module pairs as you wish, but must always have one, and ONLY one, driving program module.

When you compile a program which imports from another module you must remember to include that module name in the list of modules to link when creating the executable version of your program.

12.3 Modules: raison d'être

12.3.1 Encapsulation and information hiding

The MyIO library module can be kept, and its facilities utilized, by any program we write. When writing MyIO there was no need to worry about the exact nature of future program modules that might use it. We can add to the facilities of MyIO or alter its implementation details at any time without affecting the programs that already use it.

The use of modules:
- allows code to be reused by many programs;
- makes it much easier to write and test large programs;
- allows implementation details of a module to be changed without affecting the other program modules; a feature which makes it easier to transfer programs between different types of computer, as only machine specific modules will need to be altered.

You may find it a helpful analogy to think of a stacking hi-fi system, perhaps with a tape deck, a record turntable, a radio tuner, a CD player and an amplifier. The amplifier may make use of all the other parts and the tape deck may make use of the tuner for recording radio programs, etc. There are clearly defined connections between the parts, as well as clearly defined controls to allow you to operate the system. The units of the system are analogous to implementation modules; they are separately packaged units, independently testable and replaceable, and the electronics within are of little concern to most of us. We can certainly use the system without knowledge of the detailed internal workings; we need know only how to connect it up and how to operate the controls. Each unit has its own array of controls and connecting plugs. These are analogous to definition modules. They provide the interface through which we can get the unit to work. Even when interconnected, these modules do nothing until you operate the controls so, in this situation, you are analogous to a program module calling the functions of the system.
So, modules allow program parts to be encapsulated into neat packages, each of which hides its detailed working from the modules that use it. The nitty-gritty details are hidden, with data objects and control structures accessed and manipulated via a specified set of procedures. This is known as **information hiding**.

12.4   Definition, implementation and client modules

12.4.1   Definition modules

Definition modules can contain:
- IMPORT statements to import facilities from other modules,
- constant definitions,
- type definitions,
- variable definitions,
- procedure definitions (i.e. procedure headings only - not full declarations).

Definitions and declarations are almost the same thing, except that a definition may contain less information. Procedure declarations contain the complete code to implement the procedure, while a procedure definition consists only of its heading. A type definition may be provided in the form of its full declaration or simply by giving its identifying name.

A definition module needs to include only those facilities which are to be exportable.

Declarations and the headings of procedures used only within the implementation part are not required in the definition module.

With modern compilers, all facilities defined in the definition module are automatically exportable, but older systems required that the definition module contain a list of exportable facilities in a statement preceded by the words EXPORT QUALIFIED.

Visibility to other program parts:

All definition module facilities are available to the corresponding implementation module, with the exception, of course, of facilities imported from other modules which, remember, must be separately imported.

All definition module facilities are also available for import by other program modules.

12.4.2   Implementation modules

Apart from the word IMPLEMENTATION at the beginning, implementation modules look very much like program modules and they can contain the same kind of things:
- IMPORT statements to import facilities from other modules,
- constant declarations,
- type declarations,
- variable declarations,
- procedure declarations, and
- a module body between BEGIN and END.

The implementation module contains the code required to implement the facilities listed for export in the corresponding definition module, as well as any unexported facilities that are required locally within the implementation module. Modules can also contain local modules.

Unlike a program module, an implementation module does not always require a module body between BEGIN and END, as is the case with MyIO. We'll explain this more fully later.

Visibility to other program parts:
All of the corresponding definition module facilities are available to an implementation module so, for example, if a type is fully declared in the definition module, the implementation module may make use of it and should not try to redeclare it. However, there is an exception; facilities imported from other modules by a definition module must be imported separately by the implementation module if it also needs to make use of the same facilities.

12.4.3   Calling or client module

This can be another definition module, an implementation module or a program module. The client module does not need information on the contents of the implementation module, only on the contents of the definition module, to determine the facilities that are available and the form of call required.

The client module must contain an import statement, which can be of the form:

```
FROM LibMod IMPORT Const1,Type1,var1,ProcA,ProcB;
```

where LibMod identifies the library module from which facilities are to be obtained and Const1, Type1, var1, etc., identify the constants, types, variables and procedures to be imported.

In an alternative form of **IMPORT** statement the facilities to be imported are not explicitly listed:

```
IMPORT LibMod;
```

However, this makes it necessary to prefix (or qualify) all imported calls with the module identifying name, thus:

```
VAR
    num : LibMod.Type1;
BEGIN
    LibMod.ProcA(.............);
    ....
END;
```

12.5 A string handling module

Most Modula-2 compilers provide a library module to support character string handling. As an example, here's a small module, StringStuff, to provide three particularly useful facilities:
- to return the length of a string,
- to assign the contents of one string variable to another of different length and
- to compare the contents of one string variable with another.

Check if your compiler has a similar module. What other facilities does it provide?

The DEFINITION module:

```
DEFINITION MODULE StringStuff;

TYPE
    Result=(same,greater,less);

    PROCEDURE StringLen(s:ARRAY OF CHAR):CARDINAL;
    (*Returns the length of the string s*)

    PROCEDURE StringCopy(orig:ARRAY OF CHAR;
                         VAR copy:ARRAY OF CHAR;
                         VAR success:BOOLEAN);
    (*Copies a string from orig to copy*)

    PROCEDURE StringCompare(s1,s2:ARRAY OF CHAR):Result;
    (*Compares s1 and s2 character by character until
    **one is found to be less than the other or they are
    **found to be the same*)

END StringStuff.
```

and the corresponding IMPLEMENTATION module:

```
IMPLEMENTATION MODULE StringStuff;

    PROCEDURE StringLen(s:ARRAY OF CHAR):CARDINAL;
    CONST
        NULL=0C;
    VAR
        index:CARDINAL;
    BEGIN
        index:=0;
        WHILE (index<=HIGH(s)) AND (s[index]<>NULL) DO
            INC(index)
        END;   (*WHILE*)
        RETURN index
    END StringLen;
```

```
PROCEDURE StringCopy( orig:ARRAY OF CHAR;
                      VAR copy:ARRAY OF CHAR;
                      VAR success:BOOLEAN);
CONST
    NULL=0C;
VAR
    index:CARDINAL;
BEGIN
    index:=0;
    IF HIGH(copy)<HIGH(orig) THEN
        success:= FALSE
    ELSE
        WHILE (index<StringLen(orig)) DO
            copy[index]:=orig[index];
            INC(index);
        END;   (*WHILE*)
        copy[index]:=NULL;
        success:=TRUE
    END (*IF*)
END StringCopy;


PROCEDURE StringCompare(s1,s2:ARRAY OF CHAR):Result;
CONST
    NULL=0C;
VAR
    ch1,ch2:CHAR;
    index:CARDINAL;
BEGIN
    index:=0;
    LOOP
        IF index>HIGH(s1) THEN
            ch1:=NULL
        ELSE
            ch1:=s1[index]
        END;
        IF index>HIGH(s2) THEN
            ch2:=NULL
        ELSE
            ch2:=s2[index]
        END;
        IF ch1<ch2 THEN
            RETURN less
        ELSIF ch1>ch2 THEN
            RETURN greater
        ELSIF (ch1=ch2) AND (ch1=NULL) THEN
            RETURN same
        END;
        INC(index)
    END (*LOOP*)
END StringCompare;

END StringStuff.
```

The following program module demonstrates the use of StringCompare. Notice that we have not only had to import the procedure StringCompare, but also Result type.

```
MODULE CompareTest;

FROM StringStuff IMPORT StringCompare,Result;
FROM InOut IMPORT WriteString, WriteLn,ReadString;

VAR
    str1 : ARRAY [0..5] OF CHAR;
    str2 : ARRAY [0..5] OF CHAR;

BEGIN
    WriteString("Input a string of characters");
    WriteLn;
    ReadString(str1);
    WriteString("Input another string of characters");
    WriteLn;
    ReadString(str2);

    IF StringCompare(str1,str2)=same THEN
        WriteString("The same");
    ELSIF StringCompare(str1,str2)=greater THEN
        WriteString("The first is greater");
    ELSIF StringCompare(str1,str2)=less THEN
        WriteString("The first is less")
    END;
    WriteLn
END CompareTest.
```

Exercise 12.1

Write a procedure to concatenate (i.e. join together one after the other) two strings of characters. Incorporate this procedure into StringStuff.

12.6   Module initialization and compilation

12.6.1   Module body

You may recall from the earlier discussion on scope rules that a variable declared locally within a procedure exists only as long as the procedure is executing. When a procedure ends, so does the life of all its local variables, so values are not retained between one call and the next. This, however, is not the case with modules. Any variables declared at the outer level of a module are said to be **static**; that is they retain their value throughout the life of the program. This means that we need initialize variables belonging to a module only once at the start of program execution. To allow this to be done, Modula-2 permits an optional body section to be included in an implementation module. The body statements of all imported modules are executed ONCE before execution of the program module body begins.

The following is a module we will be making use of in Chapter 17. It provides facilities for generating 'random' numbers. The principle used is based on the 'linear congruential method' developed by D.Lehmer. To set things going, a starting number is required. This is called a seed. The method uses the seed to calculate a new value in an expression of the form:

```
seed := (MULTFACTOR * seed + ADDVALUE ) MOD MODVALUE
```

The seed is assigned a starting value, and the expression is applied to give a new value to which the expression is again applied.
MULTFACTOR, ADDVALUE, and MODVALUE are constants carefully selected to give a reasonable series of pseudo-random results.

RandomNum includes a body to initialize a random seed value.

```
DEFINITION MODULE RandomNum;
(*Linear congruential method.
**See D.Lehmer in Random Number Generators:
** Good ones are Hard to Find, Park and Miller,
**Communications of the ACM Oct 1988, p.1192
*)
(*Take a start seed value and change it on each cycle:
**
**   seed:= (MULTFACTOR * seed + ADDVALUE) MOD MODVALUE;
**
**   to produce numbers ranging from 0 to MODVALUE-1
*)

PROCEDURE Rand(VAR seed:CARDINAL):REAL;
(*Returns a 'pseudo-random' number between 0 and 1*)

PROCEDURE Random(n :CARDINAL):CARDINAL;
(*Returns 'pseudo-random' numbers exponentially
**distributed about n*)
END RandomNum.
```

```
IMPLEMENTATION MODULE RandomNum;
(*Linear congruential method.
**See D.Lehmer in Random Number Generators:
** Good ones are Hard to Find, Park and Miller,
**Communications of the ACM Oct 1988, p.1192
*)
(*Take a start seed value and change it on each cycle:
**      seed:= (MULTFACTOR*seed + ADDVALUE) MOD MODVALUE;
**  to produce numbers ranging from 0 to MODVALUE-1
*)
FROM MathLib0 IMPORT ln;
VAR
    seed:CARDINAL;

PROCEDURE Rand(VAR seed:CARDINAL):REAL;
(*Returns a 'pseudo-random' number between 0 and 1*)
CONST
    MULTFACTOR=25173;
    ADDVALUE=13849;
    MODVALUE=MAX(CARDINAL);
BEGIN
    seed:=(MULTFACTOR*seed + ADDVALUE) MOD MODVALUE;
    RETURN FLOAT(seed)/FLOAT(MODVALUE)
END Rand;

PROCEDURE Random(n : CARDINAL):CARDINAL;
(*Returns 'pseudo-random' numbers exponentially
**distributed about n*)
BEGIN
    RETURN TRUNC((-(FLOAT(n)) * ln(Rand(seed)))+1.0)
END Random;

BEGIN
    seed:=13;   (*Initialize seed value*)
END RandomNum.
```

12.6.2   Order of module initialization

To ensure that modules are initialized in the correct order, we must be certain that no module tries to make use of facilities imported from another before the imported module has been initialized. Therefore, the bodies of all imported modules must be executed before the bodies of their client modules. If a client module imports from several other modules their bodies are executed in the order that they occur in the IMPORT statement. The main program module body is always the last to be executed.

In practice the compiler takes care of these things for us but, as programmers, we need to be aware of the order in which things will happen so we can ensure we do not attempt to use uninitialized variables.

A tricky situation could occur when say, module A, imports from module B which, in turn, imports from module A. Which initialization comes first? The answer is, the compiler will make a choice, which may or may not be what the programmer had in mind.

12.6.3   Order of compilation

With compilation, order is again important. The key rules are:
- definition modules must be compiled before their corresponding implementation modules and
- as modules that import from others require the information contained in the definition modules, definition modules must be compiled before their corresponding client modules.

For example, if our program is to consist of the following modules:

```
StringStuff.def
StringStuff.mod
Sort.def
Sort.mod
MainProg.mod
```

where `Sort.mod` is to import from `StringStuff.def` and `MainProg.mod` is to import from `StringStuff.def` and `Sort.def`, the situation can be shown graphically using a module dependency diagram:

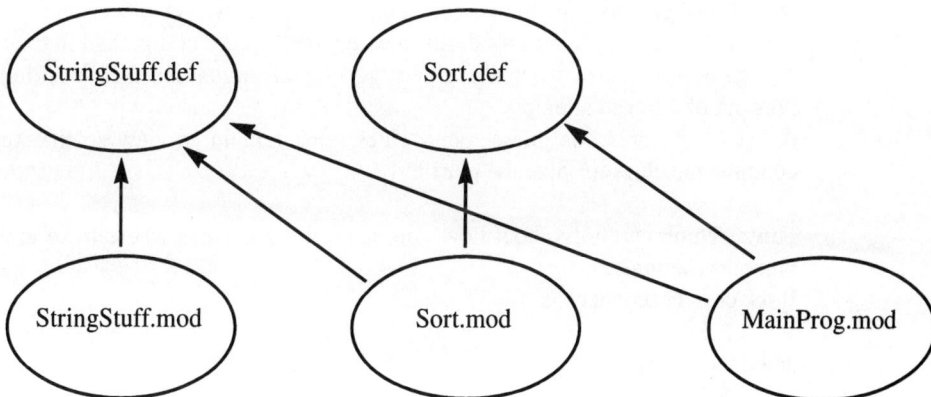

In this case there are a number of alternative compilation orders, although it is safest to compile all definition modules before compiling any implementation modules, as follows:

```
1st    StringStuff.def
2nd    StringStuff.mod
3rd    Sort.def
4th    Sort.mod
5th    MainProg.mod
```

Self test 12.1

Given the module dependency diagram described in the text, what alternative compilation orders are permissible?

Exercise 12.2

Write a guessing game program which imports RandomNum and calls for a random number in the range 0-50. It should allow, let's say, five guesses from the player before displaying the number. You may also like to include some clues, such as 'too high', 'too low', or 'very near', depending on the player's response.

Exercise 12.3

Design and write a 'Mastermind' game using four single digit random numbers (0-9) which the player needs to guess correctly and in the correct sequence. After each guess at the four digits, the player is given clues using white 'pegs' to indicate how many of the four digits guessed are the correct digit but in the wrong place, and black 'pegs' to indicate how many of the four digits guessed are the correct digit and in the correct place. The game is finished when the player guesses all digits and their position correctly or runs out of allowed attempts.

A list of the previous guesses and clues must remain in view so that the player can combine the clues to solve the puzzle.

Hint: Think carefully about how you determine the clues where there are two or more numbers the same.

If the correct sequence is

    5 2 5 4

and the guess is

    5 5 2 3

the clues given should be:

    1 black

    2 white

Allow a limit of, say, 10 guesses before revealing the answer.

Exercise 12.4

Write a program which makes use of the StringStuff procedures to read in two words and find out how many characters there are in each word. If the words are different lengths then output the longer of the two words with a suitable message. If the words are the same length then compare the words to determine whether they are identical and output the result.

Exercise 12.5

a) Design and write your own definition and implementation module for a set of
procedures to carry out and support matrix arithmetic. Begin by making the routines
work for for 2 x 2 matrices, but try to make it easy to adapt the module for square
matrices of any size.

Here are some suggested procedures for inclusion in your module:
```
MatrixRead
MatrixWrite
MatrixAdd
MatrixSubtract
MatrixTranspose
MatrixMultiply
Determinant
MatrixInvert
```

b) Write a program which imports and uses all the matrix procedures. Use this program
to test the procedures.

c) Take a copy of your matrix arithmetic module and modify it to process 3 x 3
matrices. If necessary, adapt your driver program so that you can test the new
procedures.

13   Sorting and searching algorithms

13.1   Sorting

Speed is one of the pre-occupations of computer scientists.

So how can computers be made to run faster and more efficiently?

Well, one way is to develop new and better hardware, but another method is to develop more efficient algorithms.

As computers can be particularly good at the kind of task we humans would find long, monotonous and boring, a major objective in the quest for speed has been how best to carry out long, highly repetitive jobs, such as searching through large amounts of data. This kind of task is so commonly required and so repetitive in nature, the potential for time saving is high.

Experience of searching for a number in a telephone directory will tell you that searching is a whole lot easier if the information is already sorted. Like searching, sorting is another often long and monotonous task, so both searching and sorting are potentially productive areas in which to apply fast and efficient algorithms.

We will start by looking at four sorting techniques, exploring the pros and cons of each:

* selection sort,
* insertion sort,
* bubble sort and
* 'QuickSort'.

To illustrate each of these algorithms, let's assume we are sorting an array of just five cardinal numbers:

5	4	2	6	3

and that we wish to sort them in ascending numerical order to give:

2	3	4	5	6

In the following examples, numbers in the array that have been sorted are shown in bold figures.

13.1.1   Selection sort

For this technique, we must look along the array to select the lowest value, then exchange it with the first array element. We then look for the next lowest value and exchange that with the second array element, and so on until the whole array is sorted.
So, with our example array, the start situation is:

5	4	2	6	3

We select the lowest value, which in this case is 2, and swap it with the first array value, 5, to give:

2	4	5	6	3

Now we select the lowest value in the remaining unsorted part of the array, 3, and exchange it with the second array element, 4:

2	3	5	6	4

This process continues with the next lowest value, 4, being exchanged with the third array element, 5:

2	3	4	6	5

The process continues until the part of the array to be sorted contains only the last element, which must by then be the largest, and the sort finishes.

2	3	4	5	6

Here's a procedure to sort an array of numbers using a Selection sort:

```
PROCEDURE Selection(VAR list : ARRAY OF CARDINAL);
VAR
    start,current,smallest : CARDINAL;
    temp:CARDINAL;
BEGIN
    FOR start:=0 TO HIGH(list)-1 DO
        smallest:=start;
        FOR current:=start TO HIGH(list) DO
            (*Compares to find the smallest*)
            IF list[current]<list[smallest] THEN
                smallest:=current
            END (*IF*)
        END; (*FOR*)

        IF smallest<>start THEN (*swap*)
            temp:=list[start];
            list[start]:=list[smallest];
            list[smallest]:=temp
        END (*IF*)
    END (*FOR*)
END Selection;
```

13.1.2   Insertion sort

In this sorting method the size of the sorted array is increased by one on each pass, starting with the first element. The first pass is trivial, since a single-element array needs no sorting! Effectively, the second element is taken from the array, compared and inserted in the correct sorted position relative to the first element. The first two elements now constitute the sorted part of the array. The third array element can now be removed and inserted in the correct position in the sorted front portion of the array.

So, using our example array, the start situation is:

5	4	2	6	3

The first element is considered to be already sorted in relation to itself and constitutes the sorted portion of the array:

5	4	2	6	3

The next element is compared with the first and inserted in its correct order:

4	5	2	6	3

The sorted portion of the array is now the sub-array consisting of the first two elements. Next, the third element is inserted in its correct position relative to the first two:

2	4	5	6	3

Notice how elements in the sorted portion of the array must be shifted along the array to accommodate inserted elements.

The process continues with the next element, in this case 6, being inserted in the correct position in the sorted array portion:

2	4	5	6	3

With our example numbers there is no actual movement at this step because 6 happens to be in the correct position already.

The process continues until there are no more unsorted elements remaining:

2	3	4	5	6

and the array is sorted.

Here's a procedure to sort an array of numbers using Insertion sort:

```
PROCEDURE Insertion(VAR list : ARRAY OF CARDINAL);
VAR
    start,current : CARDINAL;
    temp:CARDINAL;
BEGIN
    FOR start:=1 TO HIGH(list) DO
        current:=start;
        temp:=list[start];
        WHILE (current<>0) AND (list[current-1]>temp) DO
            (*Do swap*)
            list[current]:=list[current-1];
            DEC(current)
        END; (*WHILE*)
        list[current]:=temp
    END (*FOR*)
END Insertion;
```

13.1.3   Bubble sort

This algorithm starts by comparing the first two elements to find the larger. If necessary it swaps the element positions so that the larger element of the two occupies the second array position. The second and third elements are then compared and swapped if necessary so that the larger is in the third array position. This process continues until the end of the array is reached, at which point the largest element must have made its way into the last element position. Ignoring the last element position, the whole process is repeated to 'bubble' the next largest element to the end, and so on until the whole array is sorted.

Again, using our example array to illustrate, the start position is:

5	4	2	6	3

Firstly, 5 and 4 are compared and swapped so that the larger is moved to the right to occupy the second array position:

4	5	2	6	3

Next 5 and 2 are compared and swapped so that the larger element is moved to the right:

4	2	5	6	3

Now 5 and 6 are compared but no swap is necessary as the larger is already on the right hand side:

4	2	5	6	3

And now 6 and 3:

4	2	5	3	**6**

The end of the array has been reached so we can be sure that the largest array element is on the extreme right-hand side and this constitutes the part of the array sorted so far.

The above process continues to 'bubble' the next largest element to the right hand side of the unsorted part of the array:

Compare 4 and 2, swapping if necessary (which is necessary in this case):

2	4	5	3	**6**

Compare 4 and 5, swapping if necessary (which isn't necessary in this case):

2	4	5	3	**6**

Compare 5 and 3, swapping if necessary (which is necessary in this case):

2	4	3	**5**	**6**

The sorted right-hand portion of the array now contains two elements.
The process continues:

Compare 2 and 4, swapping if necessary (which isn't necessary in this case):

2	4	3	**5**	**6**

Compare 4 and 3, swapping if necessary (which is necessary in this case):

2	3	**4**	**5**	**6**

Finally compare 2 and 3, swapping if necessary (which isn't necessary in this case):

2	**3**	**4**	**5**	**6**

Here's a procedure to sort an array of numbers using a Bubble sort:

```
PROCEDURE Bubble(VAR list : ARRAY OF CARDINAL);
VAR
    last,current:CARDINAL;
    temp:CARDINAL;
BEGIN

    FOR last:=HIGH(list) TO 1 BY -1 DO
        FOR current:=1 TO last DO
            (*Do comparison*)
            IF list[current]< list[current-1] THEN (*swap*)
                temp:=list[current];
                list[current]:=list[current-1];
                list[current-1]:=temp
            END (*IF*)
        END (*FOR*)
    END (*FOR*)
END Bubble;
```

13.1.4   Module: `Sort`

The following program module provides a means of testing the selection sort procedure. It incorporates two counters. The first compares and counts the number of comparisons made during the sorting process. The second, swaps and counts the number of times that data elements are exchanged. This information will be useful for evaluating the relative efficiency of the different sorting methods.

```
MODULE Sort;
(*Purpose: To carry out a Selection sort on 9
**cardinal numbers
**Uses module: InOut
*)
FROM InOut IMPORT WriteString,WriteLn,WriteCard,
                                  ReadCard,Read;
CONST
    LIMIT = 9;
VAR
    list : ARRAY [0..LIMIT-1] OF CARDINAL;

PROCEDURE GetArray(VAR list : ARRAY OF CARDINAL);
VAR
    num,index:CARDINAL;

BEGIN
    WriteString('Please type in ');
    WriteCard(LIMIT,1);
    WriteString(' cardinals ');
    WriteLn;
    FOR index:=0 TO LIMIT-1 DO
        WriteString('Next number : ');
        ReadCard(list[index]);
        WriteLn
    END (*FOR*)
END GetArray;
```

```
PROCEDURE Selection(VAR list : ARRAY OF CARDINAL);
VAR
    start,current,smallest : CARDINAL;
    temp:CARDINAL;
    compares,swaps:CARDINAL;
BEGIN
    compares:=0;
    swaps:=0;
    FOR start:=0 TO HIGH(list)-1 DO
        smallest:=start;
        FOR current:=start TO HIGH(list) DO
            (*Compares to find the smallest*)
            INC(compares);
            IF list[current]<list[smallest] THEN
                smallest:=current
            END (*IF*)
        END; (*FOR*)
        IF smallest<>start THEN (*swap*)
            INC(swaps);
            temp:=list[start];
            list[start]:=list[smallest];
            list[smallest]:=temp
        END (*IF*)
    END; (*FOR*)
    WriteString('The number of comparisons was : ');
    WriteCard(compares,1);
    WriteLn;
    WriteString('The number of swaps was : ');
    WriteCard(swaps,1);
    WriteLn
END Selection;

PROCEDURE DisplayArray(list : ARRAY OF CARDINAL);
VAR
    index:CARDINAL;
BEGIN
    FOR index:=0 TO HIGH(list) DO
        WriteCard(list[index],1);
        WriteLn
    END (*FOR*)
END DisplayArray;

BEGIN
    GetArray(list);
    Selection(list);
    DisplayArray(list)
END Sort.
```

13.1.5   An aside on recursion

Before we look at a fourth sorting method, the 'QuickSort', we need to digress. Remember, that every time we call a procedure it sets aside space for its own set of local variables and formal parameter values. This means that it is possible to have many instances of the same procedure in existence at the same time. This is, in fact, what happens when a procedure calls itself. A procedure that calls itself is said to be recursive and although, at first consideration, this might seem like a pretty pointless thing to do, it is another way in which we can achieve iteration within a program. Recursion can provide a particularly neat solution to certain types of programming problem.

To illustrate the principle of recursion, consider how to calculate the factorial of a number:

$$5! = 5 \times 4 \times 3 \times 2 \times 1 = 120$$
$$4! = 4 \times 3 \times 2 \times 1 = 24$$
$$3! = 3 \times 2 \times 1 = 6$$
$$2! = 2 \times 1 = 2$$
$$1! = 1$$
$$0! = 1$$

This is an ideal candidate for a recursive procedure, and here it is:

```
PROCEDURE Factorial (num: CARDINAL) : CARDINAL;
BEGIN
    IF num<=1 THEN
        RETURN    1
    ELSE
        RETURN   (num * Factorial(num-1))
    END (*IF*)
END Factorial;
```

If the call, `Factorial(4)` is made, it returns the value of:

```
4 * Factorial(3)
```

that is, after making the call, `Factorial(3)`, which returns the value of:

```
3 * Factorial(2)
```

that is, after making the call, `Factorial(2)`, which returns the value of:

```
2 * Factorial(1)
```

that is, after making the call, `Factorial(1)`, which returns the value of:

```
1
```

Thus;

```
Factorial(1) evaluates to 1,
Factorial(2) evaluates to 2 * Factorial(1), i.e. 2,
Factorial(3) evaluates to 3 * Factorial(2), i.e. 6,
Factorial(4) evaluates to 4 * Factorial(3), i.e. 24,
```

Here's a trickier, but more graphic example of recursion. There is a programming language called LOGO, or turtle graphics, which is often used in schools to demonstrate how computers can be used for controlling a mobile object called a turtle. In its simplest form the turtle is a character displayed on a computer screen and which can be positioned, moved and made to draw patterns, using instructions like:

FORWARD 20
RIGHT 90

Suppose that we wish to write a procedure in LOGO to draw the pattern below:

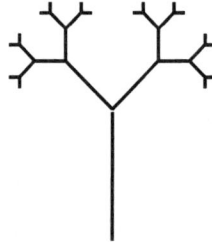

Note that the pattern is regular and symmetrical but, more importantly, it is recursive and at each node (or junction) there are smaller instances of the overall pattern.

To draw the pattern a simple basic procedure needs to be followed and repeated.

Imagine that we are going to draw the pattern by hand and have plenty of willing helpers. We could draw the first vertical line, starting at the bottom. On reaching the top, we turn 45° clockwise and get one of the helpers to draw a line, half the length of our's, in this new direction. We then turn 90° anti-clockwise and send a second helper to draw a similar line, but in this new direction. We then turn 45° clockwise and reverse back along the first line, so that we finish at the same place, and facing in the same direction as we started.
At the end of their respective lines, each helper does the same as we did, and recruits two more helpers, who do the same, and so on and so on ....

As with any iterative process, we need to have a way of stopping the repetition.

Self test 13.1

How is the iterative process stopped within our `Factorial` procedure?

We will stop our pattern drawing process when the line length is down to 1 unit.

Starting from the root, facing upwards, this is what the procedure needs to do:

DrawTree(length):
    IF (length >1) THEN
        move turtle forwards (length) units
        turn turtle clockwise by 45°
        DrawTree(length/2)
        turn turtle anti-clockwise by 90°
        DrawTree(length/2)
        move turtle back to start by turning clockwise by 45° then
        moving backwards (length) units
    END IF
END DrawTree

With an initial value of `length` equal to 32, the branches of the tree would have lengths 32, 16, 8, 4 and 2 units.

The following page shows the procedure expanded to illustrate the effect of a call to `DrawTree` with the initial value of `length` set to 4.

Incidently, there is a long standing joke amongst computer scientists that the entry for recursion in a dictionary of computing terms should be:

    Recursion: *See recursion*

Self test 13.2

What would be the result of omitting the IF statement from the `DrawTree` procedure?

```
DrawTree(4):
   IF (4 >1) THEN
      move turtle forwards 4 units
      turn turtle clockwise by 45°

      DrawTree(2):
         IF (2 >1) THEN
            move turtle forwards 2 units
            turn turtle clockwise by 45°

            DrawTree(1):
               IF (1 >1) THEN
               END IF
            END DrawTree(1)

            turn turtle anti-clockwise by 90°

            DrawTree(1):
               IF (1 >1)THEN
               END IF
            END DrawTree(1)

            move back to start by turning clockwise by 45°
            then moving backwards 2 units
         END IF
      END DrawTree(2)

      turn turtle anti-clockwise by 90°

      DrawTree(2):
         IF (2 >1) THEN
            move turtle forwards 2 units
            turn turtle clockwise by 45°

            DrawTree(1):
               IF (1 >1) THEN
               END IF
            END DrawTree(1)

            turn turtle anti-clockwise by 90°

            DrawTree(1):
               IF (1 >1) THEN
               END IF
            END DrawTree(1)

            move back to start by turning clockwise by 45°
            then moving backwards 2 units
         END IF
      END DrawTree(2)

      move back to start by turning clockwise by 45°
      then moving backwards 4 units

   END IF
END DrawTree(4)
```

13.1.6   QuickSort

This algorithm is a particularly ingenious one and, as you may have guessed, it uses recursion. It was invented by C.A.R. Hoare and works on the principle that if we can sub-divide the list to be sorted, ensuring that all values in the left part are less than the values in the right part, we can continue this sub-division process with each sub-divided part until each part is a single element. Put the parts back together and we have a sorted list.

We will illustrate using a similar list as before.

5	4	2	6	1

The first step is to select a pivot value which will mark the division between the smaller and larger values. It is not essential, but seems reasonable, to plump for the value at the middle of the list; in this case 2.

Working from the left, look for any number greater than or equal to the pivot value and, working from the right, look for any number less than or equal to the pivot value, then swap them.

1	4	2	6	5

Repeat this process until the left and right searches meet one another.

1	2	4	6	5

The values to the left of the pivot value are now all lower and the values to the right all higher.

The list is now sub-divided at the point where the searches met.

1	2		4	6	5

Each of these lists is put through the complete QuickSort process.

For the first list, let's assume we select 1 as the pivot value. No swapping takes place and the left and right searches meet immediately. The sub-division process results in individual elements, so sorting stops.

For the second list, let's assume we take 6 as the pivot value. Swapping results in

4	5	6

This list is then sub-divided into

4	5		6

The QuickSort process is applied to the left sub-list, each sub-list ends up as a single element and the process ends; the list is sorted.

Here is a QuickSort procedure in Modula-2, incorporating counts of swaps and comparisons:

```
CONST
    START = 1; (*Any CARDINAL >=1 and <FINISH*)
    FINISH = 9;
TYPE
    ArrayType = ARRAY [START..FINISH] OF CARDINAL;

PROCEDURE QuickSort(VAR list : ArrayType;
                    start, finish : CARDINAL;
                    VAR swaps, compares:CARDINAL);
VAR
    left, right : CARDINAL;
    pivot,temp : CARDINAL;
BEGIN
    left := start;
    right := finish;
    pivot := list[(start + finish) DIV 2];
    REPEAT
        WHILE list[left]<pivot DO
            INC(left);
            INC(compares);
        END; (*WHILE*)
        WHILE pivot<list[right] DO
            DEC(right);
            INC(compares);
        END; (*WHILE*)
        IF left <=right THEN
            INC(swaps);
            temp :=list[left];
            list[left] := list[right];
            list[right] := temp;
            INC(left);
            DEC(right)
        END; (*IF*)
    UNTIL (right <=left);
    IF start < right THEN
        QuickSort(list,start,right,swaps,compares)
    END; (*IF*)
    IF left < finish THEN
        QuickSort(list,left,finish,swaps,compares)
    END (*IF*)
END QuickSort;
```

13.1.7   Comparison of sorting algorithms

When sorting 5, 10 or even 20 items, it really doesn't matter which sorting method is used. However, when applied to thousands of data elements there can be large differences in algorithm performance.

In general, when choosing between algorithms, it helps to be able to quantify the merits of the alternative options. Since sorting involves comparison between data values and re-arrangement of order by swapping or shifting, keeping count of these two activities provides a way of assessing relative efficiency.

Exercise 13.1

Write new versions of the Sort program in Section 13.1.4 to obtain counts of comparisons and swaps required when running:

     a)   a selection sort,
     b)   an insertion sort,
     c)   a bubble sort and
     d)   QuickSort

on:
     (i)   randomly ordered data,
     (ii)   already sorted data,
     (iii)   partially sorted data and
     (iv)   reverse ordered data.

Conduct a number of trials and tabulate your results. Subsequently, determine the advantages and disadvantages of each sorting algorithm when compared with the others. (Remember to initialize swaps and compares to zero before calling QuickSort.)

13.2   Big O notation

Counting comparisons and swaps provides one measure of efficiency. Another approach is to examine the structure of an algorithm to ascertain the relationship between the number of items being processed, N, and the number of passes or iterations which are required.

Big O notation gives an indication of the Order of the algorithm, e.g.

An O(N) algorithm is one which takes in the order of N iterations to process N items. This type of algorithm is most likely to be one that contains a single loop, with one item processed on each pass. The time that the algorithm takes to complete the task is directly proportional to the number of items being processed.

An algorithm which contains a loop within a loop would be classed as an $O(N^2)$ algorithm.

Using the Big O notation to represent the efficiencies of sorting algorithms gives the following information:

Sort type	Data set	Order	Comments
Selection	Any	$O(N^2)$	On any trip through the data only two elements are exchanged. The number of iterations is not affected by how ordered the data is prior to the sort.
Insertion	Random order	$O(N^2)$	This is the worst case for this algorithm.
	Already partially sorted	$O(N)$	Approaches this value for partially sorted data.
Bubble	Random order	$O(N^2)$	Poor performance for a jumbled array, but can be as efficient as the insertion sort if already partially sorted.
QuickSort	Already sorted	$O(N^2)$	The worst case for this algorithm.
	Random order	$O(Nlog_2N)$	Generally significantly faster than the other sorting algorithms.

Self test 13.3

The code segment below is for a sorting algorithm:

```
FOR limit:=2 TO sortCount  DO
    temp:=val[limit]
    prev:=limit
    WHILE (prev<>1) AND (val[prev-1]<=temp) DO
        val[prev]:=val[prev-1]
        prev:=prev-1
    END; (*WHILE*)
    val[prev]:=temp
END (*FOR*)
```

Which of the following describes the nature of this sort?

a) A descending sequence Bubble Sort.
b) An ascending sequence Selection Sort.
c) A descending sequence Insertion Sort.
d) An ascending sequence Quick Sort.

Exercise 13.2

Modify each of the sorting algorithms to sort in descending order.

Exercise 13.3

By making use of the StringStuff module described in Chapter 12, modify Sort to input and sort a list of names into alphabetical order.

Exercise 13.4

The calculation of compound interest can be performed as a recursive function. The input parameters required by this function are:

- amount of money invested, i.e. the principal,
- interest rate as a percentage, i.e. the rate,
- number of years for investment, i.e. the term

On each recursive call the function must return the total value of the money invested as a function of (term-1) years:

```
RETURN CompoundInterest(principal+interest,rate,term-1)
```

    where interest: = principal * rate / 100

This constitutes a recursive call to the function.

The limiting condition, which stops the recursion, occurs when (term <= 0). In this case just the input value of principal is returned.

Write the procedure CompoundInterest in the way described, and use it in a program to calculate and display compound interest for valid values of principal, rate and term.

Exercise 13.5

The calculations to determine mortgage repayments over a given period are very similar to those used in calculating compound interest. Write a recursive procedure to calculate the monthly repayment amount for a given mortgage total, interest rate and term. Use this procedure in a program which inputs and validates the three values and outputs the results.

13.3 Searching

In this section we'll introduce some alternative strategies for searching for an item of data in a list.

13.3.1 Linear search

To begin with, consider the potentially real search problem of finding a particular car in a large car park. Car parks usually have level numbers and other spatial cues, such as the position of lifts, are normally available to help. You may not normally be absent-minded, but imagine that your perception of these cues has failed you and you have no idea where you have left your car. In this situation you might have to resort to a systematic search by starting at one end of the car park and sequentially working along the rows of cars until you find it or conclude that it has been stolen, (or that you are in the wrong car park).

Here's the search algorithm:

```
Start with first car in car park
WHILE cars left AND NOT found your car DO
     look at next car
END WHILE
IF found your car THEN
     drive home
ELSE
     call the police
END IF
```

This is a linear search and, if you're lucky, it could result in finding your car very quickly. On the other hand it may turn out that your car is the last one you look at. Even if you imagine that you had the ability to instantly transport yourself to any location within the car park it wouldn't help matters. This is the kind of search technique we used in the bar code program in Chapter 9 and the doctor's dilemma program in Chapter 10.

On average, the technique is likely to require that you check half the total number of parked cars. This gives some idea of the efficiency of this as a search technique. If there are 500 cars in the car park, then on average you would have to look at 250 of them before finding yours. So generally, if the number of items to be searched through is N, then a linear search algorithm, on average, requires N/2 cycles or iterations. Using Big O notation, this gives a worst case of $O(N)$ and an average of $O(N/2)$.

Assuming the type declarations:

```
TYPE
    WordType = ARRAY [0..50] OF CHAR;
    ListType = ARRAY [1..100] OF WordType;
```

the following procedure implements a linear search through an array of 100 names:

```
PROCEDURE Linear(list:ListType;name : ARRAY OF CHAR;
                         VAR foundWord:BOOLEAN;
                         VAR position:CARDINAL);
(*Linear name search
**Uses StringCompare from StringStuff*)
CONST
    NULL=0C;
BEGIN
    foundWord:=FALSE;
    position:=1;
    WHILE (position<=100) AND (NOT foundWord) DO
        IF (StringCompare(name,list[position])=same) THEN
            foundWord:=TRUE
        ELSE
            INC(position)
        END (*IF*)
    END (*WHILE*)
END Linear;
```

A randomly ordered telephone directory would necessitate long linear searches and would become virtually useless, but if we have some control over the way items are stored we can make searching much easier.

13.3.2   Binary search

Imagine that you have the same lost car problem, say at a race meeting, where the cars have been ushered into parking spaces as they arrived and issued with a time-stamped parking ticket to display on the windscreen. You could resort to searching in the same linear fashion as before but, in this situation, the ability to jump to any location and the fact that there is some order to the parking could help a great deal. You could start by looking somewhere near the middle of the car park and, depending on whether the middle car displayed an arrival time earlier or later than yours, you would be able to determine in which half of the car park to continue your search. You could then jump to the middle of the appropriate half, look at the time displayed and decide which quarter to search next. Repeating this process of halving the search number would eventually lead to your car.

Here's the search algorithm:

Regard the first car in car park as lower limit to section of car park to be searched
Regard the last car in car park as upper limit to section of car park to be searched
REPEAT
  Look at time displayed on middle car of current section of car park
  IF your arrival time < time displayed THEN
    Regard this location as the new upper search limit
  ELSE
    Regard this location as the new lower search limit
  END IF
UNTIL found your car OR current section of car park contains no cars
 IF found your car THEN
  drive home
ELSE
  call the police
END IF

This search strategy is called a binary search.
It requires that the items are ordered but, on average, it will be more efficient than a linear search. Each time you check a vehicle you halve the number remaining to be searched. For 500 cars in the car park you would have a maximum of 10 cars to look at in order to find your own.
This is an $O(\log_2 N)$ algorithm.

For example, if your car happened to be in position 27, the search might proceed as follows:

1. Check the car in position 250.
2. You discover that you arrived earlier than this car so you now check the car in position 125.
3. Again you find that this car arrived later than you did, so you next check position 62.
4. Yet again, you arrived earlier, so you now check position 31.
5. Next you check position 15.
6. You find that this car arrived before you, so you next check position 23; half way between 15 and 31.
7. This car arrived earlier than you, so you check car 27, which is yours, and the 7th car checked.

The following procedure uses recursion to implement a binary search through an array of 100 names:

```
PROCEDURE Binary(list:ListType;
                 name : ARRAY OF CHAR;
                 startPos, endPos : CARDINAL;
                 VAR foundWord:BOOLEAN;
                 VAR position:CARDINAL);
(*Binary name search
**Uses: StringCompare from StringStuff*)
CONST
    NULL=0C;
VAR
    midPos:CARDINAL;
BEGIN
    IF startPos>endPos THEN
        foundWord:=FALSE;
        position:=0
    ELSE
        midPos:=(startPos + endPos) DIV 2;
        IF StringCompare(name,list[midPos])=same THEN
            foundWord:=TRUE;
            position:=midPos
        ELSIF StringCompare(name,list[midPos])=less THEN
            Binary(list,name,startPos,
                                midPos-1,foundWord,position)
        ELSE
            Binary(list,name,midPos+1,
                                endPos,foundWord,position)
        END (*IF*)
    END (*IF*)
END Binary;
```

13.3.3   Hashing algorithms

Obviously if you had your own private parking place you would not be subject to the search problem described above; you could go directly to your car every time. Sometimes this might be possible, such as in a small company car park where everyone can have an individually allocated space, perhaps with their name or car registration number marking their space. However, public car parks are another matter. There are too many cars in relation to the available spaces. However, there are many ways that cars could be allocated to parking spaces to make searching easier, even though it might give a few car park managers a severe migraine. For example, we could allocate spaces according to the digits in the registration number so that car registration J345 RWK would be allocated space number 345. The main problem with this strategy is the possibility of collisions when two or more cars, e.g. J345 RWK and K345 LPN, contend for the same space. The best allocation strategy would be the one that results in the fewest collisions; perhaps applying some other formula, such as multiplying the driver's date of birth by the age of the car.

This type of allocation strategy is called hashing and, if no collisions occur, it allows an item to be retrieved immediately. If collisions are a possibility there must be some strategy for resolving them.

The following program inserts names into a hash table using the initial letter of each name to index the insertion position. Collisions are resolved simply by looking down the list for the next available free space and depositing the name there.

```
MODULE Hash;
(*Purpose: To demonstrate insertion in a hash table
**Uses module: InOut
*)
FROM InOut IMPORT WriteString,WriteLn,ReadString,Read,Write;
CONST
    NULL=0C;
TYPE
    WordType=ARRAY[0..50] OF CHAR;
    ListType=ARRAY['A'..'Z'] OF WordType;
VAR
    list:ListType;
    name:WordType;
    ch,cr:CHAR;

PROCEDURE ReadName(VAR name:WordType);
(*reads in a single name and capitalizes first letter
**Pre: None
**Post: name contains the input name with first
**letter capitalized*)
BEGIN
    WriteString("Please enter a name ");
    ReadString(name);
    name[0]:=CAP(name[0]);
    WriteLn
END ReadName;

PROCEDURE InitList(VAR list:ListType);
(*initializes the hash list by setting each cell to NULL
**Pre: None
**Post: each entry in list is initialized to NULL*)
VAR
    index:CHAR;
BEGIN
    FOR index:='A' TO 'Z' DO
        list[index,0]:=NULL
    END (*FOR*)
END InitList;

PROCEDURE DisplayList(list:ListType);
(*outputs the contents of the hash list
**Pre: list contains the hash list
**Post: None*)
VAR
    index:CHAR;
BEGIN
    FOR index:='A' TO 'Z' DO
        Write(index);
        WriteString("    ");
        WriteString(list[index]);
        WriteLn
    END (*FOR*)
END DisplayList;
```

```
PROCEDURE IsEmptySpace(word:WordType):BOOLEAN;
(*checks if a hash list space is empty
**Pre: word contains a hash list element
**Post: returns TRUE is element is empty,
**otherwise returns FALSE*)
BEGIN
    IF word[0]=NULL THEN
        RETURN TRUE
    ELSE
        RETURN FALSE
    END (*IF*)
END IsEmptySpace;

PROCEDURE IsFull(list:ListType):BOOLEAN;
(*determines whether the hash list is full
**Pre: list contains the hash list
**Post: returns TRUE if the hash list is full
**otherwise returns FALSE*)
VAR
    index:CHAR;
    full:BOOLEAN;
BEGIN
    full:=TRUE;
    index:='A';
    FOR index:='A' TO 'Z' DO
        IF IsEmptySpace(list[index]) THEN
            full:=FALSE;
        END (*IF*)
    END; (*FOR*)
    RETURN full
END IsFull;

PROCEDURE AddToList(VAR list:ListType; name:WordType);
(*takes the hash list and adds a new name.
***Pre: list contains the hash list and
**name contains the name to be added
**Post: list contains the updated hash list
**the first character of the name is used to decide
**where in the list to place the name.
**If this place is occupied, the first available
**space is used to store the name*)
VAR
    index:CHAR;
    placed:BOOLEAN;
BEGIN
    placed:=FALSE;
    index:='A';
    WHILE (index<>name[0]) AND (index<'Z') DO
        INC(index)
    END; (*WHILE*)
    WHILE (NOT placed) DO
        IF IsEmptySpace(list[index]) THEN
            list[index]:=name;
            placed:=TRUE
        ELSE
            INC(index);
            IF index>'Z' THEN
                index:='A'
            END (*IF*)
        END (*IF*)
    END (*WHILE*)
END AddToList;
```

```
BEGIN (*Main hash table program*)
    InitList(list);
    DisplayList(list);
    REPEAT
        IF NOT IsFull(list) THEN
            WriteString("Another name to add? (y/n) ");
            Read(ch);
            Read(cr);
            ch:=CAP(ch);
            IF (ch='Y') THEN
                ReadName(name);
                Read(cr);
                AddToList(list,name);
                DisplayList(list)
            END (*IF*)
        ELSE
            WriteString("Sorry the list is full");
            WriteLn
        END; (*IF*)
    UNTIL (ch<>'Y') OR (IsFull(list))
END Hash.
```

13.3.4   Comparison of searching algorithms

Of the searching techniques we have looked at, hashing algorithms are generally the most efficient, with an order of O(1) where there are no collisions. (An order O(1) means that you can go directly to the item you are searching for.) However, the search time can increase to approach that for a linear search, O(N), where there are a large number of collisions. The overhead of creating the hashing table must also be taken into account when assessing efficiency but, where there are to be a very large number of searches, any one-off set up processing may become relatively insignificant.

The binary search produces an efficient result requiring, at most, n passes to search a list of 2^n items. i.e. It is an O($\log_2$N) algorithm. The penalty to pay with this method is that the list to be searched must be sorted first.
A list to be searched, using a linear search, can be in any order, so there is no overhead in setting up the sorting conditions. However, in the worst case, a linear search will have to examine every item in the list. i.e. In the worst case it is an O(N) algorithm and, on average, O(N/2).

In conclusion;
for a small number of searches with a small list, a linear search can be quite adequate;
with large lists, or where there are to be many searches, either hashing or a binary search should be considered.

Self test 13.4

What would be the maximum number of compares required in a binary search of 4000 items?

Self test 13.5

Which one of the following best describes what the Big O notation is used for?

a) Counting swaps and compares.
b) Finding out whether algorithms work.
c) Comparing the efficiency of different algorithms.
d) Sorting and searching.

Exercise 13.6

Write a program to use a binary search to find the position of a name in a reverse ordered file of up to 100 names. Each name can consist of up to 20 characters.

Exercise 13.7

A list of 500 words, in alphabetical order, is stored in a file called `Dictionary`.
A program `SpellCheck` is required to use the list to check whether words input to the program are valid or not. On each pass of the program the user will be asked to input a word and the program will search the list for a matching word. The program will report to the user whether the word is valid (i.e. a match has been found) or invalid (i.e.no match).

a) Given that the file will be accessed using redirection of the standard input, comment briefly on the best strategy for dealing with the input/output requirements of the program.
b) Which searching algorithm would you recommend for this application and why?
c) Construct a context diagram and a level 1 data-flow diagram (DFD) for the first stage in the design of the program `SpellCheck`.
d) Draw a structure chart to bring together the DFDs, showing input and output data flows for each procedure.
e) Write a pseudocode version of the program `SpellCheck`.
f) From your design construct the program.
g) Test the program.
h) Fully document the program as described in Chapter 5.

14 A study in design

This chapter contains a design case study which we will deal with in two ways. First, we'll follow a design strategy based on functional decomposition and then we'll create an alternative design using an object-oriented approach.

14.1 A functional decomposition approach to design

14.1.1 Requirements for Registration

Personalized vehicle registration plates seem to be all the rage, if you have the cash to spare. Some sought-after registrations change hands for very large sums of money; sometimes more than the actual vehicle is worth. The car of an affluent relative sports XMA5; presumably a Christmas present, while someone else drives about looking fairly omnipotent in their Rolls registered 60D.

In Britain, each licensing office has a selection of two letter codes that appear as the last two letters of the three letter group on a normal number plate. For example, WK is issued by the Coventry licensing office, so a car with registration letters RWK must have been registered in the Coventry area. Sets of registration plate letters are assigned to particular vehicle licensing offices, so if you were content to make do with any old number, as long as the letters matched your initials, you would stand a good chance of finding a suitable car by going to garages near the licensing centre that issues licence letters which are the same as your initials.

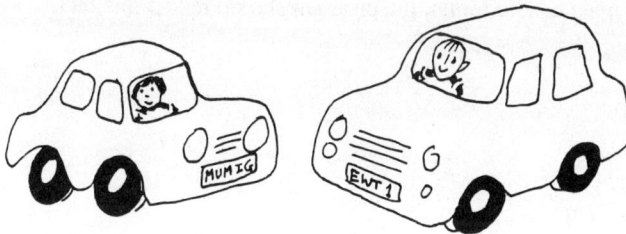

As it happens, we have a file available containing a list of two letter licence codes, AA to YY (although not all combinations are represented) followed by a licensing office code number. We also have a file listing licensing office code numbers followed by the town or city in which the office is situated. (See Appendix C.)

Sample from the LicenceCodes file:
WN59
WO13
WP64
WR31
WS10
WT31
WU31
WV09

Sample from the LicenceDistricts file:
27   Huddersfield
28   Hull
29   Ipswich
30   Kendal
31   Leeds
32   Leicester
33   Lincoln
34   Liverpool

So the best chance of getting a car with EWT on the licence plate would be in the Leeds area.

The requirement is for a program to input a surname followed by one or two forename initials and then to use the two licensing data files to find the appropriate licensing office. If none can be found, the program should report this fact.

14.1.2   Specification

After outlining the program requirements we need to think carefully about specific detail, such as what exactly is the allowed format of input to be and what will the 'not found' messages actual say. We need to produce a more detailed program specification, so here goes!

The program is to accept input of a name in the format:

surname, followed by a space, followed by either one or two forename initials, followed by a line terminating character.

e.g.

    Glendinning I

or

    Tatham EW

It should allow for input characters to be upper or lower case, or a mixture of both.
The maximum number of characters in the input line is to be 100.
The program should extract the first and last alphabetic input characters and reverse their order to give a two letter initial code.

e.g. IG or WT

The 'Licence Codes' file should be searched to find a match for this two letter code.
If a match is found, the number signifying the corresponding licence district is to be obtained, else a 'licence code not found' message is to be displayed.
The licence district number is then to be used to search the 'Licence Districts' file.
If a match is found, the corresponding district name is to be displayed, otherwise a 'district name not found' message.

Equipped with a more detailed description of exactly what is required of the program, the next stage is to use a series of data flow diagrams to represent the design. The first diagram is the context diagram which gives an overview of the whole system, including representation of the input and output devices to be used.

14.1.3   Context diagram (or level 0 DFD)

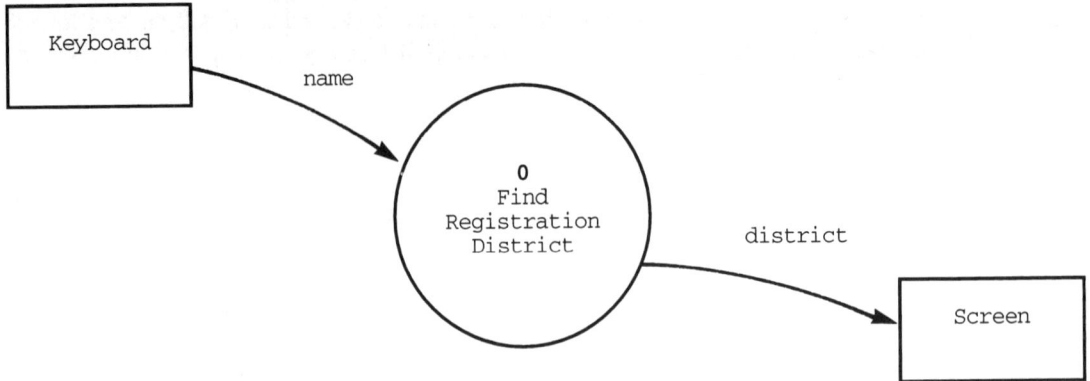

14.1.4   Refining the DFDs and developing the structure chart

The FindRegistrationDistrict process represents the action of the complete program. Into it goes a name and out comes the identity of the corresponding registration district. The FindRegistrationDistrict process is certainly not simple enough to implement easily without some further refinement, so the next stage is to expand it into component process steps. In this case, giving the level 1 DFD:

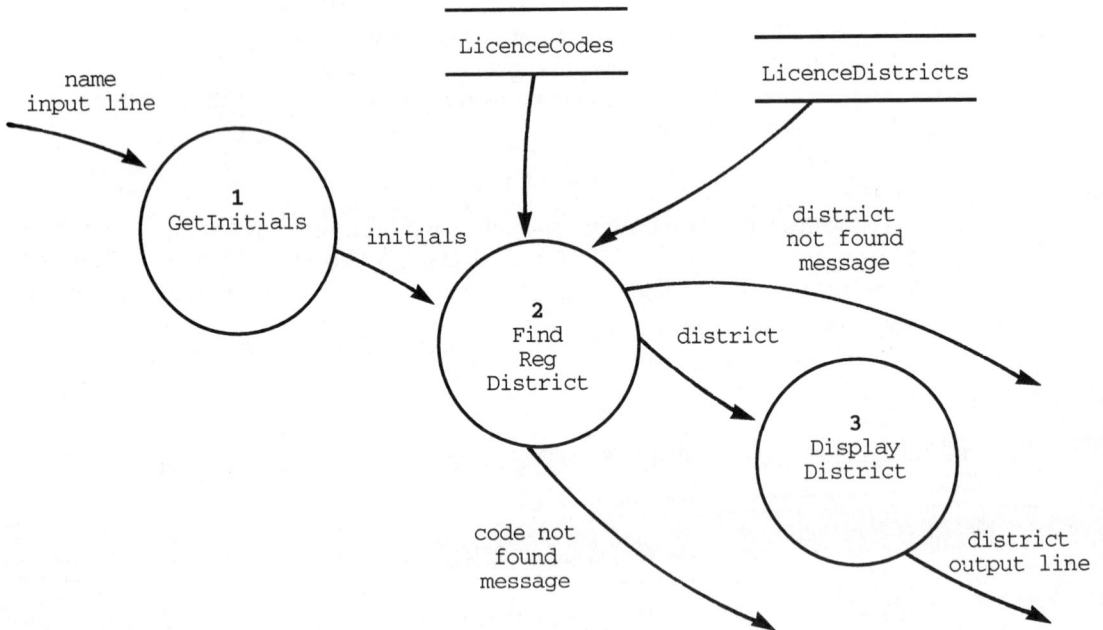

Next, we need to look at each of the processes again and decide whether they are at an easily implementable level or whether they are in need of further refinement into level 2 DFDs.

GetInitials really consists of two processes; getting the name from the user and then stripping out the initials:

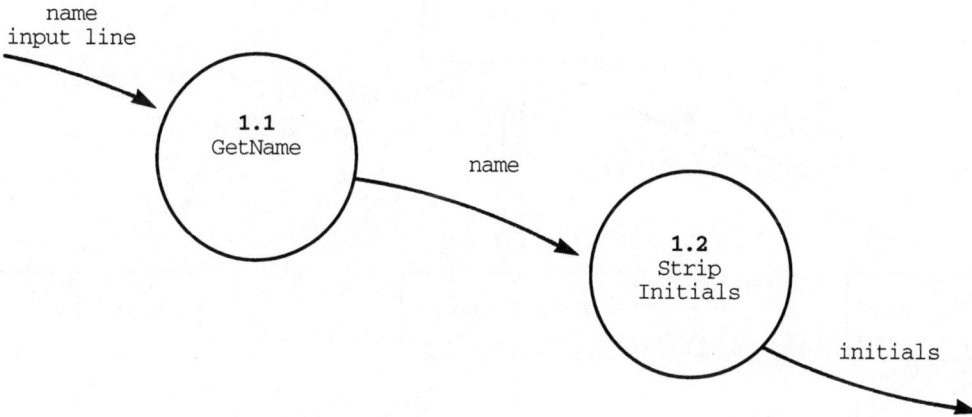

and, as there are two files to search, FindRegDistrict consists of the two steps; find the code, then find the district:

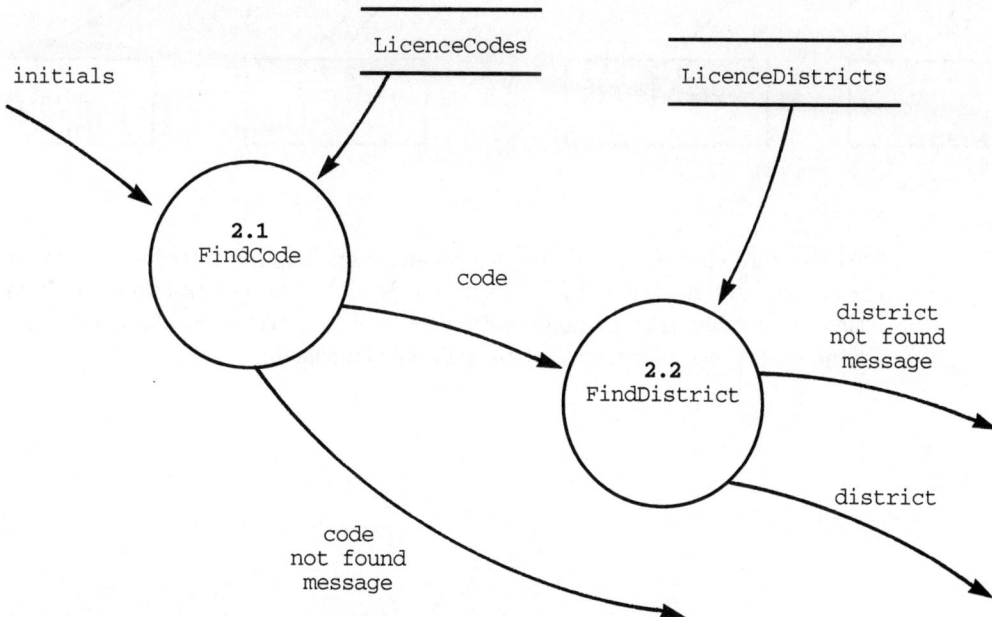

DisplayDistrict needs no further refinement.

As we are using a functional approach, we intend to write a procedure to implement each of the processes represented in the data flow diagrams. The data flows between the processes will be implemented using parameters that are passed between our procedures. The data flow diagram can be turned into a structure chart to represent the structure of our program.

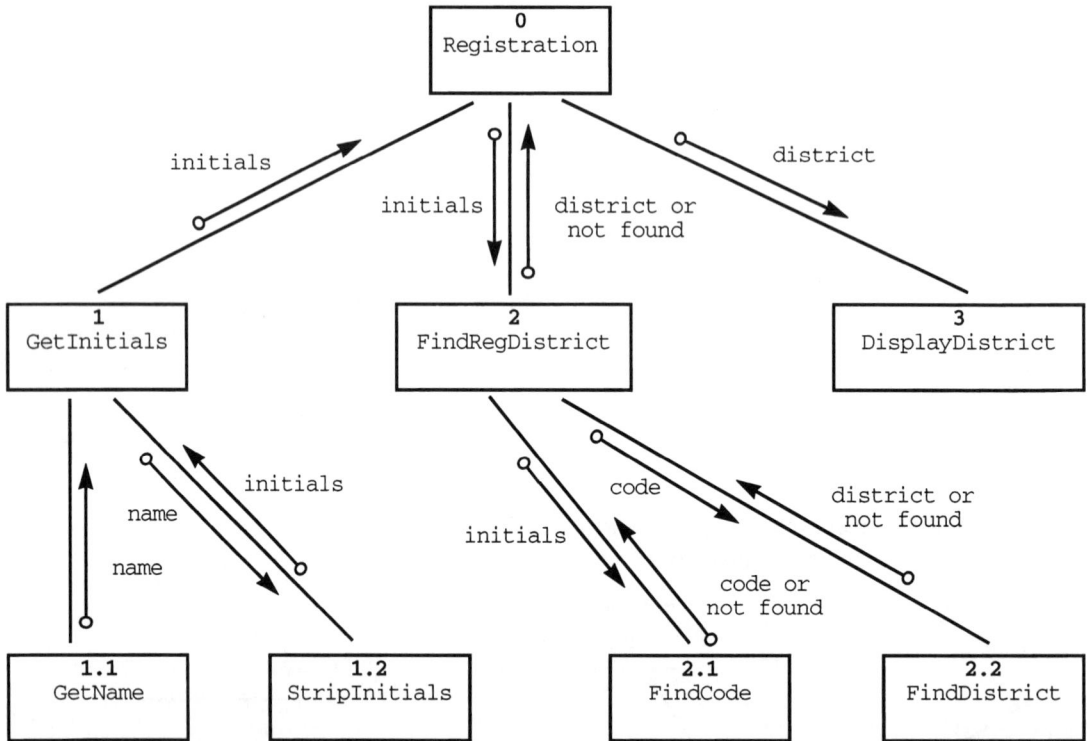

This structure chart suggests that our program will require procedures nested within procedures. Although the block structure of Modula-2 allows procedures to be nested inside one another, such nesting usually does little to enhance the clarity of a program. Grouping of related procedures is best achieved at the module level.

In our example, we can simplify things by incorporating all of our refined processes in a revised level 1 DFD.

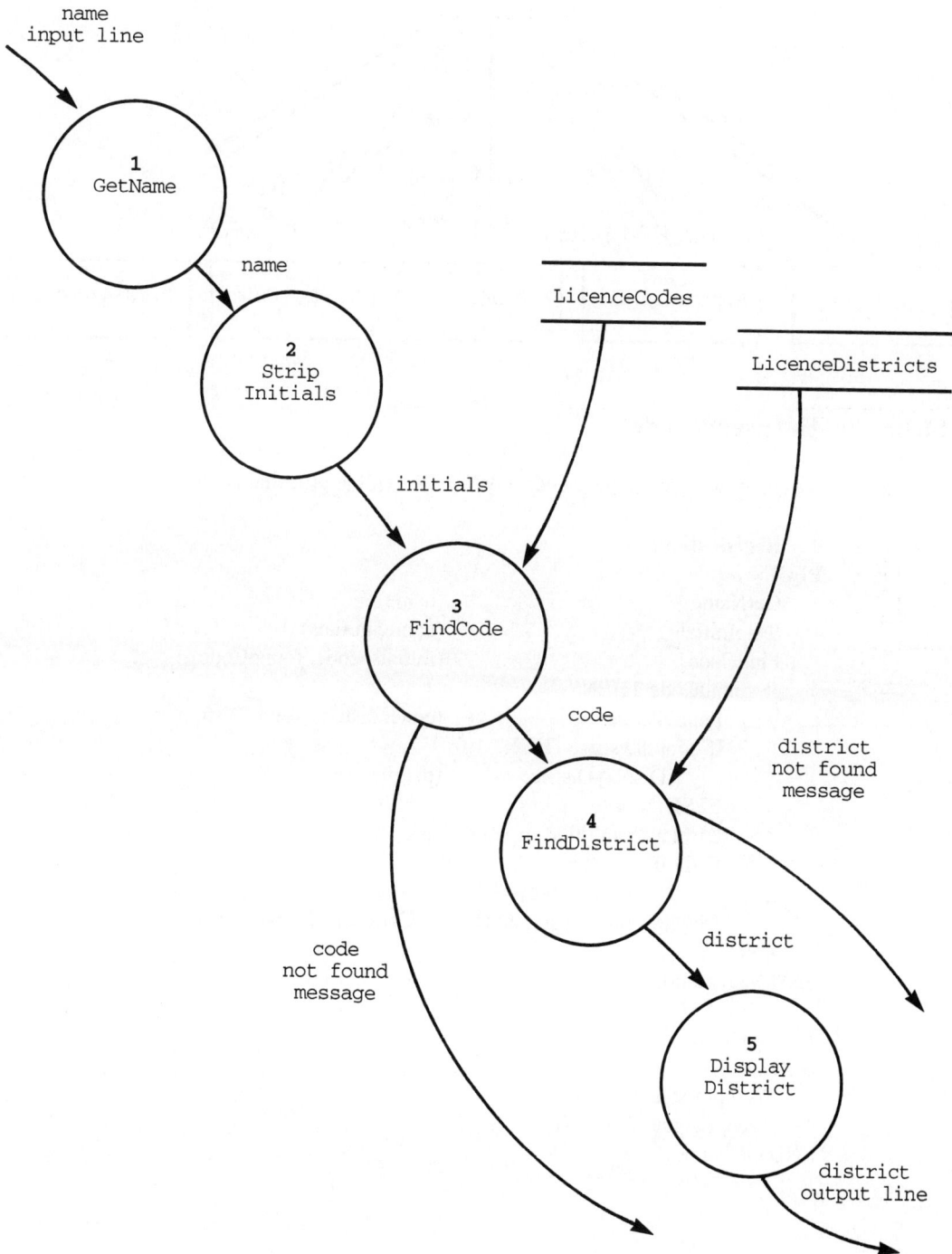

name
input line

1
GetName

name

2
Strip
Initials

LicenceCodes

LicenceDistricts

initials

3
FindCode

code

district
not found
message

4
FindDistrict

code
not found
message

district

5
Display
District

district
output line

This data flow diagram gives the structure chart:

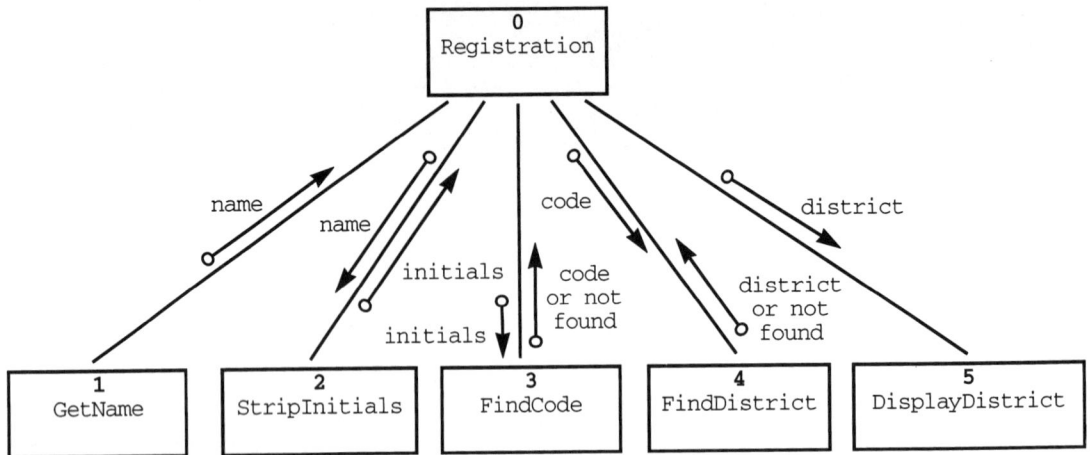

14.1.5   The pseudocode

We can now develop the pseudocode for each of the procedures.

0   Registration:
```
BEGIN
      GetName                        (name)
      StripInitials                  (name, initials)
      FindCode                       (initials, code, foundCode)
      IF foundCode THEN
            FindDistrict             (code, district, foundDistrict)
            IF foundDistrict THEN
                  DisplayDistrict    (district)
            ELSE
            Display "can't find suitable district" message
            END IF
      ELSE
            Display "no appropriate District Code was found"
      END  IF
END Registration.
```

1   GetName:
```
BEGIN
      Prompt for name input
      Accept input of name line
END GetName;
```

2   StripInitials:
BEGIN
>   Form initials from first and last alpha characters of name
END StripInitials;

3   FindCode:
BEGIN
>   Set foundCode to FALSE
>   Open Licence Codes file for input
>   Read first character from file line
>   WHILE NOT end of file AND NOT foundCode DO
>>   Read second character from file line
>>   Read district code
>>   Read line feed character
>>   IF two characters read from beginning
>>   of line match Initials THEN
>>>   foundCode is TRUE
>>>   required code:=district code
>>   END IF
>   Read first character from next file line
>   END WHILE
>   Close the file
END FindCode;

4   FindDistrict:
BEGIN
>   Set foundDistrict to FALSE
>   Open Licence Districts for input
>   Read district code
>   WHILE NOT end of file AND NOT foundDistrict DO
>>   Read district name
>>   IF required code=district code THEN
>>>   foundDistrict is TRUE;
>>>   required district:=districtName
>>   END IF
>>   Read next district code
>   END WHILE
>   Close the file
END FindDistrict;

5   DisplayDistrict:
BEGIN
>   Display district name
END DisplayDistrict;

14.1.6   Implementation

```
MODULE Registration;
(*
**Purpose:  A module to find licensing district which issues
**registration letters matching user input initials
**Uses: InOut,MyIO,StringStuff (See Chapter 12)
*)

FROM InOut IMPORT OpenInput,CloseInput,Done,ReadCard,
                  Read,ReadString,WriteString,WriteLn;
FROM MyIO IMPORT ReadLine;
FROM StringStuff IMPORT StringLen;

TYPE
     StrType = ARRAY [0..100] OF CHAR;
     InitType = ARRAY [0..1] OF CHAR;
VAR
     name,district: StrType;
     initials: InitType;
     foundCode, foundDistrict:BOOLEAN;
     code : CARDINAL;


PROCEDURE GetName(VAR name : StrType);
(*Gets name from keyboard
**Pre:   None
**Post:  name contains user name
*)
BEGIN (*GetName*)
     WriteString("Enter surname, then one or two initials");
     WriteLn;
     ReadLine(name)
END GetName;

PROCEDURE StripInitials(   name : StrType;
                           VAR initials : InitType);
(*Gets first or middle and last initial from user name
**Pre:   name represents a name in correct format
**Post:  initials contains first or middle and last
**initial obtained from name*)
BEGIN (*StripInitials*)
     initials[1]:=name[0];
     initials[0]:=name[StringLen(name) - 1]
END StripInitials;


PROCEDURE FindCode(initials : InitType;
                   VAR code: CARDINAL;
                   VAR foundCode : BOOLEAN);
(*Searches file "LicenceCodes.dat" for district code
**Pre:   Initials contains 2 initial letters
**Post:  code contains corresponding district code
**and foundCode is TRUE else foundCode is FALSE
**and code is undefined*)
VAR
     ch,reg1, reg2 : CHAR;
     districtCode : CARDINAL;
```

```
BEGIN (*FindCode*)
    foundCode:=FALSE;
    WriteString("Type Licence Codes file name");
    WriteLn;
    (*You may need to alter this; see Section 9.1.2*)
    OpenInput("dat");
    Read(reg1);
    WHILE (Done AND (NOT foundCode)) DO
        Read(reg2);
        ReadCard(districtCode);
        Read(ch); (*Read line feed if necessary*)
        IF (reg1=initials[0]) AND (reg2=initials[1]) THEN
            foundCode:=TRUE;
            code:=districtCode;
        END;   (*IF*)
        Read(reg1)
    END;   (*WHILE*)
    CloseInput
END FindCode;

PROCEDURE FindDistrict(code : CARDINAL;
                       VAR district : StrType;
                       VAR foundDistrict : BOOLEAN);
(*Searches file "LicenceDistricts.dat" for district name
**Pre:   code contains a cardinal number
**Post: district contains corresponding district name
**and foundDistrict is TRUE else foundDistrict is
**FALSE and district is undefined*)
VAR
    districtCode:CARDINAL;
    districtName : StrType;
BEGIN (*FindDistrict*)
    foundDistrict:=FALSE;
    WriteString("Type Licence Districts file name");
    WriteLn;
    (*You may need to alter this; see Section 9.1.2*)
    OpenInput("dat");
    ReadCard(districtCode);
    WHILE (Done AND (NOT foundDistrict)) DO
        ReadString(districtName);
        IF (code=districtCode) THEN
            foundDistrict:=TRUE;
            district := districtName;
        END; (*IF*)
        ReadCard(districtCode)
    END;   (*WHILE*)
    CloseInput
END FindDistrict;

PROCEDURE DisplayDistrict(district : StrType);
(*Displays the district name on the screen
**Pre:   district contains a character string
**Post: None*)
BEGIN
    WriteLn;
    WriteString("The place to buy your car is ");
    WriteString(district);
    WriteLn
END DisplayDistrict;
```

```
BEGIN  (*Main Registration program*)
    GetName(name);
    StripInitials(name,initials);
    FindCode(initials,code,foundCode);
    IF foundCode THEN
        FindDistrict(code,district,foundDistrict);
        IF foundDistrict THEN
            DisplayDistrict(district)
        ELSE
            WriteString("Cannot find suitable district");
            WriteLn
        END  (*IF *)
    ELSE
        WriteString("District Code was not found");
        WriteLn
    END  (*IF*)
END Registration.
```

14.1.7 Testing

All that remains is for us to test the program.

Here are some of the most important test cases:

1. Correct format name with one initial
2. Correct format name with two initials
3. Correct format name all upper case
4. Correct format name all lower case
5. Correct format name but with no corresponding district code
6. Correct format name with code but no corresponding district name
   (If such a case exists)
7. Name matching first entry in district code file
8. Name matching last entry in district code file
9. Name giving code matching first entry in district name file
10. Name giving code matching last entry in district name file
11. An input line of maximum number of Characters
12. Incorrect format name

Exercise 14.1

We'll leave it to you to draw up an appropriate test table and put Registration to the test.

14.1.8 Maintenance

The Registration program lends itself particularly well to a data flow design solution. There are clear, identifiable flows of data between processes and the amount of data passed is small, in accordance with our desire for minimal data coupling between the program parts.

In addition, some of the procedures may be reusable in other programs. For example, the FindDistrict procedure could be useful in any other application that makes use of the LicenceDistricts file.

Now suppose that we wish to alter things in order to log some statistical information concerning our program. We could create a loop to run our main program a number of times. Then, for example, we might wish to use a log to set up and to record the number of times the program repeats and, at the end, to furnish us with information such as the average number of comparisons with entries in the LicenceDistricts file required during the program cycles.

What alterations need to be made?

Well, we could declare a record type, LogRecord, and declare a variable of this type to represent the log.
The fields of LogRecord could be:
    cycles to represent number of current program cycle,
    limit to represent total number of cycles required and
    sum to maintain a cumulative total of search comparisons.
The average could then be calculated by dividing sum by cycles.

```
TYPE
    LogRecord =    RECORD
                       cycles,limit,sum : CARDINAL
                   END;  (*LogRecord*)

VAR log : LogRecord;
```

We can use the data in the log record to set up the loop in the main program.
We also need to count the number of comparisons made by FindDistrict as well as maintain the log record's cycles value and cumulative sum.

For example, if limit is set for five repeats of the program and the numbers of search comparison required on each successive cycle are 4, 6, 10, 3 and 12 respectively, the following changes to the variables' contents will occur:

cycles	count	sum
1	4	4
2	6	10
3	10	20
4	3	23
5	12	35

After the final cycle, the average number of comparisons can be calculated:

```
FLOAT(sum) / FLOAT(cycles) = 35 / 5 = 7
```

Here are the required alterations to FindDistrict with the alterations in bold type:

```
PROCEDURE FindDistrict(    code : CARDINAL;
                          VAR district : StrType;
                          VAR count : CARDINAL;
                          VAR foundDistrict : BOOLEAN);
VAR
      districtCode:CARDINAL;
      districtName : StrType;
      success : BOOLEAN;
BEGIN (*FindDistrict*)
      count := 0;
      foundDistrict:=FALSE;
      WriteString("Type Licence Districts file name");
      WriteLn;
      (*You may need to alter this; see Section 9.1.2*)
      OpenInput("dat");
      ReadCard(districtCode);
      WHILE (Done AND (NOT foundDistrict)) DO
          ReadString(districtName);
          INC(count);
          IF (code=districtCode) THEN
              foundDistrict:=TRUE;
              district := districtName;
          END; (*IF*)
          ReadCard(districtCode);
      END;   (*WHILE*)
      CloseInput
END FindDistrict;
```

Notice that to avoid FindDistrict directly accessing count as a global variable, it requires a additional parameter in order to return the value of count.

We can write a simple procedure to display the information we require from the log:

```
PROCEDURE DisplayLog(log : LogRecord);
CONST
      WIDTH = 10;
BEGIN
      WITH log DO
          WriteString("The number of cycles was ");
          WriteCard(cycles,1);
          WriteLn;
          WriteString("The sum of comparisons was ");
          WriteCard(sum,1);
          WriteLn;
          WriteString("The average was ");
          WriteReal(FLOAT(sum)/FLOAT(cycles),WIDTH);
          WriteLn
      END (*WITH*)
END DisplayLog;
```

Maintaining the sum total is a job that cannot be done within FindDistrict, as we need to retain the cumulative value between calls. If we made sum a variable local to FindDistrict it would lose its value after each exit from the procedure. The same applies to cycles , so we are forced to make the log record a global variable and our main program becomes:

```
BEGIN  (*Main program*)
    log.sum:=0;
    log.cycles:=0;
    WriteString("Please enter number of repeats required ");
    ReadCard(log.limit);
    Read(ch);   (*Read RETURN character*)
    WriteLn;
    WHILE (log.cycles < log.limit) DO
        GetName(name);
        StripInitials(name,initials);
        FindCode(initials,code,foundCode);
        IF foundCode THEN
            FindDistrict(code,district,count,foundDistrict);
            IF foundDistrict THEN
                DisplayDistrict(district)
            ELSE
                WriteString("Cannot find suitable district");
                WriteLn
            END  (*IF *)
        ELSE
            (*FindDistrict was not called
            **so there were no comparisons*)
            count:=0;
            WriteString("District Code was not found");
            WriteLn
        END;  (*IF*)
        INC(log.sum,count);
        INC(log.cycles)
    END; (*WHILE*)
    DisplayLog(log)
END Registration2.
```

In introducing these changes we have caused problems for any other programs wanting to use the procedure FindDistrict. It now has another parameter which may not be required in other applications. Also, we have been forced to handle log globally and we are beginning to enter a realm where we cannot functionally decompose our program into neat procedures very easily.

Imagine what would happen if we needed to make further changes along similar lines. We would end up with a very poorly decomposed program with a large number of global variables. Our procedures are likely to have increasingly long parameter lists that contravene the good design principles of low data coupling and they are unlikely to be reusable elsewhere.

In the following section we will look at an alternative design approach that overcomes these problems.

14.2   An object-oriented approach to design

The problems with software design techniques based on functional decomposition were recognized in the 1960s. It was then that the idea of Object-Oriented Programming was conceived. Object-oriented principles were first used in the Simula programming language. This inspired Alan Kay of Xerox Parc, who was working on a system using windows and graphic icons for improving the human-computer interface. He used object-oriented programming ideas in developing the SmallTalk language. In turn, these ideas led to systems such as Digital Research's GEM, the Apple Macintosh, Microsoft Windows and XWindows.

Will Watts of The Guardian outlined part of the reason for current interest in object-oriented techniques in an article published on 24th October 1991. In it he wrote:

'How does it work? Imagine an arcade game where the player is pitted against hordes of swooping alien spaceships. The traditional approach is to divide up the things to do in a top-down manner, and write a piece of code - a procedure - to perform each task. Thus, UpdateScreen could be subdivided into DrawAlien, DrawPlayersShip, and so on. Then DrawAlien is similarly subdivided into EraseCurrentPosition, CalculateNewPosition and DrawNewPosition. Eventually the level of the operating system type tasks is reached, e.g. ColourAPixel. But note that UpdateScreen must call the DrawAlien procedure once for each alien on the screen, which implies that it must know the number and type of aliens in existence.
The problems become apparent when you try to make changes. Suppose the program has to be modified to include a super alien that looks and moves in a different way. The aliens and super aliens are similar. Both perform the sequence (Erase, Move, Draw) at each animation cycle. Yet the procedural programmer will be hard-pressed to take advantage of these similarities.
He can incorporate extra tests in DrawAlien to determine the type (which will slow down his code), or write a new procedure, DrawSuperAlien. But then he has to modify UpdateScreen, to make it call DrawSuperAlien, and seek out all the other places in the program where the aliens are mentioned - initialization, sound generation, scoring, collision detection, etc.
All the code ends up being specific to the particular problem. Nothing described above could be used in, say, a game of Breakout, even though it would have an equivalent UpdateScreen procedure.
OOP is different. It lets the programmer associate procedures with data items; such procedures are called methods. So, instead of calling the DrawAlien procedure and telling it which alien to draw, we can instruct each alien to DrawYourself. This ability can be extended to other objects; super aliens, the player's ship, stars. Since the method that is called is automatically matched to the object, we do not need to write extra code within the method to determine what it is supposed to be drawing.'

For several years a major proponent of object-oriented software development has been Grady Booch, who was involved in research and implementation for the Ada programming language.

In a paper entitled *Object-Oriented Development*, which was published in *IEEE Transactions on Software Engineering Vol SE-12 No 2, February 1986*, Booch uses the design of a real-time cruise-control system to maintain the speed of a car over varying terrain to illustrate the advantages of object oriented design over functional decomposition. If you are able to obtain access to a copy, we recommend that you read this paper.

14.2.1   Redesigning `Registration`

Although Modula-2 is not a fully-fledged object-oriented programming language, it does allow implementation of many object-oriented design concepts, so let's redesign our program; this time using an object-oriented approach.

14.2.2   Identifying user tasks

As before, the first step involves identifying the requirements. We think it is useful to start by stating this purely from the user's point of view. What tasks does the user want to carry out with the system? The answer to this should be in the user's terms and have little if anything to do with implementation on a computer.

In this case, the user expects to be able to supply a person's name and to be informed of the corresponding licensing district, if any. So, the user expects to carry out just two basic tasks:

     supply a person's name and receive a district name.

To fulfil the user's requirements our application must be able to get a person's name from the user and locate the appropriate district. There are two tangible objects involved in this: a person's name and a district location and there is, from the user's point of view, just one operation to be performed on each.

A program to satisfy the user's needs would have the form:

```
BEGIN
     GetPersonName(name);
     LocateDistrict(name)
END
```

14.2.3   Identifying the method

Next, it is also useful to write an informal description of the method to be used by the program.

The `Registration` program should:

Get a name and strip the last two initials from it. Use these initials to search the 'Licence Codes' file to find a corresponding district code number, which is then used to search the 'Licence Districts' file in order to find the appropriate district name, which is then displayed.

14.2.4   Establishing the objects and operations

Now, look through the description and determine what objects are involved by identifying the nouns.

The **Registration program** should:
Get a **name** and strip the last two **initials** from it. Use these **initials** to search the **Licence Codes file** to find a corresponding **district code number**, which is then used to search the **Licence Districts file** in order to find the appropriate **district name**, which is then displayed.

The nouns are:
    Registration program
    name
    initials
    Licence Codes file
    district code number
    Licence Districts file
    district name

Thinking about what these nouns represent, we can see that **initials** are really part of **name**, **district code numbers** are in fact contained in the **Licence Codes file**, and **district names** are contained in the **Licence Districts file**.
Thus, we seem to have four significant objects:

    Registration program
    name
    Licence Codes file
    Licence Districts file

Now, go back and read the description again, this time looking for the verbs that describe operations to be carried out on the objects.

Object	Operation
Registration	(the main driving program)
name	GetName
	StripInitials
Licence Codes file	FindDistrictCode
Licence Districts file	FindDistrictName
	DisplayDistrictName

14.2.5   Implementing the method

The next stage is to write a module to implement each of the objects with its associated operations. This, in fact, constitutes an **abstract data type**, which we will discuss further in the following chapter.

As, in this example, each module is to be used to manage a program object, we have called the modules the NameManager, the CodeManager and the DistrictManager.

Here are the definition modules:

```
DEFINITION MODULE NameManager;

PROCEDURE GetName(VAR name:ARRAY OF CHAR);

PROCEDURE StripInitials(name:ARRAY OF CHAR;
                        VAR initials:ARRAY OF CHAR);

END NameManager.


DEFINITION MODULE CodeManager;

PROCEDURE FindDistrictCode(    initials:ARRAY OF CHAR;
                           VAR code:CARDINAL;
                           VAR foundCode:BOOLEAN);

END CodeManager.


DEFINITION MODULE DistrictManager;

PROCEDURE FindDistrictName(    code:CARDINAL;
                           VAR districtName : ARRAY OF CHAR;
                           VAR foundDistrict:BOOLEAN);

PROCEDURE DisplayDistrictName(code :CARDINAL);

END DistrictManager.
```

Here are the corresponding implementation modules:

```
IMPLEMENTATION MODULE NameManager;

FROM InOut IMPORT WriteString, WriteLn;
FROM MyIO IMPORT ReadLine;
FROM StringStuff IMPORT StringLen;

PROCEDURE GetName(VAR name:ARRAY OF CHAR);
BEGIN
    WriteString("Enter surname, then one or two initials");
    WriteLn;
    ReadLine(name)
END GetName;

PROCEDURE StripInitials(   name:ARRAY OF CHAR;
                           VAR initials:ARRAY OF CHAR);
BEGIN
    initials[1]:=name[0];
    initials[0]:=name[StringLen(name) - 1]
END StripInitials;

END NameManager.




IMPLEMENTATION MODULE CodeManager;

FROM InOut IMPORT OpenInput,CloseInput,WriteString,WriteLn,
                                    Read,Done,ReadCard;

PROCEDURE FindDistrictCode(   initials:ARRAY OF CHAR;
                              VAR code:CARDINAL;
                              VAR foundCode:BOOLEAN);

VAR
    ch,reg1, reg2 : CHAR;
    districtCode : CARDINAL;
BEGIN
    foundCode:=FALSE;
    WriteString("Type Licence Codes file name");
    WriteLn;
    (*You may need to alter this; see Section 9.1.2*)
    OpenInput("dat");
    Read(reg1);
    WHILE (Done AND (NOT foundCode)) DO
        Read(reg2);
        ReadCard(districtCode);
        Read(ch); (*Read line feed if necessary*)
        IF (reg1=initials[0]) AND (reg2=initials[1]) THEN
            foundCode:=TRUE;
            code:=districtCode;
        END;   (*IF*)
        Read(reg1)
    END;   (*WHILE*)
    CloseInput;
END FindDistrictCode;

END CodeManager.
```

```
IMPLEMENTATION MODULE DistrictManager;

FROM StringStuff IMPORT StringCopy;
FROM InOut IMPORT OpenInput,CloseInput,Read,Done,
            ReadCard,ReadString,WriteString,WriteLn;

PROCEDURE FindDistrictName(    code:CARDINAL;
                               VAR districtName : ARRAY OF CHAR;
                               VAR foundDistrict:BOOLEAN);
VAR
    districtCode:CARDINAL;
BEGIN (*FindDistrict*)
    foundDistrict:=FALSE;
    WriteString("Type Licence Districts file name");
    WriteLn;
    OpenInput("dat");
    (*You may need to alter this; see Section 9.1.2*)
    ReadCard(districtCode);
    WHILE (Done AND (NOT foundDistrict)) DO
        ReadString(districtName);
        IF (code=districtCode) THEN
            foundDistrict:=TRUE
        END; (*IF*)
        ReadCard(districtCode);
    END; (*WHILE*)
    CloseInput;
END FindDistrictName;

PROCEDURE DisplayDistrictName(code : CARDINAL);
VAR
    district : ARRAY [0..100] OF CHAR;
    found :BOOLEAN;
BEGIN
    FindDistrictName(code,district,found);
    IF found THEN
    WriteString("The place to buy your car is ");
        WriteString(district);
    ELSE
        WriteString("District not found")
    END; (*IF*)
    WriteLn
END DisplayDistrictName;

END DistrictManager.
```

14.2.6   Matching the user's tasks

Our aim is to create a program to satisfy the needs of the user and we now have available the tools to fulfil the user's tasks. Let's remind ourselves of what these are:

To fulfil the user's requirements our application must be able to get a person's name from the user and locate the appropriate district.

A program to satisfy the user's needs would have the form:

```
BEGIN
    GetPersonName(name);
    LocateDistrict(name)
END
```

As these are basic tasks carried out by the user in fulfilling one goal (that of finding an appropriate registration location) we can now write a module to supply just these facilities.

We have called it RegLocator and here are its definition and implementation modules:

```
DEFINITION MODULE RegLocator;

    PROCEDURE GetPersonName(VAR name : ARRAY OF CHAR);

    PROCEDURE LocateDistrict(name : ARRAY OF CHAR);

END RegLocator.


IMPLEMENTATION MODULE RegLocator;
FROM NameManager IMPORT GetName, StripInitials;
FROM CodeManager IMPORT FindDistrictCode;
FROM DistrictManager IMPORT DisplayDistrictName;
FROM InOut IMPORT WriteString;

PROCEDURE GetPersonName(VAR name : ARRAY OF CHAR);
BEGIN
    GetName(name)
END GetPersonName;

PROCEDURE LocateDistrict(name : ARRAY OF CHAR);
VAR
    initials:ARRAY[0..2] OF CHAR;
    code:CARDINAL;
    success:BOOLEAN;
BEGIN (*LocateDistrict*)
    StripInitials(name,initials);
    FindDistrictCode(initials,code,success);
    IF success THEN
        DisplayDistrictName(code);
    ELSE
        WriteString("Cannot find code")
    END (*IF*)
END LocateDistrict;

END RegLocator.
```

Finally, we need to write the final driving program module which directly reflects the user tasks identified in Section 14.2.2.

```
MODULE RegObject;
FROM RegLocator IMPORT GetPersonName,LocateDistrict;
VAR
     name:ARRAY[0..50] OF CHAR;
BEGIN
     GetPersonName(name);
     LocateDistrict(name)
END RegObject.
```

14.2.7   Dependency diagrams

The following is called a dependency diagram as it shows which of our modules will be dependent on (i.e. import) facilities provided by another.

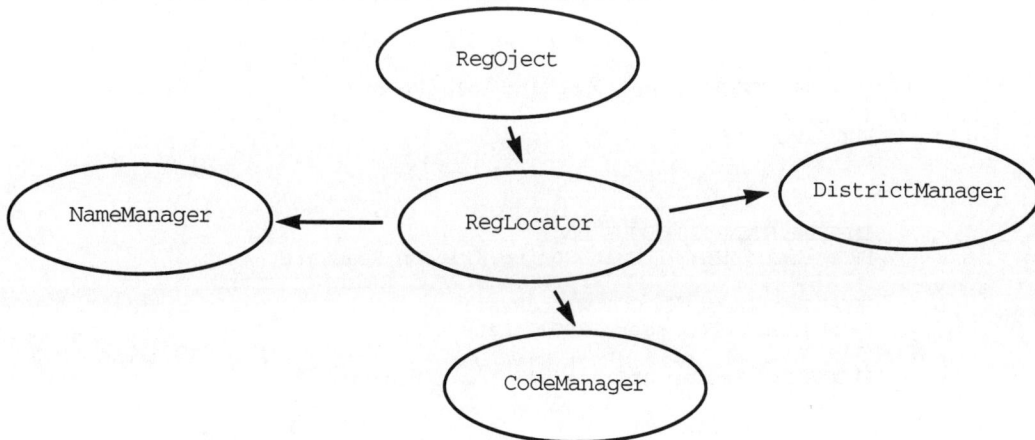

14.2.8   Maintaining our new program

Now, suppose we wish to alter things in order to log the same statistical information as before.
What alterations need to be made this time?

Well, the introduction of a log requires the introduction of a new object with its own module defining its associated set of operations.

```
DEFINITION MODULE Log;

TYPE
    LogRecord =    RECORD
                        cycles,limit,sum : CARDINAL
                    END; (*LogRecord*)
VAR
    log : LogRecord;

    PROCEDURE IncrementCycle(VAR log : LogRecord);

    PROCEDURE SetLimit(VAR log : LogRecord);

    PROCEDURE IsLimitReached(log : LogRecord):BOOLEAN;

    PROCEDURE MaintainSum(VAR log : LogRecord);

    PROCEDURE DisplayLog(log : LogRecord);

END Log.



IMPLEMENTATION MODULE Log;
FROM InOut IMPORT WriteString,WriteLn,ReadCard,
                                    Read,WriteCard;
FROM RealInOut IMPORT WriteReal;
FROM DistrictManager IMPORT ReturnCount;

PROCEDURE IncrementCycle(VAR log : LogRecord);
BEGIN
    INC(log.cycles)
END IncrementCycle;

PROCEDURE SetLimit(VAR log : LogRecord);
VAR
    ch : CHAR;
BEGIN
    WriteString("Please enter number of goes required ");
    ReadCard(log.limit);
    Read(ch); (*Read RETURN character*)
    WriteLn
END SetLimit;
```

```
PROCEDURE IsLimitReached(log : LogRecord):BOOLEAN;
BEGIN
     IF log.cycles<log.limit THEN
          RETURN FALSE
     ELSE
          RETURN TRUE
     END
END IsLimitReached;

PROCEDURE MaintainSum(VAR log : LogRecord);
BEGIN
        log.sum:=log.sum + ReturnCount()
END MaintainSum;

PROCEDURE DisplayLog(log : LogRecord);
CONST
     WIDTH = 10;
BEGIN
     WITH log DO
         WriteString("The number of cycles was ");
         WriteCard(cycles,1);
         WriteLn;
         WriteString("The sum of comparisons was ");
         WriteCard(sum,1);
         WriteLn;
         WriteString("The average was ");
         WriteReal(FLOAT(sum)/FLOAT(cycles),WIDTH);
         WriteLn
     END (*WITH*)
END DisplayLog;

BEGIN (*main module body to initialize the record fields*)
     WITH log DO
         cycles:=0;
         limit:=0;
         sum:=0
     END (*WITH*)
END Log.
```

cycles, limit and sum are each initialized to zero within the body of the module, which is executed once, before the main driving module is run (see Chapter 12).

A further operation must be made available by DistrictManager in order to return the file comparison count.
Here are the revised definition and implementation modules:

```
DEFINITION MODULE DistrictManager;

PROCEDURE FindDistrictName(   code:CARDINAL;
                              VAR districtName : ARRAY OF CHAR;
                              VAR foundDistrict:BOOLEAN);

PROCEDURE DisplayDistrictName(code :CARDINAL);

PROCEDURE ReturnCount():CARDINAL;

END DistrictManager.
```

```
IMPLEMENTATION MODULE DistrictManager;

FROM StringStuff IMPORT StringCopy;
FROM InOut IMPORT OpenInput,CloseInput,Read,Done,ReadCard,
                  ReadString,WriteString,WriteLn;
VAR
    count : CARDINAL;

PROCEDURE FindDistrictName(     code:CARDINAL;
                                VAR districtName : ARRAY OF CHAR;
                                VAR foundDistrict:BOOLEAN);
VAR
    districtCode:CARDINAL;
BEGIN (*FindDistrict*)
    count :=0;
    foundDistrict:=FALSE;
    WriteString("Type Licence Districts file name");
    WriteLn;
    OpenInput("dat");
    (*You may need to alter this; see Section 9.1.2*)
    ReadCard(districtCode);
    WHILE (Done AND (NOT foundDistrict)) DO
        INC(count);
        ReadString(districtName);
        IF (code=districtCode) THEN
            foundDistrict:=TRUE
        END; (*IF*)
        ReadCard(districtCode);
    END; (*WHILE*)
    CloseInput;
END FindDistrictName;

PROCEDURE ReturnCount():CARDINAL;
BEGIN
    RETURN count
END ReturnCount;

PROCEDURE DisplayDistrictName(code : CARDINAL);
VAR
    district : ARRAY [0..100] OF CHAR;
    found :BOOLEAN;
BEGIN
    FindDistrictName(code,district,found);
    IF found THEN
        WriteString("The place to buy your car is ");
        WriteString(district);

    ELSE
        WriteString("District not found")
    END; (*IF*)
    WriteLn
END DisplayDistrictName;

BEGIN
    count:=0;
END DistrictManager.
```

count is initialized to zero within the body of the module, which is executed once before the main driving module is run. (See Chapter 12.)

The main driving module becomes:

```
(*main driver*)
MODULE RegObject;
FROM RegLocator IMPORT GetPersonName,LocateDistrict;
FROM Log IMPORT LogRecord,SetLimit,IsLimitReached,
                 IncrementCycle,MaintainSum,DisplayLog;
VAR
     name:ARRAY[0..50] OF CHAR;
     log :LogRecord;
BEGIN
     SetLimit(log);
     LOOP
         (**)IF IsLimitReached(log) THEN EXIT END;
         GetPersonName(name);
         LocateDistrict(name);
         IncrementCycle(log);
         MaintainSum(log);
     END; (*LOOP*)
     DisplayLog(log)
END RegObject.
```

Before executing the altered program, the new `Log` module will have to be compiled. The `DistrictManager` and `RegLocator` DEFINITION and IMPLEMENTATION modules, and the main driver module, will need to be recompiled and linked.

The advantage of this object-oriented design over a functional approach is that our program matches our mental model of reality better. It directly models real objects and what the user wants to do with them rather than concentrating on the actions to be carried within the computer system, as is the case with a functional approach.

The other advantages are that any other programs that made use of the facilities provided by `DistrictManager` or `RegLocator` will only require re-linking; no amendment to their code will be necessary. Also, major changes can be made to the way the files are structured and the way data is represented without necessitating any change to the main program. Such changes are more easily localized.

Exercise 14.2

Use object-oriented principles to redesign and implement the bar code reader program from Chapter 11.

15   POINTER types

15.1   Anonymous dynamic variables

Suppose that we wish to write a program to maintain a shopping list. We could declare a character string type for variables which are to represent items to buy and we could use an array of strings to store our list. Declaring an array sets aside a fixed amount of computer memory dependent on the declared array size, so the question is, how big should the array be? Sometimes we may have only one item to buy, while on other occasions we may have a very long list. If we make it too small there may be occasions when it cannot cope, while if we make it very large we are likely to waste memory with unused array capacity. The problem with arrays, which is also true of all other data types we have met so far, is that their memory allocation is static; it is set aside once and for all when their variables are declared by name within the program.

Fortunately, many high level languages, including Modula-2, provide a solution by allowing variables to be created dynamically during program execution. Such variables are not declared by name within the program and are said to be **anonymous**. As they are anonymous we cannot refer to them directly but need to use a special POINTER type which can refer to locations inside the computer's memory. Just as numbers are used to identify houses in city streets because they provide a predictable sequence which enables a specific address to be located easily, numbers are used to identify and locate places in a computer's memory. And again, just like the number of a house, the number of a particular memory location is known as its address.

Pointers allow programmers to use memory addresses to identify variables instead of using identifier names. This can be a little confusing at first but, once you have got the hang of the technique, you have a very powerful tool for declaring and manipulating very useful data structures.

Here's an analogy that may clarify the idea of anonymous variables.
You might not know the names of everyone living in your street but you might, for example, know there is an old woman living at house number 67, a young couple with a baby at number 84, number 13 is empty and for sale, while there is a man with a white Volvo and a dog living at number 24.
You might not know their names, so in this respect they are anonymous. However, you do know something of their type and you could identify them by their addresses.
Similarly, with Modula-2's POINTER types, a variable of type POINTER can contain the address of a memory location which can in turn contain an anonymous variable of any type.
For example, consider the type declaration:

```
TYPE
    CharPtr=POINTER TO CHAR;
```

A variable of type CharPtr can contain the address of an area of memory large enough to hold a CHAR variable. A pointer type always references a specific second data type so, in this example, a variable of type CharPtr can only contain the address of an anonymous variable of type CHAR.

In this case there is no apparent advantage to using a pointer as opposed to a simple variable of type CHAR. However, there are many situations where pointers can be used in ways that would not be possible using named variables.

15.2   Using pointers

Modula-2 allows us to declare a pointer type to a record type, like this:

```
TYPE
    ItemPtr = POINTER TO ItemRec;

    ItemRec = RECORD
                  quantity : CARDINAL;
                  itemRef : CARDINAL
              END; (*ItemRec*)
```

A variable of type ItemPtr can be declared:

```
VAR
    list : ItemPtr;
```

This declaration sets aside space for a memory address only, referenced by the identifier list. Fortunately, we do not have to worry about what the actual address is; we simply use the identifier. Memory space for the record that is pointed to can be allocated dynamically as and when required during execution of the program.

When first declared, the contents of list is undefined; it could point to any available memory address. This could give rise to all kinds of problems, so Modula-2 provides a special reserved word, NIL, which acts as a POINTER constant. It can be assigned to POINTER variables to mean that the pointer is not pointing to anything, so the statement:

```
list := NIL;
```

ensures that list points nowhere.

To create an anonymous variable of a particular data type we must dynamically set aside memory space for it within our program. To achieve this there is a procedure, ALLOCATE, which must be imported from the library module Storage. ALLOCATE takes two arguments; the first must be the pointer variable and the second a CARDINAL value specifying the amount of memory required:

```
ALLOCATE(pointerVariable, sizeOfMemoryRequired);
```

The built-in function, SIZE, can be used to calculate the storage requirements of the given data type.

The following instruction will allocate space for an anonymous variable of type, ItemRec, and put its address in the pointer variable list:

```
ALLOCATE(list, SIZE(ItemRec));
```

In order to access the fields of the variable, perhaps to put some data in the record, we need to use the pointer, list. We are not interested in the actual memory address used, just the record that it points to. The distinction is achieved by the use of the caret symbol, ^ , or sometimes an upwards arrow, meaning 'dereference' or follow the pointer.

```
list^.quantity := 24;
list^.itemRef := 54321;
```

Alternatively, as for normal records, WITH can be used to simplify the use of the pointer:

```
WITH list^ DO
    quantity := 24;
    itemRef := 54321;
END; (*WITH*)
```

The diagram below describes the status of the pointers and the anonymous variables created by the above commands.

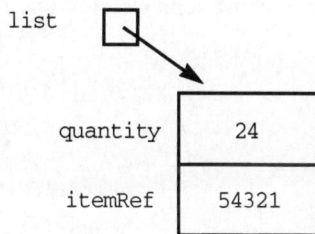

In order to free memory that has been allocated for anonymous variables, the procedure DEALLOCATE can be imported from Storage. As with ALLOCATE, DEALLOCATE takes two arguments; the first must be the pointer variable and the second a CARDINAL value specifying the amount of memory allocated to the anonymous variable.
For example:

```
DEALLOCATE(list, SIZE(ItemRec));
```

frees the memory set aside for an anonymous variable of type ItemRec pointed to by list. Strictly, the contents of list will then be left undefined, probably pointing to the area of memory now freed. This is sometimes known as a dangling pointer and following it can result in nasty consequences for your program.

Here's a brief but complete program to illustrate the use of pointers.

```
MODULE ListItem;
FROM InOut IMPORT WriteCard, WriteLn;
FROM Storage IMPORT ALLOCATE, DEALLOCATE;
TYPE
    ItemPtr =  POINTER TO ItemRec;

    ItemRec =  RECORD
                    quantity : CARDINAL;
                    itemRef : CARDINAL
               END; (*ItemRec*)
VAR
    list : ItemPtr;
BEGIN
    ALLOCATE(list,SIZE(ItemRec));
    list^.quantity := 24;
    list^.itemRef := 54321;
    WriteCard(list^.quantity,1);
    WriteLn;
    WriteCard(list^.itemRef,1);
    WriteLn;
    DEALLOCATE(list,SIZE(ItemRec))
END ListItem.
```

ListItem allocates space for the anonymous ItemRec variable pointed to by list, assigns values to its fields, displays them on the screen and then frees the memory that was occupied.

With a little example like this there is no advantage in using a pointer compared to using a straightforward record variable. Also, our list contains only one item, so let's extend things.

15.3   Linked lists

15.3.1   Setting up a linked list

The following declaration can be used to set up a linked list. It is called a linked list because each element in the list is linked to the next via a pointer.

```
TYPE
    ElementPointer = POINTER TO Element;

    Element =  RECORD
                    data: CARDINAL;
                    next : ElementPointer
               END; (*Element*);
```

This record definition contains a circular reference, since ElementPointer refers to Element and Element contains an instance of ElementPointer. Modula-2 syntax normally requires that you declare an identifier before you use it but, in this case, you are allowed to break the rule. However, the pointer must be declared before the record, otherwise an error will occur.

`Element` is a building block for an extremely useful list data structure. It contains some data (we have chosen a simple CARDINAL value, but there could be any type of data in the record) and a pointer to the next element. We will use a block like this to represent `Element` and its fields:

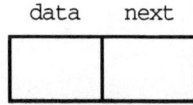

```
        data    next
      ┌──────┬──────┐
      │      │      │
      └──────┴──────┘
```

A program which uses `Element` to form data structures will require POINTER variables of type `ElementPointer`, which will be used in the dynamic creation of `Element` variables during the course of the program.

```
VAR
    firstElement, lastElement : ElementPointer;
```

Data structures can be created using records of type `Element`. The pointer field in each `Element` will contain the address of the next `Element` in sequence. `firstElement` can be used as an external pointer to access the first `Element` and the value of next in the final `Element` is set to `NIL` to indicate the end of the sequence. The diagram below illustrates this arrangement.

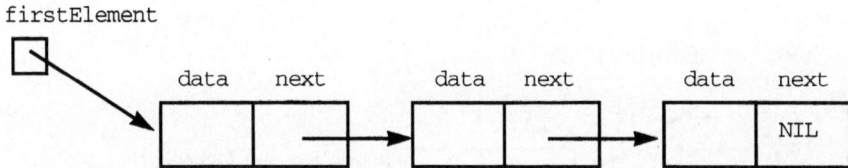

This is called a linked-list. Such a structure can be used for many different applications, some of which we will consider shortly.

Assignment is allowed between POINTER variables providing they are of the SAME type. (See Appendix B.)
So:

```
firstElement := lastElement;
```

is a legal statement.

This procedure initializes a linked list by assigning NIL to its first element:

```
PROCEDURE InitializeList(VAR firstElement : ElementPointer);
BEGIN
    firstElement := NIL
END InitializeList;
```

The following procedure, AddElement, adds another Element to the top of the list:

```
PROCEDURE AddElement (VAR firstElement:ElementPointer;
                          item : CARDINAL);
VAR
    tempPointer:ElementPointer;
BEGIN
    ALLOCATE(tempPointer, SIZE(Element));
    WITH tempPointer^ DO
        data:=item;
        next:=firstElement
    END; (*WITH*)
    firstElement := tempPointer
END AddElement;
```

Here's how it works, assuming that the list contains 3 elements and item contains the value 23.

After the statement, ALLOCATE(tempPointer, SIZE(Element));

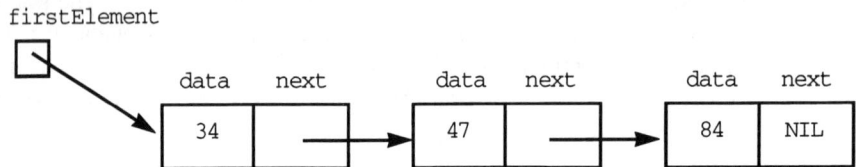

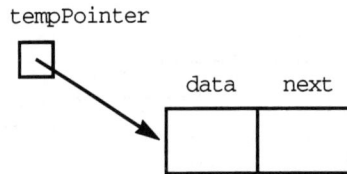

firstElement

tempPointer

After
```
    WITH tempPointer^ DO
        data:=item;
        next:=firstElement
    END; (*WITH*)
```

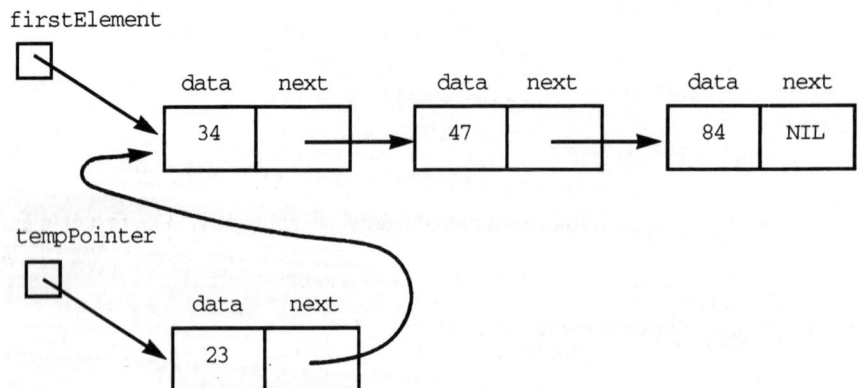

firstElement

tempPointer

After
```
firstElement := tempPointer;
```

firstElement

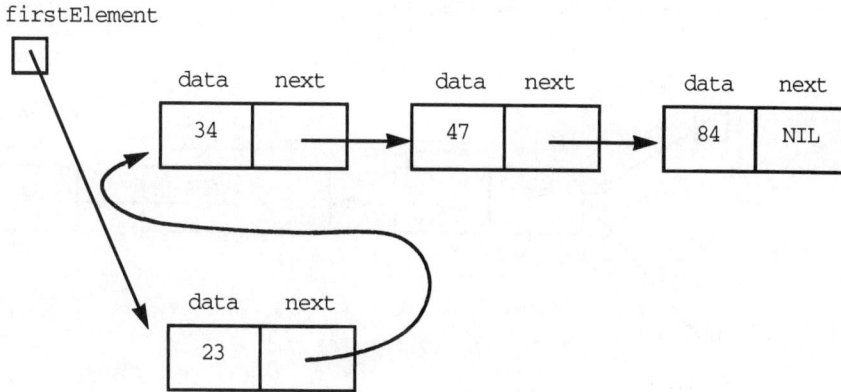

The pointer, tempPointer, ceases to exist after the procedure ends.

Visiting every element in a linked list is known as **traversal** of the list. Here is a procedure to traverse the list of elements and print out the values in sequence:

```
PROCEDURE TraverseList (firstElement:ElementPointer);
VAR
    tempPointer:ElementPointer;
BEGIN
    tempPointer:=firstElement;
    WHILE (tempPointer<>NIL) DO
        WriteCard(tempPointer^.data,1);
        WriteLn;
        tempPointer:= tempPointer^.next
    END (*WHILE*)
END TraverseList;
```

If a linked list is to be of any practical use to us we also need to be able to remove elements from it. Removal of the first element in a list can be done like this:

```
PROCEDURE RemoveFirstElement(VAR firstElement:ElementPointer;
                                  VAR value : CARDINAL);
VAR
    tempPointer:ElementPointer;
BEGIN
    (*First make sure that the list is not empty*)
    IF firstElement<>NIL THEN
        tempPointer:=firstElement;
        firstElement := firstElement^.next;
        value := tempPointer^.data;
        DEALLOCATE(tempPointer, SIZE(Element))
    ELSE
        WriteString("The list is empty");
        WriteLn
    END (*IF*)
END RemoveFirstElement;
```

Here are the steps involved:

After
```
    tempPointer := firstElement;
```

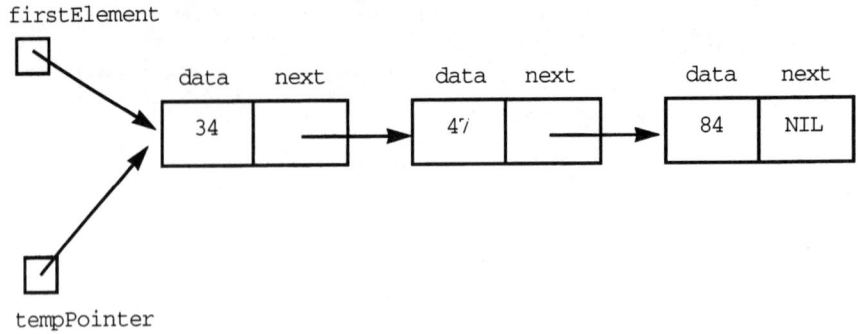

After,
```
    firstElement := firstElement^.next;
```

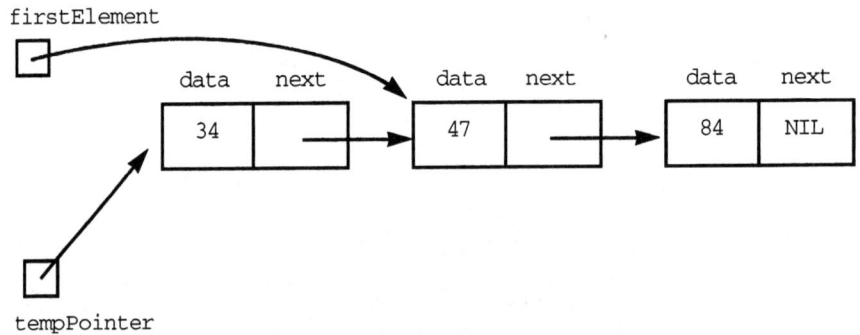

After
```
        value := tempPointer^.data;
        DEALLOCATE(tempPointer, SIZE(Element))
```

the element data is copied to the variable parameter, `value`, and the unwanted element space is freed.

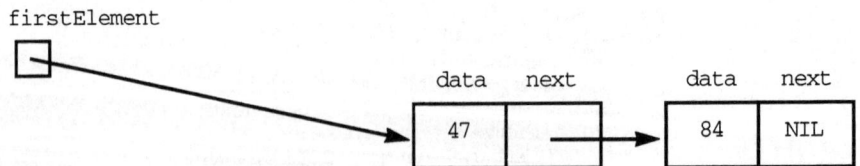

These examples are the first stage in building a set of useful procedures which can be adapted to process any linked list structure.

15.3.2   **Case study:** *the double linked list*

Assume that a program needs to validate code values as they are input from a file. If a code is valid the corresponding description record is to be printed for the user to check. On the other hand, if the code is invalid then a suitable error message is to be displayed before the user is prompted for another code value.

Also assume that for speed of searching the code records are to be read into memory.

We could use an array to store the records. However, a linked list is a better proposition because it removes the necessity to set an upper limit on the number of records allowed. Furthermore, the space allocated for an array will always be the maximum size, even if the number of records to be input is small. A linked list will require space to be allocated for just the number of records on the file.

The addition of a pointer variable converts a record declaration into a potential linked list element, thus:

```
TYPE
    TextType = ARRAY [0..20] OF CHAR;

    CodePtr = POINTER TO CodeType;

    CodeType = RECORD
                   code : CARDINAL;
                   description : TextType;
                   next : CodePtr
               END; (* CodeType RECORD *);
```

If a sequential search algorithm is to be used to search a list of these records, then this linked list is fine. However, if there is a requirement to read the list in both directions (e.g. if we decide to use a binary search) then we need to add a second pointer variable to the record. The second pointer would contain the address of the previous element in the list:

```
TYPE
    TextType = ARRAY [0..20] OF CHAR;

    CodePtr = POINTER TO CodeType;

    CodeType =    RECORD
                   code : CARDINAL;
                   description : TextType;
                   next : CodePtr;
                   previous : CodePointer
               END;   (*CodeType*);
```

A linked list with pointers in both directions is known as a double-linked list. This is what it looks like when we modify our linked list from Section 15.3.1:

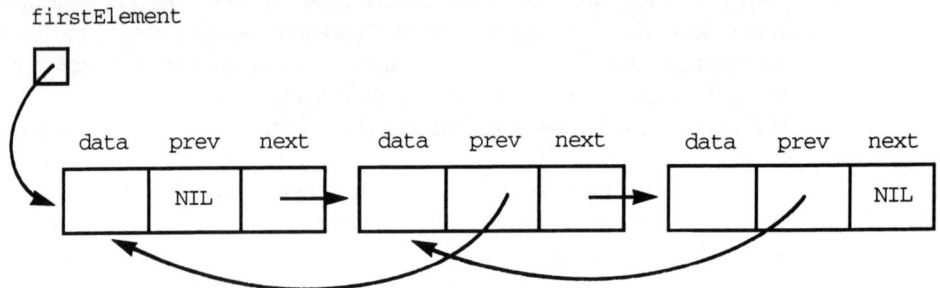

Here is the procedure AddElement revised so that it adds a new element to a double linked list and sets up next and previous pointers.

```
PROCEDURE AddElement (    VAR firstElement:ElementPointer;
                          item : CARDINAL);
VAR
    tempNext, tempPrev:ElementPointer;
BEGIN
(*save the address of the first element*)
    tempNext:=firstElement;
    ALLOCATE(firstElement, SIZE(Element));
    WITH firstElement^ DO
        data := item;
        next:=tempNext;
        prev:=NIL
    END; (*WITH*)
    tempNext^.prev:=firstElement
END AddElement;
```

A second auxiliary pointer, lastElement, is also needed to enable the reverse traversal of the list to be undertaken without first doing a forward traversal.

Self test 15.1

```
TYPE
    ListPtr = POINTER TO ListType;
    ListType  =    RECORD
                        data : CHAR;
                        next : ListPtr;
                   END;  (*ListType*)
VAR
    list : ListPtr;
```

Given the above declarations, which of the following could be legal Modula-2 assignment statements?

a)   data := 'A';
b)   list^.data := 'A';
c)   list.data := 'A';
d)   list^.next^.data := 'A';

15.4   Abstract data types

Ideally, when we write our programs we want to be able to use the programming language to implement the abstract model of the task that we have in our head. We want to use data types and operations on those types that match our abstract model. If we are trying to solve a problem the last thing we need is to have to convert everything into the computer's terms.

So far, Modula-2 has taken us a long way in this direction with its simple data types, such as INTEGER and REAL, with subrange and enumerated types, and with more complex structured types such as ARRAYS and RECORDS.

Let's now look at how we can create modules in which are packaged our own type declarations and associated operations. Such packages are called abstract data types, or ADTs for short, and lend themselves particularly well to the object-oriented programming approach introduced in Chapter 12 and pursued in later chapters.

15.4.1   Case study: *Traffic lights*

Let's assume we are to implement a program to control traffic lights. Not surprisingly Modula-2 has no built-in `TrafficLight` data type, nor built-in operations specifically for such a type, so we need to develop our own abstract data type.

In Britain, each occurrence of a real traffic light comprises three coloured lights: a red, an amber and a green. These lights can be on or off, but only the following combinations of 'on' lights are allowed:

- green alone for go,
- amber alone to warn that lights are about to go red,
- red alone for stop,
- red and amber together to indicate that lights are about to go green.

We can build the data type we require using the facilities that Modula-2 does provide. Here's how:

```
TYPE
    State = (on, off); (*an enumerated type*)

    TrafficLight = POINTER TO LightType;

    LightType  =   RECORD
                          red, amber, green : State
                   END; (*LightType*)
```

Next, we need to decide on the operations that need to be made available to create and manipulate objects of this type.

We need to be able to:
> create traffic light objects,
> dispose of traffic light objects,
> set a traffic light to signal GO,
> set a traffic light to signal STOP,
> set a traffic light to signal PREPARE TO STOP,
> set a traffic light to signal PREPARE TO GO,
> display a traffic light.

Here's the DEFINITION module:

```
DEFINITION MODULE Lights;

TYPE
    State = (on,off);
    TrafficLight = POINTER TO LightType;
    LightType =    RECORD
                        red,amber,green : State
                   END; (*LightType*)

PROCEDURE Create(VAR tl:TrafficLight);

PROCEDURE Dispose(VAR tl:TrafficLight);

PROCEDURE Stop(VAR tl:TrafficLight);

PROCEDURE PreStop(VAR tl:TrafficLight);

PROCEDURE PreGo(VAR tl:TrafficLight);

PROCEDURE Go(VAR tl:TrafficLight);

PROCEDURE Display(tl:TrafficLight);

END Lights.
```

and the corresponding IMPLEMENTATION module:

```
IMPLEMENTATION MODULE Lights;

FROM InOut IMPORT WriteString, WriteLn;
FROM Storage IMPORT ALLOCATE, DEALLOCATE;

PROCEDURE Create(VAR tl:TrafficLight);
BEGIN
    ALLOCATE(tl,SIZE(LightType));
END Create;

PROCEDURE Dispose(VAR tl:TrafficLight);
BEGIN
    DEALLOCATE(tl,SIZE(LightType));
    tl := NIL
END Dispose;
```

```
PROCEDURE Stop(VAR tl:TrafficLight);
BEGIN
    IF tl <> NIL THEN
        tl^.red:=on;
        tl^.amber:=off;
        tl^.green:=off
    END (*IF*)
END Stop;

PROCEDURE PreStop(VAR tl:TrafficLight);
BEGIN
    IF tl <> NIL THEN
        tl^.red:=off;
        tl^.amber:=on;
        tl^.green:=off
    END (*IF*)
END PreStop;

PROCEDURE PreGo(VAR tl:TrafficLight);
BEGIN
    IF tl <> NIL THEN
        tl^.red:=on;
        tl^.amber:=on;
        tl^.green:=off
    END (*IF*)
END PreGo;

PROCEDURE Go(VAR tl:TrafficLight);
BEGIN
    IF tl <> NIL THEN
        tl^.red:=off;
        tl^.amber:=off;
        tl^.green:=on
    END (*IF*)
END Go;

PROCEDURE Display(tl:TrafficLight);
BEGIN
    IF tl <> NIL THEN
        IF tl^.red=on THEN
            WriteString("Red is on");
        ELSE
            WriteString("Red is off");
        END; (*IF*)
        WriteLn;
        IF tl^.green=on THEN
            WriteString("Green is on");
        ELSE
            WriteString("Green is off");
        END; (*IF*)
        WriteLn;
        IF tl^.amber=on THEN
            WriteString("Amber is on");
        ELSE
            WriteString("Amber is off");
        END; (*IF*)
        WriteLn;
        WriteLn
    END (*IF*)
END Display;

END Lights.
```

We now have an abstract data type that will enable us to create and manipulate instances of traffic light objects. The module is self-contained and independent of other program parts so we could, for example, upgrade the traffic light module so that it displays the lights graphically and there should be no need to alter any client modules.

15.4.2   Opaque export

There is a potential snag with our `Lights` module. The procedure implementations are hidden within the IMPLEMENTATION MODULE and are not available to the client module. The data type declarations are contained in the DEFINITION MODULE, which means that the `LightType` data fields are visible (or transparent) to any client module which could access the fields of the record directly without using the procedures provided. Whether by intention or accident, it would be possible to set the red, amber and green lights all to on together which, with traffic lights, should never be allowed to happen! To ensure that client modules cannot do this, `TrafficLight` can be made into an opaque type which is exportable as a complete entity but cannot be manipulated other than via the module's procedures.

To achieve this, the type identifier is included for export in the DEFINITION MODULE and the full type declaration is given only in the implementation module.

```
DEFINITION MODULE Lights;

TYPE
    TrafficLight;    (*Opaque type*)

    (*Procedure definitions as before*)
    PROCEDURE Create.....
    .....
    .....

END Lights.



IMPLEMENTATION MODULE Lights;

FROM InOut IMPORT WriteString, WriteLn;
FROM Storage IMPORT ALLOCATE, DEALLOCATE;
TYPE
    State = (on,off);

    TrafficLight = POINTER TO LightType;
    LightType  =  RECORD
                        red,amber,green : State
                    END; (*LightType*)

    (*Full procedure declarations as before*)
    PROCEDURE Create.....
    .....
    .....
END Lights.
```

15.4.3   Encapsulation

In the above example, the type and associated operations are said to be encapsulated within the Lights module.

We can create as many TrafficLight objects as we wish, but they can be manipulated only via the procedures exported by the Lights module.

15.4.4   ADTs based on a linked list structure

A similar form of abstraction can be used with linked-list structures consisting of the data definition and a set of specific associated operations relating to the processing of a particular data type.

There are three important basic types of ADT which can be best implemented using pointers:

The stack

A stack is a 'First In Last Out' (FILO) data structure. It can be thought of as a vertical structure with only the top accessible. New elements are added to the top and elements can be removed only from the top.

This is analogous to one of those spring-loaded plate holding mechanisms you may sometimes find in cafeterias, which dispense one plate at a time. As clean plates are added to the top, the stack is pushed down, ensuring that only the top plate can be accessed at any time. When you take a plate from the stack the spring causes the plate below to pop up and take its turn as the top plate.

top

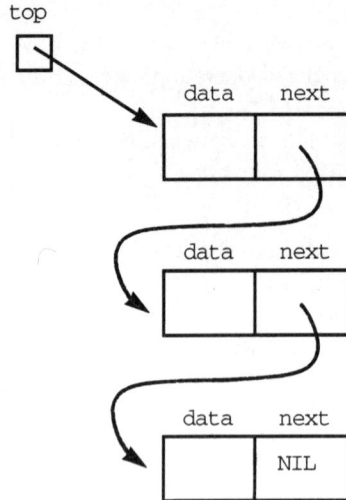

Your Modula-2 language compiler generates machine code which makes use of a stack for passing parameters to subprograms.

When a procedure is called, the address of the instruction following the procedure call is stored. When a procedure ends, the computer needs to refer to the stored address to know where to resume processing. To allow for nesting of procedures and recursive procedure calls, an unspecified number of return addresses need to be preserved. However, the return address is always the last address stored. If a stack is used to store the return addresses then the LIFO principle will always ensure that the processing continues from the correct place.

The queue

A queue is a 'First In First Out' (FIFO) data structure with a head and a tail. New elements are added to the tail (i.e. the end of the queue) and the element at the head is the first to be removed. This is analogous to a queue (or line) of people waiting to be served at a supermarket checkout. We'll be looking at a special case of a queue in Chapter 17.

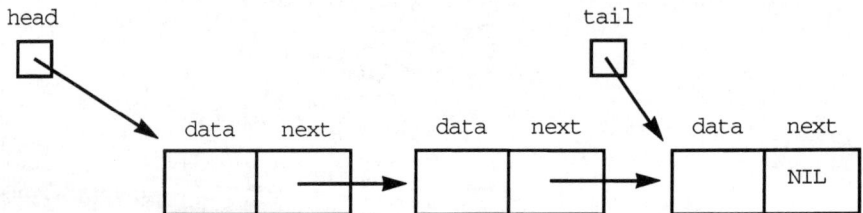

Computers use queues for such tasks as allowing access to the processor or to a peripheral device, such as a printer, when users are working with a multi-user system.

The tree

A tree is a hierarchical data structure, which can be made to 'fork' at each node. Trees merit a section of their own, so we'll defer our own 'arboreal' discussion until the following chapter.

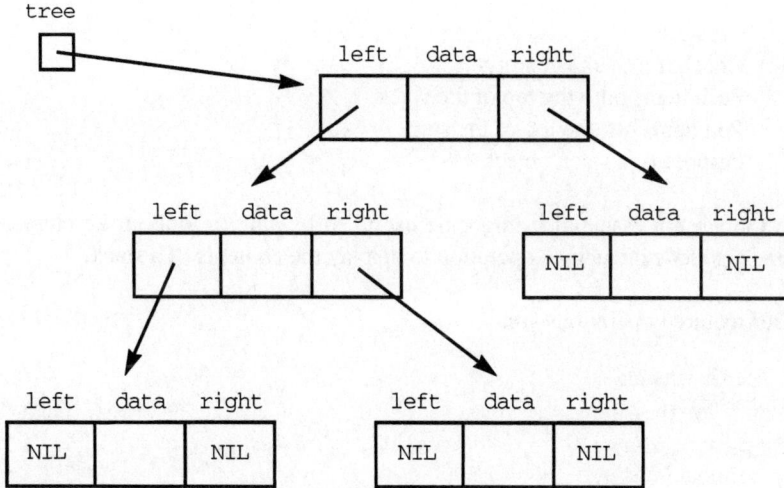

Computer systems often use tree structures to organize files into a directory hierarchy.

There are many variations in the implementation of these abstract data types and all have many applications in computer science. Any serious study of computer programming should incorporate an appreciation of the strengths of these ADTs and some practical examples of their use.

15.4.5   Case study: *the stack*

Every ADT has a number of essential procedures, or primitive operations, which are required for the creation and use of instances of objects of that type. In the case of a stack we need to be able to:

- Create stack objects,
- Check if a stack is empty,
- Push items onto the top of the stack,
- Pop items off the top of the stack,
- Dispose of a stack object.

Although not essential it might be useful to be able to look at the elements stored in a stack, so let's include an operation to display the contents of a stack.

Our required operations are:

```
CreateStack
IsEmpty
Push
Pop
DisposeStack
DisplayStack
```

You may come across the terms 'stack overflow' and possibly 'stack underflow'.
The term 'stack overflow' simply means that all the available space inside the computer has been allocated and an attempt to Push an item to a stack has failed.
The term 'stack underflow' indicates that an attempt has been made to Pop an element from an empty stack.
We can encapsulate our stack data type within its own module, which will export the stack type and all the allowable operations. Here's the DEFINITION MODULE.

```
DEFINITION MODULE Stack;
(* operates a stack; a Last-In-First-Out data structure*)

TYPE
    StackType;   (* Opaque type *)

    PROCEDURE CreateStack (VAR top :StackType);

    PROCEDURE IsEmpty (top : StackType): BOOLEAN;

    PROCEDURE Push (VAR top :StackType; inChar : CHAR);

    PROCEDURE Pop (VAR top : StackType; VAR outChar : CHAR);

    PROCEDURE DisposeStack(VAR top : StackType);

    PROCEDURE DisplayStack(top : StackType);

END Stack.
```

And here is the IMPLEMENTATION MODULE:

```
IMPLEMENTATION MODULE Stack;
(* operates a stack; a Last-In-First-Out data structure*)
FROM InOut IMPORT Write, WriteLn;
FROM Storage IMPORT ALLOCATE, DEALLOCATE;
TYPE
    StackType = POINTER TO StackRecord;
    StackRecord  =    RECORD
                          stackChar : CHAR;
                          next : StackType
                      END; (*StackRecord*)

PROCEDURE CreateStack (VAR top :StackType);
BEGIN
    top := NIL
END CreateStack;

PROCEDURE IsEmpty (top : StackType): BOOLEAN;
BEGIN
    IF top=NIL THEN
        RETURN TRUE
    ELSE
        RETURN FALSE
    END
END IsEmpty;

PROCEDURE Push (VAR top :StackType; inChar : CHAR);
(* add an item to the top of the stack *)
VAR temp: StackType;
BEGIN
    ALLOCATE(temp, SIZE(StackRecord));
    WITH temp^ DO
        stackChar:=inChar;
        next:=top
    END; (*WITH*)
    top:= temp
END Push;

PROCEDURE Pop (VAR top : StackType; VAR outChar : CHAR);
(* remove an Item from the top of the stack*)
VAR temp : StackType;
BEGIN
    IF NOT IsEmpty(top) THEN
        temp := top;
        WITH temp^ DO
            outChar:= stackChar;
            top := next
        END; (*WITH*)
        DEALLOCATE(temp,SIZE(StackRecord))
    END (*IF*)
END Pop;

PROCEDURE DisposeStack(VAR top : StackType);
(*remove all items from the stack*)
VAR outChar : CHAR;
BEGIN
    WHILE (NOT IsEmpty(top)) DO
        Pop(top,outChar)
    END (*WHILE*)
END DisposeStack;
```

```
PROCEDURE DisplayStack(top : StackType);
VAR
    outChar : CHAR;
BEGIN
    IF NOT IsEmpty(top) THEN
        Pop(top,outChar);
        Write(outChar);
        WriteLn;
        DisplayStack(top^.next)
    END (*IF*)
END DisplayStack;

END Stack.
```

An application using a stack

As an example of a way in which we could use this stack ADT, let's write a 'highly useful' program to translate English words to those used by people on the planet Htrae, which lies in a parallel galaxy to our own called the Yaw Yklim. On Htrae everything exists as in our own, but is reversed. Here's a program we have written to allow us to communicate with our counterparts, Gninnidnelg Eneri and Mahtat Cire.

As you've probably realized, all the program needs to do to translate either language is to take in a sequence of characters and reverse them. A stack is ideal for this.

As it is such a simple client program we will go straight to the pseudocode:

Translator:
BEGIN
    Create a stack object
    Load the stack with the character string to be translated
    Empty the stack, displaying each character in turn
END Translator.

LoadStack:
BEGIN
    Read char
    WHILE not EOL DO
        Push the char on to the stack
        Read next char
    END WHILE
END LoadStack;

EmptyStack:
BEGIN
    WHILE the stack is not empty DO
        Pop a char from the stack
        display popped char
    END WHILE
END EmptyStack;

HTRAE
SEMOCLEW
2ALUDOM
STNEDUTS

Here is the finished client program which uses the Stack module.

```
MODULE Translator;
(* uses a stack to reverse the characters in a name *)
FROM InOut IMPORT Read, Write, WriteString, WriteLn, EOL;
FROM Stack IMPORT StackType,CreateStack, Push, Pop, IsEmpty;

VAR  stackTop : StackType;

PROCEDURE LoadStack (VAR stackTop : StackType);
(* read characters from the keyboard and push them on to
**the stack, until EOL is read *)
VAR inChar : CHAR;
BEGIN
    WriteLn;
    WriteString("Please type in the name to translate");
    WriteLn;
    Read (inChar);
    WHILE (inChar <> EOL) DO
        Push (stackTop,inChar);
        Read (inChar);
    END (*WHILE*)
END LoadStack;

PROCEDURE EmptyStack (stackTop : StackType);
(* pop each item in turn off the stack and display the
**character returned *)
VAR outChar : CHAR;
BEGIN
    WriteLn;
    WriteString ("The translation is    ");
    WHILE (NOT IsEmpty(stackTop)) DO
        Pop (stackTop,outChar);
        Write (outChar)
    END; (*WHILE*)
    WriteLn
END EmptyStack;

BEGIN (*Main program*)
    CreateStack (stackTop);
    LoadStack (stackTop);
    EmptyStack(stackTop)
END Translator.
```

Exercise 15.1

Write a driver program that uses Lights to display the sequence corresponding to:
GO,
PREPARE TO STOP,
STOP,
PREPARE TO GO,
GO.

Exercise 15.2

Write a program using the Stack module and the StringStuff module to check for words that are palindromes (i.e. words that read the same backwards or forwards, such as, madam, noon, eve).

Exercise 15.3

a)   Write a procedure, SearchList, which searches a linked list of elements for a particular value and returns the address of the element.

b)   Write a procedure, InsertElement, to insert an element between two elements of a linked list. This procedure requires two value parameters: a pointer to the element where the new element will be inserted and a CARDINAL value as data to be stored in the element.

c)   Write a procedure to remove an element from a linked list.

Exercise 15.4

Write a program which inputs a stream of characters from the keyboard, creates a linked list of LinkType elements, as shown below, and then searches for characters within the list, outputing the sequence number of each one found.

```
TYPE
    LinkPtr = POINTER TO Link;
    LinkType  =    RECORD
                        linkChar : CHAR;
                        linkSeq : CARDINAL;
                        next : LinkPtr
                   END; (*LinkType*)
```

The field, linkSeq, is the sequence number of the character in the input stream.
Once the list has been created, the program should ask for a search character and use it to search the list. Each time a match is found the sequence number, linkSeq, is output.

There may be several occurrences of any character in the list, so the whole list should be searched. The program should continue to ask for and search for characters until the user opts to quit. At this point the list should be purged by deallocating link elements until the list is empty.

Exercise 15.5

Modify the program in Exercise 15.4 so that it plays a game of 'Hangman.' The game is played like this:

> A word or phrase is entered in secret, so that the player cannot see it. This can be done either by using a second player, or by taking phrases from a file. The letters of the phrase are put into a linked list, using LinkType elements. The player is told how many letters there are in each word, i.e. the position of the spaces and the total number of characters input. The aim of the game is to guess the phrase before a drawing of a gallows and hanging man can be completed.
> One 'go' of the game consists of the player nominating a character and being told every place where that character is used in the phrase. The player loses a life if the character is not contained in the phrase. At each lost life another piece of the gallows and hanging man is drawn. The player may substitute for a 'go' a guess at the phrase, but a wrong guess is another lost life. If the player has not guessed the phrase by the time the drawing is complete then the game is lost.
> It may be easier to have a designated number of lives to lose, e.g. 10, rather than drawing a gallows and hanging man, but that is up to your ingenuity.

Exercise 15.6

Rewrite the bar code reader program (see Chapter 11) to use a linked list for storing the records for till receipts.

Exercise 15.7

Modify the Pop procedure in the Stack module so that it reports stack underflow (an attempt to Pop from an empty stack) in the form of a BOOLEAN parameter.

Exercise 15.8

Write a client program which uses the Stack module to examine an expression to check for paired brackets. There are three types of brackets ( ) { } and [ ]. The program should follow these rules:

For each character in the expression:

- if the character is not a bracket then ignore it and continue to the next character,
- if the character is an opening bracket, push it on to the stack,
- if the character is a closing bracket pop a character off the stack,
- if the opening and closing brackets are not of the same type, or stack underflow occurred, add 1 to the mismatch count, else add 1 to the matched count,
- if the stack is not empty at the end of the expression then add one to the mismatch count for every character popped off the stack at the end.

Finally, report on how many pairs of matched and mismatched brackets were found.

16 Binary trees

16.1 Binary tree structure

A binary tree is a very useful hierarchical data structure which resembles a tree in that it consists of branching nodes.

Unlike real trees, convention has it that binary trees are represented diagrammatically with 'root' uppermost. Accordingly, the node at the top is called the root, while the nodes at the bottom are sometimes referred to as leaves.

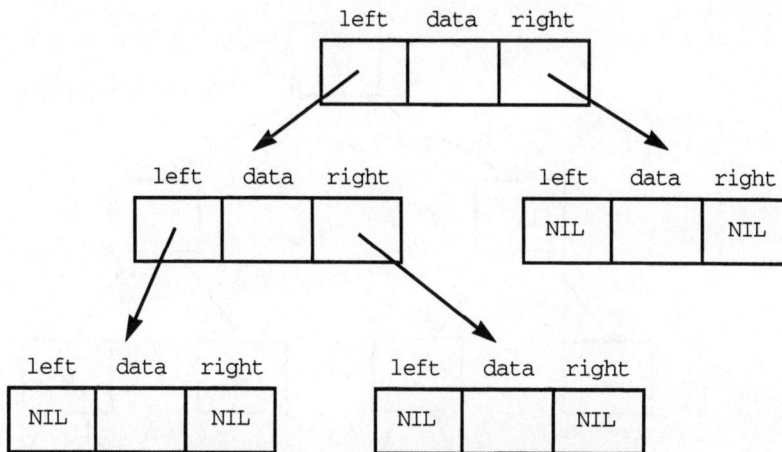

With a **binary** tree, each node contains one or more data fields and two pointers pointing to further nodes. One of the pointers points to the left descendant and the other to the right descendant of the node.

(Notice the mixing of analogies. The structure also resembles a genealogical tree. Thus, besides the terms root, branch and leaves, it is common to find terms such as parent, ancestor, child and descendant used in association with tree structures.)

A node or element type can be declared using a RECORD structure that contains two POINTERs as well as any data items to be held within the node.

```
TYPE
    BinaryTree = POINTER TO Node;

    Node  =    RECORD
                  data : DataType;
                  leftChild,
                  rightChild : BinaryTree
               END; (*Node*)
```

16.2   Tree traversal

When looking at or searching for data contained in a binary tree, we need to be able to visit each node of the tree just once. This process is called traversal and can be done in a number of ways.

In each of the examples, assume we are working with a binary tree which represents the following arithmetic expression:

$$(a + (b - c)) / (d - (e * f))$$

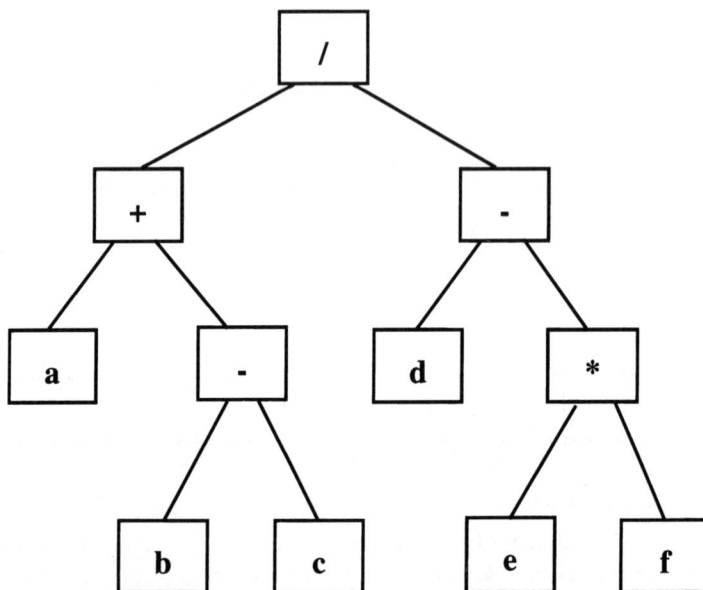

16.2.1   Pre-order traversal

Pre-order traversal proceeds by visiting the root, then traversal of the left sub-tree, followed by traversal of the right sub-tree.

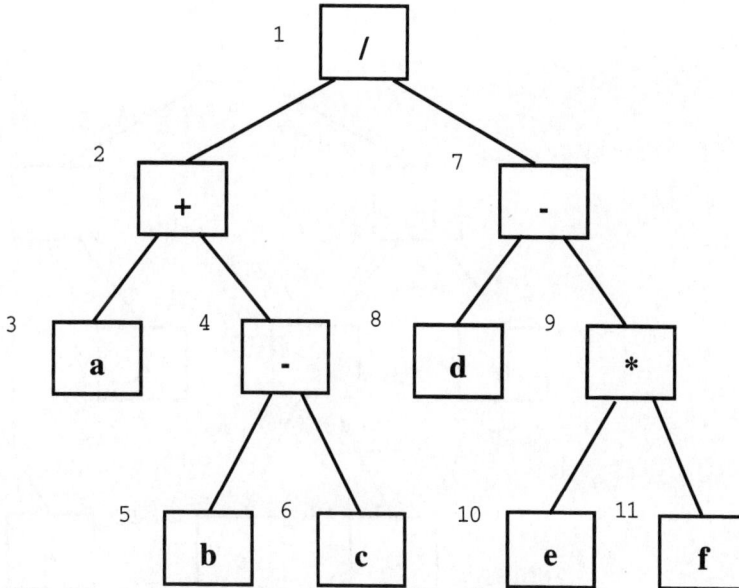

The numbers indicate the order in which the nodes are traversed.
The nodes are thus visited in the sequence:
        / + a - bc - d * e f

The pseudocode to accomplish this is:

PreOrder:
BEGIN
        Visit the root
        Traverse the left sub-tree
        Traverse the right sub-tree
END PreOrder;

This can be written as a recursive procedure:

```
PROCEDURE PreOrder(tree:BinaryTree);
BEGIN
    IF tree<>NIL THEN
        Write(tree^.data);
        PreOrder(tree^.leftChild);
        PreOrder(tree^.rightChild)
    END
END PreOrder;
```

16.2.2   In-order traversal

In-order traversal proceeds by first traversing the left sub-tree, then visiting the root, followed by traversal of the right sub-tree.

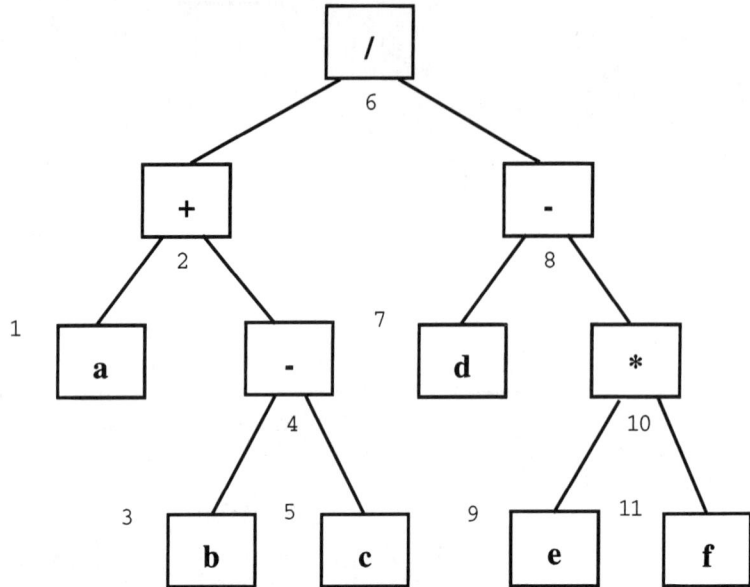

The numbers indicate the order in which the nodes are traversed.
The nodes are thus visited in the sequence: a + b - c / d - e * f

The pseudocode to accomplish this is:

InOrder:
BEGIN
    Traverse the left sub-tree
    Visit the root
    Traverse the right sub-tree
END InOrder;

This can be written as a recursive procedure:

```
PROCEDURE InOrder(tree:BinaryTree);
BEGIN
    IF tree<>NIL THEN
        InOrder(tree^.leftChild);
        Write(tree^.data);
        InOrder(tree^.rightChild)
    END
END InOrder;
```

16.2.3   Post-order traversal

Post-order traversal proceeds by traversal of the left sub-tree, followed by traversal of the right sub-tree, before visiting the root.

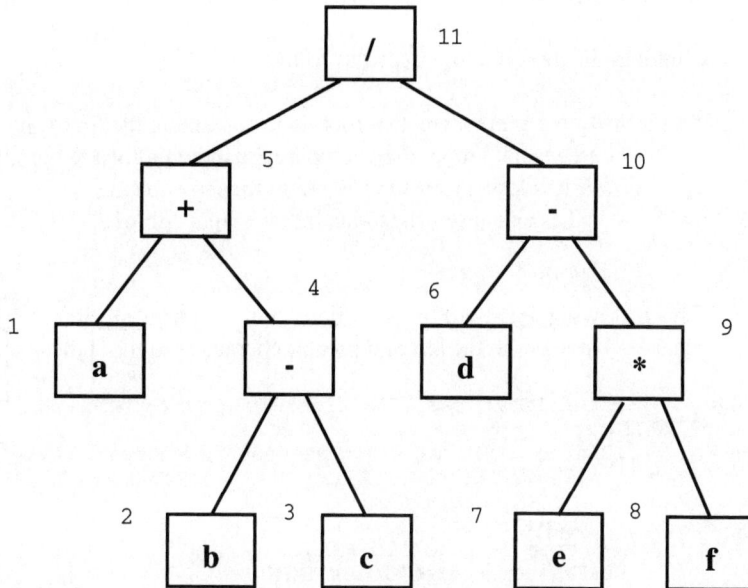

The numbers indicate the order in which the nodes are traversed.
The nodes are thus visited in the sequence: a b c - + d e f * - /

The pseudocode to accomplish this is:

PostOrder:
BEGIN
     Traverse the left sub-tree
     Traverse the right sub-tree
     Visit the root
END PostOrder;

This can be written as a recursive procedure:

```
PROCEDURE PostOrder(tree:BinaryTree);
BEGIN
    IF tree<>NIL THEN
        PostOrder(tree^.leftChild);
        PostOrder(tree^.rightChild);
        Write(tree^.data)
    END
END PostOrder;
```

The results of these traversal methods correspond to the prefix, infix and postfix (reverse Polish notation) forms of the expression.

16.3   Sorting using a binary tree

Amongst other things, a binary tree can be a convenient way of sorting. We need to be careful how we place items into the binary tree structure and then use the appropriate traversal method to extract the sorted data.

Building the tree should proceed as follows:

- if the tree is empty, create a root node containing the first value,
- if the tree is not empty then compare the incoming value with that in the root.
    If it is less, insert the value into the left sub-tree,
    otherwise insert the value into the right sub-tree.

The following `BuildTree` procedure builds a tree of characters with alphabetically smaller characters to the left and greater characters to the right:

```
PROCEDURE BuildTree (VAR tree:BinaryTree; item:CHAR);
BEGIN
    IF tree = NIL THEN   (*The tree is empty*)
        ALLOCATE(tree,SIZE(Node));
        tree^.data:=item;
        tree^.leftChild:=NIL;
        tree^.rightChild:=NIL
    ELSIF item < tree^.data THEN
        BuildTree(tree^.leftChild,item)
    ELSE
        BuildTree(tree^.rightChild,item)
    END (*IF*)
END BuildTree;
```

so, entering the letters:

d b f a c e g

produces the tree:

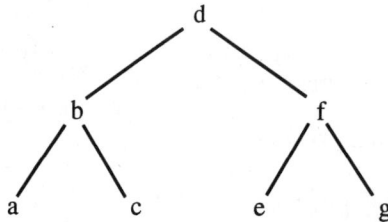

Even though different trees will result if the letters input to `BuildTree` are in a different order, notice that it always inserts them so that the `InOrder` traversal extracts them in alphabetic order.

Entering the letters:

    c f g a d e b

produces the tree:

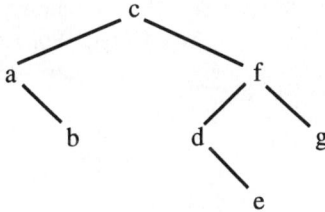

16.4   Case study: *Animal Magic*

We can use a binary tree structure to implement
a simple 'expert' system in which we 'teach' the
computer to identify different animals.

The computer is to ask us questions requiring
only a 'yes' or 'no' response to determine what
animal we are describing.

Let's assume its first guess is an elephant. So, on running the program the computer asks:
    'Is it an elephant?'
If we reply Y then the computer has finished, but if we reply N the computer asks:
    'What was the animal?'
then
    'What question should I have asked?'
and
    'What would have been the correct response, Y or N?'

If the animal we were thinking of had been a tiger, to distinguish between tiger and
elephant the question the computer should have asked could have been:
    'Does it have tusks?'
and the correct response would have been N.
The computer incorporates this information into the binary tree and, on the next run, first
asks:
    'Does it have tusks?'

Every time the computer comes across an animal it does not already know about, the
animal, together with an appropriate question, are added to the tree.

We have implemented a program to do this by setting up a binary tree structure with a single initial node containing the question:

'Is it an elephant?'

If the user responds with 'Yes' there is nothing to be done. However, if the user responds 'No', two new nodes must be added to the tree. One containing the correct animal and the other the question that should have been asked first. For example, if the user had been thinking of a tiger, the distinguishing question could have been;

'Does it have tusks?'

The tree becomes:

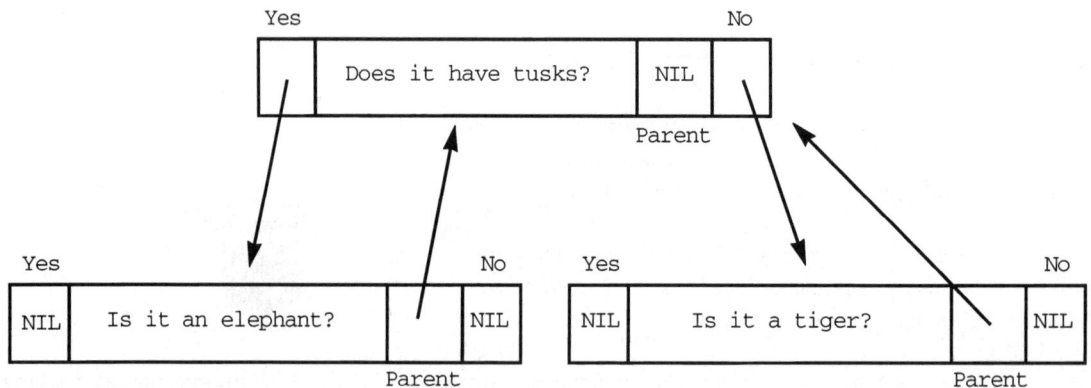

To add a node above the current node we need to include a 'parent' pointer within each node as well as pointers to each of the 'children.' On each run the program starts with the question at the root node and works down the tree on a route dependent on the Yes/No answers given by the user.

```
MODULE AnimalMagic;
(*Purpose: Uses a binary tree to play an animal
**guessing game
**Uses modules: InOut, Storage, MyIO*)
FROM InOut IMPORT WriteString, WriteLn, Write, Read,EOL;
FROM Storage IMPORT ALLOCATE, DEALLOCATE;
FROM MyIO IMPORT ReadLine;
CONST
    ESC = 33C;
    NULL = 0C;
    MAXSTR = 50;
TYPE
    Str = ARRAY[0..MAXSTR] OF CHAR;
    BinTree = POINTER TO TreeNode;

    TreeNode  =    RECORD
                        parent:BinTree;
                        message : Str;
                        yeschild : BinTree;
                        nochild: BinTree;
                   END; (*TreeNode*)

VAR
    root,tree,prev:BinTree;
    response,ch:CHAR;
    animal,question:Str;
    correct:BOOLEAN;

PROCEDURE InitTree(VAR root: BinTree);
(*Initializes the binary tree
**Pre: None
**Post: root is initialized with a single node
**containing first guess at animal name*)
BEGIN
    ALLOCATE(root, SIZE(TreeNode));
    root^.message := "Is it an elephant";
    root^.yeschild:=NIL;
    root^.nochild:=NIL;
    root^.parent:=NIL;
END InitTree;

PROCEDURE RemoveTree(VAR current:BinTree);
(*Disposes of the binary tree, freeing memory space
**Pre: current points to a binary tree
**Post: current points to NIL*)
BEGIN
    IF current^.yeschild<>NIL THEN
        RemoveTree(current^.yeschild)
    END; (*IF*)
    IF current^.nochild<>NIL THEN
        RemoveTree(current^.nochild)
    END; (*IF*)
    DEALLOCATE(current,SIZE(TreeNode));
    current:=NIL
END RemoveTree;
```

```
PROCEDURE InsertQuestion(VAR root:BinTree;
                             position: BinTree;
                             question,animal:Str;
                             answer:CHAR);
(*Inserts additional question node
**Pre: root points to the root node of the binary tree
**position points to the current position in tree
**question contains the question to be inserted
**animal contains the animal guess to be inserted
**answer contains 'Y' or 'N' to determine node
**relationships
**Post: root points to the tree with new nodes inserted*)
VAR
    tempquest,tempanimal:BinTree;
BEGIN
    ALLOCATE(tempquest,SIZE(TreeNode));
    ALLOCATE(tempanimal,SIZE(TreeNode));
    tempquest^.message := question;
    tempanimal^.message := animal;
    tempanimal^.yeschild:=NIL;
    tempanimal^.nochild:=NIL;
    IF CAP(answer)="Y" THEN
        tempquest^.yeschild:=tempanimal;
        tempquest^.nochild:=position;
    ELSE
        tempquest^.yeschild:=position;
        tempquest^.nochild:=tempanimal;
    END;   (*IF*)
    IF position^.parent<>NIL THEN
        IF position^.parent^.yeschild=position THEN
            position^.parent^.yeschild:=tempquest
        ELSE
            position^.parent^.nochild:=tempquest
        END   (*IF*)
    END; (*IF*)
    tempanimal^.parent:=tempquest;
    position^.parent:=tempquest;
    IF position=root THEN
        root:=tempquest
    END (*IF*)
END InsertQuestion;
```

```
PROCEDURE AskQuestions(tree:BinTree;
                              VAR correct : BOOLEAN);
(*Traverses tree starting at the root, traversal
**follows user's yes/no responses to questions
**Pre: tree points to binary tree
**Post: correct is TRUE if user's animal is found
**in the tree, otherwise correct is FALSE*)
VAR
    reply,cr : CHAR;
BEGIN
    WHILE tree<>NIL DO
        prev:=tree;
        WriteLn;
        WriteString(tree^.message);
        WriteLn;
        WriteString("Type 'Y' or 'N' ");
        Read(reply);
        Read(cr);   (*Read RETURN character*)
        reply:=CAP(reply);
        IF (reply="Y") THEN
            tree:=tree^.yeschild;
            correct := TRUE
        ELSE
            tree:=tree^.nochild;
            correct :=FALSE
        END (*IF*)
    END (*WHILE*)
END AskQuestions;


PROCEDURE GetNewAnimal(VAR animal : Str);
(*Sets up new animal guess
**Pre: None
**Post: animal contains a question of the form
**      "Is it a " followed by new animal name
**supplied by user*)
CONST
    PREFIX = 8;
    VAR ch :CHAR;
    i: CARDINAL;
BEGIN
    WriteString("Please name the animal");
    WriteLn;
    animal := "Is it a ";   (*Set the question prefix*)
    i:=PREFIX;
    LOOP
        Read(ch);
        IF ch=EOL THEN EXIT END;
        animal[i]:=ch;
        INC(i)
    END;
    animal[i]:=NULL;
    WriteLn
END GetNewAnimal;
```

```
PROCEDURE GetNewQuesAns(VAR question: Str;
                          VAR response : CHAR);
(*gets a new question and appropriate response
**Pre: None
**Post: question contains a new question supplied by user
** response contains correct 'Y' or 'N' response
**as supplied by user*)
VAR
    cr : CHAR;
BEGIN
    WriteString("Type in the question I should have asked");
    WriteLn;
    ReadLine(question);

    WriteLn;
    WriteString("Correct answer have been, Y or N?");
    Read(response);
    Read(cr)  (*Read RETURN character*)
END GetNewQuesAns;

BEGIN  (*main AnimalMagic program*)
    ch:=" ";
    (*Initialize the tree*)
    InitTree(root);
    REPEAT
        tree:=root;
        (*Traverse the tree, asking questions*)
        AskQuestions(tree, correct);
        (*If not correct then add new animal and
        **question to the tree*)
        IF NOT correct THEN
            GetNewAnimal(animal);
            GetNewQuesAns(question, response);
            InsertQuestion(root,prev,question,
                                   animal,CAP(response));
        ELSE
            WriteString("Aren't I clever?");
        END;
        WriteLn;
        WriteString("Press RETURN to continue, ");
        WriteString("or ESC then RETURN to exit");
        Read(ch);
    UNTIL ch=ESC;
    (*Deallocate memory occupied by tree*)
    RemoveTree(root)
END AnimalMagic.
```

17 Simulation using a priority queue

17.1 Simulation

One of the most useful features of computer spreadsheet programs is that they allow their users to do 'what if?' experiments. For example, you could use a spreadsheet to construct a table showing the annual interest payments on a loan at a given rate of interest and then investigate the effect of interest rate changes or alterations to the repayment period. In other words the spreadsheet allows you to simulate what will happen if certain variable factors change. Besides spreadsheet programs, computers can be usefully employed to simulate other aspects of the real world. For example, the government makes use computer models, which attempt to simulate the country's economy, to help predict the likely effects of national budget decisions. Obviously, the effects predicted by a computer simulation are only as reliable as the assumptions on which the model is based.

17.1.1 Continuous simulation

Often, simulation programs have a dependence on time, for example a flight simulator being used to train pilots would run in real time with an hour's 'flight' in the simulator corresponding to an hour of real flight. This type of simulation is called **continuous simulation**.

17.1.2 Discrete simulation

Sometimes a simulation program is being used in a 'what if?' experiment that involves discrete (i.e. separate) events. For example, when planning the mission of a space probe significant events may occur during the journey when the probe passes close to planetary bodies but, as the probe journeys between, there may be weeks, months or even years when nothing significant is expected. In this case it would be more practical, not to run the simulation in real time, but to hop the clock forward from event to event in discrete chunks of time. In effect we would advance the clock straight to the time of the next significant event, then the next and so on. This type of simulation is called **discrete simulation**.

17.2   Case study: *Supermarket simulation*

In this chapter we are going to use a discrete simulation for an application which is less exciting than the above but which you are much more likely to have direct experience of; queuing at a supermarket checkout.

The simulation is going to necessitate the use of two data structures, both of which are based on a linked list.

The system is to simulate what happens in a supermarket as customers arrive at the checkout, with their trolleys, and await their turn to be served. The simulation program should allow us to carry out 'what if?' experiments to see, for given service speeds, inter-customer arrival times and opening times, how long the queue gets, how long customers have to wait to be served, and how many are still waiting to be served when the shop closes.

Although, for the sake of simplicity, we will stick with a single checkout, this kind of simulation could be used to help make decisions about such things as how many checkouts should be opened at particular times and what would be the effect of introducing express checkouts (i.e. checkouts with a maximum limit to the number of items per customer).

17.2.1   The priority queue

The basis of the simulation program will be a data structure called a priority queue.

A priority queue is a special kind of linked list. Items in the queue are indexed, in this case by time, so that the highest priority items are those with earlier times. When an item is added to the queue it is inserted in order, according to the index, so that the highest priority item is at the front of the queue and the lowest priority item is at the back. When an item is removed from the queue it is always taken from the front, i.e. it is always the item with the highest priority.

In the supermarket simulator, each priority queue node represents an event and the index is the time that the event will occur. There are two types of event required for the supermarket simulation; the arrival of a customer at the checkout and the departure of a customer from the checkout.

Thus, each event node in the priority queue will consist of a record in the form:

Event node:

Time index	Type of event; arrival or departure	Pointer to the next event node	Pointer to a customer

17.2.2   Customer records

A customer will be represented by a record containing the number of items in the customer's shopping trolley as well as the customer's arrival and departure times. To help analyze the simulation after running, we will number customers as they are generated, so we'll also need to include this number in the customer record.

Customer record:

Customer No.	Items in trolley	Arrival time	Departure time

17.2.3   The checkout queue

The program will also maintain a 'first in first out' queue to represent the queue of customers waiting to be served at the checkout.

CheckOut queue node record:

Customer Pointer	next

17.2.4   Putting it all together

Our program will need two queues:
- one representing the queue of customers waiting at the checkout and
- the other, an ordered queue of events (customer arrivals and departures) that are scheduled to take place in the future.

To illustrate how these will work, consider a 'snap-shot' frozen in time. Some events will have been and gone, some may be happening now, while other events will be queuing waiting for their turn to happen.
Every time a customer arrival event is processed, the customer's departure time is calculated as a function of the number of items in his/her trolley, and a new customer's arrival time is scheduled by being added to the event queue.

At the start of the simulation we will need to specify values for the following:
- the duration of the simulation and
- the service time per item in trolley.

We can use a random number generator to supply values for:
*   customer arrival times and
*   the number of items in customer's trolley.

Departure time can be calculated when service begins by multiplying service time per item by the number of items in the trolley.

Consider the following chain of events, assuming that the current time is exactly 15 time units after the opening of the supermarket.

These are the times and events that have already occurred:

Time	Events
8	Customer 1 arrived with 16 items and went to the checkout to be served. Departure time, calculated as a function of the number of items in trolley, was set for time=19.
10	Customer 2 arrived with 22 items and joined the queue at the checkout.
13	Customer 3 arrived with 40 items and joined the queue at the checkout.

This is the event occurring right now:

Time	Event
15	The event just being removed from the event queue indicates the time is 15 and the event is the arrival of customer 4 who has 20 items and will now join the checkout queue.

These times and events are yet to take place:

Time	Events
16	Another arrival event is scheduled. Customer 5 will join the checkout queue at time=16.
19	Customer 1, currently being served, is scheduled to leave the checkout so that service of the next customer in the checkout queue can commence. The next customer's departure time is scheduled and this event is added in the correct place in the event queue.
23	Another arrival event is scheduled to take place.

The following diagram shows the current state of the event queue and the checkout queue at time=15.

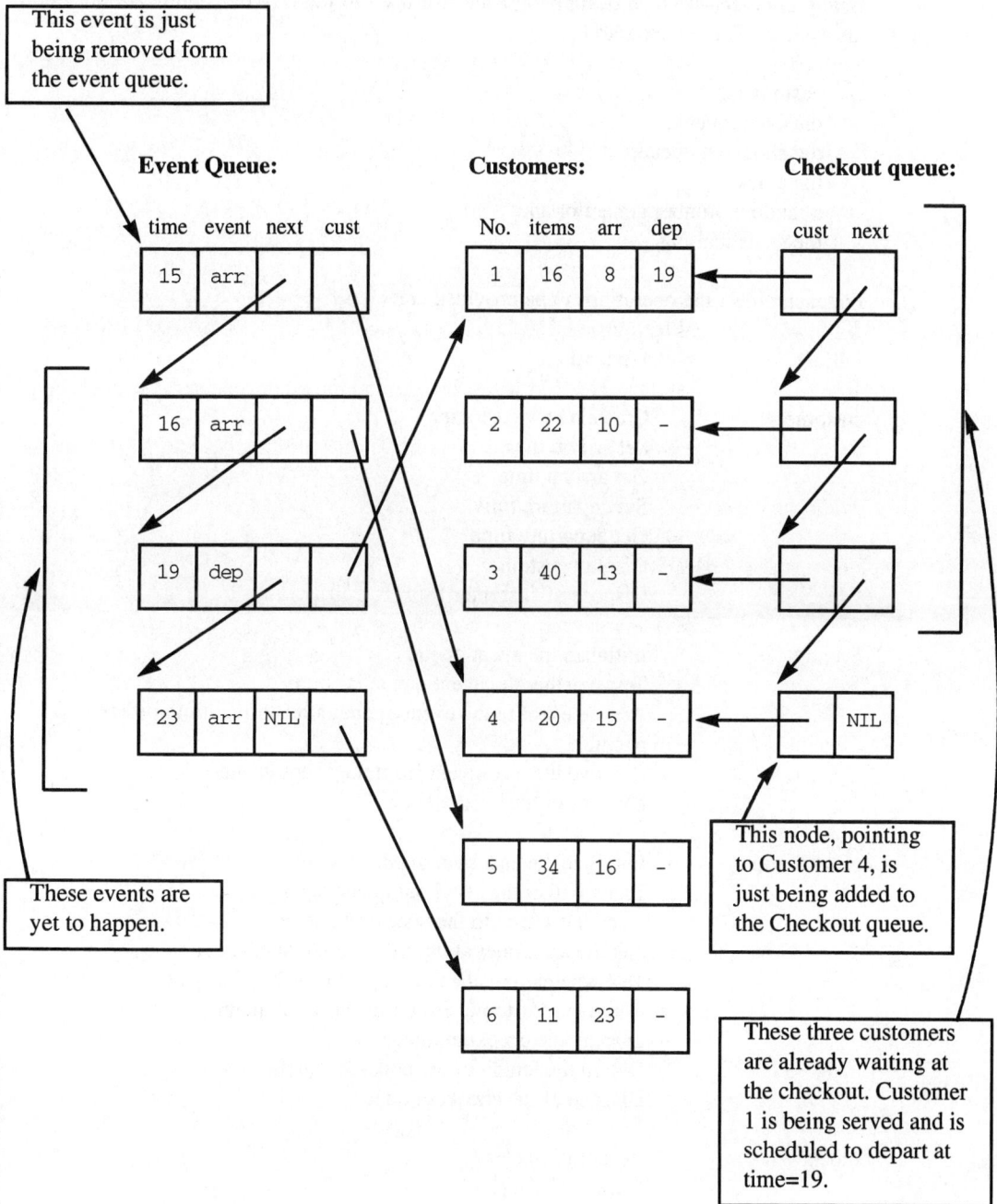

This event is just being removed form the event queue.

Event Queue:

time	event	next	cust
15	arr		
16	arr		
19	dep		
23	arr	NIL	

These events are yet to happen.

Customers:

No.	items	arr	dep
1	16	8	19
2	22	10	–
3	40	13	–
4	20	15	–
5	34	16	–
6	11	23	–

Checkout queue:

cust	next
	NIL

This node, pointing to Customer 4, is just being added to the Checkout queue.

These three customers are already waiting at the checkout. Customer 1 is being served and is scheduled to depart at time=19.

We will need to maintain a statistical log to provide information concerning the simulation to review on completion. For example, useful information could include the maximum length of the checkout queue and the total number of customers served.

Using an object-oriented design approach, we need to identify the significant objects for the system. These appear to be:

> customers,
> the event queue,
> the checkout queue,
> the clock,
> a random number generator and
> the statistical log.

For each object the operations to be provided are:

Object	**Operations**
customer	Create a new customer
	Set arrival time
	Get arrival time
	Set departure time
	Get departure time
	Display customer
	Dispose of customer
eventQ	Initialize the event queue
	Test whether the event queue is empty
	Add an event to the event queue in its correct time-ordered position
	Remove the next event from the event queue
	Dispose of the event queue
checkOutQ	Initialize the checkout queue
	Test whether the checkout queue is empty
	Add a customer to the checkout queue
	Get the customer at the front of the checkout queue
	Test whether the checkout operator is busy serving a customer
	Remove a customer from the checkout queue
	Display the checkout queue
	Obtain the length of the checkout queue
	Dispose of the checkout queue
clock	Reset the clock
	Increment the clock

randomNumberGenerator	Set the seed
	Get a 'random' number
statisticalLog	Log the checkout queue length
	Log the number of unserved customers
	Log the number of served customers
	Display the statistical log

The following diagram illustrates the module dependencies:

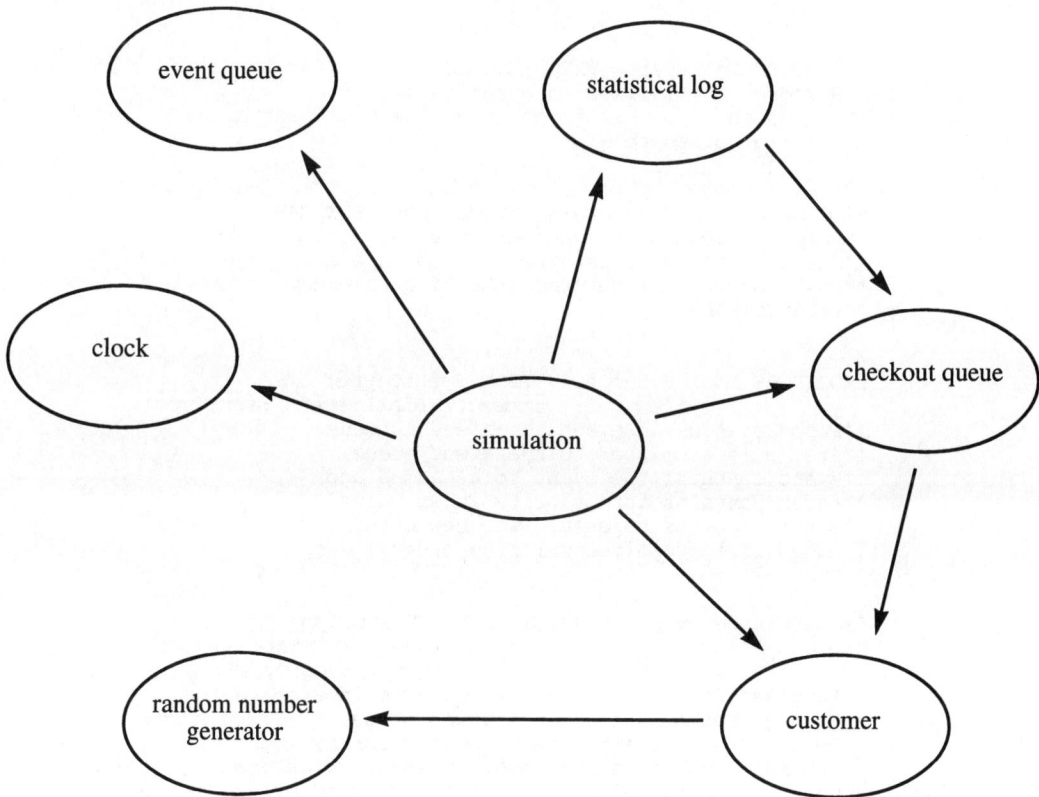

17.2.5   The priority event queue module

The priority event queue DEFINITION MODULE:

```
DEFINITION MODULE EventQ;
(*Purpose: To handle a priority queue of event nodes*)
TYPE
    EventQType=POINTER TO NodeRec;
    EventType=(arrive,depart);
    NodeRec  =     RECORD
                        index:CARDINAL;
                        event:EventType;
                        next:EventQType
                   END;  (*NodeRec*)

PROCEDURE InitEventQ(VAR q:EventQType);
(*Purpose: Initializes an event queue
**Pre: q is a pointer to an uninitialized event queue
**Post: q points to NIL*)


PROCEDURE IsEmptyEventQ(q :EventQType):BOOLEAN;
(*Purpose: Determines whether an event queue is empty
**Pre-conditions: q is a pointer to an event queue
**Post-conditions: returns TRUE if q is empty, otherwise
**returns FALSE*)


PROCEDURE AddToEventQ(    VAR q:EventQType;
                         index:CARDINAL;event:EventType);
(*Purpose: Adds an event to an event queue
**Pre: q is a pointer to the event queue;
**event contains the event to be added and
**index contains its priority index value
**Post: q points to queue with new event
**added in appropriate priority order*)


PROCEDURE RemoveFromEventQ(   VAR q:EventQType;
                              VAR index:CARDINAL;
                              VAR event: EventType);
(*Purpose: Removes the next event from an event queue
**Pre: q is a pointer to the event queue;
**Post: event contains the highest priority event
**and index contains its priority index value and q
**points to queue with the highest priority event removed*)


PROCEDURE DisplayEventQ(q:EventQType);
(*Purpose: Displays an event queue
**Pre: q is a pointer to the event queue;
**Post: None*)


PROCEDURE DisposeEventQ(VAR q:EventQType);
(*Purpose: Disposes of an event queue and deallocates memory
**Pre: q is a pointer to the event queue;
**Post: q is undefined*)

END EventQ.
```

The priority event queue IMPLEMENTATION MODULE:

```
IMPLEMENTATION MODULE EventQ;
(*Purpose: To handle a priority queue of event nodes*)
FROM Storage IMPORT ALLOCATE, DEALLOCATE;
FROM InOut IMPORT WriteString,WriteLn,WriteCard;

PROCEDURE InitEventQ(VAR q:EventQType);
(*Purpose: Initializes an event queue
**Pre: q is a pointer to an uninitialized event queue
**Post: q points to NIL*)
BEGIN
    q:=NIL;
END InitEventQ;


PROCEDURE IsEmptyEventQ(q :EventQType):BOOLEAN;
(*Purpose: Determines whether an event queue is empty
**Pre: q is a pointer to an event queue
**Post: returns TRUE if q is empty, otherwise
**returns FALSE*)
BEGIN
    IF q=NIL THEN
        RETURN TRUE
    ELSE
        RETURN FALSE
    END  (*IF*)
END IsEmptyEventQ;


PROCEDURE AddToEventQ(    VAR q:EventQType;
                         index:CARDINAL;event:EventType);
(*Purpose: Adds an event to an event queue
**Pre: q is a pointer to the event queue;
**event contains the event to be added and
**index contains its priority index value
**Post: q points to queue with new event
**added in appropriate priority order*)
VAR
    temp:EventQType;
BEGIN
    ALLOCATE(temp,SIZE(NodeRec));
    temp^.index:=index;
    temp^.event:=event;
    temp^.next:=NIL;
    IF IsEmptyEventQ(q) THEN
        q:=temp
    ELSIF  temp^.index<q^.index THEN
        (*insert in front of this one*)
        temp^.next:=q;
        q:=temp
    ELSE
        AddToEventQ(q^.next,index,event)
    END  (*IF*)
END AddToEventQ;
```

```
PROCEDURE RemoveFromEventQ(  VAR q:EventQType;
                             VAR index:CARDINAL;
                             VAR event: EventType);
(*Purpose: Removes the next event from an event queue
**Pre: q is a pointer to the event queue;
**Post: event contains the highest priority event
**and index contains its priority index value and q
**points to queue with the highest priority event removed*)
VAR
    temp:EventQType;
BEGIN
    IF NOT IsEmptyEventQ(q) THEN
        temp:=q;
        q:=q^.next;
        event:=temp^.event;
        index:=temp^.index;
        DEALLOCATE(temp,SIZE(NodeRec))
    END  (*IF*)
END RemoveFromEventQ;


PROCEDURE DisplayEventQ(q:EventQType);
(*Purpose: Displays an event queue
**Pre: q is a pointer to the event queue;
**Post: None*)
VAR
    temp:EventQType;
BEGIN
    WriteLn;
    WriteString("EVENT QUEUE");
    WriteLn;
    IF IsEmptyEventQ(q) THEN
        WriteString("The priority queue is now empty");
        WriteLn
    ELSE
        temp:=q;
        WHILE (NOT IsEmptyEventQ(temp)) DO
            WriteCard(temp^.index,1);
            WriteString("          ");
            CASE temp^.event OF
                arrive : WriteString("arrive");
            |   depart : WriteString("depart");
            ELSE
            END;  (*IF*)
            temp:=temp^.next;
            WriteLn
        END  (*WHILE*)
    END  (*IF*)
END DisplayEventQ;
```

```
PROCEDURE DisposeEventQ(VAR q:EventQType);
(*Purpose: Disposes of an event queue and deallocates memory
**Pre: q is a pointer to the event queue;
**Post: q is undefined*)
VAR
    temp:EventQType;
BEGIN
    WHILE (NOT IsEmptyEventQ(q)) DO
        temp:=q;
        q:=q^.next;
        DEALLOCATE(temp,SIZE(NodeRec))
    END;   (*WHILE*)
END DisposeEventQ;

END EventQ.
```

17.2.6   The customer module

The customer DEFINITION MODULE:

```
DEFINITION MODULE Customer;
(*Purpose: To handle customer records*)
TYPE
    CustPtr = POINTER TO CustRec;
    CustRec =   RECORD
                    custNo:CARDINAL;
                    items:CARDINAL;
                    arrival,departure:CARDINAL;
                END; (*CustRec*)


PROCEDURE SetArrival( VAR cust:CustPtr;
                          mean,time:CARDINAL);
(*Purpose: Sets a customer's random arrival time
**Pre: cust is a pointer to the customer record;
**mean contains the mean of random arrival time
**and time contains the current time
**Post: cust.arrival is set to current time
**plus a random period to elapse before next arrival*)


PROCEDURE GetArrival(cust:CustPtr):CARDINAL;
(*Purpose: Returns a customer's arrival time
**Pre: cust is a pointer to the customer record
**Post: returns the customer's arrival time*)


PROCEDURE SetDeparture(  VAR cust:CustPtr;
                          serveItem,currentTime:CARDINAL);
(*Purpose: Sets a customer's departure time
**Pre: cust is a pointer to the customer record;
**serveItem contains the time taken to serve one item
**and currentTime contains the current time
**Post: cust.departure is set to depart time*)
```

```
PROCEDURE GetDeparture(VAR cust:CustPtr):CARDINAL;
(*Purpose: Returns a customer's departure time
**Pre: cust is a pointer to the customer record
**Post: returns the customer's departure time*)


PROCEDURE NewCustomer(    VAR cust:CustPtr;
                          custNo,meanItem,meanArrive,
                          time:CARDINAL);
(*Purpose: Generates and initializes a new customer
**record
**Pre: cust points to the customer record,
**custNo contains the customer's ID number,
**meanItem contains the mean for random generation
**number of items in trolley,
**meanArrive contains the mean for random generation
**of customer's arrival time,
**time contains the current time
**Post: cust points to the new customer*)


PROCEDURE DisplayCustomer(cust:CustPtr);
(*Purpose: Displays a customer record
**Pre: cust points to a valid customer record
**Post: None*)


PROCEDURE DisposeCustomer(VAR cust:CustPtr);
(*Purpose: Disposes of a customer record and
**deallocates memory
**Pre: cust points to a valid customer record
**Post: cust is undefined*)

END Customer.
```

The customer IMPLEMENTATION MODULE:

```
IMPLEMENTATION MODULE Customer;
(*Purpose: To handle customer records*)
FROM Storage IMPORT ALLOCATE, DEALLOCATE;
FROM InOut IMPORT WriteString,WriteLn,WriteCard;
FROM RandomNum IMPORT Random;


PROCEDURE SetArrival( VAR cust:CustPtr;
                      mean,time:CARDINAL);
(*Purpose: Sets a customer's random arrival time
**Pre: cust is a pointer to the customer record;
**mean contains the mean of random arrival time
**and time contains the current time
**Post: cust.arrival is set to current time
**plus a random period to elapse before next arrival*)
VAR
    arrival:CARDINAL;
BEGIN
    cust^.arrival:=Random(mean)+time;
END SetArrival;
```

```
PROCEDURE GetArrival(cust:CustPtr):CARDINAL;
(*Purpose: Returns a customer's arrival time
**Pre: cust is a pointer to the customer record
**Post: returns the customer's arrival time*)
BEGIN
    RETURN cust^.arrival
END GetArrival;


PROCEDURE SetDeparture(   VAR cust:CustPtr;
                          serveItem,currentTime:CARDINAL);
(*Purpose: Sets a customer's departure time
**Pre: cust is a pointer to the customer record;
**serveItem contains the time taken to serve one item
**and currentTime contains the current time
**Post: cust.departure is set to depart time*)
VAR
    serveTime,items:CARDINAL;
BEGIN
    items:=cust^.items;
    serveTime:=serveItem*items;
    cust^.departure:=serveTime+currentTime
END SetDeparture;


PROCEDURE GetDeparture(VAR cust:CustPtr):CARDINAL;
(*Purpose: Returns a customer's departure time
**Pre: cust is a pointer to the customer record
**Post: returns the customer's departure time*)
BEGIN
    RETURN cust^.departure
END GetDeparture;


PROCEDURE NewCustomer(   VAR cust:CustPtr;
                         custNo,meanItem,meanArrive,
                         time:CARDINAL);
(*Purpose: Generates and initializes a new customer
**record
**Pre: cust points to the customer record,
**custNo contains the customer's ID number,
**meanItem contains the mean for random generation
**number of items in trolley,
**meanArrive contains the mean for random generation
**of customer's arrival time,
**time contains the current time
**Post: cust points to the new customer*)
VAR
    items:CARDINAL;
BEGIN
    ALLOCATE(cust,SIZE(CustRec));
    cust^.items:=Random(meanItem);
    SetArrival(cust,meanArrive,time);
    cust^.departure:=0;
    cust^.custNo:=custNo
END NewCustomer;
```

```
PROCEDURE DisplayCustomer(cust:CustPtr);
(*Purpose: Displays a customer record
**Pre: cust points to a valid customer record
**Post: None*)
BEGIN
    WriteString("Customer details: ");
    WriteLn;
    WriteString("Customer No  :      ");
    WriteCard(cust^.custNo,1);
    WriteLn;
    WriteString("Items  :     ");
    WriteCard(cust^.items,1);
    WriteLn;
    WriteString("Arrival:     ");
    WriteCard(cust^.arrival,1);
    WriteLn;
    WriteString("Depart :     ");
    WriteCard(cust^.departure,1);
    WriteLn;
END DisplayCustomer;


PROCEDURE DisposeCustomer(VAR cust:CustPtr);
(*Purpose: Disposes of a customer record and
**deallocates memory
**Pre: cust points to a valid customer record
**Post: cust is undefined*)
BEGIN
    DEALLOCATE(cust,SIZE(CustRec))
END DisposeCustomer;

END Customer.
```

17.2.7   The checkout queue module

The checkout queue DEFINITION MODULE:

```
DEFINITION MODULE CheckOutQ;
(*Purpose: To handle a queue of customers*)
FROM Customer IMPORT CustPtr;
TYPE
    CustQPtr = POINTER TO QRec;
    QRec = RECORD
                person:CustPtr;
                next:CustQPtr
           END; (*QRec*)

    PROCEDURE InitCheckOutQ(VAR custQ:CustQPtr);
(*Purpose: Initializes a checkout queue
**Pre-conditions: custQ is a pointer to an uninitialized
**checkout queue
**Post-conditions: custQ points to NIL*)


PROCEDURE IsEmptyCheckOutQ(custQ:CustQPtr):BOOLEAN;
(*Purpose: Determines whether a checkout queue is empty
**Pre: custQ is a pointer to a checkout queue
**Post: returns TRUE if custQ is empty, otherwise
**returns FALSE*)
```

```
PROCEDURE AddToCheckOutQ(VAR custQ:CustQPtr;cust:CustPtr);
(*Purpose: Adds a customer to end of a checkout queue
**Pre: custQ is a pointer to the checkout queue;
**cust points to the customer record to be added
**Post: custQ points to queue with new customer
**added to the end of the checkout queue*)


PROCEDURE GetNextCustomer(custQ:CustQPtr;VAR cust:CustPtr);
(*Purpose: Gets the customer from the front of the
**checkout queue
**Pre: custQ is a pointer to the checkout queue;
**Post: cust points to the customer at the
**front of the checkout queue*)


PROCEDURE IsServingCustomer(custQ:CustQPtr):BOOLEAN;
(*Purpose: Checks whether customer in checkout queue
**is being served by checking if departure time of
**customer at front of queue has been set
**Pre: custQ is a pointer to the checkout queue;
**Post: returns TRUE if customer's departure
**time has been set, i.e. customer being served*)


PROCEDURE RemoveFromCheckOutQ(   VAR custQ:CustQPtr;
                                 VAR cust:CustPtr);
(*Purpose: Removes the front customer from a
**checkout queue and deallocates memory
**Pre: custQ is a pointer to the checkout queue;
**Post: cust points the customer record removed from
**the front of the checkout queue and custQ points to
**the checkout queue with the front customer removed*)


PROCEDURE DisposeCheckOutQ(VAR custQ:CustQPtr);
(*Purpose: Disposes of a checkout queue and
**deallocates memory
**Pre: custQ is a pointer to the checkout queue;
**Post: custQ is undefined*)


PROCEDURE DisplayCheckOutQ(custQ:CustQPtr);
(*Purpose: Displays all of the customers in a checkout queue
**Pre: custQ is a pointer to the checkout queue;
**Post: None*)


PROCEDURE LengthCheckOutQ(custQ:CustQPtr):CARDINAL;
(*Purpose: To return the number of customers in the
**checkout queue
**Pre: custQ points to the checkout queue;
**Post: returns the number of customers in
**the queue*)

END CheckOutQ.
```

The checkout queue IMPLEMENTATION MODULE:

```
IMPLEMENTATION MODULE CheckOutQ;
(*Purpose: To handle a queue of customers*)
FROM InOut IMPORT WriteString,WriteLn,WriteCard;
FROM Storage IMPORT ALLOCATE, DEALLOCATE;
FROM Customer IMPORT CustPtr,DisplayCustomer,
                SetDeparture,GetDeparture,DisposeCustomer;


PROCEDURE InitCheckOutQ(VAR custQ:CustQPtr);
(*Purpose: Initializes a checkout queue
**Pre: custQ is a pointer to an uninitialized
**checkout queue
**Post: custQ points to NIL*)
BEGIN
    custQ:=NIL
END InitCheckOutQ;

PROCEDURE IsEmptyCheckOutQ(custQ:CustQPtr):BOOLEAN;
(*Purpose: Determines whether a checkout queue is empty
**Pre: custQ is a pointer to a checkout queue
**Post: returns TRUE if custQ is empty, otherwise
**returns FALSE*)
BEGIN
    IF custQ=NIL THEN
        RETURN TRUE
    ELSE
        RETURN FALSE
    END  (*IF*)
END IsEmptyCheckOutQ;


PROCEDURE AddToCheckOutQ(VAR custQ:CustQPtr;cust:CustPtr);
(*Purpose: Adds a customer to end of a checkout queue
**Pre: custQ is a pointer to the checkout queue;
**cust points to the customer record to be added
**Post: custQ points to queue with new customer
**added to the end of the checkout queue*)
VAR
    temp:CustQPtr;
BEGIN
    ALLOCATE(temp,SIZE(QRec));
    temp^.person:=cust;
    temp^.next:=NIL;
    IF IsEmptyCheckOutQ(custQ) THEN
        custQ:=temp
    ELSE
        AddToCheckOutQ(custQ^.next,cust)
    END  (*IF*)
END AddToCheckOutQ;
```

```
PROCEDURE GetNextCustomer(custQ:CustQPtr;VAR cust:CustPtr);
(*Purpose: Gets the customer from the front of the
**checkout queue
**Pre: custQ is a pointer to the checkout queue;
**Post: cust points to the customer at the
**front of the checkout queue*)
BEGIN
    cust:=custQ^.person
END GetNextCustomer;


PROCEDURE IsServingCustomer(custQ:CustQPtr):BOOLEAN;
(*Purpose: Checks whether customer in checkout queue
**is being served by checking if departure time of
**customer at front of queue has been set
**Pre: custQ is a pointer to the checkout queue;
**Post: returns TRUE if customer's departure
**time has been set, i.e. customer being served*)
BEGIN
    IF GetDeparture(custQ^.person)>0 THEN
        RETURN TRUE
    ELSE
        RETURN FALSE
    END   (*IF*)
END IsServingCustomer;


PROCEDURE RemoveFromCheckOutQ(   VAR custQ:CustQPtr;
                                 VAR cust:CustPtr);
(*Purpose: Removes the front customer from a
**checkout queue and deallocates memory
**Pre: custQ is a pointer to the checkout queue;
**Post: cust points the customer record removed from
**the front of the checkout queue and custQ points to
**the checkout queue with the front customer removed*)
VAR
    temp:CustQPtr;
BEGIN
    IF NOT IsEmptyCheckOutQ(custQ) THEN
        temp:=custQ;
        cust:=custQ^.person;
        custQ:=custQ^.next;
        DEALLOCATE(temp,SIZE(QRec));
    END   (*IF*)
END RemoveFromCheckOutQ;


PROCEDURE DisposeCheckOutQ(VAR custQ:CustQPtr);
(*Purpose: Disposes of a checkout queue and
**deallocates memory
**Pre: custQ is a pointer to the checkout queue;
**Post: custQ is undefined*)
VAR
    temp:CustQPtr;
BEGIN
    WHILE (NOT IsEmptyCheckOutQ(custQ)) DO
        temp:=custQ;
        DisposeCustomer(temp^.person);
        custQ:=custQ^.next;
        DEALLOCATE(temp,SIZE(QRec))
    END   (*WHILE*)
END DisposeCheckOutQ;
```

```
PROCEDURE DisplayCheckOutQ(custQ:CustQPtr);
(*Purpose: Displays all of the customers in a checkout queue
**Pre: custQ is a pointer to the checkout queue;
**Post: None*)
VAR
    temp:CustQPtr;
BEGIN
    WriteLn;
    WriteString("CHECKOUT");
    WriteLn;
    IF IsEmptyCheckOutQ(custQ) THEN
        WriteString("This checkout is empty");
        WriteLn
    ELSE
        temp:=custQ;
        WHILE (NOT IsEmptyCheckOutQ(temp)) DO
            DisplayCustomer(temp^.person);
            temp:=temp^.next
        END (*WHILE*)
    END  (*IF*)
END DisplayCheckOutQ;


PROCEDURE LengthCheckOutQ(custQ:CustQPtr):CARDINAL;
(*Purpose: To return the number of customers in the
**checkout queue
**Pre: custQ points to the checkout queue;
**Post: returns the number of customers in
**the queue*)
VAR
    len:CARDINAL;
    temp:CustQPtr;
BEGIN
    len:=0;
    temp:=custQ;
    WHILE (NOT IsEmptyCheckOutQ(temp)) DO
        INC(len);
        temp:=temp^.next
    END;  (*WHILE*)
    RETURN len
END LengthCheckOutQ;

END CheckOutQ.
```

17.2.8   The clock module

The clock DEFINITION MODULE:

```
DEFINITION MODULE Clock;
(*Purpose: To handle a clock.
**The Clock has been implemented simply as type CARDINAL
**See Exercise 17.1*)

PROCEDURE ResetClock(VAR time:CARDINAL);
(*Purpose: Initializes time to 0
**Pre: None
**Post: time is initialized to 0*)
```

```
PROCEDURE IncrClock(VAR time:CARDINAL; newTime:CARDINAL);
(*Purpose: Changes time to newTime
**Pre: newTime contains the new time setting
**Post: time is assigned the value of newTime*)

END Clock.
```

The clock IMPLEMENTATION MODULE:

```
IMPLEMENTATION MODULE Clock;
(*Purpose: To handle a clock.
**The Clock has been implemented simply as type CARDINAL
**See Exercise 17.1*)

PROCEDURE ResetClock(VAR time:CARDINAL);
(*Purpose: Initializes time to 0
**Pre: None
**Post: time is initialized to 0*)
BEGIN
    time:=0;
END ResetClock;

PROCEDURE IncrClock(VAR time:CARDINAL; newTime:CARDINAL);
(*Purpose: Changes time to newTime
**Pre: newTime contains the new time setting
**Post: time is assigned the value of newTime*)
BEGIN
    time:=newTime
END IncrClock;

END Clock.
```

17.2.9   The random number generator module

```
DEFINITION MODULE RandomNum;
(*Linear congruential method.
**See D.Lehmer in Random Number Generators:
** Good ones are Hard to Find, Park and Miller,
**Communications of the ACM Oct 1988, p.1192
*)

PROCEDURE Rand(VAR seed:CARDINAL):REAL;
(*Purpose: Returns a 'pseudo-random' number
**between 0 and 1*)

PROCEDURE Random(n :CARDINAL):CARDINAL;
(*Purpose: Returns an exponentially distributed
**'pseudo-random' number about a mean value of n*)

END RandomNum.
```

This module is discussed in Chapter 12 where you will find the corresponding implementation module.

17.2.10   The statistical log module

The statistical log DEFINITION MODULE:

```
DEFINITION MODULE StatsLog;
FROM CheckOutQ IMPORT CustQPtr;

PROCEDURE LogQLength(queue:CustQPtr);
(*Purpose: Maintains check on maximum length of
**a checkout queue
**Pre: queue points to the checkout queue
**Post: maxLength is updated to length of queue
**if it is greater than present maxLength value*)

PROCEDURE CustomersUnserved(queue:CustQPtr);
(*Purpose: Gets number of customers in checkout
**queue but still unserved
**Pre: queue points to the checkout queue
**Post: unserved is set to the length
**of the checkout queue*)

PROCEDURE CustomerServedLog;
(*Purpose: Maintains count of number of
**customers served
**Pre: global variable, served, is available
**Post: global variable, served, is incremented*)

PROCEDURE DisplayLog;
(*Purpose: Displays statistical information
**Pre: Global variables maxLength,served
**and unserved are available
**Post: None*)

END StatsLog.
```

The statistical log IMPLEMENTATION MODULE:

```
IMPLEMENTATION MODULE StatsLog;
FROM InOut IMPORT WriteString,WriteLn,WriteCard;
FROM CheckOutQ IMPORT CustQPtr,LengthCheckOutQ;
VAR
    maxLength:CARDINAL;
    unserved,served:CARDINAL;

PROCEDURE LogQLength(queue:CustQPtr);
(*Purpose: Maintains check on maximum length of checkout
**Pre: queue points to the checkout queue
**Post: maxLength is updated to length of queue
**if it is greater than present maxLength value*)
VAR
    len:CARDINAL;
BEGIN
    len:=LengthCheckOutQ(queue);
    IF len>maxLength THEN
        maxLength:=len
    END   (*IF*)
END LogQLength;
```

```
PROCEDURE CustomersUnserved(queue:CustQPtr);
(*Purpose: Gets number of customers in checkout
**queue but still unserved
**Pre: queue points to the checkout queue
**Post: unserved is set to the length
**of the checkout queue*)
BEGIN
    unserved:=LengthCheckOutQ(queue);
END CustomersUnserved;


PROCEDURE CustomerServedLog;
(*Purpose: Maintains count of number of
**customers served
**Pre: global variable, served, is available
**Post: global variable, served, is incremented*)
BEGIN
    INC(served)
END CustomerServedLog;


PROCEDURE DisplayLog;
(*Purpose: Displays statistical information
**Pre: Global variables maxLength,served
**and unserved are available
**Post: None*)
BEGIN
    WriteString("STATISTICAL LOG");
    WriteLn;
    WriteString("Maximum checkout queue length was : ");
    WriteCard(maxLength,1);
    WriteLn;
    WriteString("Number of customers served was : ");
    WriteCard(served,1);
    WriteLn;
    WriteString("Number of customers left unserved was : ");
    WriteCard(unserved,1);
    WriteLn;
    WriteString("Total number of customers was : ");
    WriteCard(unserved+served,1);
    WriteLn
END DisplayLog;

BEGIN  (*StatsLog body to initialize variables*)
    maxLength:=0;
    unserved:=0;
    served:=0;
END StatsLog.
```

17.2.11   The simulation program module

```
MODULE Simulation;
(*Purpose: The main simulation driving program
**Uses:InOut,EventQ,CheckOutQ,Customer,Clock,StatsLog*)

FROM InOut IMPORT WriteString,WriteLn,WriteCard,ReadCard;
FROM EventQ IMPORT EventType,EventQType,InitEventQ,
                   AddToEventQ,RemoveFromEventQ,DisposeEventQ;
FROM CheckOutQ IMPORT CustQPtr,InitCheckOutQ,GetNextCustomer,
                   AddToCheckOutQ,RemoveFromCheckOutQ,
                   DisposeCheckOutQ,DisplayCheckOutQ,
                   IsEmptyCheckOutQ,IsServingCustomer;
FROM Customer IMPORT CustPtr,GetArrival,SetDeparture,
                   GetDeparture,NewCustomer,DisposeCustomer;
FROM Clock IMPORT  ResetClock;
FROM StatsLog IMPORT LogQLength,CustomersUnserved,DisplayLog,
                   CustomerServedLog;
VAR
    eventQ:EventQType;
    cust,newCust,oldCust:CustPtr;
    check:CustQPtr;
    event:EventType;
    custNo : CARDINAL;
    newTime,currentTime,closeTime:CARDINAL;
    serveItemTime,meanArrive,meanItem:CARDINAL;
    closed:BOOLEAN;

BEGIN
    closed:=FALSE;

    (*Get the closing time*)
    WriteString("Enter number of secs until closing time ");
    ReadCard(closeTime);
    WriteLn;

    (*Get the service time for each item*)
    WriteString("Enter service time per item in secs ");
    ReadCard(serveItemTime);
    WriteLn;

    (*Get the mean time between customer arrivals*)
    WriteString("Enter mean time between arrivals in secs ");
    ReadCard(meanArrive);
    WriteLn;

    (*Get the mean number of items in a customer's trolley*)
    WriteString("Enter mean number of items in a trolley ");
    ReadCard(meanItem);
    WriteLn;

    (*Initialize the event queue and the checkout queue*)
    InitEventQ(eventQ);
    InitCheckOutQ(check);

    (*Reset the clock  before simulation begins*)
    ResetClock(currentTime);
```

```
(*Set customer number to 1 for first customer
**and generate the first customer's arrival*)
custNo:=1;
NewCustomer(cust,custNo,meanItem,meanArrive,currentTime);

(*Add this arrival event to the event queue*)
AddToEventQ(eventQ,GetArrival(cust),arrive);

(*Repeat while checkout is open*)
WHILE (currentTime<closeTime) DO

    (*Remove the next event from the event queue*)
    RemoveFromEventQ(eventQ,currentTime,event);

    CASE event OF

        arrive :
            (*Add customer to checkout queue and
            **generate next customer arrival*)
            AddToCheckOutQ(check,cust);
            LogQLength(check);
            INC(custNo);
            NewCustomer(newCust,custNo,meanItem,
                                meanArrive,currentTime);
            (*if the checkout is still open, add arrival
            **to event queue, otherwise dispose of
            **new customer*)
            IF GetArrival(newCust)<closeTime THEN
              AddToEventQ(eventQ,
                            GetArrival(newCust),arrive)
            ELSE
              closed:=TRUE;
              DisposeCustomer(newCust)
            END;  (*IF*)

        depart :
            (*Remove the customer from the checkout*)
            RemoveFromCheckOutQ(check,oldCust);
            CustomerServedLog;
            DisposeCustomer(oldCust);
        ELSE
    END; (*CASE*)

    (*If a customer is not currently being served,
    **start serving the next customer by calculating
    **departure time*)
    IF (NOT IsServingCustomer(check))
            AND (NOT closed)
            AND (NOT IsEmptyCheckOutQ(check)) THEN
        GetNextCustomer(check,cust);
        SetDeparture(cust,serveItemTime,currentTime);
        AddToEventQ(eventQ,GetDeparture(cust),depart)
    END;  (*IF*)
    IF closed THEN
        currentTime:=closeTime;
    END;  (*IF*)

    (*Remove comments if required*)
    (*DisplayCheckOutQ(check);*)
    cust:=newCust;
    CustomersUnserved(check);
END; (*WHILE*)
```

```
(*Display the log and deallocate space used by simulation*)
    DisplayLog;

    DisposeCheckOutQ(check);

    DisposeEventQ(eventQ)

END Simulation.
```

17.2.12   Sample output

The following is a sample run of the simulation.
Opening time is set to 1 hour and service time per item to 2 seconds. Mean time between arrivals at the checkout is set to 1 minute and the mean number of items in customers' trolleys is set to 20 items.

Example output:

```
Enter the number of secs until closing time 3600
Enter the service time per item in secs 2
Enter the mean time between arrivals in secs 60
Enter the mean number of items in a trolley 20

STATISTICAL LOG
Maximum checkout queue length was : 9
Number of customers served was : 60
Number of customers left unserved was : 1
Total number of customers was : 61
```

Exercise 17.1

Rewrite the Clock module to export a type TimeType and to handle time in hours, minutes and seconds rather than as a simple cardinal.

Exercise 17.2

Extend the Simulation program to simulate a supermarket with four checkouts. New customers arriving at the checkouts should be added to the shortest checkout queue.
You could also alter the simulation in order to find out the effect of:
a)   setting different service speeds for each checkout or
b)   introducing express checkouts for customers with less than eight items.

18   Low level facilities

Although high level languages seek to hide the details of what goes on inside the computer from the programmer, there are some situations where it is necessary for a program to manipulate individual bits (i.e. binary digits) in the computer memory. For example, writing a communications package, or handling input from a mouse, may require specific areas of memory to be written to or read from. Also, if a language is going to be used for writing system software, such as operating systems and compilers, it must be capable of handling low level detail.

The problem for the language designer is to decide just what facilities should be provided. The language needs to remain independent of the machine on which it is implemented and it is impossible to predict all the facilities that might be required in order to produce high level routines for all eventualities.

18.1   The SYSTEM module

Niklaus Wirth's solution, when designing Modula-2, was to include the concept of a pseudo-module, which has a definition part but no corresponding implementation module. The implementation code is actually built into the compiler.

The 'standard' pseudo-module that you should find included with your library modules is called SYSTEM and it should contain facilities something like the following:

```
DEFINITION MODULE SYSTEM;

TYPE
    WORD;

    ADDRESS;

    PROCESS;

    PROCEDURE ADR(anyVariable : AnyType) : ADDRESS;

    PROCEDURE TSIZE(AnyType) : CARDINAL;

    PROCEDURE NEWPROCESS (    ProcedureName : PROC;
                              location : ADDRESS;
                              approximateSize : CARDINAL;
                              VAR newName : ADDRESS);

    PROCEDURE TRANSFER(VAR    FromProcedure,
                              ToProcedure : ADDRESS);

END SYSTEM.
```

18.1.1   The type WORD

What it is
Variables of type WORD represent single words of computer memory. These are usually 16 bits (binary digits) or 32 bits, but the size depends on the computer you are using.

What you can do with it
WORD values can be used as parameters or returned by a function.
Assignment is the only operation allowed on variables of type WORD.

Other features
Type transfer functions do make it possible to perform arithmetic and relational operations on values of type WORD, although we will not explore this further here.

A formal open array parameter of type ARRAY OF WORD matches an actual parameter of any type.

18.1.2   The type ADDRESS

What it is
Variables of ADDRESS type represent the address of a word in the computer memory.
Such variables behave exactly as pointers, as though they have been declared as:

```
TYPE ADDRESS = POINTER TO WORD;
```

What you can do with it
All the operations allowed on values of type POINTER are permitted for values of type ADDRESS.
All operators that are defined for integer arithmetic should also be applicable to ADDRESS values although some compilers restrict operations that are unlikely to be meaningful for ADDRESS values, such as multiplication and division.

18.1.3   The type PROCESS

What it is
This was formerly used as a procedure type, but has since been superseded, so is included only for the sake of compatibility with older Modula-2 programs. We will not discuss it further in this book.

18.1.4   The function procedure ADR

What it is
This procedure returns the address (i.e. the memory location) of `anyVariable` during program execution.

18.1.5   The function procedure TSIZE

What it is
This procedure returns the number of bytes or words required to store a variable of `anyType`.

18.1.6   The procedure NEWPROCESS

What it is
This procedure prepares an ordinary procedure so that it can be called as a co-routine, which we will explain briefly later in this chapter. It takes as parameters:
*   the name of a procedure,
*   the start memory location set aside for the procedure,
*   the size of memory space, in bytes or words set aside for the procedure to use and
*   the name to be used in calling the procedure when using TRANSFER.

18.1.7   The procedure TRANSFER

What it is
This procedure suspends execution of one procedure in order to resume execution of another and is used for switching between co-routines.

18.2   BITSET type

BITSET is a special case of SET type, which behaves like a SET of binary digits, usually called bits. BITSET provides a way for Modula-2 programmers to manipulate single bits. The number of elements in a BITSET can vary between compiler/computer systems, but it is usually the same as the number of bits in a WORD, as defined in the module SYSTEM.

Each element of a BITSET is numbered. Usually, element zero is the least significant (right-most) bit, but some compilers may designate the most significant (left-most) bit as element zero, so beware! Assuming the usual convention, the following snippet of Modula-2 code will create two BITSET variables with the binary patterns 01010101 and 00110011 in the least significant elements.

```
VAR
    bitVar1, bitVar2 : BITSET;

BEGIN
    bitVar1 := BITSET{0,2,4,6};
    bitVar2 := {0,1,4,5};
```

As indicated above, if the SET type is omitted before the set braces, {}, the default type is BITSET but, for the sake of clarity, it is a good idea to specify the SET type.

The normal set operations apply to BITSET types. The operations are carried out on corresponding bits of the two operands and are known as 'bitwise' operations. The following simple program illustrates how BITSET variables can be declared, operated upon and output:

```
MODULE TryBitSet;
FROM InOut IMPORT Write,WriteLn;
VAR
    a,b,c,d,e,f,g : BITSET;
    card : CARDINAL;
PROCEDURE BinaryDisplay(x : BITSET);
(*Purpose: outputs the binary value of a BITSET variable,
**preceded and followed by a new line*)
VAR
    count : CARDINAL;
BEGIN
    WriteLn;
    FOR count := SIZE(BITSET)*8 TO 0 BY -1 DO
        IF count IN x THEN
            Write('1')
        ELSE
            Write('0')
        END (*IF*)
    END; (*FOR*)
    WriteLn
    END BinaryDisplay;
```

```
BEGIN (*Main program*)
  a := {0,1,4,6};
  b := {1,2,5};
  c := a + b;     (*bitwise (a OR b) i.e. set union*)
  d := a - b;     (*bitwise (a AND NOT b)
                              i.e. set difference*)
  e := a / b;     (*bitwise ((a AND NOT b) OR (NOT a AND b)
                              i.e. exclusive OR*)
  f := a * b;     (*bitwise (a AND b) i.e. set intersection*)
  BinaryDisplay(a);
  BinaryDisplay(b);
  BinaryDisplay(c);
  BinaryDisplay(d);
  BinaryDisplay(e);
  BinaryDisplay(f)
END TryBitSet.
```

Assuming a 16-bit word,
the output from this program is: Comment:

0000000001010011   (* a *)

0000000000100110   (* b *)

0000000001110111   (* a OR b *)

0000000001110101   (* a AND NOT b *)

0000000001010001   (* (a AND NOT b) OR (NOT a AND b) *)

0000000000000010   (* a AND b *)

18.3   TYPE transfer functions

Modula-2 provides TYPE transfer functions to allow conversion between variables of different data types. Type transfers may take place only between variables which occupy the same size space in the computer's memory. The name of the type transfer function is the data type that the value is being transferred to, for example:

```
VAR
    a,g : BITSET;
    card : CARDINAL;
BEGIN
    (*type transfer of BITSET to CARDINAL*)
    card := CARDINAL(a);
    (*shift left by one bit and transfer back to BITSET*)
    g := BITSET(card * 2);
END;
```

If these two statements are added to the end of the program, TryBitSet, together with BinaryDisplay(g), then the following binary number will be added to the list of results:

0000000010100110   (* the value of variable, a, shifted left by one bit *)

Our compiler issues an 'unsafe type transfer' warning for the above statements because the results are implementation dependent. These warnings do not prevent the program compiling and running, but indicate potential portability problems.

18.4   Generics

Despite the strong data typing policy of Modula-2, some functions and procedures need to accept parameters of non-specific data type. For example, the standard function, HIGH, will accept any single dimension array-type variable as a parameter. Similarly, ORD can accept any ordinal type. Procedures and functions like this are said to be generic. If you need to write a generic procedure then Modula-2 provides the data type ARRAY OF WORD, which can be used as a formal parameter type. This will be compatible with any actual parameter type.

The following procedure illustrates how ARRAY OF WORD can be used to exchange values between two variables, even if they are of different data types, providing they occupy the same size space in memory

```
PROCEDURE Exchange(VAR a, b : ARRAY OF WORD);
VAR
    temp : WORD;
    index : CARDINAL;
BEGIN
    IF HIGH(a) <> HIGH(b) THEN
        WriteString("Cannot exchange due to size difference");
        WriteLn
    ELSE
        FOR index:=0 TO HIGH(a) DO
            temp:=a[index];
            a[index]:=b[index];
            b[index]:=temp
        END (*FOR*)
    END (*IF*)
END Exchange;
```

18.5   Co-routines

In the SYSTEM module, the procedures NEWPROCESS and TRANSFER are provided to support co-routines.

A co-routine is in some ways similar to a procedure, but also has some important differences. When a procedure is called it starts executing at its first statement and continues to its end, then returns control back to its caller. However, rather than call a co-routine, we transfer control to it. When control leaves the co-routine, all variable values are preserved and when the co-routine is next activated it picks up from exactly where it left off when its action was suspended.

Co-routines can be used to simulate concurrent processes by transferring control between one another.

This has many potential uses, but has a particular application in writing computer operating systems.

When we looked at the LOOP statement, we indicated that there are a few legitimate reasons for allowing an infinite loop. The co-routine is one such reason. If two or more routines are running 'in parallel', with control passing between them, then the ability to place an infinite loop in a dependent or slave module is a very useful facility. One routine, the master module, is given the responsibility for an orderly close-down of the run.

In this chapter we have tried to provide you with a brief insight into some of the advanced features of Modula-2. To take full advantage of these facilities you will need to know something about low level (assembly language) programming and what is provided with your Modula-2 compiler.

As we've said before, experiment!

Exercise 18.1

Write a program which uses the SYSTEM module to find out the word size used with your computer/compiler.

Exercise 18.2

Write a procedure which inputs a binary number as a string of 0s and 1s and passes back a BITSET variable parameter containing the binary value. Modify TryBitSet to test your procedure. Replace the two assignment statements with calls to your procedure to input the values of the variables, a and b.

Exercise 18.3

Our notes on type transfer functions provide one method of shifting a BITSET variable one character to the left. Work out how you can provide the following binary shifts for BITSET variables, if necessary by writing a procedure:

    (i)   shift one bit to the right.
    (ii)   shift one bit to the left, circular shift (i.e. wrap around to the least significant end, any bits which 'fall off' the most significant end).
    (iii) shift one bit to the right, circular shift.
    (iv) shift half-word left, circular shift.
    (v)   shift half-word right, circular shift.

The epilogue

In the days before 24 hour television, an evening of broadcasting would end with an epilogue before you switched off making the image collapse, like a white dwarf, into a receding point of light.

Having reached the conclusion of this book we hope the effect is the opposite and that we have in part helped you to expand your skills by shedding more light on the process of developing software using Modula-2. Also, we hcpe that you don't feel ready to 'switch off'. If this is the first programming language you have studied, we are confident that you will now find it relatively quick and painless to extend your repertoire to encompass any programming language.

Appendix A - ASCII character set

Char	Decimal	Octal	Char	Decimal	Octal	Char	Decimal	Octal
nul	0	000	+	43	053	V	86	126
soh	1	001	,	44	054	W	87	127
stx	2	002	-	45	055	X	88	130
etx	3	003	.	46	056	Y	89	131
eot	4	004	/	47	057	Z	90	132
enq	5	005	0	48	060	[	91	133
ack	6	006	1	49	061	\	92	134
bel	7	007	2	50	062	]	93	135
bs	8	010	3	51	063	^	94	136
ht	9	011	4	52	064	_	95	137
lf	10	012	5	53	065	`	96	140
vt	11	013	6	54	066	a	97	141
ff	12	014	7	55	067	b	98	142
cr	13	015	8	56	070	c	99	143
so	14	016	9	57	071	d	100	144
si	15	017	:	58	072	e	101	145
dle	16	020	;	59	073	f	102	146
dc1	17	021	<	60	074	g	103	147
dc2	18	022	=	61	075	h	104	150
dc3	19	023	>	62	076	i	105	151
dc4	20	024	?	63	077	j	106	152
nak	21	025	@	64	100	k	107	153
syn	22	026	A	65	101	l	108	154
etb	23	027	B	66	102	m	109	155
can	24	030	C	67	103	n	110	156
em	25	031	D	68	104	o	111	157
sub	26	032	E	69	105	p	112	160
esc	27	033	F	70	106	q	113	161
fs	28	034	G	71	107	r	114	162
gs	29	035	H	72	110	s	115	163
rs	30	036	I	73	111	t	116	164
us	31	037	J	74	112	u	117	165
space	32	040	K	75	113	v	118	166
!	33	041	L	76	114	w	119	167
"	34	042	M	77	115	x	120	170
#	35	043	N	78	116	y	121	171
$	36	044	O	79	117	z	122	172
%	37	045	P	80	120	{	123	173
&	38	046	Q	81	121	l	124	174
'	39	047	R	82	122	}	125	175
(	40	050	S	83	123	~	126	176
)	41	051	T	84	124	del	127	177
*	42	052	U	85	125			

Appendix B - Compatibility

Modula-2 is a strongly typed language - it does not generally like you trying to mix variables of different type in the same expression.
However, the rules concerning this are not as clear-cut as you might suppose. There are, in fact, four levels of compatibility.

Types may be:

1. SAME,
2. COMPATIBLE,
3. ASSIGNMENT COMPATIBLE,
4. NOT COMPATIBLE.

The type of an actual variable parameter must be the SAME as the type of its corresponding formal parameter.

Compatibility is required between:
- the operands in an expression,
- the case labels and case expression in a CASE statement,
- the start and limit values, and the control variable in a FOR statement.

Assignment compatibility is required between:
- the assigned variable and the expression in an assignment statement,
- an array index and an expression used as the index,
- an actual value parameter and its corresponding formal parameter,
- the result returned by a function and the expression used in the function's RETURN statement.

The flow chart on the following page is designed to help you determine the level of compatibility between two types.

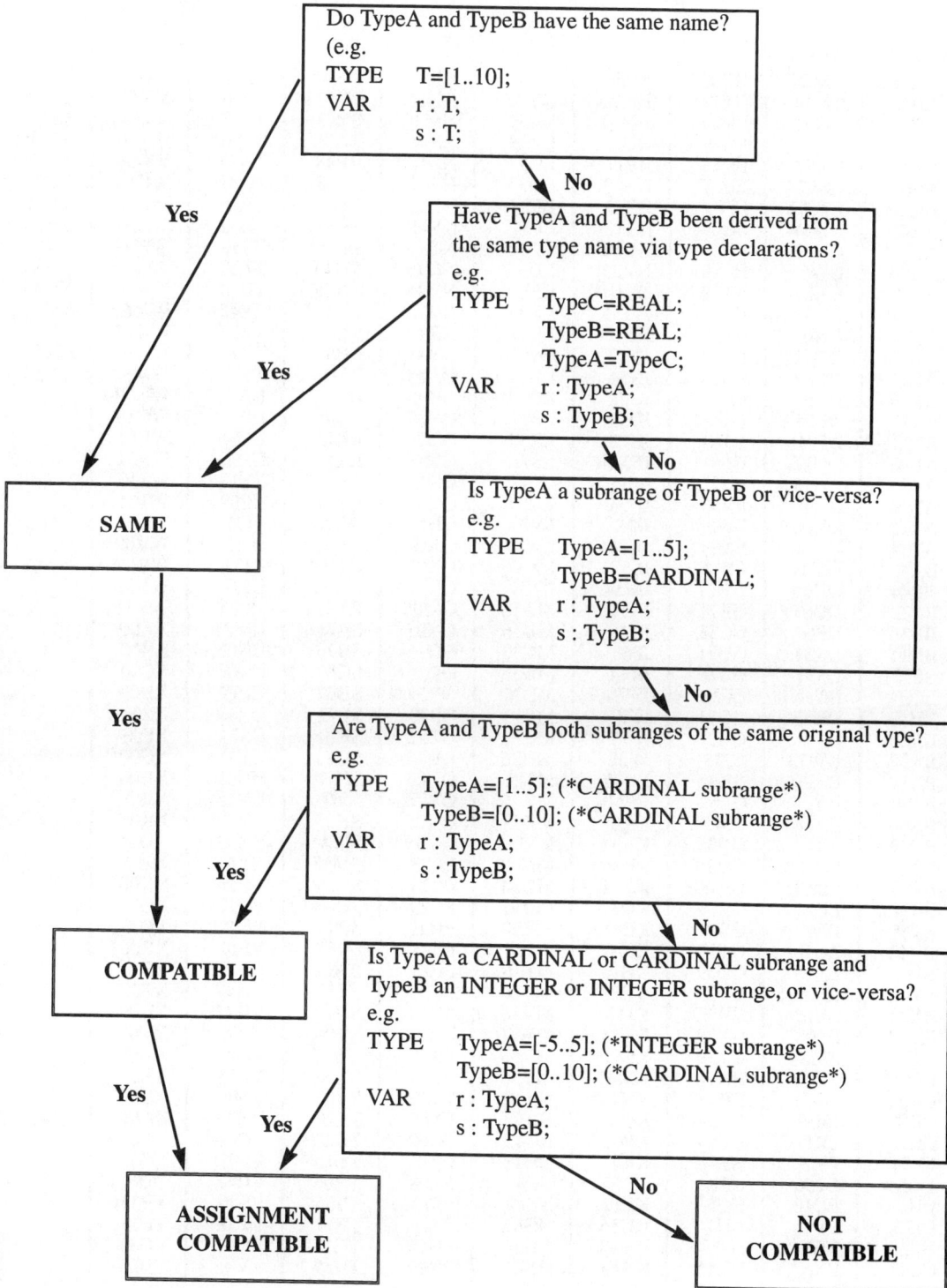

Do TypeA and TypeB have the same name?
(e.g.
TYPE   T=[1..10];
VAR   r : T;
           s : T;

No

Yes

Have TypeA and TypeB been derived from
the same type name via type declarations?
e.g.
TYPE   TypeC=REAL;
             TypeB=REAL;
             TypeA=TypeC;
VAR   r : TypeA;
           s : TypeB;

Yes

No

Is TypeA a subrange of TypeB or vice-versa?
e.g.
TYPE   TypeA=[1..5];
             TypeB=CARDINAL;
VAR   r : TypeA;
           s : TypeB;

SAME

Yes

No

Are TypeA and TypeB both subranges of the same original type?
e.g.
TYPE   TypeA=[1..5]; (*CARDINAL subrange*)
            TypeB=[0..10]; (*CARDINAL subrange*)
VAR   r : TypeA;
          s : TypeB;

Yes

No

COMPATIBLE

Is TypeA a CARDINAL or CARDINAL subrange and
TypeB an INTEGER or INTEGER subrange, or vice-versa?
e.g.
TYPE   TypeA=[-5..5]; (*INTEGER subrange*)
           TypeB=[0..10]; (*CARDINAL subrange*)
VAR   r : TypeA;
         s : TypeB;

Yes

Yes

No

**ASSIGNMENT
COMPATIBLE**

**NOT
COMPATIBLE**

Appendix C - Registration case study files

LicenceCodes file

AA55	CM34	EY02	HL56	KX40	NK40	PW47	TJ34	VW15	YJ09
AB64	CN44	FA58	HM35	KY56	NL44	PX52	TK51	VX15	YK35
AC17	CO51	FB10	HN43	LA37	NM40	PY43	TL33	VY65	YL35
AD21	CP27	FC49	HO55	LB37	NN48	RA48	TM40	WA56	YM35
AE10	CR52	FD18	HP17	LC37	NO15	RB48	TN44	WB56	YN35
AF62	CS67	FE33	HR60	LD37	NP64	RC48	TO48	WC15	YO35
AG28	CT07	FF01	HS71	LE37	NR32	RD54	TP52	WD18	YP35
AH47	CU44	FG09	HT10	LF37	NS71	RE58	TR52	WE56	YR35
AJ43	CV62	FH21	HU10	LG16	NT57	RF58	TS69	WF56	YS71
AK56	CW53	FJ20	HV35	LH37	NU48	RG44	TT20	WG56	YT35
AL48	CX27	FK18	HW10	LJ08	NV46	RH28	TU16	WH06	YU35
AM60	CY59	FL50	HX35	LK37	NW31	RJ42	TV48	WJ56	YV35
AN54	DA05	FM16	HY10	LL37	NX18	RK37	TW15	WK17	YW35
AO14	DB42	FN12	JA42	LM37	NY13	RL62	TX13	WL49	YX35
AP09	DC43	FO26	JB54	LN37	OA05	RM14	TY44	WM34	YY35
AR15	DD21	FP32	JC02	LO37	OB05	RN53	UA31	WN59	
AS72	DE25	FR53	JD35	LP37	OC05	RO40	UB31	WO13	
AT28	DF21	FS70	JE11	LR37	OD20	RP46	UC35	WP64	
AU48	DG21	FT44	JF32	LS78	OE05	RR48	UD49	WR31	
AV50	DH18	FU22	JG12	LT37	OF05	RS66	UE18	WS10	
AW57	DJ63	FV53	JH54	LU37	OG05	RT29	UF09	WT31	
AX13	DK06	FW33	JJ12	LV34	OH05	RU08	UG31	WU31	
AY32	DL45	FX08	JK24	LW37	OJ05	RV52	UH13	WV09	
BA42	DM16	FY34	JL07	LX37	OK05	RW17	UJ57	WW31	
BB44	DN65	GA71	JM54	LY37	OL05	RX54	UK05	WX31	
BC32	DO07	GB71	JN15	MA16	OM05	RY32	UL35	WY31	
BD46	DP54	GC38	JO49	MB16	ON05	SA66	UM31	XA00	
BE22	DR51	GD71	JP63	MC36	OO15	SB76	UN03	XB00	
BF58	DS71	GE71	JR44	MD36	OP05	SC70	UO03	XC00	
BG34	DT56	GF38	JS79	ME36	OR52	SD67	UP19	XD00	
BH40	DU17	GG71	JT08	MF36	OS80	SE73	UR40	XE00	
BJ29	DV20	GH38	JU32	MG36	OT52	SF70	US71	XF00	
BK52	DW13	GJ38	JV22	MH36	OU10	SG70	UT32	XG00	
BL54	DX29	GK38	JW05	MJ40	OV05	SH77	UU35	XH00	
BM40	DY24	GL62	JX27	MK36	OW52	SJ67	UV35	XJ00	
BN06	EA18	GM54	JY51	ML36	OX05	SK81	UW35	XK00	
BO13	EB11	GN38	KA34	MM36	OY37	SL69	UX57	XL00	
BP52	EC30	GO38	KB34	MN00	PA23	SM68	UY64	XM00	
BR19	ED63	GP38	KC34	MO54	PB23	SN69	VA11	XN00	
BS74	EE22	GR19	KD34	MP36	PC23	SO66	VB12	XO00	
BT65	EF43	GS40	KE41	MR60	PD23	SP69	VC17	XP00	
BU42	EG50	GT38	KF34	MS78	PE23	SR69	VE11	XR00	
BV53	EH58	GU39	KG13	MT36	PF23	SS66	VF47	XS00	
BW49	EJ01	GV29	KH28	MU36	PG23	ST72	VG47	XT00	
BX25	EK63	GW39	KJ41	MV36	PH23	SU71	VH27	XU00	
BY37	EL08	GX39	KK41	MW60	PJ23	SV00	VJ26	XV00	
CA16	EM34	GY39	KL41	MX36	PK23	SW68	VK44	XW00	
CB06	EN06	HA18	KM41	MY36	PL23	SX70	VL33	XX00	
CC02	EO04	HB13	KN41	NA42	PM23	SY00	VM42	XY00	
CD09	EP59	HC24	KO41	NB42	PN09	TA20	VN43	YA61	
CE11	ER11	HD27	KP41	NC42	PO52	TB63	VO48	YB61	
CF54	ES69	HE56	KR41	ND42	PP40	TC10	VP05	YC61	
CG55	ET56	HF34	KS77	NE42	PR08	TD06	VR42	YD61	
CH48	EU10	HG53	KT12	NF42	PS75	TE06	VS40	YE35	
CJ26	EV15	HH14	KU56	NG47	PT19	TF54	VT58	YF35	
CK53	EW50	HJ15	KV17	NH46	PU15	TG13	VU42	YG31	
CL47	EX47	HK15	KW56	NJ09	PV29	TH59	VV46	YH35	

LicenceDistricts file

01	Aberystwyth		43	Middlesbrough
02	Bangor		44	Newcastle-upon-Tyne
03	Barnstaple		45	Newport-IOW
04	Barrow-in-Furness		46	Northampton
05	Birmingham		47	Norwich
06	Bolton		48	Nottingham
07	Boston		49	Oxford
08	Bournemouth		50	Peterborough
09	Brighton		51	Plymouth
10	Bristol		52	Portsmouth
11	Cambridge		53	Preston
12	Canterbury		54	Reading
13	Cardiff		55	Salisbury
14	Carlisle		56	Sheffield
15	Chelmsford		57	Shrewsbury
16	Chester		58	Stoke-on-Trent
17	Coventry		59	Swansea
18	Dudley		60	Swindon
19	Durham		61	Taunton
20	Exeter		62	Truro
21	Gloucester		63	Warrington
22	Grimsby		64	Worcester
23	Guildford		65	York
24	Hastings		66	Aberdeen
25	Haverfordwest		67	Ayr
26	Hereford		68	Dumfries
27	Huddersfield		69	Dundee
28	Hull		70	Edinburgh
29	Ipswich		71	Glasgow
30	Kendal		72	Inverness
31	Leeds		73	Keith
32	Leicester		74	Kirkwall
33	Lincoln		75	Lerwick
34	Liverpool		76	Oban
35	London-Central		77	Selkirk
36	London-NE		78	Stirling
37	London-NW		79	Stornoway
38	London-SW		80	Stranraer
39	London-SE		81	Wick
40	Luton			
41	Maidstone			
42	Manchester			

Appendix D - Self test solutions

Self test 1.1

a) i)   A syntax error would prevent you going beyond step 4 (Compile it).

ii) A semantic error would prevent you going beyond step 6 (Test it).

b) i)   A syntax error would require you to return to step 3 (Type it) to retype part of the program.

ii) A semantic error would require you to return to step 2 (Design it) or even step 1 (Conceive it) if there was a fundamental problem.

Self test 1.2

a)   `sausage` is a legal identifier.
b)   `IMPORT` is an illegal identifier because it is a reserved word.
c)   `import` is a legal identifier because Modula-2 is case-sensitive, but it is advisable to avoid using any identifiers which may be confused with reserved words.
d)   `num3` is a legal identifier.
e)   `34numbers` is illegal because it starts with a number.
f)   `sausage&mash` is an illegal identifer because it contains &.

Self test 1.3

`'Mine's a large brandy'` will cause a syntax error if used as a literal string, because it contains an apostrophe within single quotes.
The problem is overcome by using double quotes, like this:
`"Mine's a large brandy"`

Self test 2.1

a)   0.3 + 2.8 is legal, but not very useful.
b)   24.0 * 2 is illegal because it contains two different data types: real and cardinal.
c)   23 MOD 8 is a legal expression.
d)   4.8 DIV 2.0 is illegal because DIV cannot have real operands.

Self test 2.2

a)   `total := .78;`
is illegal because reals must have at least one digit to the left of the decimal point.
b)   `sum:=0.21E06;`
is illegal because an integer cannot be assigned a real value.
c)   `balance:=sum;`
is legal.
d)   `total:=total + 0.78;`
is legal.

e) ```
   total:=balance + sum;
   ```
   is illegal:  incompatible data types.

f) ```
   sum:=balance MOD 2;
   ```
   is legal.

g) ```
   total:=sum DIV 2.0;
   ```
   is illegal: DIV requires INTEGER or CARDINAL operands.

h) ```
   sum:=sum * balance;
   ```
   is legal.

i) ```
   balance:=sum/balance;
   ```
   is illegal because / requires REAL operands.

j) ```
   sum:=(sum - 5);
   ```
   is legal.

Self test 2.3

Putting the two assignment statements together, we have:

```
class := (12 - (3 * class)) DIV 3 + 15;
```

which simplifies to:

```
class := 19 - class;
```

Self test 2.4

```
MODULE TryCard;
FROM InOut IMPORT ReadCard, WriteCard, WriteString, WriteLn;
VAR card : CARDINAL;
BEGIN
    WriteLn;
    WriteString("Please type in a cardinal number ");
    WriteLn;
    ReadCard(card);
    WriteString("Here it is again ");
        WriteLn;
    WriteCard(card,10);
    WriteLn
END TryCard.
```

Self test 3.1

a) ```
   CalculateBill(price, noOfTins, total);
   ```
   is legal.

b) ```
   CalculateBill(23, 4, total);
   ```
   is legal.

c) ```
   CalculateBill(price, noOfTins, 46);
   ```
   is illegal.  The third formal parameter is a variable parameter and a value cannot be used as the corresponding actual parameter.

d) ```
   CalculateBill(price, amount, total);
   ```
   is illegal. The second actual parameter is a REAL.

e) `CalculateBill(price, quantity, total);`
is legal because CARDINAL and INTEGER types are assignment compatible, which is the requirement for value parameters.

f) `CalculateBill(price, quantity, cost);`
is illegal because actual and formal variable parameters need to be of the same data type. `cost` and `total` have different data types.

Self test 3.2

`tax` is a formal, variable parameter.

Self test 3.3

(c) is the correct option. An actual parameter is a variable or value in brackets on a procedure call.

Self test 3.4

`GetOldMoney:`
Variable parameters: `oldPounds, shillings, oldPence`

`ConvertOldToNew:`
Value parameters: `oldPounds, shillings, oldPence`
Variable parameters: `newPence`

`DisplayNewMoney:`
Value parameter: `newPence`

Self test 3.5

A function procedure can only represent ONE output value. `ConvertNewToOld` requires three output values. Therefore, a function procedure is not appropriate for this application.

Self test 3.6

There are many possible solutions. Here is one way to do it:
```
oldPounds:=TRUNC(newPounds);
shillings:=TRUNC(((newPounds-FLOAT(oldPounds))*20.0);
oldPence:=TRUNC((((newPounds-FLOAT(oldPounds))*20.0)
                        - FLOAT(shillings)) * 12.0);
```
or
```
oldPence:=TRUNC(newPounds*240.0 + 0.5)
                        -oldPounds*240-shillings*12;
```

Self test 3.7

a) `Calc(value1+value2, value3);`
`Calc` is a normal procedure with two parameters.

b) `Calc;`
`Calc` is a normal procedure with no parameters.

c) `Calc:=total+value;`
    `Calc` is a variable.
d) `Result:=6+Calc(value1,value2);`
    This is the example where `Calc` is a function procedure.

Self test 3.8

We are looking for cases where a single value is returned and the original parameters remain unchanged.

a) This requires that the values in two variable parameters are exchanged, therefore it is not appropriate to write a function/procedure to do this.
b) Finding the cube root of a number requires a single value parameter, and returns a single value result, so a function procedure would be appropriate.
c) Incrementing requires a single variable parameter. A function procedure should not be used.
d) Printing a value requires one value parameter and no value is returned, so a function procedure is inappropriate.

Self test 3.9

A normal Modula-2 procedure is a sub-program which is called by name, qualified by the correct number and data types of parameters, in the correct sequence. A function procedure is a sub-program which returns a single value of a specific data type. There may be parameters but these should be value parameters. A function procedure call is placed on the right side of an assignment statement or may be embedded in an expression, in the same way that standard functions are used.

Self test 3.10

Constants could be placed at the beginning of the program, i.e. global constants. Here are the arguments for and against the use of local and global constants:

Global constants pros: Constants are visible, easy to find, available to other parts of the program if required. In large programs it may be difficult to find a constant embedded within a sub-program. If the constant is reused elsewhere in a program it is necessary to redeclare it in another procedure. Apart from the problems of duplication, there is no connection between these two instances of the constant, so it would be possible for them to be declared differently.

Global constants cons: Procedure is dependent on components outside itself. This increases coupling and makes program parts less portable. If a constant is only used in one procedure then the safest option is to encapsulate the constant within the procedure to which it belongs.

Self test 4.1

Visible from within procedure `C`:

local variables:	`b:CARDINAL; d:BOOLEAN; f:REAL; g:REAL;`
from procedure `B`:	`a:CHAR; c:CARDINAL;`
global variables:	`e:CHAR;`
procedures:	`A, B and C.`

Visible from within procedure B:
     local variables: a:CHAR; b:INTEGER; c:CARDINAL; f:REAL;
     global variables: d:BOOLEAN; e:CHAR;
     procedures: A, B and C.

Visible from within procedure A:
     local variables: a:CARDINAL; c:CHAR; d:INTEGER;
     global variables: e:CHAR;
     procedures: A and B.

Visible from within the main program:
     global variables: a:CARDINAL; d:BOOLEAN e: CHAR;
     procedures: A and B.

Self test 4.2

a) The **syntax error** concerns the use of the variable, area, in the main program. This has not been declared as a global variable, so it is not available in this part of the program. In any case, considering the parameter passing to the preceding procedures, it is likely that the actual parameter required here is answer. If this change is made, assuming the missing statements are completed, then the program should compile.

b) CircleArea has two value parameters as formal parameters. This is a problem because the purpose of this procedure is to calculate the area and return the result to the calling program, i.e. area should be a variable parameter. The procedure header should look like this:

```
PROCEDURE CircleArea (radius : REAL; VAR  area : REAL);
```

This change should overcome the problem of a zero result being displayed.

Self test 5.1

d) is the correct answer: The software crisis of the 1970s was caused by a significant amount of programmer time being spent on maintenance, although the other factors may have contributed to the problems.

Self test 5.2

GetInitial has one input (value) parameter, firstName, and one output (variable) parameter, initial.
Therefore the correct header is:

```
a) PROCEDURE GetInitial(firstName : StringType;
                        VAR initial : CHAR);
```

Self test 5.3

b) is true. See page 96.

Self test 6.1

If `ch:='C'` and `card:=69` (*ASCII value for 'E'*) then
a)   `ch >= 'D'` is FALSE
b)   `ch < CHR(card)` is TRUE
c)   `ch = CHR(ORD('D') - 1)` is TRUE
d)   `ORD(ch) <= (card-2)` is TRUE

Self test 6.2

Expression c) is the odd one out.

Self test 6.3

Statement b) is equivalent.

Self test 6.4

a)   This simplifies to (A=B), i.e. is TRUE if A and B are the same value.
b)   This expression is TRUE only when A and B are both FALSE.
c)   This expression is TRUE of either A or B is FALSE, or if both are FALSE.
d)   This expression is TRUE when A and B are different, i.e. A<>B.

Self test 7.1

The output will be:
20 17 14 11 8 5 2

Self test 7.2

a)   TRUE
b)   TRUE
c)   FALSE, `counterVariable` is undefined on exit from the loop.
d)   TRUE

Self test 7.3

`letter` will take values 'H', 'F', 'D' then 'B'.

Self test 7.4

There will be eight passes of the inner loop. The value of `i` on each pass is the same as the total increment to `count`,
i.e. $15 + 13 + 11 + 9 + 7 + 5 + 3 + 1$ giving 64

Self test 7.5

    a)   Valid.
    b)   Invalid.
    c)   Invalid.
    d)   Invalid.
    e)   Valid.

Self test 8.1

a) is the correct answer. The EXIT in `Thermostat3` is at the end of the LOOP, therefore it is equivalent to a REPEAT statement.

Self test 9.1

The program reads up to 101 characters from a file and writes each character to the output device.

Self test 10.1

The value of `count` on exit from the loop is 7.

Self test 10.2

    a)   Valid.
    b)   Valid.
    c)   Valid.
    d)   Invalid, it is illegal to input or output enumerated types using `WriteString`.

Self test 10.3

    a)   Legal.
    b)   Illegal.
    c)   Illegal.
    d)   Illegal.
    e)   Illegal.
    f)   Illegal.
    g)   Legal.
    h)   Illegal.

Self test 10.4

    a)   Legal if enumerated type value.
    b)   Legal.
    c)   Illegal, REAL values cannot be used as CASE labels.
    d)   Legal.
    e)   Legal.
    f)   Illegal, strings cannot be used as CASE labels.
    g)   Legal.

Self test 12.1

Alternative compilation orders for the set of modules are:

`StringStuff.def` and `Sort.def` in either order, followed by
`StringStuff.mod`, `Sort.mod` and `MainProg.mod` in any order.

Self test 13.1

The iteration stops when the function is called with a parameter value of zero. In this case, instead of calling the function once more, the value 1 is returned. This has the dual effect of correctly defining 0!=1, and allowing all instances of the function to terminate.

Self test 13.2

Omitting the IF statement in `DrawTree` would mean that only the right-most branches of the tree are drawn and the procedure does not terminate.

Self test 13.3

The correct answer is c).

Self test 13.4

A binary search of 4000 items would require a maximum of 13 searches.

Self test 13.5

The correct answer is c).

Self test 15.1

a) Legal.
b) Legal.
c) Illegal.
d) Legal.

Index